W9-AJU-181

FROM REVOLUTIONARY CADRES
TO PARTY TECHNOCRATS
IN SOCIALIST CHINA

This volume is sponsored by the Center for Chinese Studies, University of California, Berkeley

FROM REVOLUTIONARY CADRES TO PARTY TECHNOCRATS IN SOCIALIST CHINA

HONG YUNG LEE

University of California Press
Berkeley • Los Angeles • Oxford

University of California Press
Berkeley and Los Angeles, California

University of California Press, Ltd.
Oxford, England

© 1991 by
The Regents of the University of California

Library of Congress Cataloging-in-Publication Data

Lee, Hong Yung, 1939–
    From revolutionary cadres to party technocrats in
    socialist China / Hong Yung Lee.
        p.   cm.
    ISBN 0-520-06679-0 (alk. paper)
        1. Chung-kuo kung ch'an tang—History.   2. Com-
    munist leadership—China—History.   I. Title.
    JQ1519.A5L35   1990
    324.251'075'09—dc20   90-30762
                                                    CIP

Printed in the United States of America
1   2   3   4   5   6   7   8   9

The paper used in this publication meets the minimum requirements of American National Standard for Information
Sciences — Permanence of Paper for Printed Library Material, ANSI Z39.48-1984. ⊚

To Whakyung
With love and appreciation

Contents

Tables and Figures

TABLES

FIGURES

Acknowledgments

This book has taken a long time to reach fruition. In the late 1970s, I began my research to answer the simple question of which Cultural Revolution victims would be rehabilitated. Political events in China, however, overtook my original intention. All of the former victims returned to power, where they began to enact sweeping economic and bureaucratic reforms whose long-term consequences are still unclear. My research naturally followed these historical changes, which in turn shaped the contour of the book.

During the process of putting ideas on paper, I changed my institutional base several times, moving from Marquette to Yale, then to the East-West Center, and finally arriving at the University of California. The intellectual and personal benefits I gained from colleagues along the way are too numerous to be fully acknowledged in this limited space. However, I would like briefly to mention a few individuals of particular note.

With his commitment to the understanding of China and his devotion to the scholarly life, Professor Tang Tsou has been a powerful source of inspiration throughout my academic career. Lowell Dittmer read several drafts of the manuscript, providing accurate criticism and warm encouragement. The book benefited enormously from lively discussions with Helen Siu, Marc Blecher, Brantly Womack, and Deborah Davis. I would also like to thank to other scholars who commented on the manuscript, including professors Robert Scalapino, Chalmers Johnson, Frederic Wakeman, Joyce Kallgren, Michel Oksenberg, Kenneth Liberthal, Lynn White, Merle Goldman, and Susan Shirk. Professors Joseph LaPalombara, James Scott, and Jonathan Spence of Yale were unsparing with their time and suggestions. Sheila Levine and Betsey Scheiner went beyond professional obligation in helping me fine-tune my writing.

Research grants from the Woodrow Wilson Center, the Social

Science Research Council, and the Center for International and Areas Studies of Yale enabled me to travel to China and to concentrate on writing this book. In addition, I would like to express my gratitude to Jong-Hyun Chey for his generous encouragement. Lee-Jay Cho and Jae Yul Kim have been very supportive of the research.

Finally, this book would not have been written without the support of my family. During the prolonged gestation period, Sonya and Sunyoung have increasingly taken part in editing the manuscript during their growing years in high school and now in college. This book is dedicated to Whakyung whose unfaltering love and confidence have sustained me during agonizing moments. Although I am solely responsible for any shortcomings of the book, its merits should be shared by those who assisted me in various ways.

1

Introduction

This is a study of the structure, personnel, and historical formation of the cadre system in China with an emphasis on the period from the Cultural Revolution (CR) to the post-Mao reforms. More specifically, through a careful analysis of China's cadre recruitment policy, its effect on the operation of the political system at subsequent stages, and its role as a key issue in conflicts among the elite—particularly during the CR—this book traces the transformation of the Chinese Communist Party (CCP) leaders from revolutionary cadres to bureaucratic technocrats.[1]

Unlike the Eastern European socialist countries, where former revolutionaries started to co-opt technical experts into the ruling elite immediately after seizure of political power, the elite transformation in China took place over a period of almost three decades after the foundation of the new regime. Moreover, the prolonged and tortuous transition was frequently marked by inner elite conflicts, purges, and rehabilitations. Therefore, this study of the evolving cadre system in China hopes to make sense of complex CCP politics by illuminating four basic issues: (1) the reason for the sustained revolutionary momentum during Mao's era, (2) the intensity of elite conflicts over cadre issues during the CR, (3) the impetus of sweeping reforms after Mao's death, and (4) characteristics of the political system emerging as a result of the reforms.

These four issues can be explained briefly as follows. Recruited from the poorly educated peasant class, the original revolutionaries brought a rural orientation to nation building after 1949: the former revolutionaries continued to recruit cadres after 1949 from lower rungs of the social hierarchy for their political reliability, and they created a structure of the party-state whose effective opera-

---

1. The questions addressed in this book are the ones that Barrington Moore left untouched in his seminal work, *Social Origins of Dictatorship and Democracy* (Boston: Beacon Press, 1966), which traced Communist revolutions back to peasant rebellions.

tion largely depended on cadres. Consequently, the cadres owed their ascendency to official positions in the party-state and willingly carried out radical policies according to their leaders' orders; at the same time, they enjoyed enormous power to make decisions directly affecting ordinary Chinese people's daily lives. Their revolutionary eagerness, the Chinese people's resentment of their privileges, and Mao's own ideological vision resulted in the CR, which produced four new groups: initiators, beneficiaries, survivors, and the purged. Each elite group had a different power base, which defined the group's political interests and determined its policies on the issues of purging and recruiting cadres.

Eventually, after many power struggles, almost all the CR victims—the purged—returned to power. Because of their bitterness over their experiences during the CR as victims of the system they had helped to create, the rehabilitated cadres became born-again reformers once they regained power. The shift of the regime's main task from revolutionary change to economic development resulted in a change in the composition and recruitment of the cadres. With the replacement of senior political leaders and a large number of revolutionary cadres by bureaucratic technocrats, China's new political leaders were, and still are, trying to restructure the sociopolitical and economic systems so that they will be able to balance both the political needs of the Leninist party and the structural prerequisites of economic development. However, the market, although essential to economic development, is incompatible with the existence of the Leninist Party and its version of socialism. Continuing tensions erupted into the student democratic movement in the spring of 1989, which the regime ruthlessly suppressed. In the long run, however, the tensions will probably produce an authoritarian regime with a more market-oriented economic system.

ANALYTICAL FRAMEWORK:
CADRES AND STRUCTURE

The analytical framework of this book blends the concept of political choice with a structural approach, thereby rejecting the extreme view of structural determinism on the one hand and the total autonomy of political action on the other. The structure, broadly defined to refer to everything that lies outside a political actor, sets limits to what is politically possible at any particular time.[2] In turn, political actors respond to and attempt to modify or change the structure through "dynamic manipulations."[3]

The cadres serve as a direct link between political choice and structure. A given cadre recruitment policy is chosen within the limits of environmental constraints and as a means of carrying out a specific core task at a given moment. A series of policy decisions on cadres at a given moment produces a cadre system, which in turn decisively influences the structure, orientation, and capability of the political system (which includes the decision-making process, the conflict structure, and the way the party-state interacts with society). Although a political system at any given moment enjoys a certain amount of autonomy in selecting its main task and its subsequent cadre policy, its choices are also constrained by the interests, perceptions, and preferences of the existing cadre corps. The choices made in recruiting cadres thus produce a structure that constrains the policy choices at the next stage. In this sense, the cadres are creators as well as agents of the state structure; the cadres create political, economic, and social structures that largely reflect their ideological vision. Once this basic structure is established, however, it operates as a constraint on the cadres' behavior.

This conceptualization of the cadres is particularly appropriate for the CCP, which has tried to modify its environment first through political revolution, then through social revolution, and now through economic development. This perspective also enables us to visualize the dynamics of Chinese politics fully by focusing on the process of evolving structure.

CADRES:
POLITICAL ELITES AND BUREAUCRATS

Originally developed in the context of the Russian revolution, and then translated into Chinese, the term "cadre" (*ganbu*) referred to the backbone of the revolutionary movement—people whose high

2. For the purpose of this book, the term "structure" includes, among other things, the social or class relationship, the organizational principle of the party-state, and the conflict structures among the top-level decision-makers with the party-state.

3. William H. Riker, "The Heresthetic of Constitution-Making. The Presidency in 1987, with Comments on Determinism and Rational Choice," *American Political Science Review*, no. 1, March 1984, 1–16.

level of political consciousness qualified them to assume responsibility for specific political tasks. In this original sense, cadres are the leaders, in contrast to the masses, who are the followers in a revolution. However, after the CCP became the ruling party, the meaning of cadre expanded to include all those who were paid from the state budget but not engaged in productive manual labor.[4] Thus, the current Chinese concept of cadre includes two analytically distinct categories: the political elite and the functionaries staffing the huge party-state apparatus.

However, the conventional definition of the elite as a small group of leaders at the top of the political system or as a small social stratum in the class structure is not useful in the case of China. First, no social elite (or, using Suzanne Keller's term, "strategic elite") exists independent of the party-state.[5] A series of campaigns eliminated any source of power in society, whether in the form of class, social institution, or political group; and the party-state imposed its bureaucratic structure on every functional field of society for the sake of the socialist revolution. Consequently, in China, possession of political power because of an official position in the bureaucratic system is what defines elite status. The sole channel of upward mobility for ambitious individuals has been through the bureaucracy—a channel that the party-state has easily controlled through its prerogative over the personnel management of cadres.

Second, to distinguish political leaders from bureaucrats both functionally and structurally within the Chinese bureaucracy is extremely difficult. The idea that politicians make policy and bureaucrats implement it turns out to be invalid even in Western democratic countries, where the two groups have different institutional bases (the first in state agencies and the second in parliaments), career track systems (the first as representatives of the people's will through election and the second as instruments for the state), and social origins (the first from the lower class and the second from the upper class).[6] No such formal distinction has existed in China up to now. On the contrary, both the Leninist princi-

4. *Xinming Zidian* [Dictionary of New Names], no. 5, 1985, 14; *Guoji Tongxun* 1 (34) (1984): 215.
5. Suzanne Keller, *Beyond the Ruling Class* (New York: Random House, 1963), 20.
6. Joel D. Aberbach, Robert D. Putnam, Bert A. Rockman, *Bureaucrats and Politicians in Western Democracies* (Cambridge, Mass.: Harvard University Press, 1981).

ple of "democratic centralism" and the notion of the "mass line"—
which, at least in theory, obliges the party to pay attention to the
actual needs and opinions of ordinary people—regard policy-
making and its implementation as a continuous process, and when
no strong leader such as Stalin or Mao exists, the interests and
preferences of low-level cadres frequently influence the policy-
making.

Structurally speaking, the political elite in the Chinese bureaucracy includes not only top-level political leaders, but also the
"leading cadres" (or "responsible persons") of the various functional units such as economic enterprises and business units (*shiye
danwei*). Moreover, the leading cadres are stratified according to
their rank and position and the administrative status of the units
they lead. In other words, an elite group at each level is subject to
tight control by its superiors, who have the authority of appointment and removal over it. In addition, leading cadres are usually
promoted from among ordinary cadres within a unit, as was the
case in traditional China where the path to high political position
was through the bureaucracy.

For these reasons elite politics, political conflict, and the bureaucratic system are inextricably interrelated in China. Top-
level politics are shaped by and reflect the power base that each
elite group controls within the bureaucratic system. Indeed, the
political conflicts frequently center on how to shape the bureaucratic systems.[7]

Existing studies tend to focus exclusively on one of these dimen-
sions, particularly on the changing profile of the top political leaders as largely defined by the membership of the party's Central
Committee, whereas cadre recruitment, conflict over issues, and
the resultant impact on the bureaucratic system have been largely
neglected.[8] For instance, Doak Barnett and Harry Harding deal exclusively with the formal structure of the Chinese bureaucratic system, while leaving the issue of the cadres within the bureaucratic
machine untouched.[9] The existing literature on the CR and other

7. Harry Harding, *Organizing China: The Problems of Bureaucracy, 1949–1976*
(Stanford: Stanford University Press, 1981).

8. Robert Scalapino, ed., *Elites in the People's Republic of China* (Seattle: University
of Washington Press, 1972).

9. Harding, *Organizing China*; A. Doak Barnett, *Cadres, Bureaucracy, and Political
Power in Communist China* (New York: Columbia University Press, 1967).

elite conflicts tends to stress power struggles organized along factional lines, while overlooking the crucial importance of cadre policy as one of the focal points of the dissension. As a result, most
existing studies tend to be static, atheoretical, or theoretically excessive; they fail to offer a dynamic macro-view of the CCP's political process.

I have purposely employed the three different modes of analysis
associated with elite study, political conflict, and bureaucratic systems, using each mode of analysis as needed. For instance, I ana-
lyze elite profiles in order to substantiate the long-term trend of
bureaucratic technocrats replacing old revolutionaries; relate the
CR elite conflicts to cadre issues and discuss the cadre structure in
order to highlight the changing practice of cadre management. My
chapters, however, are not explicitly organized around these three
topics; rather, the topics are discussed in each chapter in light of
relevant theoretical insights drawn from existing studies.

IMPORTANCE OF CADRES IN CCP
POLITICS

It has been widely accepted since Mosca and Pareto that a political
elite exerts enormous influence in shaping a political system.[10]
This point is particularly true of traditional China where a well-
defined elite of scholar-bureaucrat-landlords dominated not only
political but economic and cultural life. China's embrace of socialism reinforced historical tradition. A socialist system, with ultimate
faith in the rationality of the human mind, substitutes allegedly
chaotic market control with decisions consciously made by the
political elite located in a hierarchically constructed organizational
setting. Because of the centrality of the political elite in the socialist
system, many social scientists attribute regime transformation to
the rise of a new type of elite, "the new technocratic elite," "the
managerial modernizers," or "the technically trained bureaucrats."[11]

10. Vilfredo Pareto, *The Mind and Society: A Treatise on General Sociology*, vol. 1
(New York: Dover, 1965); Gaetano Mosca, *The Ruling Class* (New York: McGraw-
Hill, 1965).
11. M. H. Lowenthal, "Development vs. Utopia in Communist Policy," in Chalmers Johnson, ed., *Change in Communist Systems* (Stanford: Stanford University

Even contemporary debates on the "relative autonomy of the state" focus mainly on the issue of political elites. For instance, some Marxists point to the alleged homogeneity of political and social elites in capitalist countries as key evidence for the lack of state autonomy.[12] Even the proponents of state autonomy cannot avoid the issue of the political elite. "[The state] refers to all those individuals who occupy offices that authorize them and them alone to make and apply decisions that are binding upon all segments of the society."[13]

The impact of the personal and idiosyncratic features of a political elite on the nature of structure varies inversely with the degree of institutionalization of the "offices"; the less institutionalization, the greater the likelihood that officials will exhibit personal idiosyncrasies in performing their official duties.[14] The Chinese political process has never been highly institutionalized for several obvious reasons. First, the idea that rule by man supersedes rule by law has long been a part of the Confucian political tradition. Second, because Communist ideology has never clearly defined the relationship between ideology and organization, the institutionalization of the state has been uncertain.[15] Third, Mao's belief that all human and social problems are political in nature and therefore should be analyzed from the class perspective denies an autonomous role to rules of procedure, which include administrative laws. Moreover, the question of how far the state should be regulated and institutionalized was the focus of ideological controversy between Mao and his political adversaries.

The political structure set up by the old revolutionaries since 1949 reinforced the crucial importance of cadres in the Chinese political process. What the Chinese call "unit ownership," along

Press, 1970); W. A. Welsh, "Toward a Multi-Strategy Approach to Research on Contemporary Communist Political Elite: Empirical and Quantitative Problems," in F. J. Feron, ed., *Communist Studies and Social Science* (Chicago: Rand McNally, 1969); and Peter Ludz, *The Changing Party Elite in East Germany* (Boston: MIT Press, 1972).

12. Ralph Milliband, *The State in Capitalist Society* (New York: Basic Books, 1969).

13. Eric Nordlinger, *On the Autonomy of the Democratic State* (Cambridge: Harvard University Press, 1981), p. 11.

14. For institutionalization of the state, see Samuel Huntington, *Political Order in Changing Societies* (New Haven: Yale University Press, 1968).

15. For the relationship between ideology and organization, see Franz Schurmann, *Ideology and Organization in Communist China* (Berkeley and Los Angeles: University of California Press, 1968).

with the practice of organizing each unit to be self-sufficient in meeting most of its members' social needs—the principle known as "big and complete, small and complete" (*da er quan, xiao er quan*)—has allowed the leading cadres of each unit to make decisions not only on matters pertaining to the unit's tasks, but also on issues relating to the private lives of the unit members "from birth to death."[16] Official guidelines on any policy have always been broad and ambiguous, giving a great deal of leeway to the leading cadres at each level. Furthermore, allocation of most necessary resources, services, and finances through administrative decisions rather than through the market has minimized the need for communication and interaction among units and among individuals belonging to different units. The little coordination that was necessary was conducted only through a superior authority. The practice of keeping one cadre for a long time in a unit—known as "the life-tenure system"—made it easy for leaders to "privatize" their formal authority. Although local cadres were held accountable to the upper echelon, the mechanisms needed for ordinary members of the unit to supervise their leading cadres have been nonexistent or extremely weak. Mass participation in political campaigns, leadership participation in labor, and criticism and self-criticism have become formalized rituals and empty rhetoric without much impact on the operation of the overall system.

ORGANIZATION

This study is based on recently available materials published in China as well as information obtained through interviews in Hong Kong and elsewhere. These sources are supplemented by biographical information about top-level leaders that I have been collecting for the past several years. I completed the manuscript before the Chinese student demonstrations of 1989. Except for minor changes, I have attempted no major revisions in light of these tragic events. Organized largely chronologically and partially topically, the book consists of four parts.

Part I describes the background of the party-state by first examining how the CCP developed the strategy of recruiting poorly

16. *Zhengzhi Yu Zhengzhi Kexue* (Beijing: Qunzhong Chubanshe, 1983), 95; *Jingji Fazhan Yu Tizhi Gaige*, no. 7, 1986, 7–12.

educated poor peasants after trying several other methods during the revolutionary period (chapter 2), then by analyzing the cadre policies the former revolutionaries pursued as the political leaders of the bureaucratized party-state in the 1950s and the early 1960s (chapter 3).

Part II analyzes the manipulation of cadre issues by the various elite groups during the CR. The four chapters in this section are organized chronologically. After reviewing the structures of the elite conflicts, chapter 4 promotes the concept of the "situational group" as the most useful tool for understanding the elite conflicts during the ten years of the CR. Lin Biao's power base and his strategy to succeed Mao are discussed in chapter 5. Chapter 6 analyzes the conflict between the Gang of Four and the Zhou Enlai group in terms of their divergent cadre policies. Hua Guofeng's cadre policy is contrasted with that of Deng Xiaoping in chapter 7.

The chapters in Part III, dealing with the current bureaucratic reforms, are arranged in part thematically and in part chronologically. Chapter 8 argues that the personal experiences of having been purged during the CR prompted the old cadres to initiate sweeping reforms when they were rehabilitated after Mao's death. Chapter 9 discusses the basic structural problems of the cadre corps, focusing on its size, age structure, and level of education. Chapter 10 discusses Deng Xiaoping's preparation for the change in leadership by stressing the development of new criteria for cadre recruitment, the development of a special retirement system for veteran cadres (*lixiu*), and the purge of the CR rebels from leadership positions. Chapter 11 analyzes the composition of the new leadership in terms of age, education, and possible ideological orientation. Chapter 12 focuses on the CCP's effort to readjust itself to the new task of economic development.

Part IV contains two chapters. The first one analyzes the personnel dossier system, which constitutes the basis for the personnel management system. Chapter 14 discusses the changing role of the party in managing cadre affairs in the context of the current endeavor to separate the party from the government and other functional authorities and the shifting locus of decision-making authority on personnel matters within the party-state bureaucracy. In chapter 15 I summarize my basic arguments and speculate on the characteristics of the political system now in the making.

PART I

POLITICAL ELITES
OF THE PARTY-STATE

2

Recruitment of Revolutionaries: The Future Political Elites

Originally founded by a handful of intellectuals, the CCP struggled for almost three decades in pursuit of political power, frequently adjusting its revolutionary strategy to fit the changing political environment. During this period, the party's perception of its environmental constraints and its main task at a given moment largely determined the criteria used for membership recruitment. After the urban-oriented revolutionary strategy supported by Moscow failed miserably, Mao shifted the focus of membership recruitment to the rural peasant. The task of fighting the invading Japanese and its concomitant united front strategy enabled the party to recruit its members from diverse social groups—including intellectuals and the middle peasants, who worked their own land without hiring laborers.[1] But with Mao's assertion of ideological orthodoxy in the Yanan rectification campaign and the initiation of land reform as a preparation for the forthcoming civil war, the previous tendency of stressing class background in cadre policy reemerged, intensifying until Mao's death in 1976.

This chapter, which surveys the growth in the number of CCP members during the revolutionary period, helps us understand the process by which the revolutionary elites who dominated Chinese politics after 1949 were recruited.

---

1. "Intellectuals" in China refers to those with some education, in contrast to those with no formal education. Initially, all those with a middle school education were called intellectuals. But as the number of educated people increased, the term came to refer to those with a college education. Because of the limited number of college graduates in China, the term "intellectual" is also used to refer to those in certain occupations—usually those with professional careers. Although intellectuals do not constitute a class in a strict sense in China, they are treated almost like a class.

DURING THE GREAT
REVOLUTIONARY WAR

The CCP was born out of the crises that China encountered in the 1920s. Concerned with China's survival in the face of foreign pressure, warlordism, and social disintegration, thirteen intellectuals, representing fifty-seven members of the various regional Marxist groups, set up a national organization of the Communist Party.[2]

These thirteen were from the best-educated group in China at the time. Five of them had studied abroad, and all but two, who were high school graduates, had college-level educations. They were very young, with an average age of twenty-nine. None of them appears to have studied natural sciences, concentrating instead on the humanities and social sciences, so that they resembled Lasswell's "symbol manipulators." Although there is little available background information on the fifty-seven original party members, a Chinese source reports that all but four of them were intellectuals.[3] Thus, the founders of the CCP belonged to the May 4 generation of intellectuals who had been searching for the solution to China's political, economic, and social problems.[4]

Although they learned from Marxism-Leninism the importance of organization as a tool for their political actions, the founders did not quite know how to create a revolutionary party. The platform of the First Party Congress (1921) was vague and broad: it did not require any specific class background for membership. "Anyone who is willing to accept the party's platform and policy and agrees to be loyal to the party" could join the party with an introduction from a party member.[5] Even members of bourgeois parties had

2. Cao Yunfang and Pan Xianying, eds., *Zhongguo Gongchandang Jiquan Fazhan Shi* (Beijing: Zhongguo Renmin Daxue Dangan Shi, 1984), 11–20.

3. For "symbol manipulators," see Harold Lasswell and Daniel Lerner, eds., *World Revolutionary Elites* (Cambridge, Mass.: M.I.T. Press, 1965). *Dangshi Yanjiu*, no. 2, 1981, 65; *Zhonggong Dangshi Cankao Ziliao*, 1982, 5:163. Another Chinese source reports that the CCP had fifty-three members when it was founded. The occupations of forty-seven of them were as follows: seven professors and teachers, seven editors and reporters, one lawyer, one leftist KMT member, six primary school teachers, thirteen college students, five middle school students, and two workers. Zhu Chengjia, ed., *Zhonggong Dangshi Yanjiu Lunwen Xuan* (Changsha: Hunan Renmin Chubanshe, 1983), 1:212.

4. Jerome B. Grieder, *Intellectuals and the State in Modern China: A Narrative History* (New York: Free Press, 1981).

5. *Zhongguo Gongchandangzhang Huibian* (Beijing: Renmin Chubanshe, 1979), 1–4, 41.

Table 1.   Background of the Thirteen Founding Members of the CCP

Members	Area of Representation	Province	Life Span	Education
Li Hanjun	Shanghai	Hubei	1890–1927	Tokyo Imp. Univ.
Li Da	Shanghai	Hunan	1890–1966	Tokyo Imp. Univ.
Zhang Guotao	Beijing	Jiangxi	1897–1979	Beijing Univ.
Liu Renjing	Beijing	Hubei	1902–	High School attached to Wuhan Univ.
Chen Gongbo	Guangdong	Guang-dong	1892–1946	Beijing Univ.
Pao Huizeng	Guangdong	Hubei	1890–1927	Tokyo Imp. Univ.
Tung Piwu	Wuhan	Hubei	1886–1975	Studied in Japan
Chen Tanqiu	Wuhan	Hubei	1896–1943	Wuchang Normal Univ.
Mao Zedong	Changsha	Hunan	1893–1976	First Normal School of Hunan
He Shuheng	Changsha	Hunan	1876–1935	First Normal School of Hunan
Deng Enming	Jinan	Guizhou	1901–1931	First Middle School of Jinan
Wang Jinmei	Jinan	Shandong	1898–1925	First Normal School of Shandong
Zhou Feihai	Japan	Hunan	1897–1948	Seventh Normal School of Japan

Source. Dangshi Cailiao Zhengli Weiyuan Hui, no. 7, 1986, 20–28. Also see Shin Wu-jun, Zhonggong Dangce Jianshe Lilun Zhi Yanjiu (M.A. thesis, National Political University of Taiwan, 1978), 117.

only to sever their ties to join the Communist Party. Instead of the probation period adopted later, the rule specified two months of investigation.

But when the Second Party Congress decided to join the Third International in 1922, the party made requirements for membership more strict in order to make itself a "proletarian revolutionary party."[6] Admission of any candidate from outside the working

6. The resolution adopted at the Second Party Congress declared: "We are neither lecturing intellectuals, nor fanatic revolutionaries. We don't want to enter universities, research institutes, or libraries. Since our party is the fighting party of the proletariat, we have to go to the people and organize a 'mass party.'" Zhonggong "Dangde Jianshe" Yuanshi Wenjian Huibian (Taipei: Sifa Xinzhengbu Diaochaju Bianyi, 1979), 2:15.

Table 2. Growth of CCP Membership, 1921–87

Year	Population (millions)	Party Members
First revolutionary civil war		
1921 (1st Cong., 23 July)		57[a]
1922 (2d Cong., 16–23 July)		123[a]
1923 (3d Cong., 12–20 June)		432[a]
1925 (4th Cong., 11–22 Jan.)		950[a]
1925 (Nov.)		10,000[g]
1926 (July)		30,000[g]
1927 (5th Cong., 27 Apr.–9 May)		57,965[a]
1927 (after 12 Apr.)		10,000[a]
Second revolutionary civil war		
1928 (6th Cong., 18 June–11 July)		40,000[a]
1929 (2d plenum of 6th Cong., June)		50,000[g]
1930 (3d plenum of 6th Cong., Sept.)		60,000[g]
1930		122,318[a]
1931 (4th plenum of 6th Cong., Jan.)		68,000[g]
1932 (Aug.)		107,000[g]
1933		200,000[g]
1934 (5th plenum of 6th Cong.)		300,000[a]
1937 (after the Long March)		40,000[a]
Anti-Japanese War		
1938 (Jan.)		200,000[g]
1939		300,000[g]
1940		800,000[a]
1941		763,447[a]
1942		736,151[a]
1943		700,000[g]
1944		853,420[c]
1945 (7th Cong., 23 Apr.–11 June)		1,211,128[a]
Third revolutionary civil war		
1946		1,348,320[a]
1947		2,759,456[c]
1947		1,700,000[d]
1948		3,065,533[a]
1949 (Sept.)	541	4,488,080[a]
PRC		
1950	551	5,821,604[a]
1951		5,762,293[a]
1952	574	6,001,604[a]
1953	589	6,612,254[a]
1954	602	7,859,473[a]
1955 (June)		8,545,916[b]
1955	614	9,393,394[a]
1956 (8th Cong., 15–27 Sept.)	628	10,734,384[a]
1957	646	12,720,000[a]
1959	672	13,960,000[a]

Table 2.   (*continued*)

Year	Population (millions)	Party Members
1961	658	17,000,000[a]
1964	704	
1965 (end of 1965)		18,000,000[e]
1966 (Aug.)		18,000,000[h]
1969 (9th Cong., Apr.)	806	22,000,000[b]
1971 (June)	852	17,000,000[h]
1972 (Oct.)		20,000,000[h]
1973 (10th Cong., 24–28 Aug.)	892	28,000,000[c]
1976 (Sept.)		34,000,000[h]
1977 (11th Cong., 13–19 Aug.)	949	35,000,000[b]
1979 (Jan.)		36,000,000[h]
1980 (Mar.)	987	38,000,000[h]
1981 (6th Plenum of 11th Cong.)		38,923,569[f]
1981 (12th Cong., 1–11 Sept.)		39,657,212[h]
1983 (June)		40,000,000[h]
1984 (end)		41,000,000[i]
1987 (13th Cong., 26 Oct.)		46,000,000[i]

Sources. a. Franz Schurmann, *Ideology and Organization in Communist China* (Berkeley and Los Angeles: University of California Press, 1968), 129.
b. *Zhonggong Gongchandang Lici Daibiao Dahui* (Shanghai: Shanghai Renmin Chubanshe, 1983), 11.
c. James R. Townsend and Brantly Womack, *Politics: China* (3d ed.), 285.
d. Xian Fu, *Xin Shigi Zhengdang Jianghua* (Beijing: Xinhua Chubanshe, 1984), 147.
e. *Renmin Ribao*, 14 Apr. 1980.
f. *Dangde Jichu Zhishi Wenda* (Henan: Henan Chubanshe), 96.
g. Shin Wujun, *Zhonggong Dangde Jianshe Lilun Zhi Yanjiu* (M.A. Thesis, National Political University of Taiwan, 1978), 186, 263.
h. *Zhongguo Zhonglan*, 1984, 24.
i. *Renmin Ribao*, 26 Oct. 1987.

class now had to be approved by the central organs; workers could be admitted by district party committees.[7] Later the CCP further tightened up the recruitment procedure. Joining the party required two letters of recommendation from members of longer than six months' standing. The application procedure required the approval of two additional upper-level organs—one from the local committee and another from the district (*qu*) committee. Also introduced was the idea of a probationary period: three months for laborers, six months for nonlaborers.[8]

7. Ibid. 1:43.
8. *Dangshi Yanjiu*, no. 2, 1981, 69.

Socioeconomic conditions, however, were not conducive to a working-class party. Despite the rapid spread of the workers' labor movement in 1922–23, when the Third Party Congress was held in June 1923, it was still a party of disgruntled intellectuals: although 25 percent of party members were workers, none held a leading position in the party.[9] When the second plenum of the Third Party Congress was held on 24 November 1923, the number of party members had increased by merely 100 persons in the preceding five months.

After the first united front with the Kuomintang (KMT), the CCP's recruitment policy changed: the party decided to make itself "a true mass party" by rapidly expanding its membership. Accordingly, the probation period was reduced to one month for workers and peasants and a mere three months for intellectuals.[10] Chen Duxiu was particularly enthusiastic about the new policy direction. Declaring that "not increasing the number of party members is a kind of sabotage and a counterrevolutionary activity," he developed a plan to bring the number of party members to 40,000 by the Fifth Party Congress. A recruitment quota was set up for each area.[11]

The new direction in the recruitment policy coincided with the Nationalists' northern expedition and the May 13 movement. Between 1925 and 1927, party membership jumped from 950 to 58,000 (see table 2). As can be seen in table 3, the increase was largely due to an influx of workers, who constituted the majority of all party members in 1926 and 1927, while the percentage of peasant party members declined.[12] The surge also reflected a successful military operation by the Nationalist northern expedition forces. As the Nationalist forces approached and the warlords' forces disintegrated, peasants began to rise against the landlords—totally spontaneously according to Mao's famous "Hunan Report," but more probably with the help of revolutionary organizations and army

9. Ibid.
10. Cao and Pan, eds., *Zhongguo Gongchandang*, 49; *Dangshi Yanjiu*, no. 3, 1982, 37.
11. Ibid., 49.
12. *Dangshi Yanjiu*, no. 2, 1983, 38; Harold Isaacs reports that more than half of the party members—53.8 percent—were workers at the time of Zhiang's coup. Harold Isaacs, *The Tragedy of the Chinese Revolution* (Stanford: Stanford University Press, 1961), 440.

Table 3. Class Composition of CCP Members by Years, 1921–31

Class	1921	1922	1923	1/1926	4/1927	6/1928	1929	3/1930	9/1930	1931
Intellectuals	53 93%	174 81%	327 75%	(27.35%)	11,073 19.1%	10,060 7.2%				
Workers	4 7%	21 19%	105 25%	(60%)	33,627 58%	13,122 11%	(3%)	(2.5%)	(1.6%)	(0%)
Peasants				(11.75%)	10,842 18.7%	99,822 76%				
Military					1,797 3.1%	1,263 0.82%				
Small merchants					289 0.5%					
Others					4,522 7.8%	4,643 3.5%				
Total	57	195	432	18,526	62,150	128,910				

Sources. Percentages in parentheses are from the statistics of Guangdong, Beifang, Jiangzhe, and Hunan party committees. Compiled from information in *Dangshi Yanjiu*, no. 2, 1981, 65–69; no. 3, 1981, 39; no. 2, 1983, 40.

officers. In any case, the CCP was in a position to mobilize the peasants and exploit their enthusiasm. The CCP made the greatest gains in those areas captured by the northern expedition forces. In Hunan, which Nationalist forces entered in July 1925, the CCP's membership registered a quantum leap from a mere 702 in October 1925 to 4,570 by December 1926, and then to 13,000 by July 1927, with a recruiting average of 100 new members per week.[13]

Chiang Kai-shek, probably alarmed at the CCP's rapid spread in areas his troops had liberated from the warlords' forces, moved against the CCP when his troops entered Shanghai in April 1927. His coup almost completely destroyed the party's previous four years' work, reducing CCP strength from 57,000 to 10,000.[14] Seriously affected were worker party members; their share of the total party membership dropped to about 10 percent, and no single healthy party branch remained among industrial workers.[15] Despite the party's renewed efforts to recruit them, the percentage of workers in the party steadily decreased. By 1929 workers accounted for only 3 percent of members, and by 1931 the figure was approaching zero (see table 3).[16]

The CCP responded to Chiang's "double cross" with an extreme leftist policy closely paralleling the Comintern line. Qu Qiubai, the newly elected leader, blamed Chen Duxiu's rightist opportunism for the disaster and decided to make the party "Bolshevik" by replacing the nonproletariat intellectuals in the leadership with members from worker and peasant backgrounds.[17] Quotas of cadres with working-class backgrounds were instituted for each level of the party organs. The party began to attach primary importance to class background (*jieji chengfen*), favoring workers while downgrading the role of the intellectuals who had founded the party.[18] As contemporary Chinese historians argue, "rightist op-

13. *Dangshi Yanjiu*, no. 2, 1982, 32.

14. *Zhonggong Dangshi Jiangyi* (Liaoning: Liaoning Renmin Chubanshe, 1984), 57.

15. Isaacs, *Tragedy of the Chinese Revolution*, 440.

16. Shin Wujun, *Zhonggong Dangde Jianshe Lilun Zhi Yanjiu*, M.A. thesis, National Political College of Taiwan, 1978, 264.

17. Cao and Pan, eds., *Zhongguo Gongchandang*, 76.

18. At that time some party leaders reportedly insisted that "since intellectuals are no longer useful, [it is therefore necessary to] completely restructure the party [by] removing [intellectual leaders]." Shin, *Zhonggong Dangde*, 297.

portunism" was replaced by the equally erroneous "leftist adventurism."[19]

Even after the Sixth Party Congress (PC) held in Moscow deposed Qu Qiubai for his "leftist adventurism," the leftist tendency continued, moving in an even more radical direction. The party constitution adopted by the Sixth PC increased the importance of class background in joining the party.[20] Depending on class backgrounds, different numbers of recommendations were needed: one for workers; two for peasants, artisans, intellectuals, and low-ranking staff persons; and three for high-ranking officials of the various organs. The congress also decided to concentrate its recruitment effort on industrial workers in order to reconstruct party organs in industrial areas. As a result, "many intellectuals with abundant practical experience such as Liu Shaoqi and Yun Daiying" were replaced by workers.[21]

Whether or not it was because of the stress placed on recruiting workers and peasants or other reasons, the CCP rapidly regained strength after the Sixth PC. By 1930, the party had recovered from the 1927 setback with 60,000 members.[22] This rapid recovery was largely due to new membership in the Soviet area, over which the party center, now dominated by Li Lisan, did not have control. But the party was also recovering in urban areas. The labor movement was reactivated in major cities like Shanghai, Tianjin, and Wuhan, and the total number of worker branches increased to 229.[23] According to Li Lisan's report, in the latter six months of 1929, the party recruited 13,000 workers.[24]

The party, however, was still far from having the numbers needed to stage urban uprisings. On 22 March 1932 Li Lisan issued an order, which specified the minimum quota of workers for each province to recruit during April and May. Local party organs were instructed to report recruitment results by June 1930, with a reminder that their work would be evaluated by their fulfillment of the

19. Cao and Pan, eds., *Zhongguo Gongchandang*, 72.
20. *Dangshi Yanjiu*, no. 1, 1986, 53.
21. Ibid.
22. Cao and Pan, eds., *Zhongguo Gongchandang*, 104.
23. *Zhonggong Dangshi Jianyi*, 76.
24. *Zhonggong Zhongyang Guanyu Gongren Yundong Wenjian Xuanbian* (Beijing: Dangan Chubanshe, 1984), 2:9.

quota.[25] Li's effort proved futile when his effort to initiate "an urban uprising and concentrated Red Army attacks on the big cities" ended in disaster.[26]

Though criticizing Li Lisan, the new leadership, which was dominated by twenty-eight Chinese students who had just returned from training in the Soviet Union, basically continued his policy, attaching even more importance to class background and adding "international standards" to their program in order to recruit more industrial workers, as in the Soviet Union. Among peasants, only "hired laborers and poor peasants" would be considered for party membership. Wang Ming, the leader of the returned student group, relied on an organizational approach to supervising recruitment work and set up "inspection teams," which frequently visited the lowest level branches, gathering information, helping lower-level cadres, and supervising the cadres' implementation of official policies. Each party member living in an industrial sector was required to recommend at least one person for the party every month with the aim of bringing worker membership to about 10 percent of the total party membership.[27]

In his desire to recruit more industrial workers, Wang Ming stepped up discrimination against intellectuals. He suspected that the majority of the central Soviet's leading bodies were in the hands of intellectuals. In an allegedly ruthless purge of intellectuals (which included executing fifteen hundred people), Zhang Guotao publicly declared, "If worker cadres make mistakes, the party can understand; but if intellectuals make mistakes, the punishment should be tripled." Kang Keqing succinctly recaptures the mood of the time: "Only if you have a fountain pen in your front pocket do you face the danger of being persecuted as an intellectual; only if you wear eyeglasses do you encounter difficulties."[28]

In retrospect, the party's strategy of focusing exclusively on

---

25. Ibid., 26–30.
26. On 10 June, the CCP Politburo adopted the now famous resolution, "The new revolutionary tide and victory in one or a few provinces." *Zhonggong "Dangde Jianshe,"* 3:87–98.
27. Ibid., 2:122–82.
28. *Fuyang Shifan Xueyuan Xuebao,* no. 4, 1984, 32–41.

industrial workers and utilizing them for armed uprisings was doomed to failure. Even if Chinese workers had acted as an ideal proletariat from the Marxist-Leninist viewpoint, willing to forego immediate economic interests for long-term political ones, conditions in China were still not favorable for an urban revolution. The size of the working class was too small, and the Nationalist repressive capability in urban sectors was too strong. Such CCP leaders as Qu Qiubai, Li Lisan, and Wang Ming, however, had largely overlooked this simple point either because of their orthodox view of Marxism-Leninism or because of the Comintern's domination. For them, Marxism-Leninism operated as "an ideology acting as a higher authority, which stripped individuals of freedom in action except that of submission to it."[29] In brief, they pursued an unrealistic option dictated by a Soviet interpretation of Marxism, while overlooking a feasible alternative based on actual conditions in China.

MAO'S STRATEGY AND THE
ANTI-JAPANESE WAR

Mao was developing a different strategy based on the concrete conditions of China's reality: because of a paucity of industrial workers Mao focused recruitment on peasants. This shift raised theoretical and practical problems. First, the CCP was not powerful enough to revise the tenets of Marxism-Leninism to fit China's reality and pressure from the Comintern to conform continued. Peng Zhen lucidly described the CCP's dilemma:

> According to the Fifth Congress of the Comintern, "the party should be reformed on the basis of an industrial branch," "only the industrial branch can be the foundation of the party," "the street branch [jiedao zhibu] is only an auxiliary organization." If we want to follow these principles, what should we do? We cannot afford not to have any organizations. Our branches should be organized according to administrative areas. Villages are the primary units of our revolutionary bases, and they are everywhere.

29. Martin Carnoy, The State and Political Theory (Princeton: Princeton University Press, 1984), 92.

What could be done? Peng answered:

> Therfore, we cannot automatically guarantee the social background [shehui chengfen] and the class character of our party by relying on branch organizations. Only by relying on the class backgrounds of the leaders of the branches, making the workers, the hired laborers, and the poor peasants a majority among the branch members, and educating those branches, can we ensure [the class nature of our party].[30]

Second, even if the peasants—the poor peasants—had already demonstrated ample revolutionary potential in their willingness to revolt against the existing order, there were obvious basic differences in both economics and politics between industrial workers and peasants. Mao resolved this problem by emphasizing political and ideological education for the peasants. Through education, peasants would obtain a "proletarian political consciousness," thereby transcending their peasant mentality. The Confucian tradition of emphasizing education thus reinforced the CCP's practical need to instill peasants with workers' political consciousness. But despite the enormous stress placed on political education, the CCP very much remained a party imbued with a peasant mentality throughout Mao's era.

There is not much information about Mao's policy on party building during the time he spent in Jinggangshan and Jiangxi, the period from 1927 to 1935. Nonetheless, we know that party growth was quite rapid. By 1930, almost one-third of the 300,000 party members were in Mao's central Soviet area. Although we do not know the precise class composition, it is obvious that most of these 100,000 members were peasants, including some middle peasants. According to a contemporary Chinese historian, during this period Mao changed the party from a "proletarian party to a mass party" by recruiting "a large number of members from revolutionary elements among the peasants and petty bourgeoisie."[31]

The fact that Mao allowed many middle peasants to join the party can be indirectly substantiated by the change in his land re-

30. Peng Zhen, Guanyu Jin-Cha-Ji Bianqu Dangde Gongzuo He Juti Zhengce Baogao (Beijing: Zhongyang Dangxiao Chubanshe, 1981), 200.
31. Ma Jipin and Zhou Yi, eds., Mao Zedong Jiandang Sixiang Yu Dangshi Yanjiu (Changsha: Hunan Renmin Chubanshe, 1984), 167.

form policy. In Jinggangshan, Mao initially followed the Comintern's hard line on that subject. The land reform law of December 1928 declared the confiscation of all lands and put them under state ownership. Every peasant, regardless of sex and age, was given an equal amount of land to cultivate, though not to own. Land sale was strictly prohibited.[32] This radical policy was modified in Jiangxi. The new land reform law confiscated land only from landlords and clans. Moreover, the new policy promised "not to strike down the rich peasants, and not to cause any loss to the middle peasants." It recommended mere adjustment, "using the original cultivating land as a basis, and adding more and taking less." Even in implementing this adjustment, "the rich and middle peasants were allowed to keep good land for themselves, and less fertile lands were given to others."[33] For this rich peasant line and "narrow empiricism," Mao was criticized by—and eventually lost power to—the twenty-eight returned students.[34]

As shown in table 2, CCP membership suffered a major setback in the mid-1930s when the CCP was forced by the Nationalists' fifth encirclement campaign to embark on the Long March. Altogether, 300,000 started the march, but just over one-tenth (40,000) arrived at Yanan. This group of dedicated Communists, "steeled by the epic experiences of the Long March," proselytized with amazing success during the anti-Japanese war. Under Mao's leadership, it eventually became strong enough to defeat the Nationalists.

Many factors contributed to the CCP's success, and many Western scholars have advanced different explanations depending on their theoretical perspective.[35] Mao, however, attributed the success to the "three treasures": the united front, armed struggle, and party organization.

> The past eighteen years' experience tells us that the united front and the armed struggle are the two basic weapons with which to defeat the enemy. The united front means a united front of armed struggle.

32. For Mao's policy see *Zhonggong Dangshi Jiangyi*, 75.
33. Ibid.
34. Zhu Chengjia, ed., *Zhonggong Dangshi*, 2:324–26.
35. Chalmers Johnson, *Peasant Nationalism and Communist Power* (Stanford: Stanford University Press, 1962); Lucian Bianco, *Origins of the Chinese Revolution* (Stanford: Stanford University Press, 1971); Franz Schurmann, *Ideology and Organization in Communist China* (Berkeley and Los Angeles: University of California Press, 1968).

The party organization is the heroic soldier who, using two weapons, can defeat enemies. The three are interrelated.[36]

The united front not only relieved the CCP base areas from Nationalist military pressure, but it also legitimized the party as a de facto government in the "red" areas. The Japanese strategy of advancing rapidly with their forces, while leaving only small garrisons to hold urban areas, created a power vacuum that the CCP's guerrilla forces could easily exploit. By 1939, the number of soldiers in the Red Army jumped from 40,000 to 500,000, controlling 150 counties inhabited by a total population of about 100 million.[37]

The CCP had to set up a new power structure in these newly liberated areas, but it did not have enough reliable party members and cadres. To deal with this shortage of manpower (renhuang), the party decided to expand as rapidly as possible by admitting "activists during the anti-Japanese war—workers, hired laborers, leftist intellectuals in urban areas, and leftist KMT officers." Admission procedures were also relaxed. For instance, the probation period for workers and hired laborers was abolished, and it was reduced to one month for poor peasants and artisans and three for leftist intellectuals, lower-level employees (xiao zhiyuan), and noncommissioned officers of the KMT. Others had to go through a six-month probation period, although this could be shortened, depending on the circumstances.[38] The new policy enabled various base areas to increase their membership as rapidly as possible.[39]

The united front led the CCP to moderate its land reform policy even further. In Yanan, the party decided not to confiscate rich peasants' property, and in the case of redistribution, rich peasants were entitled to the same share as poor or middle peasants.[40] Even landlords with family members in the Red Army were exempted from confiscation.[41] At other revolutionary bases such as Jin-Cha-Ji,

36. Shin, Zhonggong Dangde, 306. Also for the united front policy, see Lyman Van Slyke, Enemies and Friends: The United Front in Chinese Communist History (Stanford: Stanford University Press, 1967), 59.

37. Cao and Pan, eds., Zhongguo Gongchandang, 161.

38. Hunan Shida Xuebao, March 1985, 25–29.

39. For the CCP's resolution of March 1938 to "recruit party members on a large scale," see Zhonggong "Dangde Jianshe," 2:192.

40. Mark Selden, The Yenan Way in Revolutionary China (Cambridge, Mass.: Harvard University Press, 1971), 97.

41. Ibid., 99.

a policy of "reducing rents and interest rates" eventually replaced land reform, allowing landlords to continue to exist.[42] The moderate land reform policy made it possible for middle peasants and rich peasants to join the party.

The CCP also changed its mind about intellectuals. To correct the "erroneous view" that "intellectuals can remain revolutionary only for three days and that recruiting them is very dangerous," the party decided to recruit intellectuals on a large scale. Insisting that the Chinese revolution was also anti-imperialist (a position that appealed to intellectuals), the decision, reportedly drafted by Mao, flatly declared that "without the participation of intellectuals, a Chinese revolution is impossible to achieve."[43] Party members recruited in 1938 were known as the "38-style cadres," a group that included a large contingency of intellectuals.

The CCP's united front policy appealed to patriotic Chinese intellectuals, many of whom had migrated to Communist-controlled areas in order to fight the Japanese. The party welcomed them "as long as they are pure, firm, and willing to accept hardship, regardless of age, sex, occupation, and educational level." Many of them eventually joined the party.[44] Among the intellectual groups migrating to Yanan during this period, the best known is the December 9 group, which derived its name from the December 9 student movement in 1935 that protested Chiang Kai-shek's policy of "first eliminating the Communist bandits and then resisting the Japanese invasion."[45] As the best-educated people in the CCP, many members of this group rapidly moved up the hierarchy after 1949. Women members of the group later married such party leaders as Lin Biao and He Long. However, when the CR started, the group suffered greatly because of its complex relations with the KMT before the move to Yanan.

During the united front period, the CCP decided to obtain the release of party leaders in Nationalist prisons. On instruction from the central authorities, Liu Shaoqi authorized these leaders,

42. For the details of the rent and interest reductions in Jin-Cha-Ji border areas, see Xu Yi, ed., *Jin-Cha-Ji Bianqu Caizheng Jingjishi Cailiao Xuanbian* (Tianjin: Nakai Daxue Chubanshe, 1984), vol. on agriculture, 1–244.

43. *Hunan Shida Xuebao*, March 1985, 25–29.

44. *Dangshi Tongxun*, March 1984, 46.

45. John Israel, *Student Nationalism in China, 1921–1937* (Stanford: Stanford University Press, 1962).

through secret channels, to write false confessions, which the Nationalist authorities demanded as a precondition to their release. Many of these leaders later became important, but they too were attacked during the CR for having surrendered to the KMT.[46]

The Red Army was instrumental in building up the party quickly. From the beginning it was organized to fight as well as to propagate the party line and to mobilize the masses. To ensure that "the party controls the gun," it had penetrated the military.[47] According to a Chinese source, all officers above the rank of battalion commander—90 percent of company and platoon leaders and 20 percent of all regular soldiers—were party members by the beginning of the anti-Japanese war.[48]

After tightening its control, the CCP relied on the military to expand the party. As early as 1930, Mao flatly declared that since "the experience of the Red Army is richer than that of the local party," they "should therefore endeavor to help local party committees and train local party cadres." When the Eighth Route Army left Yanan to penetrate the territories occupied by the Japanese, Mao specifically told Chu De, the commander, that the "Sino-Japanese war is the best opportunity for our party to expand. Our policy is to spend 70 percent of our efforts on expansion, 20 percent on our compromise [with the KMT], and 10 percent on fighting the Japanese."[49]

When a Red Army unit entered an unfamiliar village for the first time, it usually employed the following methods to establish a new power structure and party branch.[50] First, military representatives used "administrative methods" by ordering the leader of the village to convene a villagewide mass meeting. Even though he was appointed by the KMT, the leader was compelled to call for a mass meeting and formally to introduce Red Army representatives. The representatives would explain the need to set up a mass organization against the Japanese. Sponsorship by the power elite in each locality helped to legitimize the representatives and to break the ice

46. Shin, *Zhonggong Dangde*, 304.
47. Cao and Pan, eds., *Zhongguo Gongchandang*, 145, 167.
48. Ibid., 144.
49. Shin, *Zhonggong Dangde*, 306.
50. Peng Zhen, *Guanyu Jin-Cha-Ji*, 134–44. Subsequent quotations are from this source.

in establishing contact with the masses. According to the CCP, this method was necessary because of "the peasants' dependency and conservativism" prior to their mobilization.

Second, membership in the anti-Japanese organization was open to almost anyone in the village, including "speculators, class enemies, and alien elements [yiji fenzi]," because "the task facing the party was enormous and urgent, whereas the available manpower was very limited."

Third, the CCP representatives skillfully nursed the anti-Japanese organizations, letting them gradually take over functions previously performed by village leaders, which created a "dual power structure." The official guidelines contained specific instructions to avoid the forcible removal of the village leader; instead, he was to be drawn into the anti-Japanese mass organization so that whatever legitimacy he had could be transferred to it.

Fourth, once the umbrella anti-Japanese mass organization had set up offices in charge of different projects, party representatives kept a careful eye on the active workers, hired laborers, and poor peasants who appeared to have the trust of the masses and who demonstrated leadership ability. Once potential candidates were selected, the party representatives told them to set up peasants' and workers' associations. Naturally, when these organizations were formed, the activists assumed leadership.

Fifth, the representatives led the associations to discuss current socioeconomic conditions in the village, often explaining Marxist theory along with CCP's policy on these problems. These specialized associations eventually demanded reduced rents, increased wages, and shorter working hours. As class-conflict-related issues arose, some of the former activists from the economically better-off groups withdrew. Vacancies were filled by persons with good class backgrounds whose interests were tied to the CCP program.

Sixth, those original leaders with questionable motivations and backgrounds were replaced by more reliable elements who had proven their activism, dedication, and leadership ability. This replacement ensured that each mass organization—including the original united front organization—would operate as the party wished.

Seventh, in selecting the cadres, the most reliable people were approached, tested, and given the option of joining the party. If they responded positively, they were groomed as members. After joining the party, each person was sent to a higher level to receive training. Then, he or she was returned to the native area to recruit other members.

In this way, the CCP developed layers of organizations. At the outer rim was the anti-Japanese association, whose membership was open to all; then came the peasants' and workers' associations, with membership largely determined by economic position. At the core was the party branch, which the CCP staffed with carefully selected people from a hired laborer or poor-peasant background. The party branch controlled mass organizations through the cadres. In building up these layers, it exploited the prestige and ability of the existing elite to establish mass organizations, while taking over the organizations by introducing more reliable elements and getting rid of unreliable ones.[51]

As a result of this program, CCP membership grew at an amazing rate in the first few years of the second united front. The total number of members increased by twenty times in a mere three years—from 40,000 in 1937 to 800,000 in 1940.[52]

There is not much information on the class composition of the mass organizations and party branches. What fragmented information that is available, however, indicates that although poor peasants dominated party branches, rich and middle peasants were tolerated in both the united front organization and the formal government structure, which was staffed by equal numbers of communists, noncommunist leftists, and middle-of-the-roaders (a structure known as the 3:3:3 system). Table 4 breaks down the social and economic backgrounds of low-level government functionaries elected through the 3:3:3 system.

Table 4 shows that the higher one goes up the administrative hierarchy, the more educated people, rich peasants, and middle peasants were elected. Also, the table indicates a crude correlation between the level of education and class background; undoubtedly

51. Ibid.
52. Cao and Pan, eds., *Zhongguo Gongchandang*, 139, 161; Peng Zhen, *Guanyu Jin-Cha-Ji*, 142.

Table 4.   Characteristics of Persons Elected to Leadership Positions in
Rural Governments in Jin-Cha-Ji Border Areas, 1941

Characteristics	Village (cun)	District (qu)	County (xian)
Sex			
Male	92.8	94.20	100.0
Female	7.1	5.88	0
Age			
Young	27.6	21.50	42.8
Middle-aged	55.2	76.48	57.2
Old	17.2	1.94	0
Class background			
Workers	7.6	3.18	0
Poor peasants	40.1	35.29	14.4
Middle peasants	40.2	58.89	42.8
Rich peasants	6.7	1.94	42.8
Landlords	0.1	0	0
Merchants	5.3	0	0
Education			
Illiterate	17.6	3.88	0
Primary school	80.0	74.54	0
Middle school	2.3	21.58	100
College	0.1	0	0

Source. Peng Zhen, *Guanyu Jin-Cha-Ji Bianqu Dangde Gongzuo He Juti Zhengce Baogao*
(Beijing: Zhongyang Dangxiao Chubanshe, 1981), 40–42.

the rich and middle peasants were better educated.[53] In contrast to
the heavy representation of the rich and middle peasants in the
elected government position, hired laborers and poor peasants
constituted a majority in the party membership.

Table 5 gives credence to Yang Shangkun's report that poor
peasants made up between 60 and 83 percent of the entire party
and that intellectuals constituted about 5–10 percent—even 25 percent in some units.[54] One must also notice the significant presence
of middle peasants. However, when the CCP intensified the class
struggle after 1945, the middle peasants' chances of joining the party diminished.

53. *Shaan-Gan-Ning Bianqu De Jingbing Jianzheng* (Beijing: Jiushi Chubanshe,
1982), 113.
54. According to Yang Shangkun, only 2 percent of party members were female.
Zhonggong "Dangde Jianshe," 1:104.

Table 5. Class Background of Party Members in Jin-Cha-Ji Border Areas, 1940 (percentage)

Class	Beiyu District	Jinzhong and Jindong Districts
Workers	6.57	6.3
Hired laborers	7.41	
Poor peasants	68.07	72
Middle peasants	10.42	18
Intellectuals	3.82	1.8
Others	2.82	1.9

Source. Peng Zhen, *Guanyu Jin-Cha-Ji Bianqu Dangde Gongzuo He Juti Zhengce Baogao* (Beijing: Zhongyang Dangxiao Chubanshe, 1981), 201.

Although politically reliable, most hired laborers and poor peasants were illiterate or had a minimal education, which prevented them from becoming cadres. The majority of cadres, particularly at the county level and above, were composed of intellectuals. Chen Yun, director of the central organization department, reported that, as of November 1939, "eighty-five percent of the middle-echelon cadres of the party and government are intellectuals. During the anti-Japanese war [we] absorbed some intellectuals, and later the political cadres, except for the old Red army, relied on that group, who were from these 38-style cadres."[55] Table 6 also indicates that middle peasants had a better chance of joining cadres at the county and district levels, while the percentage of poor peasants dropped from 72.5 percent at the branch level to 10 percent at the county level.

Local cadres during the anti-Japanese war were made up of two groups—intellectual cadres at the middle level and poor-peasant cadres largely limited to the lower level. One official document of the Shaan-Gan-Ning border government reports on the problems of these two groups:

> More than 90 percent of the district- and village-level cadres were activists in the local area. They are very familiar with local conditions, can maintain good relationships with the ordinary people,

55. Chen Yun, *Chen Yun Wenxun*, 145. Quoted in *Fuyang Shifan Xueyuan Xuebao*, no. 4, 1984, 32–41.

Table 6.   Class Backgrounds of Party Cadres in Beiye, 1940
(percentage)

Class	County	District	Branch	Party Members
Workers	3.30	7.70	4.70	6.30
Hired laborers	1.10	6.50	2.77	6.02
Poor peasants	10.00	46.10	72.50	70.30
Middle peasants	7.80	17.54	14.97	2.07
Intellectuals	73.30	20.30	4.39	3.68
Others	4.50	1.75	0.59	2.62

Source. Peng Zhen, *Guanyu Jin-Cha-Ji Bianqu Dangde Gongzuo He Juiti Zhengce Baogao*
(Beijing: Zhongyang Dangxiao Chubanshe, 1981), 202.

and usually carry out their responsibilities. But their level of education is very low and their attachments to place and family are very
strong.

Most of the county-level cadres were of peasant origins; the proportion of those with primary school and junior high school educations came to about 40 percent; they have had much experience with
the practice of revolutionary struggle, but their theoretical level is
low, and their cultural level is insufficient. They often work from the
narrow perspective of empiricism and cannot handle new, complex
situations; they lack innovative attitudes because they have been
working in the same positions for long periods of time.

The report continues:

More than 70 percent of the district cadres are revolutionary young
intellectuals; they are rich in fresh perception, enthusiastic about
their work, and active. Unfortunately, they lack practical experience
as well as the attitude of seeking truth from the facts. On the whole,
the cadre corps are good, but there remain some problems with corruption, particularly at the district, county, and village [*xiang*]
levels.[56]

When the general political and military situation worsened
around 1940, the CCP responded with a policy of retrenchment; its
recruitment strategy shifted from "emphasizing quantity" to
"emphasizing quality," with the slogan of "firmly and cautiously,
paying attention to details" as if "carving with care." At the same

56. *Shaan-Gan-Ning Bianqu*, 113.

time, the party started to attach increasing importance to class background in its recruitment. This was not a surprise because even during the heyday of the united front, Marxist bias had persisted. Many CCP leaders, particularly those closely associated with the twenty-eight returned students, had insisted that the ratio between workers and peasants in the party should increase. Knowing that most intellectuals joined the party because of its resistance to the Japanese rather than its commitment to the socialist revolution, they stressed the need to cultivate "intellectuals from poor economic categories" for cadre positions.[57]

Another reason for the renewed emphasis on class background was a practical one, although it was based on Marxist assumptions. The CCP had already formed the habit of relying on class background to determine loyalty—a practice that continued until the recent past. Party leaders knew that landlords, merchants, and rich peasants were cooperating with the party because of its coercive power. Despite their outward support of the CCP, these classes hoped for its failure. When the base area was vulnerable to infiltration by enemy agents and the final battles with the Japanese and the Nationalists were yet to come, the political loyalty of members to the party was crucially important.

The party thus adopted a "Resolution Regarding the Investigation of Party Members' Class Background" in November 1939.[58] In order to consolidate the party, the resolution called for it to check the class background of members very carefully, expelling all alien elements (yiji fenzi), landlords, rich peasants, merchants, speculators, and enemy spies. Various localities reported the expulsion of between 2 to 3 percent of their members.[59] Party members with a middle-peasant background were reassigned from party leadership positions to other mass organizations, while poor-peasant members were promoted to branch leadership. Intellectuals from areas controlled by either the KMT or the Japanese ("white" areas) were also subjected to careful scrutiny by the party. Through this method, Dingbei county reduced the percentage of middle-peasant

57. *Zhonggong "Dangde Jianshe,"* 1:210–15.
58. Ibid., 195–205.
59. Peng Zhen, *Guanyu Jin-Cha-Ji,* 158.

members in the party branch leadership from 70 to 24 percent and Tang county from 50 to 14 percent.[60]

By 1943, the CCP had launched a counterattack and recovered many base areas, resuming party expansion.[61] When the collapse of the Japanese military became imminent, the CCP convened the Seventh Party Congress in April 1945. Attended by 547 delegates, the congress symbolized the triumph of the CCP, which had expanded from 40,000 members after the Long March to 1.2 million, powerful enough to challenge the KMT. It also epitomized Mao's personal victory: his peasant-oriented strategy was vindicated. The congress decided, among other things, to expand party membership as fast as possible and eventually to have an open party construction in the liberated areas.[62]

DURING THE CIVIL WAR

In the four years between 1945 and 1949, when the CCP was engaged in its final battles with the Nationalists, membership jumped from 1.2 million to over 4.4 million. This increase was due to the party's conscious decision to push its growth as rapidly as possible. That decision may or may not indicate that the CCP was expecting a military confrontation with the KMT. However, by the time the CCP decided to carry out land reform in May 1946, it had certainly realized that military confrontation was unavoidable. The party must have calculated that land reform would create social groups that would support it in the forthcoming civil war. Land reforms also enabled it to recruit a large number of activists. Together, party expansion and land reform were intended to strengthen the party's mass base for the civil war, which put an end to the united front and intensified class conflict.

The party publicly declared its new criteria for membership:

> The anti-Japanese war is already over, and now class struggle will become the important issue. . . . What kind of people should be recruited? In recruiting new members, special attention should be

60. Ibid., 155–56.
61. Cao and Pan, eds., *Zhongguo Gongchandang*, 170.
62. For the composition of delegates to the Seventh CC, see Peter Vladimirov, *Yenan Diary*, cited in Shin, *Zhonggong Dangde*, 327.

given to class backgrounds. The main targets are workers, coolies, hired hands, poor peasants, and young intellectuals who have determination, are politically pure, and have actually participated in the struggle. Since today's struggle is mainly a democratic struggle against feudalism, the conditions are not the same as during the anti-Japanese war. Therefore, our party's class background should be more pure. But this does not mean that all with good class backgrounds can join the party. Only those proletariats and semiproletariats convinced of the need for struggle can join the party.[63]

Party documents gradually rounded out the criteria for membership. The first prerequisite was "pure class background," as stated above.[64] The second requirement was a clean history—no one who had joined the KMT or collaborated with the Japanese, for example, was eligible. Good class background alone was no guarantee, however, for even people with such backgrounds collaborated with the Japanese or the KMT. The third condition was political expression as proven in various mass struggles—"class struggle, struggle against the enemy, struggle against renegades, and struggle for production." Among soldiers, "those who have proven themselves in investigating deserters and renegades," that is, those who had betrayed their friends to the party, were considered more desirable.

Three groups of people were never to be recruited. In the first were people with undesirable class backgrounds, lumped together with those who had served in either the Manchu puppet government set up by the Japanese or the KMT. The second group included members of religious groups. The third group consisted of those who had been making a living "in immoral ways"—speculators, hooligans, and opium smokers.[65]

As usual the required procedure for joining the party differed according to class background. The probationary period was six months for workers, coolies, hired hands, poor peasants, and the urban poor; one year for middle peasants, white-collar workers, free professionals, and intellectuals; and three years for others.[66] Party members on probation could not act as sponsors, but because

63. *Jiandang* (Harbin: Heilongjiang Danganshi, 1984), 82–83.
64. Ibid., 19.
65. Ibid., 91–92.
66. *Zhongguo Gongchandangzhang Huibian*, 48.

of the shortage of old party members, reliable new members with good class backgrounds could be authorized to recommend new recruits. Candidates with desirable class backgrounds were approved by a district party committee; the others had to be approved by county-level party committees.

The rapid increase in the number of party members was largely due to large-scale recruitment in Manchuria. When the party adopted the policy of "defending the south and expanding to the north," the CCP dispatched 100,000 troops with 20,000 cadres headed by one-quarter of the Politburo to Manchuria.[67] Eventually, they established party networks throughout Manchuria, thus increasing the total size of party membership to 3 million by 1948.

The national trend of the growth rate varied year by year during the period from 1945 to 1949. The low growth rate of 1946 reflected the uncertainty about the CCP's future strategy and the fluid political situation. However, once the CCP shifted its land policy from "reducing rents" to "distributing land to the tillers," party building gained momentum. The expansion slowed down in 1947 when the party launched a rectification campaign. By 1949, when the CCP was sealing its victory, it started openly to recruit new members for the first time. An approximate 1.2 million new members were admitted in the final year of the civil war.

Fluctuation in party expansion largely corresponds to the stages of land reform in Manchuria. In the first stage, from December 1945 to June 1946 (i.e., before the beginning of land reforms), the Heilongjiang provincial party committee adopted a strategy of "careful and controlled development," because the main task at that moment was the struggle against renegades; land reform had not yet started. Originally, 301 cadres—including some nonparty members—entered the area right after the Japanese surrendered. In the first year they recruited 618 new party members, mostly from military and municipal organs. This left the vast rural areas without any party organizations or members.[68]

The second stage started right after the June 1946 conference, which decided how land was to be distributed. The provincial par-

67. Cao and Pan, eds., *Zhongguo Gongchandang*, 184.
68. Of 618, 289 were in the military, 223 in municipal organs, and 106 in rural areas. *Jiandang*, 50–53.

Table 7.   Increase in Number of Party Members by Year,
Heilongjiang Province, 1945–49

Date	No. of New Recruits		No. of Party Branches	Total No. of Members	
11/1945		302			
5/1946	Total	618			
	Military	289			
	Urban	223			
	Rural	106			
9/1946	Total	2,566			
	Military	240			
	Urban	414			
	Rural	1,854			
10/1947		2,141	309	Total	5,285
				Rural	3,758
1/1948	No development				
Spring 1948	Total	2,869	754	Total	8,154
				Urban	2,022
				Rural	5,532
12/1949	Total	9,768	1,325	Total	18,903
	Rural	8,774		Urban	4,094
				Rural	14,309

Source. *Jiandang* (Harbin: Heilongjiangsheng Danganguan, 1985), 50–63.

ty committee moved to set up party organizations as fast as possible, sometimes even circumventing existing regulations. It sent work teams of 933 members to rural areas where there were no party members. The work teams recruited 2,566 new members (in 206 branches) to act as "seeds" in developing the rural party organizations. In other areas, the party expanded more rapidly. Songjiang province reports that membership increased by 600 percent in the four months after the May 4 decision. During this period, many individuals made extreme efforts to gain new members: one cadre recruited 140 people in three months, averaging 1.5 persons per day.[69]

The third phase of recruitment started after October 1946 when

69. Ibid. After 1945, the CCP set up five provinces and one special municipality. They were Songjiang, Hejiang, Heilongjiang, Nenjiang and Suijiang (later, Mudanjiang) provinces. By 1954, all of them were combined into the present Heilongjiang province.

the campaign to "cook raw rice" started. In this campaign, hired hands and poor peasants became the dominant political force, and activists from their class were recruited on a large scale by a policy of "actively and cautiously increasing party members" initiated by the Heilongjiang provincial party committee. In the Beian district, 260 old party members recruited 2,141 new ones, many of whom were immediately promoted to leadership positions. In the entire province, a total of 11,842 new members was promoted to cadres, bringing the total number to 22,387.

In the fourth stage, between November 1947 and January 1948, the movement began dividing the land. During this period, party recruitment temporarily stopped, and rectification started. After finishing the distribution of land, the recruitment drive resumed.[70] Before the beginning of open party building in August 1948, the total number of members had increased to 8,154—a 50 percent increase compared with the previous figure—and every county, district, and village had established a party branch.[71]

The last phase was open party building. By August 1948 when the Red Army was winning the civil war, the party felt safe enough to begin membership recruitment openly so as to set up party branches in every village by March 1949. This time, not the work teams, but the county and district party committees took responsibility for recruiting members and setting up basic organs.

The open party building followed well-defined stages. First, the party launched a vigorous propaganda campaign to dispel all kinds of erroneous views.[72] Then the county and district party committees set up a plan for recruitment and trained "organization persons" (zuzhi yuan) whose main job was to interview and evaluate candidates for party membership.

In mass meetings, party leaders explained the purpose of open party building. Then anyone who was interested in joining the party made a self-report (zibao), in which he reported his own candidacy. The public then discussed the qualifications of those who had nominated themselves. If they passed the public debate, they were finally screened and approved by the appropriate party

70. Ibid., 86–105.
71. Ibid.
72. Peng Zhen, Guanyu Jin-Cha-Ji, 142.

organs. About one-quarter of the self-nominated candidates were accepted.[73]

During the four years between 1945 and 1949 the party grew dramatically in Manchuria. A small number of old members recruited new ones with amazing speed. In Mudanjiang province, sixty old members who had moved into the area recruited 4,000 new members, who totaled 0.45 percent of the population in the area.[74] In Nenjiang province, 772 old members recruited 16,254 people (or 0.6 percent of the total population). Heilongjiang was reported to have recruited 9,768 new members in the three months from September through November 1948, 8,774 of them in 517 rural party branches.[75]

To ensure that party branches were set up in every village, a recruitment quota for each area was usually assigned.[76] The counties in the Jinsui base area were instructed to increase party membership by 33 percent in three months.[77] Each area authorized individual members to recruit a certain number of people.

Not surprisingly, use of the quotas for party expansion had many undesirable consequences. In some areas lower-level units blindly tried to meet the quota by accepting unqualified persons. Some units tried to overpass "internally decided targets" and "complete the work before the timetable," thereby sacrificing standards of quality. Since only members could recruit new members and many localities did not have any branches, there was much corruption and inefficiency. If a recruiter was corrupt, his new members would often be unfit for membership. One party member who had concealed his class background was made chairman of a peasants association because of his activism during the land reforms. When the party told him to recruit seventy new members, he personally recruited forty persons, including a "policeman, a spy, and a former bandit."[78] One of his relatives also recruited twenty candidates, many of whom were unsuited for membership. Recruiters tended to look for candidates only among personal ac-

73. *Jiandang*, 33.
74. Ibid., 232.
75. Most of the information in the following discussion is from *Jiandang*, and from experiences of Party building in the former five provinces.
76. *Jiandang*, 44.
77. Ibid.
78. Peng Zhen, *Guanyu Jin-Cha-Ji*, 142.

quaintances or people with whom they had something in common. For instance, some members only recruited new members from the same province. One member from Shandong province recruited only Shandong people, and when there were no more hired hands and poor peasants to recruit, he approached "bad elements." Some people followed the organizational ties of the anti-Japanese associations, and when there were no good people in the anti-Japanese associations, they accepted bad ones. Others recruited only school classmates and colleagues.[79]

Moreover, even those recruited from the good classes did not have the appropriate "political consciousness" in the eyes of the Chinese leaders. They suffered from a "peasants' diffused conservativism." Some members flourished economically after the land reforms and wanted to become rich. Such thinking weakened the party members' ties to their classes. It was hoped that rectification would solve all these problems.

Moreover, as the land reform movement developed, it directly threatened the interests of cadres from the exploiting class, whereas the poor peasants' demand for land increased.[80] The well-known case of Pingshan county was typical. There, pressure from the peasants forced the party to purge its local party. Pingshan was an old liberated area, but the local leadership was allegedly under the control of "liu-mang, landlords, and rich peasants," who resisted the poor peasants' demand for a thorough redistribution of land. Even work teams sent down by the higher level could not resolve the conflict between the poor peasants and the local party committee. Eventually, the committee had to be reorganized in a public meeting where nonparty poor peasants were allowed to participate.

From the beginning, the party knew that rapid expansion would introduce many undesirable elements. It instructed local committees to use the "wave style" in recruiting members: to "recruit some, immediately train them, and then recruit another group." This pattern of expansion, immediately followed by a rectification campaign, was a well-established procedure.

On 17 July 1947 a meeting chaired by Liu Shaoqi reviewed land

79. Ibid.
80. *Jiandang*, 79.

reform works and decided to carry out the rectification. Mao agreed. Its objective was to check "class backgrounds, ideology, and work style," while consolidating organization, ideology, and work style.[81] Party members from such exploiting classes as landlords, rich peasants, and degenerates were to be expelled.

Among these three objectives, determining class background was the easiest task for lower-level party leaders to carry out. Various methods were used. "In some areas, the determination of class status was based on individual report and public discussion; in other areas, each individual was required to write down his class background on the form; in other areas, the decision was made at a meeting where poor peasants participated."[82]

Once their class status was determined, party members with undesirable class backgrounds were under great pressure, even though the official policy was supposed to take into account their actual political performance. By contrast, those with desirable class backgrounds demanded revenge on the other classes. Some units under the leadership of poor peasants advanced such simplistic slogans as "organize the poor peasant party members into a 'small group of poor peasants,' unify the middle-peasant cadres, and attack the cadres of the landlord and the rich peasant class," and "poor and hired peasants conquered the world, and they will control the world." As has happened many times in China, once the official policy was set, social groups with vested interests in the policy pushed it to an extreme.

Thus, a leftist tendency appeared, pushing land reform in a radical direction by violating the rights of the middle peasants and emphasizing class background over political performance. Deng Xiaoping reportedly wrote a letter to the center, pointing out that class background should not be overstressed in party rectification; instead, "standpoint" should be considered. Deng also said that in some areas party members from the landlord and rich-peasant classes were being indiscriminately expelled. Mao agreed with this view by publishing "On Our Current Task," which criticized the leftist trend.[83] Central party leaders allegedly corrected the leftist

81. Cao and Pan, eds., *Zhongguo Gongchandang*, 199.
82. *Jiandang*, 84.
83. Ibid.

tendency but did not uproot it. They could not do so because the leftist tendency originated from hired-laborer and poor-peasant backgrounds, the political elite, and for this reason the leftist tendency reasserted itself again and again.

LEGACY OF THE CCP'S
REVOLUTIONARY EXPERIENCES

The preceding discussion demonstrates that the party's major expansion took place only when it had strong military forces to protect its operation.[84] The CCP's membership grew rapidly during the first united front in the areas which the KMT forces physically controlled, and then in the Jiangxi Soviet area, where the party set up a state within a state. After the Long March, the enhanced military capability of the CCP, operating in the power vacuum created by the Japanese invasion, facilitated a large increase in party membership. During the civil war, the party again expanded most rapidly in Manchuria, which it controlled militarily. This reliance on the military to create a political atmosphere conducive for implementing party policies has had a long-term effect on Chinese leaders' view of political power.

The crucial role played by the military, however, does not diminish the organizational skill and capability that party leaders demonstrated. Without superb organizational capabilities, party leaders could not have exploited the political, economic, and social grievances of various classes and groups in China while adjusting their programs and policies to the changing situation. As Roy Hofheinz rightly concludes, neither "contextual" nor "motivational" theories that do not take into account the behavior of the Chinese Communists themselves can explain the success of the CCP.[85] Without the flexible and skillful leadership of the party, whatever revolutionary potential Chinese society had would have remained as mere potential.

One of the CCP's remarkable organizational capabilities was its

84. For the latest publication on this issue, see Yung-fa Chen, *Making Revolution* (Berkeley and Los Angeles: University of California Press, 1986).

85. Roy Hofheinz, "The Ecology of Chinese Communist Success," in A. Doak Barnett, ed., *Chinese Communist Politics in Action* (Seattle: University of Washington, 1969), 3–77.

adaptability to the changing socioeconomic conditions of China
and its ability to restructure itself in line with a new task. When the
pre-Mao era leaders insisted on building the proletarian party exclusively on the working class, their policy was doomed from the
beginning, not because of any logical flaws in Marxism-Leninism,
but because they overlooked China's concrete conditions. Under
Mao's leadership the party shifted its focus to rural problems,
adopted a mild land reform policy, and recruited party members
from a broader segment of the population. The united front
allowed the party to utilize the expertise and knowledge of intellectuals while minimizing the potential resistance of landlords and
rich peasants. However, when the CCP renewed class warfare in
rural areas for land reform in 1946, it shifted the focus of recruitment to poor peasants and hired hands, while discriminating
against intellectuals, most of whom came from the well-to-do social
class. In this sense, the revolution was made by the counter-elite
rather than "coming by itself" out of the structural conditions of
China.[86] Any explanation of the CCP's success in political revolution has to take into account Mao's role in selecting a "feasible
alternative" revolutionary strategy.

The most amazing organizational skill that the CCP leadership
demonstrated during this period was not their success in building
a dedicated revolutionary party along Leninist principles, but their
masterful development of several layers of organization that still
kept the party at the core. They set up the anti-Japanese mass
organizations, peasants associations, workers associations, and
other types of mass organizations, while maintaining the party's
control over them through dedicated party members. By keeping
the membership requirements for each mass organization broad
and general, but preserving the strict requirements for its membership, the party mobilized different social groups, while maintaining control over them. This concept of a layered organization
appears to be at the heart of Mao's political strategy; even when he
stressed the need to be "unified with 95 percent of the people," the
implicit assumption was that a core leadership existed. Although
the notion of auxiliary organizations first came from Lenin, Mao

86. Theda Skocpol, *State and Social Revolution* (Cambridge: Cambridge University Press, 1979).

used it very effectively, thereby compensating for the deterministic thread of thinking in original Marxism.

These layered organizations helped the CCP achieve two seemingly conflicting tasks in eastern and central China during the anti-Japanese war: building an effective administrative hierarchy at all levels while allowing peasants at the basic level to seize power almost spontaneously from the traditional local elite, the two concomitant processes that, according to Yungfa Chen, eventually led the CCP to its final victory.[87] They also provided the CCP with the organizational channels necessary for effective use of the mass line, mass mobilization, and mass campaigns.

By the time the CCP captured political power, it had accumulated thirty years of revolutionary experience with almost 4.5 million seasoned party members. Most were poorly educated young people from the most disadvantaged social groups.[88] For instance, among 18,903 party members in Heilongjiang province, the family background of 21 percent was worker, 49 percent hired hand, and 25 percent poor peasant. These three categories comprised 95 percent of the party membership.[89] Fifty-one percent of the Heilongjiang party membership was illiterate, and 23 percent "could barely recognize the characters," the sum of the two amounting to 74 percent. Those who had attended primary school constituted 23.4 percent, whereas only a mere 2.4 percent attended middle schools.[90] The overall educational level of CCP members in 1949 was much lower than that of their counterparts in the Soviet Union in 1927.[91]

Although we do not have national aggregate data showing the percentage of party members holding cadre positions, it is fair to assume that the rate was very high at that time and that those without official positions became cadres after 1949. For instance, in a Heilongjiang county with 600 party members, the "cadres-party members" constituted 95 percent.[92] These figures are extremely

87. Chen, *Making Revolution*.
88. Among all the party members of Heilongjiang, 37 percent belonged to the 18–25 age group and 54.4 percent to the 25–40 age group. *Jiandang*, 59.
89. Ibid.
90. Ibid.
91. Jerry Hough, *Soviet Leadership in Transition* (Washington, D.C.: Brookings Institution, 1980), 28.
92. *Jiandang*, 119.

high for a time when only 0.65 percent of the rural population and about 0.2 percent of the urban population were party members.[93]

Heilongjiang may be an extreme case. However, in every sense, the party members were from the least educated and the most disadvantaged social groups in the rural area. Nonetheless, they served the party well when its main task was fighting a guerrilla war. The type of leaders needed by the party at that time was a heroic, selfless guerrilla fighter dedicated to the cause, rather than an educated professional with specialized knowledge or administrative skills. An effective guerrilla commander had to take care of all the needs of a given base area's members by mobilizing the support of the available sources. The peasant youth could readily provide these leadership qualities.[94]

To summarize, the type of leadership, the policy goals of the CCP, the organizational setting, the techniques of mass line and mass mobilization, and the practice of recruiting political leaders from poor peasants—all these factors complemented one another in helping the CCP to achieve its political victory in 1949. However, some of these factors, ironically, turned out to be constraints when the CCP faced its new task of state building and economic development. Among the many revolutionary experiences that influenced the CCP's political process after the foundation of the People's Republic of China, the most obvious continuity consisted of the former revolutionaries who first founded the new regime, then ruled China for the next thirty years, most remaining as generalists, except for a few working in the economy.[95]

93. In 1948 already 40–45 percent of all cadres in Heilongjiang province were party members. Ibid.

94. James Scott identifies geographical isolation, pervasive personal ties, the absence of a division of labor, self-reliance, millenarian idealism, and egalitarianism as prominent features of a peasant society. "Hegemony and the Peasantry," *Politics and Society*, no. 3, 1977, 267–96.

95. Of course, there were exceptions. For instance, Yao Yiyuan and Zhao Ziyang became experts on economics and finance. For those who developed a speciality in economics, see Kenneth Liberthal and Michel Oksenberg, *Bureaucratic Politics and Chinese Energy Development* (Washington, D.C.: U.S. Department of Commerce, 1986).

3

Staffing the Party-State, 1949–66

This chapter analyzes various social groups that were recruited for the party and the state bureaucracy in terms of "virtue," "ability," and "seniority"—the three criteria that the CCP claims to have used—and the implications of the cadre policy for the political process. To the party, "virtue" meant political loyalty and reliability—one's commitment to Marxism-Leninism as well as to the Leninist principle of the party—which were frequently inferred from one's class background, political history, social relationships, and family background. In addition, political loyalty has also been assumed from political activism and support for a particular policy line at a given moment.

During the guerrilla war period, "ability" referred to the capacity to mobilize people for the specific political task of fighting a guerrilla war. After 1949, despite the functional requirements of managing urban sectors and developing the economy, the CCP by and large continued to use the old idea of ability, although it was usually measured in terms of educational level as well as performance not only in specific functional work but also in political leadership. "Seniority" was based on when a person joined the party or revolutionary movement. Unlike virtue and ability, seniority has never been officially recognized as an important criterion in personnel management. But it has been the most important factor in China, more important than in any other bureaucratic organization, because seniority symbolizes both proven political loyalty and accumulated "practical experiences."

Although the specific meaning and relative weight of the three criteria have changed, often becoming the focus of inner elite conflict, the overall trend has been for the CCP to increasingly stress virtue, while downgrading the relevance of ability in personnel management. The trend reflected the continuing rural orientation of the revolutionary elite who founded the new regime and the

47

CCP's failure to adjust its cadre policy to the requirements of economic development and modernization after its successful political revolution.

STAFFING THE PARTY-STATE APPARATUS

The party approached the task of setting up a power structure in the newly liberated areas as it had previously dealt with the problem of setting up a new base area: it dispatched cadre groups that worked as "frames"—nuclear groups—and supplemented their strength with cadres recruited locally.[1] Once these cadres (commonly known as "southbound cadres") moved into a newly liberated province, they were usually reinforced by local underground party members, as well as by local guerrilla forces. When the People's Liberation Army (PLA) moved to the front, some units—known as "localized forces" (*zhuli difang hua*)—were usually left to be used locally. However, the combination of all these groups was not sufficient to administer the vast liberated areas. For instance, in Hunan province there were about 15,000 civilian cadres with about one division of the PLA to govern its population of 18 million.[2]

Despite the heavy reliance on military personnel, the CCP encountered a keen shortage of qualified personnel to fill 2.7 million positions when the People's Republic of China was founded. The problem was particularly serious at the local level.[3] The CCP drew from six different groups to ameliorate the cadre shortage.[4] They were (1) existing cadres generally known as "old cadres," (2) young high school or college graduates, (3) activists from mass movements such as land reform (most of them came from the worker and peasant classes), (4) old nonparty intellectuals who

---

1. Cao Zhi, ed., *Zhonghua Renmin Gongheguo Renshi Zhidu Gaiyao* (Beijing: Beijing Daxue Chubanshe, 1985), 102–4.

2. *Hunan Dangshi Tongxun*, no. 1, 1985, 15.

3. Harry Harding, *Organizing China: The Problems of Bureaucracy, 1949–1976* (Stanford: Stanford University Press, 1981), 36.

4. For the recruitment of cadres the regime made a distinction between "absorption" (*xishou*) and "recruitment" (*luyong*). Absorption implied those who were automatically qualified for the cadre positions, whereas recruitment implied selection from a large group of people. The two groups of people who were absorbed into the cadre ranks were graduates of colleges and high schools and demobilized soldiers. Recruitment of cadres was made from worker and peasant activists as well as from unemployed people in the society. Cao Zhi, ed., *Zhonghua Renmin*, 20.

were scattered throughout the society, (5) demobilized PLA men, and (6) selected officials from the former Nationalist government.

We do not know how much each of these groups contributed to the total cadre pool. Even though Harding reports that only 750,000 old party members were qualified, a larger number of them must have eventually landed cadre positions.[5] The total number of college graduates in 1950 was only 40,000, so their contribution cannot have been great.[6] The number of available intellectuals was also very small: China had produced only 210,000 college graduates between 1923 and 1949, and only 10,000 of these had studied abroad.[7] About 100,000 of these older intellectuals were sent to special "people's revolutionary universities" for political education between 1950 and 1952, and others were given ideological training in short courses.[8]

Since the combination of the three groups was not sufficient to remedy the shortage of cadres, the CCP relied heavily on former Nationalist government officials. They must have constituted the largest proportion of the cadre class immediately after liberation, particularly in low-level technical positions.[9] Since their political loyalty was dubious, their recruitment could only have been a temporary one. Relying on these groups, the regime set up a basic structure, and by 1952 the cadre shortage was somewhat alleviated.[10] By the mid-1950s, the Chinese cadre corps was composed of several different groups, each of which had different degrees of seniority, ability, and virtue.

The first group was the old cadres, the most senior group who had "conquered the world." Their political reliability was unquestionable, but their average educational level was not high; the highest-level group included intellectuals who had joined the movement during the anti-Japanese war, but many of the middle- and lower-level cadres were from "desirable class backgrounds" and had relatively little education. For ability, all the old cadres

5. Harding, *Organizing China*, 35.
6. Ibid., 36.
7. *Zhongqing Shehui Kexue*, no. 3, 1985, 42; another Chinese source reports the figure to be 180,000, *Shehui Kexue Cankao*, 20 July 1986, 11.
8. Harding, *Organizing China*, 37.
9. Ibid.
10. Ibid., 38.

could claim the "long practical experience" of fighting a guerrilla war.

The old cadres were also divided into two smaller groups: those from the "red" areas, also known as "southbound cadres," who constituted a majority of the old cadres, and those who had done underground work or fought the guerrilla war in the "white" areas. Since most underground work was done in a person's native area, these people were "native cadres," and their educational level was much higher than that of their red-area counterparts, whom they considered as "outsiders." Former underground workers also tended to have more complicated relations with the KMT; some had been arrested; others had close contacts with KMT authorities. Their class backgrounds and "complicated historical problems" made them easy prey for a politically motivated investigation in the early 1950s. The campaign against "localism" eventually weakened their power in local politics.[11]

On the whole, the old cadres occupied leading positions at every level of the party-state organs down to the county. They were also heavily concentrated in such politically powerful positions as secretary of the party committee. Even old cadres with little education—gong nong bing—landed leadership positions at the county and commune levels. Thus, after a careful study of local leadership, Michel Oksenberg concluded that "the generation which seized power during the early years of the revolution continued to monopolize the center of power at the local level, at least until the start of the CR."[12]

The second group, officials retained from the old regime, could claim neither seniority nor virtue, and very few of them were allowed to join the party. Their only reliable asset was their ability. Even those who were kept were mere functionaries within specialized organs. A series of campaigns, including the Three Antis (san-fan), directed against corruption, waste, and bureaucratism, and the Five Antis (wufan), aimed against bribes, fraud, tax evasion, and those in the business community who were leaking state eco-

---

11. For this reason, many of the "localists" joined the rebel faction during the CR.
12. Michel Oksenberg, "Individual Attributes, Bureaucratic Positions, and Political Recruitment," in A. Doak Barnett, ed., Chinese Communist Politics in Action (Seattle: University of Washington Press, 1969), 155–57.

nomic secrets, eventually removed these officials from office, and by 1956 most of them had been dismissed.[13]

The third group consisted of old intellectuals. Some, with national fame, received honorary positions because they had been targets of the CCP's united front policy. Others were assigned to specialist positions where they could utilize their expertise. Old intellectuals could not claim virtue or seniority, but they possessed knowledge that the regime needed, and it helped them to survive in functional positions.[14]

The fourth group consisted of young intellectuals—the new high school and college graduates at the time of liberation—who joined the southbound teams or were assigned to cadre posts right after liberation. Many of them came from undesirable classes, but they could claim that the old bourgeois ideology had not influenced them as much as it had the old intellectuals. Most of them were assigned to functional fields of the party-state structure. Almost thirty years later, the few members of this group with the right family background, political attitude, and connections emerged as national leaders.

The fifth group was made of demobilized soldiers. Generally, the military preferred to discharge only those not suitable for their needs—such as female officers, former KMT officers who had voluntarily surrendered to the CCP, and those "old in age, physically weak, and low in cultural level," although sometimes "young intellectuals and specialists" whom key industrial projects needed were transferred as well.[15]

Reassignment was uniformly managed by the center. Every year the military set up a plan to discharge a certain number of PLA men, and then the Military Affairs Commission coordinated the task with the civilian government to allocate the number of persons to each local authority, which assigned people to appropriate posts. When an army officer was transferred to the civilian sector, he was entitled to a post equivalent to his military rank in terms of salary, level, and fringe benefits.[16] Since military seniority was

13. Ezra Vogel, "From Revolutionary to Semi-Bureaucrat: The 'Regularization' of Cadres," *China Quarterly*, no. 29, January–March 1965, 36–60.
14. Ibid.
15. Cao Zhi, ed., *Zhonghua Renmin*, 20–34.
16. For a comparison of the ranks of military personnel and civilian cadres, see ibid.

based on the date of enlistment and seniority was transferrable,
former soldiers could usually claim high seniority. Their political
loyalty had been tested on the battlefield, and their contribution
to the final defeat of the KMT forces was readily recognized.
Many of them were party members of long standing, but they were
generally poorly educated.[17] Given these strengths and weaknesses, it is not surprising that many demobilized soldiers were
assigned to coercive organs and to political positions that required
only low-level technical competence, such as the political department in a factory.[18]

The largest pool for political cadres was that of worker and
peasant activists. They were politically reliable because they were
recruited from the poorest sector, which had benefited most from
the Communist revolution. But their lack of education was a draw-
back. Nonetheless, the regime justified their promotion to cadre
positions for the reason that "once on the job, their rich practical
experience and firm class standpoint enable them to learn administrative practice quickly."[19] This group filled vacancies at the lower
levels, usually serving in their native locality. Their career pattern
leading to the cadre position was first as an activist in the mass
movement, then joining the party, and finally occupying a leadership position in a new party-state institute.

Among virtue, ability, and seniority, seniority was clearly the
most important factor, which in turn reinforced old cadres' dominance at not only national but also municipal- and county-level
politics. For instance, according to Ying-mao Kau, 68 percent of the
Wuhan municipal elite were party members; 83 percent of the
party members had joined before 1949; over one-half of the elite
(58 percent) were revolutionists who had made their careers in the
Communist movement before the beginning of the third revolutionary civil war; only 18 percent of them had any technical
training.[20] While old party members monopolized key positions
within the bureaucracy, the rank and file of the party expanded
rapidly.

17. Oksenberg, "Individual Attributes."
18. Ibid.
19. Harding, *Organizing China*, 20.
20. Ying-mao Kau, "The Urban Bureaucratic Elite in Communist China: A Case
Study of Wuhan, 1949–65," in Barnett, ed., *Chinese Communist Politics*, 216–67.

PARTY MEMBERSHIP RECRUITMENT

During the last stage of the civil war, party membership jumped from 1.3 million (in 1946) to almost 4.5 million by the time the CCP proudly declared the founding of the new state in 1949. Membership increased to 5.8 million, and 250,000 party branches were organized by 1951[21] (see table 2).

The rapid expansion compromised the quality of new recruits.[22] In addition, there was a need to spread party membership evenly in all localities because the heaviest concentration was in central-north China (*hua bei*)—almost one-third of all party members. The CCP decided in March 1951 to expel "bad elements" and educate party members with Communist ideology to achieve "purity and quality and to improve the combat capacity of the party."[23] The qualifications of all party members were carefully checked against official guidelines, which specified the types of people to be expelled as well as eight requisites for party members that were more stringent than those of the 1945 party constitution.[24] Consequently, 328,000—about 5 percent of party members—were expelled.[25]

When the rural cooperativization drive started, party leaders decided to accelerate membership recruitment in rural areas to prepare for the forthcoming agricultural collectivization. Hunan province reportedly recruited 120,000 peasants—an astonishing 42 percent of all its party members—in 1956. Most peasants recruited during this period were activists of "unified purchase" or "backbone elements" of the agricultural cooperation movement, and

21. Although rural members constituted the majority (3 million), the PLA ranked first in terms of the ratio between the total number of people employed and party members in a given sector (1.6 million party members were in the military). Seven hundred thousand party members were employed in state organs, whereas workers accounted for only 200,000 members. Wang Yifan and Chen Mingxian, *Zhongguo Congchandang Lice Zhengdang Zhenfeng* (Harbin: Heilongjiang Renmin Chubanshe, 1985), 123; *Zhonggong Dangshi Cankao Ziliao* (Renmin Chubanshe, 1974), 87.

22. For the quality problems of party members, see Wang and Chen, *Zhongguo Congchandang*.

23. Ibid., 87; *Shenhui Kexue Cankao* (Qinghai), 30 September 1984, 2–7. For the official resolution on party rectification, see *Zhonggong Dangshi Cankao Ziliao*, 121.

24. For the types of persons to be expelled and the requirements of members, see *Zhonggong Gongchang Lice Zhongyao Huiyi Ji* (Shanghai: Shanghai Renmin Chubanshe, 1983), 2:13–15.

25. *Zhibu Shenghuo* (Beijing), no. 1, 1984, 19.

almost all of them—95 percent in some cases—were classified as poor peasants at the time of the land reform.[26] After joining the party, new members led collectivization movements and then assumed leadership roles in the newly established cooperatives.[27]

The party had also expanded rapidly in urban areas, particularly in industrialized areas where few members existed before 1949, in preparation for the socialist transformation of industry. For instance, in the Anshan Iron and Steel Company, only 2,800 people joined the party between 1950 and 1953; but the party admitted 72,000 workers (90 percent of whom were youths) in 1953–54 alone.[28] The city of Zhengzhou reported that the number of party members among construction workers increased fourteenfold in one year. As was the case in rural collectivization, new party members led the peaceful transformation of industry and eventually landed cadre positions in enterprises. "Model workers, advanced workers, and pioneers in technology" were also accepted in order to effectively promote technical innovation.

The party also admitted a fair number of intellectuals immediately after 1949 when their cooperation was indispensable, particularly in propaganda, education, culture, and the arts.[29] The introduction of the first five-year-plan further accentuated the need for the cooperation of intellectuals. Therefore, the regime adopted a lenient policy of "unifying, educating, and transforming intellectuals." The CCP granted the class status of "staff" to those who worked in big organizations and "laborer" to self-employed professionals (e.g., reporters, artists, and athletes) on the grounds that they earned their income by selling their labor.[30] Even "those who are receiving high salaries, such as engineers, professors, and specialists, are also classified as staff."[31] Only a small number of intellectuals were classified as "reactionary" or "national bourgeoisie." Consequently, some intellectuals managed to join the party and to become cadres after undergoing ideological reform.[32]

26. *Daily Report*, 28 February 1956, AAA25.
27. Ibid., 6 July 1956, AAA14; 16 December 1954, AAA22.
28. Ibid., 2 July 1954, AAA6.
29. For the occupational distribution of about 2 million intellectuals, see *Zhongqing Shehui Kexue*, March 1985, 42–48.
30. *Renda Fuyin*, February 1985, 53.
31. Ibid.
32. For a survey showing intellectuals' attitudes toward the CCP, see *Zhongqing Shehui Kexue*, March 1985, 42–48.

However, the CCP gradually tightened its control over intellectuals. Many of them became the target of mass struggle in such political campaigns as the Three Antis, the Five Antis, the suppression of counterrevolutionaries, opposing America and aiding Korea. The CCP's continuing emphasis on class background, the imposition of official ideology, and the nationalization of educational institutions were bound to clash with the intellectuals' propensity to be critical and independent. The campaign against Hu Feng, a prominent literary figure, for his alleged counterrevolutionary views served as a chilling warning, particularly to intellectuals in creative fields.

As the morale of intellectuals gradually deteriorated, Zhou Enlai found it necessary to improve their political position in 1956. Declaring that 80 percent of intellectuals supported the CCP and that they constituted a "formidable force in the socialist construction program," he urged the party to improve their living and working conditions as well as their political status.[33] Endorsing Zhou's suggestion, An Ziwen, director of the organizational department, instructed lower-level party committees "first to accept famous specialists and authorities, and then investigate their qualifications," while criticizing lower-level party leaders' reluctance to admit intellectuals as an expression of fear on the part of those members without any education.[34] Consequently, the proportion of intellectuals to the total number of party members increased from about 12 percent in 1956 to about 15 percent in 1957 (see table 8). In Hunan the total number of intellectuals admitted to the party during the first five months of 1956 amounted to 1 percent of total party membership, and 21 percent of the 1956 new recruits in Beijing were intellectuals.[35]

Between 1953 and 1956, the number of party members took another quantum leap. By the time of the Eighth Party Congress in 1956, membership had grown to 10 million, almost two party members for every 100 Chinese, an increase of nearly 1,000 percent from

33. *Current Background*, no. 376, 7 February 1956, 7.
34. *Keyan Pipan*, nos. 4–5, 1968, in *Hungweibing Ziliao Xianbian* (Washington, D.C.: Center for Chinese Research Materials, 1980), vol. 2, 0587; see also Guangdong Shengwei Zuzhibu, ed., *Zai Zhishifenzizhong Fazhan Dangyuan* (Guangdongsheng Renmin Chubanshe, 1956).
35. *Daily Report*, 10 April 1956, AAA36; *Survey of China Mainland Press*, no. 1325, 10 July 1956, 19.

Table 8.   Background of Party Members in 1956 and 1957

Class	1956		1957		Net increase 1956–57	
	No.[a]	%	No.[a]	%	No.[a]	%
Workers	1,503	14.0	1,740	13.7	237	11.9
Peasants	7,417	69.1	8,500	66.8	1,083	54.5
Intellectuals	1,256	11.7	1,880	14.8	624	31.4
Others	558	5.2	600	4.7	42	2.1
Total	10,734	100.0	12,720	100.0	1,986	

Source. James C. F. Wang, Contemporary Chinese Politics: An Introduction (Englewood Cliffs, N.J.: Prentice-Hall, 1980), 84.

a. In thousands.

1945. Compared with this national trend, the increase of members in the areas liberated during the last stage of the civil war was even more dramatic.[36] Most of the new recruits were young people.

We have no comprehensive demographic information that shows the composition of party members recruited in the first surge of recruitment after the founding of the People's Republic of China. Data from Zhejiang province may adumbrate the national trend (see table 9).

The composition of those recruited in Zhejiang between 1949 and 1957 approximates the pattern of composition of the entire party as reported at the Eighth Party Congress (see table 8). The percentages of workers and peasants are very close to the national figures. Table 9 indicates that 11.3 percent of the newly recruited were government employees. Although we do not have any information on the total number of cadres in the province, 27,000 must have constituted a large portion of all government employees at that time.

In sum, party membership increased substantially after the founding of the People's Republic of China. From 1949 to 1957, the number of cadres almost tripled—from 2.9 million to 8.1 million (see table 32). By 1956, about 63 percent of those who belonged to

36. From the date of its liberation to 1956, Qinghai recruited 41,609 party members (2.1 percent of its total membership), 5,944 new members per year on average. Shehui Kexue Cankao, 30 September 1984, 2–7.

Table 9.   Occupations of Party Members Recruited in Zhejiang Province,
1949–56

Occupation	No.	%
Worker	31,000	13
Peasant	161,000	67
Government personnel	27,000	11.3
Teacher or student	8,000	3.3
Urban resident[a]	1,000	0.4
Literary	9,000	3.7
Total[b]	237,000	

Source. Baoya Shiyuan Xuebao, Feb. 1982, 46–53.

a. Generally refers to housewives and other unemployed residents.
b. Since about 61,000 who joined the party before 1949 were transferred from other areas, more than 92 percent of the 237,000 (218,040) were admitted during the period of the first five-year plan.

the party had been recruited after liberation. Most of them were recruited during mass movements, which exclusively relied on political criteria (including class background). Their revolutionary potential was impressive; most of them came from classes that had little reason to protect the old society, and they proved their loyalty to the party by demonstrating activism in various campaigns. But a basic weakness was a low level of education and a lack of specialized knowledge—the basic requirements for leading a nation toward industrialization and rapid economic development. However, those party members without cadre positions expected their political virtue to be rewarded with such positions.

THE ANTIRIGHTIST CAMPAIGN

By the time of the Hundred Flowers campaign during the mid-1950s, however, the need for new cadres had decreased, thus intensifying the conflict among the various social groups for cadre positions.[37] At the same time, the bureaucracy was hopelessly

37. About the increasingly severe competition for upward mobility among university and middle school students, see Jonathan Unger, Education Under Mao (New York: Columbia University Press, 1982); and Susan Shirk, Competitive Comrades: Career Incentives and Student Strategy in China (Berkeley and Los Angeles: University of California Press, 1982).

overstaffed, and many cadres had no specific work to do.[38] The campaign to "simplify the administrative structure and to reduce the number of cadres" further heightened tensions within the Chinese bureaucracy, tensions that had been building up since 1949.

Harding identifies four areas of conflict at the time of the Hundred Flowers campaign: (1) between local cadres and "outsiders," (2) between the educated and noneducated, (3) between junior and senior cadres, and (4) between party and nonparty officials.[39] These tensions usually overlapped in any one case; however, the main conflict was between virtue and ability, the first represented by a majority of the party members, who had less education, and the second by intellectuals, who tended not to be party members. As noted, nonparty member cadres owed their positions to their ability; native cadres were better educated than "outsiders," junior cadres better than senior ones, and nonparty officials better than those who belonged to the party.

In fact, the party had been stepping up discrimination against nonparty member cadres as the total pool of members increased after 1949. By 1957 total party membership had reached the 12.7 million mark (see table 2), almost a threefold increase from 1949. Once the party came to have a large reservoir of its own members, it probably tried to fill cadre positions with new members—who expected to be rewarded with tangible benefits—while making a genuine effort to increase party member cadres' technical competence through short-term training programs.[40]

---

38. For a detailed study of the administrative simplification, see *Gongfei "Xiafang" Wenti De Tuishi* (Taipei: Diaochaju, 1958). The monograph reports:

> In the thirteen provincial corporations in Qinghai, 73 percent of cadres on the average had nothing to do. For example, there is one accountant who fills in only one accounting form in a day; another manages only food coupons; another is in charge of the tickets for getting haircuts. Managing the bath tickets needs one full-time person, and managing furniture requres another. As a result, male workers wander around the streets, and female workers do needlework.

Guangdong province reported that in some commercial corporations, the ratio of cadres to workers was 13:12. In some colleges and high schools, the teacher-student ratio was 1:1 (39).

39. Harding, *Organizing China*, 145–47; Ying-mao Kau, "Urban Bureaucratic Elite," 236.

40. *Dazhong Bao*, 25 August 1957.

The proportion of nonparty cadres probably declined steadily after 1949. By 1957, about 60 percent of cadres were party members, a substantial increase from the estimated 13 percent in 1949.[41] Moreover, party members dominated leading positions, whereas those nonparty members who managed to hold their positions saw their administrative authority diminish because they had no access to information allowed only to party members.[42] The increasing domination of member cadres can be noted in the changing official formulas for the united front strategy. Before 1949, the party insisted on the proportion of 3:3:3; in 1956 Zhou Enlai was urging that at least one-quarter of government jobs be given to non-members.[43] If in 1956 2 mil on nonparty cadres did hold 25 percent of all government positions, party member cadres numbered 6 million, and there were probably another 6 million members who did not hold cadre positions. The conflict between the better-educated nonparty member intellectuals and party member cadres surfaced in the Hundred Flowers campaign.

When the intellectuals were induced to air their grievances in the Hundred Flowers campaign, they vented their rage on the dictatorial power of the party-state, particularly its tight monopoly of authority over cadres and its increasing emphasis on virtue. They charged that party cadres considered themselves made of "uncommon stuff" while looking down on nonparty people as knowing nothing of politics.[44] Although they agreed with the CCP that cadres should be appointed on the basis of virtue and ability, they disagreed with the party on what they meant, rejecting the official practice of regarding party members as uniquely virtuous. To them, virtue, as defined by the party, meant "absence of talent."[45] They were bitter about the old cadres whom they regarded as *tubaozi*, "without education and devoid of virtue," relying instead on their "seniority to eat unearned rice." The CCP was also accused of having put officials retained from the Nationalist era in the "freezer" as "materials to be preserved," but with the ulterior intention of

41. *Qinghai Ribao*, 15 August 1957; *Nanfang Ribao*, 17 August 1957.
42. Frederick Teiwes, *Politics and Purge in China* (Armonk, N.Y.: M. E. Sharpe, 1979), 260.
43. *Wenhui Bao*, 24 September 1957.
44. Teiwes, *Politics and Purge*.
45. *Qingdao Ribao*, 14 September 1957.

dumping them as "waste." After experiencing "eight years full of difficulties, and difficulties without end," the retained officials did not "have any hope."[46]

The party's initial response to the intellectuals' charge was rather subdued and defensive. To the criticism that party members lacked virtue, the official news media rather lamely argued that "true virtue" referred to such qualities as "unlimited loyalty to the proletarian class and the socialist task, a high degree of organizational discipline, and lofty political qualities"—all qualities the old revolutionaries presumably possessed.[47] The official media defined ability in a similar way: it was the ability to fight guerrilla wars and to lead mass campaigns against class enemies.

Furthermore, it seems that the party pleaded for understanding about the difficulties inherent in managing personnel matters.

> When we promote those from worker-peasant backgrounds, they [rightists] accuse us of "solely emphasizing background"; when we promote old cadres, they criticize us of "exclusively relying on seniority"; if we promote cadres with strength in functional ability, they blame us for "overemphasizing ability at the expense of virtue"; they oppose the promotion of politically reliable cadres who lack vocational ability, calling them "water barrel cadres"; if we promote female comrades, they accuse us of being engaged in "skirt relations," pointing out the few wives of leading cadres; if we promote cadres from the lower level, they charge us with egalitarianism; if we promote those from the upper level, they insist that we officials protect one another. They object to others being promoted once in five years. But when they themselves are promoted once a year, they continue to complain that their talents are wasted. On the one hand, they criticize those loyal to the party and the party leaders as "following a leadership line" and "docile dogs." On the other hand, they praise liberals resisting leaders for their determination to struggle for and uphold truth.[48]

However, once the antirightist campaign began, the defensive tone changed to harsh denunciation. Mao reversed Zhou Enlai's estimate made one year before by insisting that 80 percent of intellectuals were "bourgeois intellectuals."[49] Deng Xiaoping played a

46. Ibid.
47. Guangxi Ribao, 1 August 1957.
48. Ibid.
49. Mao Zedong Xuanji (Beijing: Renmin Chubanshe, 1977), 5:484.

key role in the antirightist campaign. In his "Report on the Rectification Movement" delivered at the third extended conference of
the Eighth Party Congress, he declared that intellectuals belonged
to the bourgeois class because of their family backgrounds and the
type of education they received. This represented a drastic shift
from the past practice of emphasizing that most intellectuals
earned wages. Party members who had spoken out against the
party were condemned as spokesmen for the bourgeois class who
had entered the party "surreptitiously." Accepting the view that
the antisocialist political ideology of the intellectuals came from
their class background rather than from the possession of any
objective knowledge, Deng advocated training "proletarian intellectuals" and "revolutionary specialists" by promoting young
workers and peasants to carry out the tasks usually performed by
the intellectuals.[50]

Following Deng's reports, the center issued specific criteria for
defining rightists. The basic criterion was whether or not a person
opposed socialism, but how to determine intention was undefined,
leaving room for abuse.[51]

Rectification mainly affected intellectuals in party and government organs above the province and municipality levels as well as
in "business units"—such as educational institutions, research units, newspapers and the publishing industry, literature and art
groups, and public health organizations. Many informants insisted
that during the campaign higher authorities sent down a quota of
rightists to each unit, and each unit in turn had to meet the quota,
even by manufacturing rightists if none was found. The way to
detect a rightist was by first checking the records of speeches and
then by mobilizing the masses to recall questionable statements,
speeches, and problems. Through these methods, the CCP produced about half a million "rightists," which represented 10 percent of all intellectuals.[52] Probably those who earned the rightist

---

50. Zhonggong Zhongyang Dangxiao Dangshi Yanjiushi, ed., *Zhonggong Dangshi Cankao Ziliao* (Beijing: Renmin Chubanshe, 1979), 8:635–66.

51. For the official criteria used for selecting rightists, see ibid.

52. Harding, *Organizing China*, 149. According to Frederick Teiwes (*Politics and
Purge*), between 15 and 40 percent of the leadership of the democratic parties and
between 2 and 3 percent of the members of the CCP itself were labeled rightists
during the antirightist campaign. The label, in many cases, was not removed until
after Mao's death.

stigma were the most outspoken, independent, and honest intellectuals. After the antirightist campaign, no one dared to challenge the party.

On the other hand, the ferocious opposition to perceived rightists that a large number of party members demonstrated is understandable when one looks carefully at the basic structure of the party. More than half of the twelve million party members had been recruited after 1949. Many of them were from worker or peasant backgrounds with little education, and they obviously owed their positions to political loyalty. As the beneficiaries of the new order, through land reform and the socialization of industry, they knew very well that without the Communist Party they would not have risen so far. Thus, they were genuinely eager to defend their interests and reacted violently when intellectuals criticized the party. In this sense the campaign symbolized the peasant mentality not only of Mao but also of the party as a whole. The antirightist campaign has been called the peasants' challenge to intellectuals.[53]

The Hundred Flowers period was the last time the issue of member versus nonmember cadres was publicly aired. With the antirightist campaign, it seems that the Chinese people accepted the party's prerogative over personnel management and the domination of party cadres in all leadership positions. The process of extending political power over other functional fields is best exemplified by the concurrent appointments of top party leaders to professorships at various universities.[54]

AFTER THE ANTIRIGHTIST CAMPAIGN

Party member recruitment came to a standstill during the Hundred Flowers period, but it resumed immediately after the antirightist campaign. As was the case with the preceding movement, the groups targeted for recruitment were those who had proven themselves in the previous antirightist campaign.[55] Heilongjiang province reportedly acquired 6.4 percent and Guizhou province 10

53. "Discussion of 1957," in *Qingnian Lundan* (Wuhan), 1985.
54. For instance, Tao Zhu, Kang Sheng, Zhou Yang, and Ko Qingxi were appointed to professorships at universities and colleges.
55. *Daily Report*, 1 July 1959; 11 July 1959.

percent of their total party membership in this manner.[56] A particularly sought-after group were women: Zhejiang province recruited 10,500—27.2 percent of all women members—in 1959.[57] The recruitment drive continued throughout the Great Leap Forward period. During the euphoric period in which the party sought to build an immediate socialism—known as the "Communist wind"—the party again resorted to quotas for basic units. As a result, "the recruitment work was sloppy, and some localities blindly pursued quantity, thus lowering the quality of the party members."[58]

Despite the antirightist movement, the official line continued to emphasize a balance between ability and virtue.[59] Obviously China needed able cadres to carry out the economic development that the Eighth Party Congress had promised. However, the party changed its policy to combining the "red" and "expert" in each cadre by training experts from the peasant and worker classes instead of relying on party member cadres for virtue and the intellectuals for ability. Liu Shaoqi instructed the party to "cultivate a large number of cadres, raise their ability, and promote the specialization of cadres."[60]

The leftist tendency of the Great Leap Forward, however, pushed aside the moderate leaders' efforts to create "proletarian experts." During that period, the built-in anti-intellectual bias among cadres from worker and peasant backgrounds reasserted itself, frequently equating intellectuals with their former exploiters.

> The class background of intellectuals is not good, their social relations are complicated, and their ideology is backward. Although their living conditions in the old world were not as good as the capitalists', they were much better than the workers'. The workers are the only creators of values, but intellectuals exploit them just as the capitalists do.[61]

When the Great Leap Forward resulted in disaster, Mao withdrew from the front line, while Liu Shaoqi renewed the effort to

56. *Survey of China Mainland Press*, 26 August 1959, 6.
57. *Daily Report*, 9 March 1959, C3.
58. *Shehui Kexue Cankao*, 30 September 1984, 2–7.
59. *Dazhong Bao*, 14 May 1958.
60. *Renmin Ribao*, 1 May 1958.
61. *Zhongqing Shehui Kexue*, March 1985, 42–48.

"raise the technical and scientific level of the cadres and to promote cadres with special expertise to the leading posts." Under his leadership, the party decided to stop the recruitment and to carry out a "fresh registration."[62] At the same time, Zhou, who had been desperately trying to provide adequate working conditions for specialists by guaranteeing five-sixths of their working hours for their speciality, organized the Guangzhou conference in 1962.[63] Realizing the essential functions that experts and specialists perform in running a modern society, moderate leaders were ready to co-opt intellectuals into the party-state apparatus. But this effort did not last. Instead, the CR began.

As the crisis generated by the Great Leap Forward came to a close, Mao, coming out of semiretirement, advanced the slogan "Never forget class struggle." By 1964, as China's ideological dispute with the Soviet Union intensified, Mao advocated the cultivation of "millions of revolutionary successors." "This is a matter of great, extremely great, importance, a matter of life and death for the fate of the party and the nation." Revolutionary successors had to be (1) real Marxist-Leninists, (2) revolutionaries, (3) proletarian politicians who could be one with the majority of the people, (4) models in practicing the party's democratic centralism, and (5) modest, aware of the danger of being arrogant, and good at self-criticism.[64]

Mao did not mention anything relating to ability. None of the five conditions, which were exclusively related to virtue, touched upon the essence of Leninism—party spirit. Instead, Mao strongly emphasized three abstractions: Marxism-Leninism, revolution, and the masses. With the new criteria for revolutionary successors, the party embarked on a policy of "actively, and cautiously absorbing new party members on a comparatively large scale" by means of the Socialist Education Movement (SEM). Qinghai province recruited 10,530, the largest group of new members ever admitted in

62. *Shehui Kexue Cankao*, 30 September 1984, 2–7.

63. For the radicals' criticism of the Guangzhou conference, see *Xiju Zhanbao*, 24 June 1964. Enjoying the new freedom, some party intellectuals such as Wu Han and Deng To published articles subtly satirizing Mao's "petty bourgeois fanaticism," criticism which later started the CR.

64. *Renmin Ribao*, 4 July 1964.

one year.[65] Another source estimated that about 2.2 million were recruited during this period.

By the time of the CR, party member cadres completely dominated the party-state. Oksenberg reports that almost 100 percent of even county-level and district-level cadres were party members—90 percent at the multivillage level, 83 percent at the village level, and 60 percent at the subvillage level.[66] Kau reports a similar situation among the Wuhan municipal elite: the old party members dominated the higher echelons of the municipal bureaucracy. Party member cadres monopolized politically influential positions, whereas cadres without party membership—who possessed 93 percent of all technical and professional skills in the bureaucracy—languished in functional placements, which had neither influence nor prestige.[67]

POLITICAL IMPLICATIONS OF THE CADRE POLICY

After founding the new regime in a 1949, the former revolutionaries continued to recruit cadres largely through mass campaigns, using the methods of centrally assigned recruitment quotas, recruiting large numbers in groups—known as the "wave style," and party rectification. Immediately after 1949, when the CCP faced the urgent tasks of setting up a new state, restoring social order, and reviving the war-shattered economy, the founding fathers of the new regime tried to balance virtue and ability in selecting cadres. At that time the CCP adopted a pragmatic and lenient policy toward intellectuals in order to utilize their functional expertise and political support. Once the CCP succeeded in solving such immediate urban problems as controlling inflation and launching the first five-year plan, the delicate balance between competency and political loyalty gradually shifted in favor of the latter. The intellectuals' criticism of the party's cadre policy and the subsequent antirightist campaign decisively tipped on the side of

65. By the end of 1966 Qinghai had a total of 77,665 party members, 3.3 percent of the population. *Shehui Kexue Cankao*, 30 September 1984, 2–7.
66. Oksenberg, "Individual Attributes," 180.
67. Ying-mao Kau, "'Urban Bureaucratic Elite.'"

political reliability. The practice of looking at class background to gauge political attitude continued until Mao's death.

The radical faction led by Mao was largely responsible for the anti-intellectual bias that persisted in the new China. But the bias also had a deeper root: it reflected the diffused sentiment of the rank and file of party members and the cadre corps at that time. When land reform started in 1946, peasant cadres challenged the intellectual cadres because they were from the well-to-do social classes. When competency was briefly emphasized for the selection and promotion of cadres during the first five-year plan, many of the former guerrilla fighters complained bitterly because their contribution to "conquering the world" was not fully appreciated and because their guerrilla war skills were no longer needed—"the heroes have no place to use their weapons." During the antirightist campaign, top party leaders could easily mobilize the former revolutionaries as well as newly recruited party members to crush the demands calling for increased attention to professional competency, thus making it possible for "the old heroes to have a place to use their weapons."[68]

The class-based cadre policy made it impossible for the political elite to maintain a proper balance between social revolution on the one hand and economic construction and nation building on the other. The cadre policy was less dysfunctional in the rural areas where the regime's task was rather simple and the educational level of the cadre corps was not particularly low compared with that of the average rural population. But in urban areas, the educational level of the cadres was not much higher than that of the urban population they governed, although urban efforts required more sophisticated, diverse, and specialized knowledge. Moreover, the experiences of the revolutionary elite were less relevant to the efficient management of urban areas.

Not only did the CCP recruit its cadres from social groups that were ill-equipped to act as "proctors," but it also failed to train them for the complexities of economic development and management in modern society, as Stalin did in the Soviet Union during

68. From interview in Beijing in 1986. For fragmented data on the class background of lower-level cadres immediately after the establishment of the PRC, see Zhongnan Junzhengweiyuanhui Tugai Weiyuanhui Diaocha Yanjiushi, *Zhongnanqu Yibaifenzhi Diaocha* (Wuhan: Diaocha Yanjiuchu, 1953), 322.

the 1930s.[69] Consequently, the educational level of the top elite during the 1950s was actually lower than that during the Jiangxi period of the early 1930s. For instance, according to Derek Waller, about 31 percent of the Jiangxi elite had a college-level education, whereas only 26 percent of the Eighth Central Committee members had a similar level of education.[70] Intellectuals constituted 14 percent of all CCP members in 1957, whereas the same category amounted to 43 percent of the Polish Communist Party in 1960.[71]

In the early 1950s Chinese leaders tried to improve the cultural and technical standards of the existing cadre corps by setting up an "intensive middle-school program specially designed for the workers and peasant cadres" as well as cadre training institutes. China had about 347 cadre training institutes—34 managed by central organs and 313 by provincial and municipal governments.[72] By 1956, 1.27 million cadres had received training in their specialized fields and in basic political theory. All remaining cadres were scheduled to receive similar training by 1962. In addition, existing educational institutions organized special classes for cadres on active duty.[73]

Training efforts, however, had substantially declined by the time of the Hundred Flowers campaign and gradually came to an end as the overall political orientation shifted. First, the center gave jurisdiction over cadre schools to the provinces and municipalities. Then, by August 1961, it was decided to stop cadre training for three years, and many school facilities were used for other purposes. In 1964, the regime finally closed the remaining training institutes.[74]

In reflecting on what went wrong with the Chinese political sys-

69. Stalin systematically trained children from the working class into "proletarian experts." After the great purge of the first generation of revolutionaries in 1930, he promoted them to leadership positions. Sheila Fitzpatrick, "Stalin and the Making of a new Elite, 1928–1939," *Slavic Review* 38 (September 1979): 377–402. Also see her *Education and Social Mobility in the Soviet Union, 1921–1934* (London: Cambridge University Press, 1979).

70. Derek J. Waller, "The Evaluation of the Chinese Communist Political Elite, 1931–56," in Robert Scalapino, ed., *Elites in the People's Republic of China* (Seattle: University of Washington Press, 1972).

71. Samuel Huntington, *Political Order in Changing Societies* (New Haven: Yale University Press, 1968), 34..

72. Cao Zhi, ed., *Zhonghua Renmin*, 59–98.

73. Ibid.

74. Ibid.

tem he himself helped build, Lu Dingyi, former director of the propaganda department, candidly attributed Maoist radicalism to the low educational level of the cadre corps.

> [At the beginning of the liberation we] should have sent some party members [from peasant and worker backgrounds] to receive an education—not short-term training, but a regular college education. If [we had followed] that way for ten or twenty years, it would have been very good for our construction. Not pushing for that idea was largely my responsibility. That was a big mistake.
>
> If a mistake has been made, it is better to recognize it. I am a graduate of Jiatong University, but I have worked for a long time in propaganda, education, and cultural fields, and I have not paid special attention to the importance of intellectuals. That was a great mistake! Any army without culture [*wenhua*] is a stupid army. Without culture, how can one know what a democratic legal system is and thereby avoid promoting feudalistic [policies], such as promoting backyard furnaces to the extent of cutting down trees and stressing grain to the extent of eliminating sideline farming? [The lack of culture] led to blind commandism at the top level and to blind compliance at the lower level; both of them are equally ignorant. Ignorance led to the persecution of the intellectuals.[75]

Having been recruited from the poorest sector of society, the Chinese cadre corps did not have a power base independent of the party-state, nor any vested interests such as wealth, prestige, or political influence to protect. They derived whatever they possessed exclusively from the bureaucratic positions they held in the state apparatus. In this respect, the Communist elites were quite different from traditional elites, who came mainly from landlords and wealthy families and who had their own social and economic interests to defend. At the same time, as scholar-officials appointed by the imperial court after passing the civil service examination, traditional elites also represented the state's authority. Their dual role helped maintain the balance between society and state.[76]

Although the party-state recruited its cadres from the lower classes, most of them have acted more or less as agents of the state rather than as representatives of their class. The idea of state

75. *Minzu Yu Fazhi*, no. 4, 1983, 3.
76. Siku-kai Lau, "Monism, Pluralism, and Segmental Coordination: Toward Alternative Theory of Elite, Power, and Social Stability," *Journal of the Chinese University of Hong Kong*, 3, no. 1, 187–206.

bureaucrats representing the concrete interests of specific social groups has never been legitimized in China. Despite the notion of the party as the "vanguard," the CCP condemned those who were sensitive to the perceived interests of the masses for making the mistake of "tailism," a pejorative term for blindly following the lead of the masses, even though urging the cadres to practice the mass line and mass mobilization.[77] As a result, instead of serving as a channel for the perceived interests of the Chinese masses as originally intended, the mass movement and mass mobilization became mere tools for implementing the radical policy chosen for ideological reasons.[78] Furthermore, even though their economic interests lay with private farming, the basic-level rural cadres who had obtained their positions because of their poor-peasant background and political activism during the land reform faithfully carried out the collectivization policy. This clearly demonstrates that political interests were more important than economic ones as far as the bureaucrats were concerned. In other words, positions within the bureaucracy rather than economic interests largely dictated the political behavior of the cadres.[79] As a result, the cadres were more responsive to their superiors in the party-state than to the particular class from which they were recruited.

Although the former revolutionaries set up a state structure ostensibly modeled after the Soviet's, the Chinese party-state was more centralized and with less structural differentiation and routinization. (For a detailed discussion of the structure, see chapter 9.) For the sake of making a socialist revolution, the party deeply and completely penetrated not only all the auxiliary mass organizations but also the state apparatus, imposing "monistic" leadership and thereby losing the flexibility that the layered organizations had previously offered. At the same time the party-state was never fully institutionalized to the extent of effectively regulating the behavior of each officeholder. Consequently, the group of cadres occupying

77. Chalmers Johnson, "Chinese Communist Leadership and Mass Response," in Ping-ti Ho and Tang Tsou, eds., *China in Crisis* (Chicago: University of Chicago Press, 1968), 1:397–447.

78. Tang Tsou, *The Cultural Revolution and Post-Mao Reforms* (Chicago: University of Chicago Press, 1986), xiiv.

79. For the distinction between class position and class situation, see Nicos Poulantzas, "The Problem of the Capitalist Class," in Robin Blackburn, ed., *Ideology in Social Science* (London: Collins, 1972).

political office represented the party-state more realistically than did the abstract notions of political structures, offices, and roles. This means that the political elite's values, habits, and style, which derived from their social characteristics and previous revolutionary experiences, had a deep influence on the evolution of the political institutions and their actual operation. As a result, distinguishing between the authority of the offices and that of the occupants is a difficult task in the party-state.

Subject to the personnel decisions of their superiors, the cadres were hierarchically organized according to well-defined ranks—which were initially devised for a salary scale but eventually became social status symbols. Although the cadres did not have any discretionary power over the "value premise"—which was Mao's prerogative as the guardian of official ideology—they enjoyed a substantial amount of discretionary power over the "factual premise."[80] They were selected on the basis of political loyalty rather than competency and expected to use political criteria, which were open to subjective interpretation by the decision-makers, rather than any other functional criteria. The extensive personal networks existing among the old cadres and the Maoist pressure for constant contact with the masses made it difficult for the revolutionary cadres to operate exclusively on an impersonal basis. General rules and guidelines that in other bureaucracies operate to circumscribe the behavior of the occupants of office were vague and frequently couched in ambiguous ideological terms that allowed varying interpretations. In short, the cadres were expected to play the role of revolutionary leaders mobilizing the masses for social revolution rather than efficient and effective administrators.

The cadre system that the CCP developed immediately after 1949, including the practice of recruiting cadres from the most disadvantaged social groups on the basis of their loyalty as proven in political campaigns, buttressed the CCP's attempt to consolidate its own political structure through social transformation. Free from any external restraints encountered during the revolutionary era,

80. For the distinction between the two, see Herbert Simon, "Decision-Making and Administrative Organization," in Robert K. Merton, ed., *Reader in Bureaucracy* (New York: Free Press, 1967), 185–94.

the party-state initiated a series of social revolutions that completely eliminated any social force that could have raised political demands or worked as a check on the ever-expanding party-state;
ideological campaigns, quite often backed by coercion, broke the
will of any of the Chinese people considering resisting the revolutionary changes.[81] Each of these campaigns, which generated
many activists recruited to fill cadre positions, further consolidated
the party-state's domination over society.

Land reform brought an end to the political influence of the
landlord class, which had frequently played the role of "guardian
of society" when the traditional state adopted policies adverse to
its interests. The collectivization of agriculture shifted control over
economic resources from individual peasants to the state, thus depriving society of resources with which to challenge the party-
state's authority. A continuous effort to equalize peasant incomes
and an artificial intensification of class struggle in the rural areas
prevented any peasant group from gaining substantial economic
resources.

The peaceful transformation of industry deprived the capitalist
class, which had never developed much political influence, of any
control over resources, while absorbing some of them individually
into the state apparatus as managers of enterprises. The introduction of the material allocation system through the state plan politically emasculated the urban population, making it completely dependent on the state for its income. As a result, individuals lost
control over such crucial decisions as savings, consumption, labor
allocation, occupational choice, and physical movement across
administrative boundaries.

Workers in state enterprises are owners in theory, but they have
never been allowed to exercise any substantive influence even in
factory management. That was the case with the "one-man management system" of the early 1950s, as well as "the manager responsibility system under the leadership of the party committee"
during Mao's era.[82] Even when the Workers Mao's Thought prop-

81. Tang Tsou, "Reflections on the Formation and Foundation of the Communist Party-State in China," in his *Cultural Revolution*, 259–334.
82. For the change from the first to the second, see Franz Schurmann, *Ideology
and Organization in Communist China* (Berkeley and Los Angeles: University of California Press, 1968).

aganda teams were sent to higher learning institutes during the CR, it was the military rather than the workers who exercised real power.

Intellectuals do not constitute an independent class, but because of their education and training they can provide the regime with the educated manpower necessary for industrialization and modernization. At the same time, in many societies intellectuals tend to acts as critics of the existing social and political order. This has been particularly true in modern China. Nonetheless, a series of campaigns after 1949 undermined their social prestige and political influence. Worst of all, the state extended its control over all "business units" and brought professional associations under its control, thus transforming what had been individual, practicing professionals into members of bureaucratized organizations. Finally, the antirightist campaign of 1958 muzzled outspoken intellectuals and blacklisted almost 10 percent of the intellectual population, thus ending the active political role that Chinese intellectuals had played since the May 4 movement. Thereafter, neither a social group that could check for the abuse of political power by the party-state nor a forum where political issues could be discussed existed.

There are cultural as well as historical reasons for the CCP's reliance on the political power of the party-state to initiate social change. Unlike the case of Western Europe, the state as an institution with an active role has never been problematic in China, Japan, or Korea, where the origin of the state—regardless of how one defines it—can be traced back several thousand years. Particularly in China, with its long tradition of centralized bureaucracy headed by an emperor, the state's existence has been historically, intellectually, and culturally accepted.

The personal experiences of senior party leaders reinforced the cultural tradition. The Communist movement from the beginning viewed a powerful state with overwhelming political power as a solution to the incessant internal civil wars among the warlords and to the external pressure from the imperialist powers. China's acceptance of Marxism-Leninism further contributed to the rise of the powerful party-state. From the beginning, Marxism-Leninism appealed to Chinese radical intellectuals as a political ideology rather than as scientific laws governing social development. Mao's sinification of Marxism-Leninism—or "creative integration of the universal truth of Marxism-Leninism to the concrete conditions of China," to use the official Chinese phrase—can be summarized as the politicization of Marxism-Leninism. The fact that the CCP came to power only through a full-scale civil war against the Nationalists also favored a dominant state.[83]

In retrospect, although they successfully defeated the Nationalists, the founders lacked the wisdom needed to maintain a proper balance between social revolution on the one hand and economic construction and nation building on the other. Nor did they demonstrate the ability to build an efficient party-state that could continuously adapt to new situations and perform the complex task of coordinating many specialized functional units in a modern society.

The failure is largely due to Mao's radicalism. As was the case with Wang Ming, who accepted the dogmatism of Russian Leninism, Mao's thought, which had resolved the basic problems of the Chinese revolution, also put the Chinese elite in a straitjacket after 1949.[84] As a contemporary Chinese historian argues, "for a long period, Comrade Mao lived in China's backward countryside. He did not understand modern, socialized, large-scale industry. This caused him to sink, with regard to the question of socialist economic construction, even more into subjective utopianism marked by impatience for quick success."[85]

Stressing the rural orientation of Mao cannot explain the question of why he had so much power.[86] The root of the Maoist ultraleftist tendency should therefore be traced back to the cadre corps that the regime created after 1949. Largely from the lower

83. For an attempt to explain the post-1949 policy in terms of the preceding revolutionary experiences, see Theda Skocpol, *State and Social Revolution* (Cambridge: Cambridge University Press, 1979).

84. His experiences in the Yanan period remained central to his way of thinking, even after liberation when they were not as relevant. See Johnson, "Chinese Communist Leadership."

85. Stuart Schram, "The Limits of Cataclysmic Change," *China Quarterly*, no. 108, December 1986, 612–24.

86. By "rural orientation," I mean the tendency to view political processes in moral and ethical terms with millenarian expectations, to reject functional specialization and a market mechanism, and to emphasize self-sufficiency and distribution over production. For the peasantry's political outlook, see James Scott, "Hegemony and the Peasantry," *Politics and Society*, no. 3, 1977, 267–96.

rungs of society and without many vested interests to protect, cadres could be readily co-opted into the party-state apparatus and induced to act as the state's agents in its encroachment upon society. In their political outlook the cadres retained the peasants' viewpoint while remaining ignorant of the complex requirements of modern industrialized society. Whenever such pragmatic leaders as Liu Shaoqi and Zhou Enlai attempted to adjust the cadre policy to such prerequisites of modernization as functional differentiation, specialization, professionalism, and routinization of administrative procedures, the powerful party, with its large number of uneducated members accustomed to political movements, resisted the changes with Mao's encouragement. Instead, the former guerrilla fighters—largely recruited from among poor peasants—sustained the mass mobilization even to run the economy, bringing their "small producers' mentality" and "guerrilla mentality" to the complex problems of managing a modern industrialized complex society.[87] In this sense Mao's peasant mentality represented rather than shaped those of the majority of cadres, who, according to Liao Gailong, one of the best-known party historians, "not only worshiped authority, but also corrupted the party with egalitarian thinking."[88] An extreme historical irony is that it was precisely Mao's success in mobilizing the peasants that later proved to be the basic limitation to China's political development.

87. *Qingnian Lundan*, no. 2, 1985, 92–98; Andrew Walder, *Communist Neo-Traditionalism* (Berkeley and Los Angeles: University of California Press, 1986), 114–22.
88. Schram, "Limits of Cataclysmic Change."

PART II

ELITE CONFLICTS
AND CADRE ISSUES DURING THE
CULTURAL REVOLUTION

4

Conflict Structures

Historically speaking, by the time of the CR, the cadre system had displayed many structural weaknesses. Although it was originally conceived as an instrument for revolution, social transformation, and control over society, the cadre corps developed an identity different from that of the masses. Comfortably entrenched in the bureaucratic apparatus, they exercised enormous powers as agents of the party-state, enjoying many privileges. At the same time, opportunities for entering privileged positions were decreasing as the expansion of the party-state's bureaucracy and overall economic growth slowed down and competition for educational opportunities, the first step toward upward mobility, intensified.[1] All these factors produced accumulated but suppressed tensions in the society, which affected intraparty debate.[2]

The cadre system itself became the focus of elite conflicts. Worrying that the cadres were becoming a new ruling class, negating the very ideal of the revolution, Maoist leaders saw the need to redistribute scarce goods, including educational opportunity and political power, as a remedy. In contrast, Liu Shaoqi and his followers were more sensitive to the interests of the cadres and were willing to co-opt middle-class intellectuals into the cadre corps because their skills and expertise were needed for economic development, which would in turn expand the chance for upward mobility. To the Maoist leaders, accepting professional elites into the ruling structure was a betrayal of the revolutionary goal of raising

1. Jonathan Unger, *Education Under Mao* (New York: Columbia University Press, 1982); Stanley Rosen, *Red Guard Factionalism and the Cultural Revolution in Guangzhou (Canton)* (Boulder, Colo.: Westview Press, 1982).
2. James Townsend, "Intra-Party Conflict in China: Disintegration of an Established Party System," in Samuel P. Huntington and Clement H. Moore, eds., *Authoritarian Politics in Modern Society* (New York: Basic Books, 1970), 284–310.

the status of peasants and workers, who were the backbone of the Chinese revolution.

Political considerations also entered into the ideological dispute. Mao was losing his control over the gigantic party-state bureaucracy largely because of his hostility toward the bureaucratization of the cadre corps. By contrast, Liu Shaoqi was gaining popularity with his pragmatic policies and his respect for the vested interests of the cadre corps.[3] The highly centralized cadre system further intensified the competition for control over the corps; any elite group that controlled the cadres could control the party-state. Moreover, the absence of a retirement system and the monopoly of political power by cadres made it a life-and-death matter for each individual cadre to maintain his or her position.[4] In brief, the rigidity of the cadre system further aggravated the inner elite conflict.

When Mao initiated the CR by removing the party-state's control over society and mobilizing the masses against the elites, a multitude of social conflicts that the party-state had previously suppressed surfaced, allowing the divided elites to exploit them for their own political interests. How to deal with the issues that the unprecedented scale of mass mobilization constantly raised further divided the elites and masses. Each phase of the CR raised new ideological and political questions. And each decision made to resolve these difficulties produced new groups that either benefited or suffered from the official decision, thereby changing the existing conflict structure.

THE PURGE PATTERN

At the initial stage of the CR, the question of who should be purged was decided in the process of mass mobilization, not by the party organizations with due authority. The Chinese masses in every unit split into numerous factions, often forming alliances with mass organizations outside their units. The bureaucrats also manipulated the question to protect themselves or to lead the movement in the direction of their choice. Of course, official policy was

3. For Liu Shaoqi, see Lowell Dittmer, *Liu Shao-Ch'i and the Chinese Cultural Revolution* (Berkeley and Los Angeles: University of California Press, 1974).
4. Michel Oksenberg, "Exit Patterns from Chinese Politics and Its Implications," *China Quarterly*, no. 67, September 1976, 501–18.

to purge only the "powerholders taking the capitalist road." But often the chaotic and factionalized mass movement could not make a distinction between cadres who followed the alleged revisionist line and Maoist cadres who followed the "proletarian road."

As chaotic as the decision on a particular cadre might have been, the basic cleavage between the radicals and the conservatives, which cut across the horizontal demarcation line of the elite and masses, shaped the outcome of the purge. Each side had its own ideology and policy preferences, which were largely determined by the characteristics of each side's membership.[5]

The radical forces, represented by the Jiang Qing group at the top and recruited largely from discontented social groups—which existed primarily outside the locus of power in the Chinese ruling structure—saw their interests best served by drastic political change. They consistently pursued a radical policy, defending the reforms of the CR or even demanding further reform. They used the basic goals of Marxism and the political principles as defined in Mao's thought to justify their challenge to the structural legitimacy of the party organizations.

In contrast, the conservative mass organizations, mainly consisting of better-off social groups and supported by the military establishment, shared the party organization's interest in maintaining the status quo. The conservative forces tried to limit changes to a minimum or to reverse the radical reforms implemented during the CR. By stressing the structural legitimacy of the party organization in the name of Leninist tenets, the conservative forces emphasized the organizational principle in order to defend the correctness and legitimacy of decisions reached by due process. Each camp, of course, justified its position in ideological terms. But they were also more than willing to push their views to the extreme for maximum political gain.

Differences between radicals and conservatives crystallized over the questions of who should be purged and how to evaluate the cadres. Maoist radicals tended to emphasize the horizontal cleavage between the masses and the elite as the demarcation line be-

5. For details of the conflict along the cleavage, see Hong Yung Lee, *The Politics of the Chinese Cultural Revolution* (Berkeley and Los Angeles: University of California Press, 1978).

tween participants and targets. The Liuist leaders stressed the vertical cleavage between those inside and those outside the party. As a result, the scope of the purges expanded gradually from "bourgeois academic authorities," to "black gangs" (who protected the academic authorities), to "monsters and freaks," and finally to "powerholders taking the capitalist road within the party." The radicals pushed for a more comprehensive purge, while party leaders endeavored to keep it as narrow as possible. When the Maoists pinpointed more categories to purge, the party organization responded by attempting to restrict the targets to those specifically mentioned. Consequently, the party organization was continually one step behind the Maoist leaders.

Over the question of how to evaluate the cadres, the Jiang Qing radical group stressed the cadres' political performance over class background, political action over intention, and performance records in "the fifty days" (at the early stage of the CR) over the past seventeen years' records. By contrast, the conservatives stressed class background, party membership, and past records, while condemning the radicals as anti-Communist elements simply exploiting the CR to vent their resentment of the CCP.

We do not know how the two conflicting views determined the actual outcome of the purge. But since we know who was purged during the two years of mass mobilization between 1966 and 1968, tables 10–15, constructed with biographical data on individual cadres, allow us to glimpse the purge pattern (from which we can infer the CR conflict structures).

Table 10 demonstrates the devastating impact of the CR on the formal authority: about 60 percent of the top political leaders lost their positions in the CR. Particularly affected were party and government organizations, whereas the impact on the military was the least. Although the elite conflict was not organized along institutional lines, the differential impact was due to the different functional areas for which each institution was responsible and the different political powers each institution wielded. Not only was the military least affected, but it also aggrandized its political influence by default.

Although the career background of each individual cadre is not exactly the same as the type of organization he belonged to, table 11 shows that the leaders whose careers had evolved around poli-

Table 10. Impact of the CR by Type of Organization, as of 1969

Type of Organization	Purged		Survived		Total	
	No.	%	No.	%	No.	%
Party	202	73	76	27	278	100
Government	380	77	117	23	503	100
Military	122	29	292	71	414	100
Mass	34	77	10	23	44	100
Total	738	60	495	40	1,239	100

Source. Compiled by the author from biographical information.

Note. The sample includes all those who served in positions of the Central Committee, ministers and vice ministers, heads of central military organs, directors of central party organs, provincial party secretaries, chairmen and vice chairmen of provincial revolutionary committees (governors and vice governors), and military commanders of large military regions and provincial military districts.

Table 11.   Impact of the CR by Area of Specialty, as of 1969

Area of Specialty	Purged		Survived		Total	
	No.	%	No.	%	No.	%
Political	468	78	130	22	598	100
Military	122	29	290	70	412	100
Functional	101	67	50	33	151	100
Total	692	60	470	40	1,161	100

Source. Compiled by the author from biographical information.

Note. The sample includes all those who served in positions of the Central Committee, ministers and vice ministers, heads of central military organs, directors of central party organs, provincial party secretaries, chairmen and vice chairmen of provincial revolutionary committees (governors and vice governors), and military commanders of large military regions and provincial military districts.

tical works suffered the most, and 67 percent of the specialists lost their positions. By contrast, professional soldiers suffered the least. This again indicates that the mass movement was squarely directed against the powerholders. In table 12 the 70 percent purge rate of central leaders (in contrast to only 54 percent of local leaders) indicates that the impetus to radicalism came from the center, and the Gang of Four's influence was quite limited at local levels.

Kang Sheng allegedly condemned eighty Central Committee

Table 12.   Impact of the CR by Locality, as of 1969

Locality	Purged		Survived		Total	
	No.	%	No.	%	No.	%
Central	337	70	144	30	481	100
Noncentral	398	54	335	45	733	100
Total	735	61	479	40	1,214	100

Source. Compiled by the author from biographical information.

Note. The sample includes all those who served in positions of the Central Committee, ministers and vice ministers, heads of central military organs, directors of central party organs, provincial party secretaries, chairmen and vice chairmen of provincial revolutionary committees (governors and vice governors), and military commanders of large military regions and provincial military districts.

Table 13.   Impact of Kang Sheng's Accusation, as of 1969

Members	Purged		Survived		Total	
	No.	%	No.	%	No.	%
Not accused	30	48	32	51	62	100
Accused	66	82	14	18	80	100
Total	96	68	46	32	142	100

Sources. Zuigao Renmin Fayuan Yuanjiushi Bian, Zhonghua Renmin Gongheguo Renmin Fayuan Tiebei Fating Shenpan Lin Biao, Jiang Qing Fangeming Jituan Zhufan Jishi (Beijing: Falu Chubanshe, 1982). Also compiled by the author from biographical information.

Note. The sample includes all Eighth CC members whom Kang Sheng blacklisted.

members, of whom sixty-six were purged, only fourteen surviving (table 13). This indicates that Kang Sheng—and by inference the Gang of Four—exerted enormous influence in selecting who was to be purged. The surviving fourteen must have been leaders with their own political influence who were powerful enough to protect themselves or people who were protected by Mao. The fact that thirty persons who were not accused by Kang were purged indicates the complexity of the conflict at the top level. Although not being accused by Kang does not necessarily mean that they were protected by the radicals, it is obvious that the radicals' influence on the matters of purge and survival was not total.

    Table 14 shows that field army affiliation was clearly correlated

Table 14.   Impact of the CR by Field Army Affiliation, as of 1969

Field Army Affiliation	Purged		Survived		Total	
	No.	%	No.	%	No.	%
1st, 2d, 3d, 5th and 6th	350	55	282	45	632	100
4th	85	42	113	57	198	100
Total	435	52	395	48	830	100

Sources. Field army information is based on data provided by W. Whitson, *The Chinese Command: A History of Communist Military Politics, 1927–71* (New York: Praeger, 1973), which includes the civilian leaders. Information on purges was compiled by the author from biographical information.

Table 15.   Impact of the CR by Military Generation, as of 1969

Generation	Purged		Survived		Total	
	No.	%	No.	%	No.	%
1st	83	59	57	41	140	100
2d	55	42	77	58	132	100
3d	35	25	103	75	138	100
4th–8th	11	20	43	80	54	100
Total	184	40	280	60	464	100

Sources. Field army information is based on data provided by W. Whitson, *The Chinese Command: A History of Communist Military Politics, 1927–71* (New York: Praeger, 1973), which includes the civilian leaders. Information on purge was compiled by the author from biographical information.

with the rate of purge. Former officers of the Fourth Field Army fared much better than those of other field armies. The rise of Lin Biao might have reduced the possible charge against the former Fourth Field Army officers, whereas the purge of the leaders of other field armies (Peng Dehuai, Deng Xiaoping, and Chen Yi) made their officers more vulnerable. Or Lin Biao might have protected his field army officers, who would otherwise have been toppled. That 42 percent of the former Fourth Field Army officers were purged, however, indicates that the conflict in the CR was not exclusively along the line of field army affiliations.

Table 15 demonstrates that seniority affected the political fate of the military officers; the older they were, the more likely they were to be purged. Obviously, the CR centered conflict among the senior party leaders with substantial political power. Even most of the purged Fourth Field Army officers were senior ones with political status independent of Lin Biao. They either refused to join Lin's group, thus forfeiting his possible protection, or he might have actively tried to remove them as obstacles to his rise to power. Whichever was the case, Lin Biao's strategy was to protect the junior officers who had affiliations with his field army, thereby reinforcing the existing ties by renewing their indebtedness to him. The CR offered the younger generation an opportunity to be promoted, with less room for the older generation of officers, who had already reached top positions. Actually, 57 percent of the third to eighth generations were promoted whereas only 16 percent of the first generation of military leaders were promoted during the CR. On the whole, my biographical data indicate that the purge rate among high-ranking cadres was higher than among low-ranking cadres. Particularly vulnerable to the purge were those who had enjoyed rapid promotion before the CR and those who held multiple positions at the time of the CR. Also, of the ninety-four persons who had studied abroad, about 64 percent of them were purged, with only 36 percent surviving.

This purge pattern reveals that the CR destroyed the formal authority of the party-state because the powerholders or leading cadres represented the formal authority when the degree of institutionalization was low. As the powerholders defended themselves by invoking the structural legitimacy of the organization, the rebels rejected the organizational norms, rules, and procedures in the name of the higher authority of Mao's thought.

The only political authority that was formally accepted as a standard for judging all political conduct was the radicalized version of Mao's thought and his personal decisions, frequently known as "great strategic decisions." Every political actor claimed to follow Mao's line and ideology, but each political group interpreted the meaning of Mao's thought and his specific instructions in light of their particular political interests. Almost anyone, regardless of position and organizational affiliation, was vulnerable to the charges of anti-Maoism from some quarter. That one was following an order coming through the regular channels of authority neither guaranteed safety nor implied that one was a good cadre. On the contrary, those who stuck to the Leninist organizational principle were condemned as "docile tools" with a "slave mentality." Colleagues often blamed one another, and subordinates challenged superiors, quite often disguising their political ambition in the name of the revolution. The mass movement challenged the moral and ethical foundations of the entire political community.

As a witch-hunt atmosphere permeated the entire society, the choice available for each individual was either to purge or to be purged, and people quickly learned that it was better to accuse before being accused. There were many grounds for accusation and persecution: opposing Mao's line, having a bad class background or blotted political record, and so forth. Caught in the dilemma between what they really believed to be right and what they saw as politically advantageous, some people refused to compromise their conception of basic human decency, but the more opportunistic were willing to go against their own conscience by laying false charges and providing concocted evidence. Others were compelled to do so under coercion and torture.

As the mass movement created terror and chaos, which resulted in struggle, dispute, and policy changes, and exposed most cadres to the charge that they made some errors (according to the criteria used at any given moment), only personal trust allowed people to share their inner feelings and maintain confidentiality.[6] Usually trust came from personal ties based on friendship, belonging to the same unit, or sharing the same birthplace, but even these bonds provided no security against betrayal. The CR offered many temptations for the self-interested to betray trust. In brief, the importance of informal ties increased in inverse proportion to the weakening of the formal authority.

SITUATIONAL GROUPS
AND REHABILITATION

The purge pattern indicates that the conflicting groups during the CR do not fit neatly into any of the conflict groups suggested in the standard literature. They were too complex to be explained as "tendency groups," those people with a similar ideological pro-

---

6. S. N. Eisenstadt and L. Roniger, *Patrons, Clients, and Friends* (Cambridge: Cambridge University Press, 1984).

pensity that leads them to take similar positions on various specific issues.[7] Nor can they be called "opinion groups," which are issue-specific, because the elite conflicts were too intense, severe, and well structured. Although the conflicts involved institutional cleavages among the party, the government, and the military, the formal authority of Mao, which all institutions accepted, and the diffused power bases of the various conflict groups limited the applicability of "institutional groups" on which the theory of bureaucratic politics has developed. Many informal groups based on personal ties were active in the CR, but it is difficult to ascertain to what extent they became political groups actually affecting the outcome of the conflicts. It is a "faction" concept that has been most widely used in analyzing the dynamics of the CR. By definition, a faction is very limited in size and capability, and, therefore, factional politics result in "immobilism."[8] The idea of a micro-group such as a faction is of limited use because the CR conflicts involved almost all Chinese, including both the masses and the political elite. The CR conflicts, moreover, caused many ideological and policy disputes, which frequently ended in real changes in these areas—a situation that runs counter to the meaning of a faction.

Because of the large number of political groups that emerged during the chaotic process of the elite conflicts and mass mobilization, the numerous issues over which they clashed, and the constantly forming and changing coalitions, it is extremely difficult to identify convincingly the factors that led to the CR. Instead, looking at how conflicts were structured in terms of the various groups that came into existence as a result of the mass mobilization, I propose to use the concept of "situational group," referring to the

7. Franklyn Griffiths, "A Tendency Analysis of Soviet Policy-Making," in Gordon Skilling and Franklyn Griffiths, eds., *Interest Groups in Soviet Politics* (Princeton: Princeton University Press, 1971), 335–77.

8. For the factional model, see W. Whitson, "The Field Army in Chinese Communist Military Politics," *China Quarterly*, no. 46, 1963, 668–99; Andrew Nathan, "A Factional Model for CCP Politics," *China Quarterly*, no. 53, 1973, 34–66; Tang Tsou, "Prolegomenon to the Studying of Informal Groups in CCP Politics," *China Quarterly*, no. 65, 1976, 98–113; Lucian Pye, *The Dynamics of Factions and Consensus in Chinese Politics* (Santa Monica, Ca.: Rand Corporation, 1981); Ralph W. Nicholas, "Faction: A Comparative Analysis," 55–74, and James C. Scott, "Patron-Client Politics and Political Change in Southeast Asia," 123–46, both in Steffen W. Schmitt, James Scott, Carl Lande, and Laura Guasti, eds., *Friends, Followers, and Faction* (Berkeley and Los Angeles: University of California Press, 1977).

position in which a group finds itself as a result of a particular state policy.[9] This concept is particularly appropriate to Chinese revolutionary politics, which relies heavily on political power to change the entire social structure. Because of the decisive and omnipresent role of the party-state in China, many groups—for example, the poor and the unemployed, which in Western countries would be labeled sociological groups—are more accurately defined as situational groups. The members of a situational group may or may not have a common group identity, but they are keenly aware that their situation is the result of state policy.

One situational group was composed of victims of the CR— the purged. Although they were off the political stage for a while (depending on when they were rehabilitated), they constituted a coherent political group, and after Mao's death they became the "rehabilitated cadres" who regained power. Among them were different subgroups. Some were officially denounced as "renegades, spies, and traitors" and then expelled from the party (e.g., Liu Shaoqi). Others were condemned as "powerholders taking the capitalist road," imprisoned for a while, and then released (e.g., Deng Xiaoping). There was also a group of cadres who were criticized and put aside by the masses. Their cases were never officially concluded. This situational group had many personal reasons to challenge the validity of the CR. They recognized Mao's mistakes, while holding the Gang of Four and Lin Biao responsible for the hardships they had suffered.

A second group consisted of leaders who were criticized but never officially purged or demoted; despite the profound crisis, this group of cadres managed to survive. As purge and counterpurge continued, they became more important in the overall distribution of power. Three examples are Zhou Enlai, Li Xiannian, and Ye Jianying. Although they enjoyed close personal relations with Mao, they had ample sympathy for their less fortunate comrades whom the CR victimized. They had no reason to defend the CR other than protecting Mao's position in Chinese history.

A third group included cadres who occupied middle-echelon positions in the party-state at the beginning of the CR and who were promoted upward (regardless of their desires) as the purges

9. William Gamson, *Power and Discontent* (Homewood, Ill.: Dorsey Press, 1968).

beneficiaries

created vacancies at the top. As the de facto beneficiaries of the CR, they developed a deep personal loyalty to Mao, although they may have had personal reservations about some of his decisions. They tended to defend the CR on the whole, while rehabilitating some of its innocent victims as long as Mao's overall reputation was not undermined. Hua Guofeng and Wu De are examples of this type of cadre.

The fourth and last group consisted of those who initiated the CR and spurred the mass movement. Within this group were two subgroups: the Gang of Four, who controlled propaganda, and Lin Biao's group, which consisted mostly of military officers. Both used Mao's thought to initiate the CR, and both contributed to the development of Mao's personality cult. They had every reason to defend the CR while resisting the rehabilitation of cadres, particularly senior ones, whose return would threaten their own power position.

Analyzing the CR elite conflicts in terms of situational groups offers several advantages that the other types of conflict groups cannot. First, the situational group can accommodate ideological differences among the elites. Broadly speaking, the victims of the CR were on the right of the ideological spectrum, whereas the initiators of the CR were on the left. The survivors and the beneficiaries were between the two extremes. Second, the situational model can deal with the problem of size in conflict groups. Since the CR involved all the cadres as well as a large number of ordinary Chinese, the factional model based on personal ties cannot fully explain its dynamics and outcome. Moreover, unlike the factional model, the situational group does not assume that major elite conflicts are organized along cleavages based on informal ties, thus avoiding the question of formal and informal authorities. At the same time, the situational group differs from an opinion group—in which one can change one's position depending on the issue— because its members' positions are largely determined by their own political interests. In addition, the situational group possesses more group cohesiveness than the tendency group.

Most important, with this concept one can effectively address the question of rehabilitation, the issue around which elite conflicts centered. Understandably, all members of each situational group saw their crucial personal interests at stake in this issue.

The practice of allowing purged cadres to return to the political scene seems to be unique to the CCP, contrasting sharply with Stalin's policy.[10] The traditional Chinese belief that man is fallible and yet also malleable through education provided the philosophical justification for cadre rehabilitation. Mao strengthened this traditional belief by emphasizing the need to reeducate cadres who made mistakes and by departing from some Leninists' view that the Communist Party is infallible.[11]

Rehabilitation, when fairly used, can perform several positive functions. It can work as a mechanism for administering justice and for allowing cadres to ask for reviews of their cases. Without such minimal protection, no political system can survive for long. At the same time, rehabilitation helps the decision-makers to correct their mistakes, assuage their guilt, and learn from their experiences. For ordinary Chinese citizens, the existence of rehabilitation can act to sustain their faith in the sincerity and, therefore, the legitimacy, of the party. Rehabilitation also benefits the Chinese political system by serving as a vehicle for keeping the cadres united by bringing back those who have strayed from the correct path. In addition, the political system can make good use of disgraced cadres' experiences.

Ideally, rehabilitation should be decided on the basis of the correctness or incorrectness of the original decision. But many political factors influenced each decision. First, whether the original decision was right or wrong depended on both subjective political judgment and the official line at a given moment. Since declaring a decision was wrong also raised the question of the decision-makers' culpability, those who made the decision usually defended it; the opposition, of course, capitalized on any problematic decisions.[12]

Most important, whom to rehabilitate, particularly among

10. In Chinese, "rehabilitation" (*pingfan*) implies the overthrowing of an original disciplinary decision. The reasons most often cited for such reversals include false accusations, calumnious evidence, or excessively severe punishment. Rehabilitation usually entails the restoration of honor, the reinstatement of the disgraced cadre in his original position, and the payment of the wages he would have received during the period of his disgrace.

11. *Pingfan Ziliao Huibian* (Guangdong, 19 January 1968), in *Hongweibing Ziliao Huibian* (Washington D.C.: Center for Chinese Research Material, 1978), 5010–5022.

12. For this point, see Hong Yung Lee, *Politics of the Chinese Cultural Revolution*.

upper-echelon political leaders, had (and always has) profound ramifications for the distribution of power as well as for policy. For this reason the distribution of power at a given moment decisively influenced cadre rehabilitation, and whenever a major change occurred in power distribution, the demand for rehabilitation increased.

From the beginning, the CR was concerned with who should be purged and who should be protected or rehabilitated. Although all cadres were attacked in one way or another during the mass movement, some of the attacked managed to survive or to be liberated at early stages of the mass movement. More cadres were liberated when Mao proceeded to set up a new power structure in the form of a revolutionary committee. The three-in-one formula offered some cadres opportunities to join the new power structure as "revolutionary cadres." But who was qualified to be a "revolutionary cadre" was heatedly disputed, and every faction tried to maximize its power position in the new revolutionary committee by supporting the cadres of its own choice. Generally, PLA representatives in each unit, who had access to cadres' dossiers, made personnel decisions on cadres. The Jiang Qing group exerted its influence in the units with which it was concerned—generally those at central and provincial levels. However, at these high levels, the group could find only a few "revolutionary cadres," and worse still, most of them happened to have "other political problems."[13] The radicals' influence over the formation of revolutionary committees at lower levels was further diluted because decisive authority came from the provincial revolutionary committee, which was dominated by local PLA leaders with the support of conservative mass organizations.

Large-scale "liberation" took place in 1968, when Mao launched the campaign to purify class ranks. Part of this campaign was known as "settling cases" (*dingan*) by rendering official judgment on each cadre. At that time the cadres' status was uncertain: almost

---

13. For instance, Liu Geping of Shansi, Wang Xiaoyu of Shandong, and Pan Fusheng of Heilongjiang joined the rebels. However, almost all such cadres had disappeared by the Ninth Party Congress (1969), probably because their "political problems which—referring to past mistakes"—made them vulnerable to attack by conservative forces.

all of them were criticized by the masses, but they were neither removed from their posts nor formally reinstated.

Unlike the case in earlier phases, this time new formal authorities—the revolutionary committees, Workers Mao's Thought Propaganda Teams, or the Military Affairs Commission—investigated each cadre, particularly focusing on class background (i.e., whether the one in their dossier was correct or not) and any suspicious past problems. Final decisions were supposed to be made impartially and objectively, but because of rampant factionalism, simplistic charges abounded, and even a single accusatory letter from the masses or an accusation in a mass meeting could trigger a lengthy process of investigation. As a result, many (what were later called) "false accusations," "mistaken decisions," and "trumped-up charges" were produced in the campaign.

After two years of chaotic mass mobilization, it was not easy to determine who was good and who was bad. All the decision-making bodies were split between radicals and conservatives, who violently disagreed even on basic standards of right and wrong. Moreover, two years of prolonged struggle exposed the weaknesses of every cadre. The chaos of the mass movement made it difficult to separate cadres who sought only their own interests from those who pursued what they believed to be the public good. Some cadres stood firmly for what they considered the right course, but unfortunately they turned out to be on the wrong side—at least from the Maoist viewpoint. Other cadres found in Mao's call to criticize powerholders a chance to vent accumulated resentments against their superiors. Still others were wholly opportunistic and unprincipled, changing their allegiance to whichever side seemed to be winning.

Another group of cadres, known as "wanderers" (xiaoyao pai), withdrew from the whole movement, adopted an indifferent attitude, and tried to enjoy themselves. Many cadres who honestly reported their class origin and political history to the party were victimized because of "bad records"; those who managed to keep their records clean by lying claimed to be true revolutionaries. Dedicated Communist cadres who had faithfully carried out official policies prior to the CR drew heavier criticism from the masses than the "old good persons" (lao hao ren). There was a compelling need to untangle things and bring some semblance of justice and order to the situation. Veteran revolutionary cadres, who had led the Chinese revolution to success, came under fire from former KMT partisans. Many opportunists, who had compromised with the Japanese, the KMT, and the CCP, also surviveϕd the CR without having passed a "soul-searching test."

To make matters even more complex, the official definition of those to be purged was ambiguous and constantly changing. At the initial stage, the official target was defined as the "bourgeois academic authority." Then it expanded to include "powerholders taking the capitalist road," but the radicals and conservatives disagreed on how to define "capitalist roaders." The radicals insisted on purging all the cadres guilty of "the bourgeois reactionary line" (which suppressed the spontaneous mass movement). However, since almost 90 percent of the cadres had carried out the wrong line, the official policy changed to distinguishing between people who had willingly carried out the mistaken line and those who had simply followed orders coming down through regular organizational channels.[14] Eventually, even those who were guilty of the bourgeois reactionary line were allowed to repent when the official description changed to "stubborn powerholders who took the capitalist road, but refused to reform."[15]

Eventually the official category to be purged was reduced to "renegade and spy." Capitulating to the enemy by revealing party secrets and by selling out comrades, even when captured by the enemy, is against the principles of Leninism. To call a cadre a renegade is the most effective tactic for discrediting any party cadre in the public eye. Unlike other political mistakes, whose seriousness diminishes over time and with the introduction of different interpretations, being a renegade is an almost unforgivable sin. For this reason, Liu Shaoqi was labeled a renegade. Once applied, these labels substantially decreased anyone's chance for a verdict reversal, even when the political atmosphere changed drastically. In fact, those who had been condemned as renegades—mostly those from the "white" areas—were the last to be rehabilitated.

14. *Gongren Zaofan Bao,* 10 April 1969.
15. *Renmin Ribao,* 1 January 1964.

R,

Figure. 1.   Distribution of Rehabilitation by Years

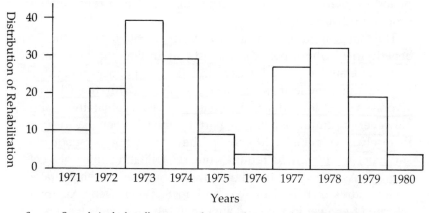

Source. Sample includes all persons who served on any of the Eighth to the Twelfth Central Committees.

I don't see this.

The concept of situational groups, their coalitions, and their conflict over the issue of rehabilitation are powerful tools in explaining the process and outcome of elite conflicts (see fig. 1).

Despite two years of mass mobilization, many old cadres managed to survive under the protection of Zhou Enlai. They represented continuity for the regime. Mao did not have either the capability or the will to purge all the old cadres. Besides their continued existence, there was the Lin Biao incident, which further weakened the political forces who had initiated the CR. The incident also deprived the Cultural Revolution Small Group, dominated by Madam Mao and her followers, of a powerful coalition partner, with whom it shared a common interest in safeguarding the accomplishments of the CR.

Immediately following Lin's death in 1971, a large number of senior cadres were rehabilitated (see figure 1). This intensified the Gang of Four's (Jiang Qing, Zhang Chunqiao, Yao Wenyuan, and Wang Hongwen) conflicts with the survivors, in spite of Mao's effort to make the two groups cooperate. The Jiang Qing group renewed the mass campaign under the excuse of criticizing Confucius and Lin Biao in order to promote the CR rebels and to strengthen their power positions, while accusing the senior cadres of attemping to "reverse the achievements of the CR." During this period of intensifying conflict, 1975–76, the rate of rehabilitation dropped substantially.

The Gang of Four even failed to form a coalition with the CR beneficiaries, whose political interests lay in limiting the number of rehabilitated cadres. Instead, the Gang's political ineptitude pushed the beneficiaries to form a coalition with the CR survivors—a coalition which eventually moved against the Gang. However, by cutting a potential partner, the CR's beneficiaries left themselves vulnerable. Moreover, they could not persuade the survivors of the CR to refrain from rehabilitating their old colleagues. As shown in the figure 1, the number of rehabilitated senior cadres increased in 1977 and 1978. When Deng Xiaoping returned to power in 1978 and almost all the CR victims were reinstated, the de facto beneficiaries were doomed.

After easing out Hua Guofeng, Deng formed a broad coalition with the rehabilitated and the survivors, both of whom had suffered greatly. Since the winning coalition had no vested interest in the CR, it could totally repudiate it and initiate political and economic reforms. While inducing the rehabilitated cadres to retire through a special retirement system (see chapter 10), Deng Xiaoping promoted the younger generation of technocrats to the highest positions in the Thirteenth Party Congress.

[Handwritten margin notes, left side:] but Deng came back against the gang, didn't he? The lines between the 4 groups are not clear when considered over time. but they were all colleagues.

[Handwritten margin notes, bottom left:] focus on pol. interests of the people seems okay) but how to specify what they are?

[Handwritten margin note, bottom center:] why had survivors suffered?

5

Lin Biao: Military Man

After two years of mass mobilization that almost paralyzed the formal authority of the party-state, there were three contending situational groups at the top level. One was Zhou Enlai, the leader of the government functionaries, to whom not only the surviving cadres and the beneficiaries but also the purged leaders increasingly looked for leadership. The Lin Biao and Jiang Qing groups were the initiators of the CR; the former controlled the "gun" while the latter controlled the "pen." Mao had close personal relationships with these three groups. One could even say that Mao was using Zhou Enlai to handle the administrative function of the party-state, the Gang of Four to mobilize the masses and ideologically justify the CR, and Lin Biao to control the military, on which he increasingly depended to maintain social order.

The political interests of the three groups converged and clashed. At the beginning of the CR in 1966, the Jiang Qing group and Lin Biao shared common interests. Both wanted to remove a large number of central political leaders to create vacancies within the bureaucracy for their own followers. Furthermore, cultivating Mao's personality cult served the interests of both groups, which were close to Mao.

However, the two groups had disparate support bases. The core members of Jiang Qing's group were the ideologues whose political interests lay with the mass mobilization of the disadvantaged social groups and who wanted to change the existing power structure. By contrast, Lin Biao's support came from military officers, whom he skillfully protected and then promoted to leadership positions during the CR. Although Lin's formal position was second only to Mao's, he lacked Mao's charisma, his contact with the masses was very limited, and his influence over the civilian bureaucracy was minimal. Lin Biao's political aim, therefore, was not to mobilize the masses and then modify the existing system but to take over the system from within. Lin used his formal authority to develop a factional network by promoting his personal followers to key positions in the military and expanding the military's influence over the civilian bureaucracy. Perceived as Mao's faithful disciple and as a close collaborator of the Gang of Four, Lin Biao had to produce a continuous flow of rhetoric.

The political interests of the two groups diverged when local mass organizations clashed with local military leaders. The Jiang Qing group, mostly composed of what the Chinese call "petty intellectuals," wanted to use the masses to seize military power at the local level, whereas Lin Biao had to be sensitive to the institutional interests of the military, particularly those of local military leaders. Lin thus found himself under opposing pressures: pressure from the Jiang Qing group to support the radical Red Guards and pressure from local military leaders to defend the PLA's interests. Caught in this dilemma, he cooperated with the Jiang Qing group against the senior leaders, at the same time competing with the radicals to fill vacancies created by the purges with his own people.[1]

Zhou Enlai must also be factored into this uneasy relationship between the Jiang Qing and Lin Biao groups. Whether it was because of a lack of personal ambition or his skillful maneuvering, Zhou succeeded in building a public image as an impartial premier honestly trying to carry out Mao's policy within objective constraints. He protected the party and government leaders as far as his power and influence allowed, but when it became impossible to do so without a serious confrontation with other elite groups, he publicly dropped his defense and acted as a conciliator and moderator rather than as an advocate of any partisan position. Apparently, he used universal criteria rather than particularistic ones in selecting targets and defending victims. Perhaps he did not need to engage in factional politics because his administration of the government was essential to the daily life of the society. The combination of political skill, a consistently moderate position, high prestige among the entire cadre corps, and Mao's trust caused

1. For this point, see Zuigao Renmin Fayuan Yanjiusuo, ed., *Zhonghua Renmin Gongheguo Zuigao Renmin Fayuan Tebie Fating Shenpan Lin Biao, Jiang Qing Fangeming Jituan Zhufan Jishi* (Beijing: Falu Chubanshe, 1982); and Nie Rongzhen, *Nie Rongzhen Huiyilu* (Beijing: Jiefangjun Chubanshe, 1984), vol. 3.

even the Jiang Qing group to respect him, at least publicly, although privately the radicals regarded him as the "third head-quarters" commanding the cadres' loyalty—a man who somehow managed to survive the CR's turbulence.

Zhou and Lin were both opposed to the Gang of Four's strag-tegy of mass mobilization, and both had very practical views on policy. If they could have formed a coalition against the Gang of Four, it would have been very powerful.

POWER BASE

SELECTING THE NINTH
CENTRAL COMMITTEE

The three groups clashed over the issue of who should be pro-moted to the Ninth Central Committee. The Gang of Four wanted to promote the CR rebels—"those who have proven themselves in the CR"—while removing "all the hidden class enemies in the party."[2] The Zhou Enlai group tried to strengthen cadre repre-sentation in the new Central Committee, whereas Lin Biao was in favor of giving a large share of political power to military leaders.

When the twelfth plenum of the Eighth Party Congress was con-vened in October 1968, only forty Central Committee members out of ninety-seven (ten had died), less than a quorum, were allowed to attend. The meeting, therefore, first decided to promote ten alter-nate members in order to reach a quorum. In addition, some lead-ers of the revolutionary committees and some PLA leaders also participated with voting rights.[3] The meeting expelled Liu Shaoqi as a traitor and renegade.

Since local party committees had not yet been restored, each provincial revolutionary committee selected delegates to the next National Party Congress. Tension along the border after a brief clash with the Soviet Union caused the national delegates, instead of directly attending in person, to select a presidium that would

2. For reconstruction of the party, see the untitled monograph [Materials on Party Reconstruction], in *Hongweibing Ziliao Huibian* [Washington D.C.: Center for Chinese Research Materials, 1978], 5029–42.

3. Zhonggong Zhongyang Wenxian Yanjiushi, ed., *Guanyu Jianguo Yilai de Rugan Lishi Wenti de Jueyi* (Beijing: Renmin Ribao Chubanshe, 1983), 389.

exercise authority in the name of the congress. The presidium first chose its own leaders and then made basic decisions on how to select new Central Committee members: it limited the number of full and alternate members to 250 and the number of Eighth CC members to be reelected to 53, and it also specified the groups whose members would be automatically "elected."[4]

Each provincial delegation nominated candidates to the CC and forwarded their names to the presidium. After collecting all the names, the presidium first voted on the lists of names, most of which had more candidates than could be elected, and then reviewed the qualifications of each candidate. The discussion developed into a heated clash among Zhou Enlai, the military, and the Gang of Four, which wanted to bring in many rebels.[5] After negotiating about each name to appear on the final list, members of the presidium each cast one vote for or against the list. It was approved unanimously. "Because there were too many nominees from the military and the mass representatives," 279 members were elected to the CC, exceeding the limit set up by the presidium. It took almost ten days for the presidium to select the CC members.[6]

As table 16 demonstrates, the PLA was the group that gained the most from the CR. Its local representation at the Ninth CC also increased substantially as a result of the loss of leaders from the central party and the government, a sign that power had become decentralized. But the gains made by local leaders did not benefit provincial party leaders, for the local leaders were PLA members who took power at the expense of their civilian counterparts. According to my preliminary estimate, out of 225 provincial party secretaries at the time of the CR, only 98 (43 percent) managed to survive. By contrast, of the 8 regional PLA leaders at the Eighth CC, only 1 was permanently purged.

Conflict over the selection of Politburo members was more intense. Mao reported to the congress:

4. Zhonggong Zhongyang Dangxiao Dangshi Jiaoyan Ziliaozu, ed., *Zhonggou Gongchandang Lice Zhongyao Huiyiji* (Shanghai: Shanghai Renmin Chubanshe, 1983), 2:242; Zhongguo Zhongyang Dangshi Yanjiushi, ed., *Zhongguo Gongchandang Lice Daibiao Dahui* (Beijing: Zhongyang Dangxiao Chubanshe, 1983), 66–72.
5. Zhongguo Zhongyang Dangshi Yanjiushi, ed., *Zhongguo Gongchandang.*
6. Ibid.

Table 16.   Representation on the Ninth Central Committee, as of 1969

Membership	PLA		Cadre		Mass		Total	
	No.	%	No.	%	No.	%	No.	%
Full member	71	42	62	36	37	22	170	100
Alternate Member	50	46	18	16	41	38	109	100
Total	121	43	80	29	78	28	279	100
Power Weight[a]	192	43	142	31	115	26	449	100

Source. Compiled by the author from biographical information.

a. Calculated by giving two points to full members and one point to alternate members.

> I have faith in some of my old comrades who made mistakes. Originally there was a long list of twenty people [of old cadres], and I considered it good to make all of them Politburo members. Later someone advanced a shorter list of ten people, and I thought the list was too short. Most [of the old cadres] are middle roaders, and [I] am opposed to the long and the short lists and favor a medium size list of about twenty persons.[7]

The twenty-person Politburo included eight new members. Six of them turned out to be from Lin Biao's group; the Jiang Qing group obtained four seats.[8]

LIN BIAO'S FOLLOWERS

Tables 17–19, constructed on the basis of biographical information that I have collected, attempt to identify Lin's power base by analyzing those purged with him. Lin's political influence in the Ninth CC was quite modest: only 16 percent of its members were purged with him. Moreover, his modest political influence was largely limited to the military; forty-nine of sixty-six members purged with him were military men (constituting 40 percent of all military representatives in the committee), whereas only 5 percent of the mass representatives and 16 percent of the cadres failed to make it into

7. *Zhonggong Dangshi Jiaoxue Cankao Ziliao; Wenhua Dageming Shiqi* (Beijing: Zhongguo Renmin Zhengzhi Xueyuan, 1983), 4, no. 4 (1983): 278.

8. The Lin group include Ye Qun, Chen Boda, Huang Yongsheng, Qiu Huizuo, and Wu Faxian. The Jiang Qing group members were Xie Fuzhi, Jiang Qing, Zhang Chunqiao, and Yao Wenyuan.

Table 17. Impact of Lin Biao's Fall on Ninth Central Committee
Members, as of 1973

Membership	Purged		Survived		Total	
	No.	%	No.	%	No.	%
Cadres	13	16	129	84	142	100
Military	49	40	72	60	121	100
Masses	4	5	115	95	119	100
Total	66	16	316	84	382	100

Source. Compiled by the author from biographical information.

Table 18. Impact of Lin Biao's Fall by Field Army Affiliation, as of 1973

Field Army Affiliation	Purged		Survived		Total	
	No.	%	No.	%	No.	%
4th	32	28	82	72	114	100
1st, 2d, 3d, 5th and 6th	61	19	260	81	321	100
Total	93	21	342	79	435	100

Sources. Field army information is based on data provided by W. Whitson, *The Chinese Command: A History of Communist Military Politics, 1927–71* (New York: Praeger, 1973), which includes the civilian leaders. Information on purges was compiled by the author from biographical information.

the Tenth CC. Despite his impressive array of formal titles, his political influence in the Chinese bureaucracy was rather limited. As a professional military man, he had no experience to help him as the head of a civilian bureaucracy. Nor did he possess any charismatic qualities, either physical or intellectual.

Even within the military, Lin Biao drew his supporters largely from former Fourth Field Army officers (see table 18). Moreover, as shown in table 19, most of his supporters were from the second (32 percent) and third (27 percent) generations of military leaders, whereas his influence on the first generation of senior military leaders was quite limited (18 percent).

This skewed distribution of Lin Biao's followers within the military demonstrates that his control was very tenuous, and the military was not free from factional, regional, and organizational rivalries. Furthermore, Mao, as chairman of the Military Affairs Commission, was not about to give him a free hand.

Table 19.   Impact of Lin Biao's Fall by Military Generation, as of 1973

Generation	Purged		Survived		Total	
	No.	%	No.	%	No.	%
1st	11	18	49	82	60	100
2d	27	32	57	68	84	100
3d	29	27	77	73	106	100
4th–8th	9	23	31	77	40	100
Total	76	26	214	74	290	100

Source. Field army information is based on data provided by W. Whitson, *The Chinese Command: A History of Communist Military Politics, 1927–71* (New York: Praeger, 1973), which includes the civilian leaders. Information on purges was compiled by the author from biographical information.

None of the most senior leaders (except Chen Boda) was implicated in the Lin Biao affair. Many of them apparently did not take him seriously, as indicated by Luo Ruiqing's remark: "I never though that guy would fill the position [of Defense Minister]."[9] Even during the CR, when Lin's power was rapidly increasing, many senior military leaders looked at his political maneuvers with contempt and tried to distance themselves from him and the Gang of Four. Lin could not pressure them to join his informal group because they had direct access to Mao, which they used to clarify their status.[10]

Lin Biao's most loyal followers were from the second echelon of military leaders, mostly from the former Fourth Field Army, which had been close to him for a long time. These followers were Huang Yongsheng, former commander of the Guangdong military region (who was promoted in 1968 to be chief of staff), Qiu Huizou, director of the quartermaster department, Li Zuopeng, commander of the navy, and Wu Faxian, commander of the air force. All of them helped Lin purge Lo Ruiqing by secretly collecting incriminating information against him. During the CR, Lin enhanced their dependency on him by personally protecting them at the most crucial moment—when they were criticized as powerholders by the masses. In return, these former Fourth Field Army officers de-

9. Interview in Beijing, 1988.
10. Nie Rongzhen, *Nie Rongzhen Huiyilu*, vol. 3.

veloped personal loyalties to Lin, regarding him not only as a formal superior but also as an informal leader.

In addition to these high-level leaders, Lin Biao also cultivated a group of loyal followers among junior air force officers, with whom he did not have any direct work relations. The key link between Lin and these personal followers was his twenty-one-year-old son, Lin Liguo, who was a physics student at Beijing University when the CR started. Lin Biao first asked Wu Faxian to take care of his son during the initial stages of the CR. Later he instructed Wu to make his son deputy director of the air force's management office and operational department so that Lin Biao himself could help the development of air defense strategy through his son. Wu was more than willing to oblige. He convened the party committee of the air force, which decided that "every matter in the air force should be reported to Lin Liguo, and everything should be under his control and command." In addition, the political department of the air force adopted five measures: "Think of Lin Liguo all the time, ask him about everything, protect him everywhere, take him as our leader, sincerely comply with his demands and his every command."[11] Under the protection of Wu Faxian, Lin Liguo gathered together a dozen middle-level air force officers.[12]

The Lin Biao group closely approximates an archetypical faction. First, its key membership included a few former Fourth Field Army officers and second- and third-generation military officers from other field armies who owed their promotion to him. They developed very close personal ties, which resulted in complex mutual obligations. For instance, Lin Biao protected Wu Faxian, and in return Wu accepted Lin's son into the air force, helped him get promoted into key positions, and tolerated his factional network within the air force.

Moreover, the second layer of Lin Biao's group, which consisted of ambitious air force officers, whom his son recruited through the secret channels of patronage, also approximates the typical factional model: the faction was based exclusively on personal ties, the officers were motivated by ambition, and they were dedicated to

11. Yan Jiaqi, *Wenge Shinian Shi* (Tianjin: Tianjin Renmin Chubanshe, 1986), 341–42.

12. For the Lin Liguo group, see ibid., 319–97; Zuigao Renmin Fayuan Yanjiusuo, ed., *Zhonghua Renmin*.

their patrons without much consideration for formal rules. Because they did not have their own power base, they were willing to engage in factional activities, deeply involving themselves in preparing the 571 program (*wu chi yi*, a Chinese homonym with armed uprising). Obviously, they expected to be rewarded if their plan succeeded.

However, Lin Biao's senior military followers—Huang Yongsheng, Li Zoupeng, Wu Faxian, and Qiu Huizuo—were not directly involved in the conspiracy, according to available data revealed during their trial. They behaved circumspectly during the critical period; although they apparently knew Lin Liguo's plan, they neither actively participated in it nor exposed the plan to an appropriate authority. At the same time they gave Lin Liguo all the support they could mobilize through their formal authority and transmitted to Lin Biao the content of the speeches that Mao made during his trip to military regions. Probably their positions were too high for them openly to participate in obvious antiparty activities.[13]

This pattern of behavior again reveals a complex and subtle mix of formal and informal ties in Chinese politics. Because of a strong tradition of formal bureaucracy, incumbents of formal organizations tend to use their discretionary powers to help their factional interests, but not so far as to jeopardize their formal authority.

REHABILITATION

At the Ninth Party Congress Mao emphatically stressed the need for unity. Lin Biao also endorsed a policy of moderation. He urged that only cadres of the three categories be purged and that "good people who made the mistake of following the capitalist road" be set free, "if they raise their determination and if the masses are willing to forgive them."[14] Thereafter, the news media began to publish articles discussing cadre rehabilitation. However, instead of urging large-scale rehabilitation, these articles simply reported some experiences of rehabilitated cadres to prove a general point.

13. Zuigao Renmin Fayuan Yanjiusuo, *Zhonghua Renmin*.
14. *Zhonggong Dangshi Jiaoxue*, no. 4, 1983, 278.

On the question of how to evaluate cadres, an article about an experience in Shanghai suggested that the regime should (1) consider each cadre's major characteristics and actions rather than minor ones; (2) look at the circumstances and historical conditions in which cadres made mistakes (and forgive those whose mistakes resulted from following instructions passed down through organizational channels); (3) survey the entire history and work of each cadre, not just his work during the CR; (4) evaluate each cadre's performance throughout the CR, not just during a particular period; and (5) take into account the cadre's attitude toward his own mistakes. This formula represented a clear victory for the moderates and a setback for the radicals, who insisted on using cadres' performance records from the early stages of the CR as the major criterion for rehabilitation.[15] When the entire work record was used as the principal criterion, most cadres passed the test and were consequently liberated.

A statement accompanying the liberation of Liu Bing, former deputy secretary of Qinghua University, shows how the five conditions worked in one case.

> Liu Bing joined the revolution in his youth. Having investigated and researched his record after 1949, particularly after he came to Qinghua in 1956, everyone came to the following conclusion. He had a very close relationship with a handful of counterrevolutionary revisionists, but this relationship derived from his work [rather than from personal ties]. Liu Bing never took part in counterrevolutionary activities. In his work, he followed the counterrevolutionary education policy, but never with the intention of restoring capitalism or of opposing Chairman Mao's revolutionary education policy; and he never took part in any criminal activity. Because of the insufficient transformation of his bourgeois worldview, he spread rightist views, but he did not violently attack the party or socialism. By his failure to put proletarian politics first, he overemphasized "functional work" and employed a few bad persons. Yet he never surrendered to the renegades.[16]

Newspaper discussions also offered some examples of "good cadres who made mistakes." For instance, before the CR a Shanghai cadre set up three mottoes to observe personally: (1) not to be economically corrupt, (2) not to lead a decadent life, and (3)

15. *Renmin Ribao*, 3 March 1969.
16. Ibid., 1 June 1969.

not to pursue fame. Despite this cadre's personal integrity, he implemented the bourgeois reactionary line during the CR.[17] Obviously this type of cadre was regarded as a "good person who had made mistakes." Another criterion used to determine whether a cadre was good or not was class background. Any cadre who came from a family who had suffered exploitation was presumed to be good.

Newspapers also addressed the subject of the masses' opposition to cadre rehabilitation. There was still strong resistance to rehabilitation from mass organizations because the masses were afraid of retaliation from cadres against whom they had once struggled.[18] And the lingering effects of CR factionalism often made those in charge of cadre rehabilitation unable to reach a consensus on a particular cadre.

Although we do not know how these model cases were applied to each individual cadre, we know that most of the cadres liberated before Lin Biao's fall were specialists whose expertise was greatly needed to help units function smoothly. A preliminary count has revealed that only thirteen provincial-level cadres, but a much larger number of government leaders, were liberated before Lin Biao's purge. Most of the 127 ministerial-level government cadres freed by June 1971 were former vice ministers.[19]

It is very likely that the Gang of Four would have opposed rehabilitating any cadres, if possible, whereas Zhou Enlai would have brought back as many cadres as possible. Documentary evidence about Lin Biao's attitude toward cadre rehabilitation is contradictory; he was accused, on the one hand, of having opposed it and, on the other, of having schemed to use the grievances of purged cadres in his own move against Mao.[20] His real position seems to have been between these two extremes; he was willing to rehabilitate lower-level cadres, but he refused to allow the return of high ranking cadres because they would have posed a threat to his position. In fact, most of the cadres at the basic production level were liberated prior to Lin Biao's fall.[21]

17. Ibid., 28 March 1969.
18. Ibid., 14 April 1969.
19. For instance, see Zhonggong Yanjiu 4(9) (July 1972):42–51.
20. Ying-mao Kau, The Lin Biao Affair (White Plains, N.Y.: International Arts and Science Press, 1975), 84; Daily Report, 21 June 1976.
21. China News Analysis, no. 311, 8 May 1969; no. 315, 12 June 1969; Hong Qi, no. 6, 1978.

POLITICAL STRATEGY

Although Lin Biao is known as a brilliant military strategist, he rose to power primarily because he actively encouraged the cult of Mao. He introduced Mao's approach of "politics in command" to the PLA and succeeded, to a certain extent, in restoring that body's sagging morale after the purge of Peng Dehuai. During the CR, he pushed Mao's personality cult to new heights. "Every sentence in Chairman Mao's work is a truth. One single sentence of his surpasses 10,000 of ours. . . . We must carry out not only those instructions we understand, but also those we fail to understand for the moment, and in the course of carrying them out, we must try to understand them."[22]

Lin Biao's thought pattern, aptly labeled a "barracks communism" by Lowell Dittmer, shows the traits of a military man, particularly in his penchant for reducing complex and ambiguous matters to simple propositions.[23] During the CR, he divided the leading cadres into two categories: those who paid attention to important matters and those who were preoccupied with minor matters. Although we do not know whether he undertook any serious study of Marxism-Leninism or any other theoretical literature, he left several boxes of cards containing excerpts from various Marxist writings, organized under such headings as "relations between superior and subordinates," "cadre policy," "seeking truth," and "dialectics."[24]

Although Lin Biao rose to be Mao's official successor during the CR, as vice chairman of the CCP, his real power was precarious because his influence was overshadowed by Mao, who was too powerful and unpredictable to be trusted. Lin knew about Mao's habit of using confidants and then dropping them.[25] Although he was fourteen years younger than Mao, his poor health made it doubtful that he would outlive him.[26] As defense minister he was legally subordinate to Premier Zhou Enlai, his for-

22. *New China News Agency* (Beijing), 23 January 1968.
23. Lowell Dittmer, *China's Continuous Revolution: The Post-Liberation Epoch, 1949–1981* (Berkeley and Los Angeles: University of California Press, 1987).
24. *Zhonggong Dangshi Jiaoxue*, no. 4, 1983, 336.
25. Ying-mao Kau, *Lin Biao Affair*.
26. Hu Hua, "Marching on a Tortuous Road and Socialist New Victory During New Line" (unpublished paper), 1987, 24.

mer teacher at Whampao Military Academy. In the propaganda field he had no reliable partners except for the Gang of Four, over whom he did not have any formal authority.

With his power base limited to military officers, largely from the Fourth Field Army and those from the second and third generations, Lin attempted, first, to strengthen the political authority of the military, second, to obtain formal authority over the bureaucracy as chairman of the state, and, third, to mobilize his factional followers for a coup attempt.

USING THE MILITARY

Although Mao had to rely on the military to restore any semblance of order after two years of chaotic mass mobilization, the elite groups' interests in the military's deep involvement in politics diverged. For Mao, who invented the phrase "the party controls the gun," military involvement was a temporary measure to control the mass movement. The Gang of Four saw that their interests lay in weakening the military's political influence while increasing that of the rebels in the newly established power organs at the local level. Zhou Enlai shared Mao's view, regarding use of the military as an expedient measure to prevent civil war.

Given Lin Biao's heavy reliance on the military for his support, it is clear that he benefited from the institution's increasing political influence during the crisis of the CR, although he did not totally control it. For example, as vice chairman in charge of the daily operations of the Military Affairs Commission, he could legitimately interfere with the operations of the military control commissions that were imposed even on some central government ministries.

The rising tension along the Sino-Soviet border in 1969 helped the military to maintain its active involvement in politics. After the armed clash in Chenbao island, Lin Biao expanded the military's control over industry at the expense of the State Council under Zhou Enlai.[27] Using the need to prepare for war as an ex-

---

27. On the border clash, see Thomas Robinson, "The Sino-Soviet Border Dispute," *American Political Science Review*, vol. 66, December 1972, 1175–1202. For Lin Biao's exploitation of the incident, see *Jingji Jihua Yanjiu*, 20 November 1983.

cuse, he extended the military's authority over many industries at the expense of the State Council.[28] He also gave the military jurisdiction over small industries that could produce small weapons, and he planned to set up an "independent and complete national defense industry" under his control. Furthermore, Lin Biao reportedly intervened in the work of the economic planning agency by ordering it to replace "balance" as the main guiding principle of economic planning with "the battle perspective." Subsequently, the military share of the national budget increased by 34 percent in 1969, by 15 percent in 1970, and by 17 percent in 1971. In these years, defense industry and science received more than 11 percent of the total reinvestment of the state (in 1968 it had received only 9 percent). The state bureaucracy under Zhou Enlai was losing its jurisdiction over a large portion of industry.

Lin Biao reportedly issued Order no. 1 on 18 October 1969 "behind the [back of] Chairman Mao." Under the pretext of "strengthening war preparation to prevent the enemy's sudden attack," this order put the entire military on alert, set up command structures, and appointed officers to command posts.[29] After Order no. 1, Lin's followers dispersed old senior leaders to different parts of China.[30] The objective was to remove them from the decision-making process at the center and to prevent them from forming a coalition against Lin. It was easy to keep close surveillance over them through the reliable local military units, and Lin took the precaution of forbidding these older leaders from communicating with one another.[31] Only on 19 October did Lin Biao report to Mao (by telephone recording), "following the practice of first beheading and then reporting," therefore forcing Mao to acquiesce in his decision. Upon hearing the report, Mao's first comment was that the order should be burned.[32]

Not surprisingly, after Lin Biao's death all his decisions made in the name of war preparations were reversed. All industry was returned to the control of the State Council. In contrast to Lin's

28. *Jingji Jihua Yanjiu*, 23 November 1983.
29. Ibid.
30. Nie Rongzhen, *Nie Rongzhen Huiyilu*, vol. 3.
31. Ibid.
32. The implication of Mao's comment was that the order should be regarded as if it had not been issued. Ibid.

strategy of preparing for war, which inevitably increased the power of the military, Mao Zedong and Zhou Enlai opted for the goal of
overcoming China's diplomatic isolation by improving Sino-
American relations. In addition, Mao attempted to limit the power
of the military: he later reduced its involvement in local politics by
sending soldiers back to their barracks and transferring political
authority to provincial party committees. "At the moment [our
military] promotes politics [wen], but does not promote military
affairs [wu], and it has already become a cultured army [wenhua
jundui]."[33] By February 1971, the center decided to transfer the authority to investigate May 16 elements to the national committee
headed by Wu De, thus depriving the local military of the chance
to use this investigation to increase their political influence.[34]

ISSUES OF STATE CHAIRMANSHIP

Lin and his followers tried to overcome his weakness in the civilian bureaucracy by making him the formal head of the state, as
chairman of the PRC, the position that was abolished with Liu
Shaoqi's purge.[35] The Gang of Four apparently wanted to exploit
the issue in order to weaken Zhou Enlai's position.[36] Viewing the
revision of the state constitution as "an opportunity for the redistribution of power," the Gang of Four argued that the new constitution should include an article stating that "on the basis of
the Central Committee of the CCP's nomination, the premier
and members of the State Council will be appointed and dismissed." According to this draft, the chairman of the CCP
would concurrently be "a head of the proletarian dictatorship,"
whereas the premier would also be a "first minister" in charge
of management offices under the chairman.[37]

Mao, probably happy with the three groups conflicting and
cooperating under his authority, expressed several times his ob-
jection to restoring the state chairmanship. Zhou Enlai was

33. *Zhonggong Dangshi Jiaoxue*, no. 4, 1983, 301.
34. Ibid., 298.
35. For Lin's maneuver at Lushan, see Zheng Derung and Zhu Yang, eds.,
Zhongguo Gongchandang Lishi Jiangyi (Jilin: Jilin Renmin Chubanshe, 1982), 181–93.
36. Chen Hefu, ed., *Zhongguo Faxian Leibian* (Beijing: Zhongguo Shehui Kexue
Chubanshe, 1980), 353.
37. Ibid.

more than happy with Mao's opposition. But Lin Biao pushed the issue. He made an unauthorized move by stating "Chairman Mao is a genius," and the "chairmanship of the state should be established" in his opening speech at the second plenum of the Ninth Party Congress held in August 1970 in Lushan. Lin's followers endorsed his speech, demanding that it be distributed and studied.[38]

Mao counterattacked. Declaring "it is unprecedented for a few persons to attempt to confuse 200 Central Committee members," he personally convened a Politburo meeting, which decided to stop discussion of Lin Biao's speech, to cancel the central-north China group's report prepared by Chen Boda, and to order Chen to submit to self-criticism. A few days later, Mao wrote "My Opinion," which repudiated Lin's and Chen's theories of genius. In addition, probably alarmed at Lin's move, Mao took several additional measures to weaken Lin's position. He ordered the PLA to rectify its work style (*zuofeng*) by initiating the campaign "against arrogance and complacency" and by placing Zhou Enlai in charge of the campaign. Mao also dispatched Ye Jianying to work in the management section of the Military Affairs Commission in order to let "some air in" and reorganized the Beijing military region by transferring the Thirty-eighth Field Army, which was suspected of being loyal to Lin Biao, out of Beijing—the strategy Mao himself described as "digging out Lin's wall."

COUP ATTEMPT

After the Lushan conference Lin Biao realized not only that his plan for peaceful succession had failed but that he had also exposed his purpose so fully that he was in political trouble. He thus concluded, "Struggle by words will not do; only using weapons can work." Knowing Mao well enough to realize that he would probably move against him at the forthcoming third plenum of the Ninth Party Congress (planned for September 1971), Lin thought it

38. According to the official interpretation, proclaiming Mao's genius was intended to achieve two objectives for the Lin Biao group. First, it would discredit Zhang Chunqiao, who failed to recognize Mao as a genius. By criticizing Zhang, Lin Biao could seize hegemony over ideology from the Jiang Qing faction. The second objective was to establish the triumvirate of Marx, Lenin, and Mao, with a parallel triumvirate of assistants—Engels, Stalin, and Lin Biao. Hu Hua, "Marching on a Tortuous Road."

would be better for him to move first. His son and his factional followers developed a secret contingent coup plan of the 571 program.[39]

Not sitting idly by, Mao was maneuvering to further isolate Lin Biao politically. From mid-August to 12 September 1971 Mao traveled around the south talking with leaders of the big military regions, provinces, and municipalities. In his talks, he made his displeasure with Lin Biao amply clear: "A certain person is impatient to be the state chairman; he wants to divide the party and seize power. . . . Making one's own wife the management office chief is not appropriate." With regard to his role in Lin Biao's rise, he said, "Of course, I have some responsibility."[40]

After being informed of Mao's move by means of two different sources, Lin Biao ordered the activation of the 571 program.[41] Lin Liguo's group busily discussed possible methods of assassinating Mao, ranging from using napalm and rockets to destroy Mao's train to sending assassins to murder him. Probably because he had been informed of "some abnormal action" on the part of Lin Biao's followers, Mao changed his travel schedule and immediately returned to Beijing.[42] When the Lin Liguo group discovered that Mao had left for Beijing, they changed their coup plan and decided to escape to Guangdong. In Canton, they planned to convene a meeting of cadres above the divisional level and then to use the radio broadcast system to declare the establishment of a separate regime. Reportedly, they planned to ask for help from the Soviet Union.[43]

"A comrade in the central management office" (probably Wang Dongxing) informed Zhou of Lin Biao's plan to escape to the Soviet Union.[44] Zhou ordered that no plane take off without the joint approval of Mao, Zhou, Huang, Wu, and Li Zuopeng, commander

39. Lin Liguo called his secret group a "fleet" in admiration of the Japanese naval spirit as depicted in the movie *Tora! Tora! Tora!* For the most detailed information on his coup plan, see Yan Jiaqi, *Wenge Shinian Shi*, 356; Zuigao Renmin Fayuan Yanjiushi, ed., *Zhonghua Renmin*.

40. *Jiefangjun Bao*, 25 November 1980.

41. Zuigao Renmin Fayuan Yanjiushi, ed., *Zhonghua Renmin*, 112.

42. Hu Hua reports that Zheng Shiqing, the head of Jiangxi province, informed Mao at Nanchang (at the end of August) of Lin Liguo's activities. Hu Hua, "Marching on a Tortuous Road."

43. Zuigao Renmin Fayuan Yanjiushi, ed., *Zhonghua Renmin*, 142–49.

44. *Dangshi Yanjiu*, no. 3, 1981, 59.

of the navy, who was responsible for airport security. Nonetheless, at midnight, Lin Biao, Ye Qun, and Lin Liguo decided to escape, probably because they had heard about Zhou's suspicions. Around 2 A.M., when Lin's plane was getting close to the limits of Chinese air space, Wu Faxian asked Zhou whether or not to shoot the plane down. Zhou went to Mao for a decision. Mao said, "Heaven wants to rain, and a woman wants to marry. Let him go."[45] On the afternoon of 14 September, Zhou received a report from the Chinese embassy in Mongolia stating that the plane had crashed. We still do not know why.[46]

45. Ibid.
46. Some speculate that the plane was shot down; others guess that the plane ran out of fuel. *Hangkong Zhishi*, no. 9, 1981, 26–29.

6

The Gang of Four: Ideologues

Lin Biao's fall reduced the contending political groups to radical ideologues and bureaucrats, the latter headed by Zhou Enlai. Mao tried to bring the two warring groups together, relying on the ideologues to maintain a revolutionary momentum, while counting on the bureaucrats to preserve order and run the economy. However, the two groups were bound to clash on many issues created by the Lin Biao incident. The innocent victims of Lin's conspiracy had to be rehabilitated. But thorny issues were who the innocent victims were, how many of those purged should be rehabilitated, and who should fill the power vacuum created by the purge of Lin's followers and the military's return to barracks. Understandably, Zhou's group wanted to reinstate disgraced cadres in order to correct Lin Biao's mistakes and to remedy the "absolute shortage of experienced cadres," whereas the Gang of Four wanted to promote CR rebels in order to establish their power base within the party-state apparatus.

POWER BASE

The official news media often referred to the CR radicals as "the Gang of Four's factional system" (*xitong*), which "had its own platform, line, policy, theory, and supporting members." The two contradictory terms "faction" and "system" accurately capture the complexities of the CR radical group. The behavior of the four radical leaders—Jiang Qing, Zhang Chunqiao, Yao Wenyuan, and Wang Hongwen—displayed all the characteristics of a faction. Thanks to close personal ties with Jiang Qing, Zhang Chunqiao and Yao Wenyuan became members of the Cultural Revolution Small Group in the initial stage of the CR and then were promoted to the Politburo with her. Wang Hongwen, a leader of the radical workers organization in Shanghai, probably owed his rise to

Zhang Chunqiao and Yao Wenyuan, who must have recommended him to Mao. United by friendship, the four radicals thought as one on every issue, and each of them developed complex factional networks involving subleaders and their followers. They frequently gathered followers into "study groups" or "writing groups," which acted as confidential networks for their factional activities.[1]

But the Gang of Four was more than a faction because it had developed a well-defined ideology and political program. It regarded itself as representing "Chairman Mao's proletarian headquarters" at the central level and the "new, rising political forces" at the mass level. Often the Gang of Four managed to make official its radical ideology, program, and policy so that they were implemented at the organizational level. It mobilized disadvantaged and discontented social groups against the existing political authority. The recruitment of such well-known followers as Zhang Tiesheng and Wen Hongsheng was based not on narrowly defined personal ties but on what they had done and stood for during the CR. Only after recruitment did followers become close to the Gang of Four. The well-known followers represented a certain type of person rather than unique individuals. The Gang of Four's power base both reflected and shaped its cadre policy.

SELECTING THE TENTH CENTRAL COMMITTEE

Immediately after the Lin Biao incident, Zhou Enlai, who was delegated by Mao to manage the daily work of the center, took a moderate domestic and international course for China.[2] In dealing with the chaotic domestic scene, he demonstrated his political acumen, deftly compromising with the radicals in order to restore a semblance of political stability.

Thanks to Zhou's willingness to compromise with the Gang of Four, the two sides apparently reached an agreement on how to convene the Tenth Party Congress at an extended Central Commit-

---

1. *Daily Report*, 29 June 1977, p. E2; *Hong Qi*, no. 11, 1977; no. 5, 1979.
2. In the rural area, Zhou initiated a moderate policy of paying attention to the needs of collectives and individuals, and in the foreign policy arena, he diffused military pressure from the Soviet Union by inviting President Nixon to Beijing.

tee meeting held in May 1973. Qualifications for delegates to the congress included "good political performance during the CR," a criterion that the radicals may have insisted on. As for old cadres who had "made serious mistakes, if they underwent self-criticism, they should be allowed to be delegates." However, a veteran cadre with a "questionable history" was not to be elected. The delegation would be selected by "negotiation" and "voting." A quota probably demanded by the radicals was set up for each occupational category: 30 percent for workers, 25 percent for lower-middle and poor peasants, 19 percent for "revolutionary" cadres, and 5 percent for "revolutionary" inellectuals. The Jiang Qing group also managed to set up an age quota for the delegation: 80 percent of the worker and peasant delegation had to be between eighteen and fifty-five; the same age group had to constitute about 60 percent of the military delegates, cadres, and revolutionary intellectuals.[3]

Preparations for the congress proceeded secretly; delegates from each province met in its capital under the pretense of "study classes."[4] These meetings selected an election committee of 104 members with Wang Hongwen as chairman.[5]

The election committee used the Ninth CC members as the basis for selecting new CC members, first removing Lin Biao's followers (a total of forty-seven people) and then filling the vacancies with those selected by the election committee from the pool of nominees recommended by provinces and municipalities. Heated debate between the two groups ensued. The Zhou Enlai group managed to place some rehabilitated cadres (such as Deng Xiaoping, Wu Lanfu, Wang Jiaxiang, Tan Zhenlin, and Li Jingquan, all of whom were Eighth CC members, but had failed to enter the Ninth CC).[6] The Gang of Four, by contrast, argued vehemently on behalf of the CR rebels, even nominating nonparty member CR rebels on the grounds that they "had joined the party ideologically, although they have not yet joined the party organizationally." A substantial

3. Zhongguo Zhongyang Dangshi Yanjiushi, ed., *Zhongguo Gongchandang Lice Daibiao Dahui* (Beijing: Zhongyang Dangxiao Chubanshe, 1983), 107.

4. Ibid., 111.

5. In addition, Wang Hongwen was in charge of revising the party constitution, and he assumed the chairmanship of the preparatory committee for electing the Tenth CC. Zhou Enlai, Kang Sheng, Ye Jianying, Jiang Qing, Zhang Chunqiao, and Li Desheng were vice chairmen. Ibid.

6. Ibid., 112.

number of the young CR rebels entered the Central Committee. For example, Zhang Chunqiao pushed hard for Zhu Gejia, a Shanghai student who had been sent to Xinjiang, in spite of objections from Zhou's group. The final meeting, which was attended by all delegates and lasted only four days (from 24 to 28 August), approved the final list of Tenth CC members.[7]

Officially labeled "a congress of unity, a congress of victory, and a congress full of vigor," the Tenth Party Congress produced a well-balanced outcome in terms of the membership of the Central Committee; 30 percent were from the PLA, 33 percent were cadres, and 37 percent were representatives from the masses.[8] This balance was achieved by removing 40 percent of the PLA's Ninth CC members from office and adding twenty-five PLA candidates (six were liberated PLA leaders), forty-three cadres, and forty-eight leaders of the masses. This kind of balance would have been impossible without a conscious effort to maintain equilibrium. Theoretical justification for such equal representation came from the principle of the three-in-one formula—which was first introduced in 1967 as a means to form the revolutionary committees with representatives from the cadres, the military, and the mass organizations—on which the Jiang Qing group probably insisted in order to increase mass representation.

The radicals had reason to be satisfied with the outcome of the Tenth Party Congress. Mass representation made spectacular gains in the Tenth CC, mainly at the expense of PLA leaders; it increased from a mere 25 percent in the Ninth CC to 37 percent in the Tenth CC. By contrast, the PLA's proportion decreased from 43 percent in the Ninth CC to 30 percent, whereas cadre representation increased slightly from 31 percent to 33 percent. In terms of numbers of representatives, cadres were behind the masses. Yet if we take into account the difference between full members and alternate members by giving double weight to each full member, we see that cadres had more power than delegates from the masses.

7. For the heated debates at the meeting, see ibid., 117–18.
8. In the Tenth CC, some of the old cadres—Deng Xiaoping, Wang Jiaxiang, Wu Lanfu, Li Jingquan, Li Baohua, Liao Chengzhi, Yang Yong, Chen Chiwei, and Wang Zhen—entered the Tenth CC. But such Gang of Four followers (who were known to have "horns on the head, and scars on the body") as Wang Xiuzhen, Xu Jingxian, Ma Tienshui, Yu Huiping, Jin Zumin, Zhou Hongbao, Chu Chiayao, Dang Zhishan, Xia Fangen, and Xie Zhengyi were also added. Ibid.

Table 20.   Representation on the Tenth Central Committee, as of 1973

Membership	PLA No.	PLA %	Cadres No.	Cadres %	Masses No.	Masses %	Total No.	Total %
Full member	62	32	79	40	54	28	195	100
Alternate member	34	27	25	20	65	52	124	100
Total	96	30	104	33	119	37	319	100
Power Weight[a]	158	31	183	35	174	34	514	100

Source. Compiled by the author from biographical information.

a. Calculated by giving two points to full members and one point to alternate members.

Table 21.   Impact of the Gang of Four's Fall on Members of the Tenth Central Committee, as of 1977

Membership	Purged No.	Purged %	Survived No.	Survived %	Total No.	Total %
PLA	35	37	59	53	104	100
Cadres	18	17	86	83	94	100
Masses	66	55	55	45	121	100
Total	132	41	187	49	319	100

Source. Compiled by the author from biographical information.

FOLLOWERS IN THE TENTH CENTRAL COMMITTEE

Since we know who among the Ninth CC members was purged with the Gang of Four, tables 21–26 attempt to delineate their power base among the three groups. In table 21 we see that under half of the Tenth CC members (41 percent) were removed from their seats when the Gang of Four fell. The scope of this purge indicates that the gang's influence was much more powerful than Lin Biao's: almost twice as many people were purged in Lin Biao's group as purged in the Gang of Four's. Of the 41 percent of the Tenth CC members who failed to make it into the Eleventh CC, 55 percent were mass representatives (54 percent of all the mass representatives at the Tenth CC), 26 percent were PLA representatives (37 percent of all the PLA representatives), and 19 percent

Table 22.   Impact of the Gang of Four's Fall by Organizational Affiliation, as of 1977

Membership	Purged		Survived		Total	
	No.	%	No.	%	No.	%
Party	8	11	63	89	71	100
Government	49	25	150	75	199	100
Military	75	45	93	55	168	100
Masses	40	59	28	41	68	100
Multiple[a]	87	71	31	39	121	100
Total	259	36	455	64	714	100

Source. Compiled by the author from biographical information.

Note. This sample includes all those who had held positions of leadership at central and provincial levels of party, government, and military organizations.
a. Those who were concurrently holding positions in party, military, and government organizations at the provincial level and below.

were cadres (17 percent of all the cadres). Needless to say, the Gang of Four controlled the majority of the mass representatives at the Tenth CC.

Table 22 shows a similar distribution of the Gang of Four's influence nationwide: their supporters were heavily drawn from the mass organizations; the 59 percent purge rate among the mass representatives is likely to be lower than the actual figure, because many of the mass leaders who had originally made it into the Eleventh Party Congress were later dropped. The radicals' influence among the PLA was surprisingly high; about 45 percent of PLA members in the sample were identified as having been purged with the Gang of Four. The radicals' weakest point was among party leaders: only 11 percent of them disappeared with the Gang of Four. Twenty-five percent of the government leaders were also purged with the Gang. The 71 percent purge rate of those who held multiple positions clearly indicates that the main power base of the Gang of Four was the former rebels whom they had promoted to leadership positions after Lin Biao's fall.

Table 23 examines the correlation between the number of promotions after 1971 and the probability of being purged with the Gang of Four. Undoubtedly, their followers were those whom the radicals worked hard to place in leadership positions—the beneficiaries

Table 23.   Impact of the Gang of Four's Fall by Promotion Grade
During the CR

	Purged		Survived		Total	
Promotion Grade	No.	%	No.	%	No.	%
1	129	23	274	67	403	100
2–9	114	45	139	55	253	100
Total	243	37	413	63	656	100

Source. Compiled by the author from biographical information.

Note. This sample includes all those who had held the positions of leadership at the central and provincial levels of party, government, and military organizations.

Table 24.   Gang of Four Followers in the Eighth Central Committee

	Purged		Survived		Total	
Membership	No.	%	No.	%	No.	%
Politburo	1	11	8	89	9	100
Full Members	1	5	18	94	19	100
Alternate Members	4	12	30	88	34	100
Total	6	10	56	90	62	100

Source. Compiled by the author from biographical information.

of the gang's cadre line. By contrast, table 24 clearly demonstrates the unpopularity of the radicals among the senior cadres; only six members of the Eighth CC were identified as members of the Gang of Four group.

Table 25 shows that the Gang of Four's ties with any particular field army were very weak because none of the radical members had any particular field army ties—except for Xie Fuzhi. Most of the military leaders who were purged with the Gang of Four were junior officers whom the gang patronized, promoting them to leadership positions on the basis of their "revolutionary spirit." This point is made particularly clear in table 26, which shows that 38 percent of the fourth to eight generation of military leaders were purged with the Gang of Four, although they constituted only 14 percent of all military leaders who reached a high enough level to be included in the sample.

Table 25.   Impact of the Gang of Four's Fall by Field Army Affiliation

	Purged		Survived		Total	
Field Army Affiliation	No.	%	No.	%	No.	%
1st, 2d, 3d, 5th, and 6th	74	23	252	77	326	77
4th	27	28	70	72	97	23
Total	101	24	322	76	423	100

Sources. Field army information is based on data provided by W. Whitson, *The Chinese Command: A History of Communist Military Politics, 1927–71* (New York: Praeger, 1973), which includes the civilian leaders. Information on purges was compiled by the author from biographical information.

Table 26.   Impact of the Gang of Four's Fall by Military Generation

	Purged		Survived		Total	
Generation	No.	%	No.	%	No.	%
1st	4	6	58	94	62	100
2d	17	27	47	73	64	100
3d	29	39	46	61	75	100
4th–8th	13	38	21	62	34	100

Sources. Field army information is based on data provided by W. Whitson, *The Chinese Command: A History of Communist Military Politics, 1927–71* (New York: Praeger, 1973), which includes the civilian leaders. Information on purges was compiled by the author from biographical information.

In short, the Jiang Qing group did well at the Tenth Party Congress, partly thanks to Mao's support and Zhou Enlai's willingness to compromise for the sake of unity. They succeeded in making Wang Hongwen vice chairman of the party, probably as a representative of the masses and the younger members. However, a closer look reveals the weakness of the Gang of Four's position. First, they could not command a majority in the Politburo: the radicals controlled five votes (including Kang Sheng), whereas the beneficiaries, headed by Hua, had eight, the survivors had seven, and the rehabilitated had only one. In terms of simple arithmetic, the Gang of Four obviously needed the cooperation of Hua Guofeng's group to carry any majority vote in the Politburo.

More seriously, the ideologues' power base at the provincial level was very tenuous. None of the mass representatives of the Tenth CC carried the title of first or second secretary to a provincial party committee. Moreover, twenty-eight of the mass leaders at the Tenth CC did not even sit on the standing committee of their provincial party committees. Many of them were instead chairmen or vice chairmen of provincial trade unions, which controlled the newly organized militia. Despite the two years of mass mobilization that disrupted the entire ruling structure, the CR radicals failed to find entry into party committees once they were reactivated. For this reason, radicals wanted to "open the party committees and make revolution," while "relying on the leftists, not on the party."[9] In their inability to control the party committees, they frequently set up new party committees—"officials of movement," "underground fighting groups," or "artillery brigades"—to replace the existing leadership of the party organ.[10] Unlike the Lin Biao group, which tried to seize power from within, the Gang of Four used mass mobilization to seize party committees' power from the outside. They publicly declared, "We must support the revolt of large numbers of the masses in factories against the factory leadership and certain leaders of the third ministry. [We] should seize the power that must be seized."[11]

CADRE POLICY

IDEOLOGY

The Gang of Four developed an elaborate ideology, which, while eloquently articulating some of Mao's basic concerns (e.g., the bureaucratization of the party), also directly served its political interests. A good example is Zhang Chunqiao's 1975 article, "On Exercising All-Around Dictatorship over the Bourgeoisie," which addressed a central theoretical question: how can one explain the existence of class struggle in a society where the means of production are collectivized and in a Communist Party that theoretically represents the working class? Zhang's answer politicized the concept of "class," making explicit points already discernible in Mao's writing. According to Zhang, not just the distribution of the means

9. *Hong Qi*, no. 5, 1979.
10. *Daily Report*, 29 June 1977, E2.
11. *Dagong Bao* (Hong Kong), 27 January 1977.

of ownership but also economic reward and political power can serve as the basis for forming a class. By arguing that the inequality stemming from differential wages as well as from differential power distribution can also be a basis for class formation, Zhang logically justified in Marxist terms the existence of class struggle in socialist China and in the Communist Party. Any party leader advocating a policy that aggravated the differential distribution of power and wealth could be considered a capitalist roader. In this regard Zhang's view resembles Djilas's devastating criticism of the Communist elite as the "new class," a view articulated by such ultraleftist organizations as the May 16 group and Sheng Wu Lien.[12]

To the concept of a politicized "class," Zhang Chunqiao added the notion of a "new stage": each new stage of revolution even within a socialist country requires new leadership and new enemies. Whatever the validity of his argument may be, its political significance is clear: he provided a theoretical justification for attacking veteran party leaders and social groups that had benefited from the Chinese revolution—in the name of continuing the revolution.

In order to reach the point where some party leaders could be made into targets of a new revolution, Zhang proposed a distinction between ideology and organization, which the Leninists believed to be inseparable.

> There are undeniably some comrades among us who have joined the Communist Party organizationally but not ideologically. In their world outlook they have not yet overstepped the bounds of small production and of the bourgeoisie. They approve of the dictatorship of the proletariat at a certain stage and within a certain sphere and are pleased with some victories of the proletariat because they gain from them. Once they have secured their spoils, they feel it is time to settle down and feather their cozy nests. As for exercising an all-around dictatorship over the bourgeoisie and as for going farther than the first step on the 10,000-*mile* [*li*] march, sorry, let others do the job: here is my stop—I must get off the bus.[13]

12. Zhang Chunqiao, *On Exercising All-Around Dictatorship over the Bourgeoisie* (Beijing: Foreign Languages Press, 1975); Milovan Djilas, *The New Class: An Analysis of the Communist System* (New York; Praeger, 1957).
13. Zhang, *On Exercising All-Around Dictatorship*, 18.

Once ideology and organization were separated, it became possible to argue that those who had led the CCP to the establishment of the People's Republic of China were plausible objects of this new revolution. Zhang allegedly declared, "The current targets of revolution are the democrats who used to eat bran in the old society, were wounded in the war resisting Japanese aggression, shouldered guns in the war of liberation, and crossed the river [the Yalu River] in the movement to resist U.S. aggression and aid Korea."[14] Those who joined the revolution after 1949 were not exempt. "The poor and middle peasants reaped the benefits of land reform. They do not demand a socialist revolution and do not have a revolutionary character any more, whereas the landlords and rich peasants who have been suppressed for almost twenty years are opposed to the capitalist roaders, and their rebel spirit is the strongest."[15] To the CR radicals, the party's leaders had too much interest in retaining the status quo. "When the war ended, they made profits and rose to the positions of influence; because of their vested interest in the new status quo, they can no longer advance."[16] In the realms of ideology and policy, "they practice revisionism; in dealing with foreign countries, they practice capitulationism."[17] These people should be the major targets of the revolution, not "traitors or secret agents, and not types engaged in corruption and degeneration."[18]

Zhang Chunqiao analyzed workers in a similar fashion. He divided them into four age groups. The first group consisted of "veteran workers" who had started work before the liberation, usually as foremen or technical workers receiving high wages. Their political consciousness, according to Zhang, was not sufficient because "their position has changed and their livelihood has changed." The second group worked initially as "apprentices" both before and after liberation. Although "they had good feelings toward the party and are now the 'backbone' of the factories, they

14. *Hong Qi*, no. 8, 1977, 60.
15. *Renmin Ribao*, 4 June 1977.
16. "Document of the Central Committee (*Zhongfa*), No. 37, 1977," *Issues and Studies*, 14(7) (July 1978):81–102.
17. *Renmin Ribao*, 4 June 1977.
18. Ibid.

are influenced too much by 'Soviet revisionism,' and therefore they are too much concerned with material incentives."[19]

The third group of workers entered factories around 1958 as

> contract and temporary workers who suffered under the revisionist line. They rose to the revolution in 1966. Their understanding of line struggle is high, and they have excellent morale and good feelings toward the CR. The problem is that their understanding of the party is rather poor, and their attitude to labor is not quite satisfactory. They don't know what they can and cannot do. Some people have selfish motives in fomenting rebellion. They always go backward after seizing power. In a certain sense they are the new lumpen-proletariat. Zeng Guofan used this kind of person to suppress the Taiping Rebellion, and Chiang Kai-shek used to rely on them. These are part of the foundation of our party.

The fourth group covers "new worker," those who became workers after participating in the CR as Red Guards. "They are enthusiastic, simple, eager to learn, with quick reflexes and very few experiences of struggle; they are childish and need tempering."[20]

RECRUITMENT

While attacking the veteran cadres, the Jiang Qing group endeavored to promote "the new rising forces" (i.e., the CR rebels) who had proven to be "highly sensitive to the two-line struggle, strong in their class view, willing to defend Mao's revolutionary line, and courageous in their opposition to revisionism."[21]

More specific criteria advocated by the CR radicals included "daring to struggle against the bourgeois reactionary line," "being willing to go against the tide," having a "clear standpoint," being "familiar with leadership" or "being supported by the masses," and "cherishing deep feelings." All these phrases refer to rebels willing to take on the existing leadership. A Yunnan rebel summarized Zhang Chunqiao's elaborate argument in the following way: "The major contradiction at the socialist stage is between capitalist roaders and rebels. 'Rebels' are advanced elements and the basic

19. *Beijing Informer*, 16 June 1977.
20. Ibid.
21. *Hong Qi*, no. 2, 1977, 7–12.

force for the revolution; they are 'the essence of humankind.' . . .
[One] should take rebel ideology as the guiding principle, and
democracy should be given to only rebel factions."[22]

Since the term "rebel" was too controversial and too vague to be
an official criterion and since most of the rebels were young, the
Gang of Four advocated the promotion of "young" people, insisting that "the group around twenty-five years old should have one-
third of all leadership positions; those forty-five or older are not fit
for such positions."[23] Simple-minded rebels made slogans such as
"the older, the more revisionist; the older, the more inclined to the
right; the older, the more counterrevolutionary."[24] At the radicals'
insistence, the meaning of the three-in-one formula was altered so
that it referred to the young, the middle-aged, and the old, not to
the PLA, the revolutionary cadres, and the mass representatives.
Having one-third of every leadership group consist of young people became an official policy.

The radicals were accused of having used "two surprise
attacks." One recruited unqualified persons to the party, and the
second promoted them to high office by skipping several grades—
the practice that Deng Xiaoping satirically labeled "helicopter
promotion." For example, a Shanghai rebel who had graduated
only from middle school was sent to a northeastern province
where he became deputy director of the provincial propaganda department. Another Shanghai rusticated youth was ordered into the
party by the Gang of Four and was eventually elected to the Tenth
CC.[25] Some people who were not yet party members became party
secretaries.[26]

The radicals apparently used several illegal methods to promote
their followers to positions of power. First, when the radicals controlled a unit's organizational department, they used it arbitrarily
to replace lower-level leaders with their own followers. Second,
they relied on their factional communications channels to scout for

22. The simpler-minded radicals used "high grade and high wage" to determine
who were the powerholders. *Renmin Ribao*, 4 June 1977.

23. Among the leaders of the revolutionary committee of Linxian county in
Henan about 40 percent were "young people." *Renmin Ribao*, 5 June 1974. Also for
promotion of "young people," see *Renmin Ribao*, 19 October 1973; 25 October 1973.

24. *Renmin Ribao*, 6 October 1977.

25. Ibid., 26 April 1978.

26. *Hong Qi*, no. 2, 1977, 7–12.

potential candidates. For the central government leadership, "they prepared a list of a dozen persons to be appointed to the posts of minister, vice minister, and department and bureau director under the ministries. Some Shanghai cadres were so appointed." Third, "when the former rebels were not allowed to join the party, they complained to Jiang Qing, who specifically instructed the party committees involved to admit them on the grounds that they had 'rebelled and have revolutionary enthusiasm. . . . If you are not willing to introduce them, I will do so. . . . You should rely on that kind of people.'"[27]

Another widely used illegal method of effecting promotions was the study session. More than 65 percent of the graduates of the Anhui provincial study session attended by workers and peasants were appointed to leadership posts above the county (*xian*) level. Similarly, the Anhui provincial party school was a key instrument for recruiting factional members and placing them in leadership positions. When a particular rebel was rejected by party branches at his workplace, the Gang of Four's followers often used their authority to take the case to another unit or to set up a new, temporary branch, which admitted the person. This way of joining the party was known as "entering the party after flying over the sea."[28] Thus, the Gang of Four "violated party rules and regulations, randomly destroyed the party's cadre management principle, and disregarded materials in the dossier, frequently changing the conclusions that had been reached organizationally and adding forged materials." Through such means, a railway party committee recruited 106 persons in eight days. The CR rebels openly declared, "the party charter is only for consultation"; "rebelling is the only qualification for joining the party, and the best application to it."[29]

Since most radicals, at least at the beginning of the CR, came from undesirable class backgrounds, the people they recruited were vulnerable to charges of being "political riffraff, reactionary, literary radicals, the scum of society, and dregs and monsters carrying a counterrevolutionary black banner." Since many of them had been politically backward before the CR and were imprisoned

27. *Renmin Ribao*, 14 March 1977.
28. Ibid.
29. Ibid.

by the military because of their challenge to the PLA in 1967, they were also condemned: "Those who stank in the past now smell fragrant because they are out of prison."[30] Since they were activists in the CR, they were also accused: "Their 'heroes going against the trend' were criminals—corrupt thieves, speculators, degenerates, and violators of state laws. Their comrades included those who participated in beatings, lootings, and destruction—the hooligans who disrupted the social order." What the Gang of Four called those with the strongest revolutionary enthusiasm were those who sent secret intelligence to them, filed complaints with them, and wrote pledges of loyalty to them. What they called "new rising forces were those who did not go to work every day, who were unproductive, undisciplined parasites."[31]

We have no way of knowing how many former rebels were made cadres and then promoted. However, the scattered official figures available seem to indicate that personnel changes in some basic units were sweeping. For instance, the seventh machine-building ministry changed almost 80 percent of the leadership in Beijing factories under its jurisdiction in 1976.[32] At Wuhan Steel Mill, seven of eleven secretaries were ousted, and the remaining four ran away, reducing production by 45 percent in 1976.[33] New cadres accounted for 39 percent of the Wushun municipality revolutionary committee.[34] Radicals in one district allegedly appointed ninety-five new members to county-level standing committees. In Zhengding county 126 young cadres were promoted to deputy secretaries of twenty-five communes.[35] In one county of Qinghai province, almost 380 cadres were subjected to struggle meetings, more than half of all commune-level cadres were purged, and 201 out of all 321 production-brigade-level cadres were replaced by rebels. Shunde county, in Guangdong province, reported that 25 percent of brigade party committee members were young cadres.[36] More than two-thirds of all cadres in twenty-three brigades of a Jiangxu province commune were young people (the

30. Ibid., 4 June 1977.
31. Ibid., 17 May 1977; ibid., 4 June 1977.
32. "Document of the Central Committee (*Zhongfa*), No. 37, 1977," 139.
33. Ibid.
34. *Renmin Ribao*, 9 June 1973.
35. Ibid., 10 July 1974.
36. Ibid., 21 March 1973.

average age was thirty; they had proven themselves during the CR). Another source reported that new cadres amounted to 61 percent of 176 production team cadres.[37]

During this period, many workers were promoted to cadre positions. At one factory in Henan county, twenty-five workers out of a total of 1,000 were promoted to cadre status.[38] The Beijing Transformer Factory reported that 30 percent of its cadres and 70 percent of its leading cadres were newly promoted.[39] The Fuzhou railway bureau reported that one-third of its leadership was composed of newly promoted young people.[40] In brief, many basic-level units carried out official policy by staffing approximately one-third of their revolutionary committees with the young, but not all of the young people were adherents of the Gang of Four. Who was promoted depended largely on the old cadres' choices.

In 1969, when party rebuilding started, official policy was "to eliminate wastrels, renegades, spies, counterrevolutionaries, and stubborn capitalist roaders." A commune in Henan province reported that it had expelled 3.4 percent of its party members; 1.8 percent more were subjected to various disciplinary measures. Although we do not know what percentage of new recruits entered the party with the aid of the Gang of Four's network, the increase in party membership during the period was very rapid. One Chinese source claimed that "a substantial portion of the 6 million recruited in 1969–73 is suspected to have been composed of rebels."[41] In the ten years of the CR, the total number of party members doubled to 32 million. This means that on the average, 1.6 million new members were recruited each year.

A majority of the new recruits were under the age of thirty.[42] At the Gang of Four's insistence, women were actively recruited. Beijing reports that "the overwhelming majority of new recruits were under thirty-five years of age, and women constituted 25 percent of the total."[43] As a result, the proportion of women among new

37. Ibid., 14 September 1973.
38. Ibid., 19 February 1974.
39. Ibid., 22 October 1973.
40. Ibid., 27 August 1973.
41. *Dangshi Yanjiu*, no. 2, 1985, 57–64.
42. *Beijing Review*, 1 July 1973; *New China News Analysis* (Shanghai), 30 June 1973; *New China News Agency* (Shenyang), 2 July 1976.
43. "Comrade Wang Hongwen's Report at the Central Study Class," *Issues and Studies* 11(2) (February 1975):94–105.

party members increased from about 10 percent in 1966 to 27 percent in 1973.[44] Another group that the regime actively recruited during this period were ethnic minorities.[45] Youths who had been sent to rural areas provided a large pool of young people from which new members were recruited.[46] Most new recruits had good class backgrounds. For instance, 45,000 of the 60,000 new members admitted by the Beijing party committee between 1966 and 1973 were "workers, former poor and lower-middle peasants or children of such families"; just under 3,000 were "revolutionary intellectuals working in the fields of culture, health, science and education."[47]

REHABILITATION

The fall of Lin Biao, one of the main architects of the CR, put decision-makers in Beijing in a quandary: they had to rehabilitate Lin's victims, but they could not reverse official decisions made during the CR, decisions that usually originated from Lin Biao and were endorsed by Mao. It proved extremely difficult to distinguish Lin's decisions from those made by others during the CR. Many purged cadres demanded rehabilitation on the grounds that they had been his innocent victims.[48] According to the Gang of Four's charge, Deng Xiaoping, with tears in his eyes, declared in one of his self-criticism sessions that he was "the arch enemy of Lin Biao" and consequently Lin had wanted to "put him in a death situation."[49] Moreover, the Zhou Enlai and the Jiang Qing groups disagreed about who should be rehabilitated.

According to a Taiwanese source, Wang Dongxing, vice chairman of the CCP at this time, sent a list of ten types of cadres to be liberated and ten types not to be liberated to a specially convened work conference. He ended his instructions by remarking, "This is party 'policy.' If there are any errors, I request comrades to point

44. Joan Mahoney, "Problems in China's Party Rebuilding," *Current Scene* 15(3) (March 1977); Robert Martin, *Party Recruitment in China: Pattern and Prospect* (New York: Columbia University, Occasional Papers of the East Asian Institute); *Renmin Ribao*, 27 June 1973.
45. *Renmin Ribao*, 6 October 1973.
46. NCNA (Beijing), January 21, 1975; *Beijing Review*, no. 22, May 31, 1974, 20.
47. Ibid.
48. *Daily Report*, 7 November 1978.
49. *Xuexi Yu Pipan*, no. 5, 1976, 18–20.

them out. I personally assume responsibility."[50] This blunt statment implies how sensitive the issue was.

Official policy granted rehabilitation to all cadres who had been purged because of their opposition to Lin Biao's line and to his rise within the party. All those who had been purged for errors in "supporting the left" during the CR were exonerated. As noted, many cadres had supported conservative mass organizations during the CR, and for that reason they were rejected by the radicals. Now all cadres who were active in the CR for either conservative or radical organizations became eligible for rehabilitation. Another category included those who were dismissed from office for their lack of "enough revolutionary drive," one of the criteria advanced by Lin Biao for evaluating cadres.[51]

Official policy also declared that "renegades, enemy spies, and alien classes" should not be rehabilitated even if they had opposed Lin Biao in the past. It also made a distinction between decisions made with Mao's approval and decisions made by Lin Biao alone. Decisions not to be reversed included those made "in accordance with conclusions drawn by our organization after Lin Biao and Chen Boda had reported to the central authority for intructions and obtained approval." Another point reads:

> During the great proletarian CR the central authority, acting on Mao's instruction or his approval, made certain resolutions pursuant to the comments submitted by the central departments and provinces. Except for some individual cases which were not properly handled because Lin and Chen had furnished wrong information or issued false orders and directives in Mao's name, which are now being further studied, the overwhelming majority of cases were correctly handled. This should be affirmed and no reversal of the verdict on any of these cases should be allowed.[52]

Regardless of how these ambiguous and somewhat contradictory policy lines were actually applied to an individual cadre, many high-ranking cadres purged during the CR reappeared, not in a group, but one by one, after Lin Biao's fall. On 1 August 1972, the founding day of the army, such old cadres as Chen Yun, Wang

50. *Daily Report*, 24 March 1975, E5.
51. Ibid.
52. Ibid.

Zhen, and Zheng Daiyuan appeared. At every important occasion thereafter, Zhou Enlai brought some more old cadres forward. For instance, Chen Zaidao, the commander responsible for the open challenge to the central authorities by the Wuhan workers in 1967, made his first public reappearance on Army Day, in 1972.

The most surprising comeback was that of Deng Xiaoping, who made his first public appearance in March 1973 escorted by Wang Hairong, Mao's niece. According to a Chinese source, Deng wrote a letter to Mao exposing Lin Biao in August 1972. Commenting on the letter, Mao said,

> He does not have historical problems. In the Soviet period he was rectified by leftist opportunist Wang Ming. . . . During the liberation war, he helped Liu Bocheng to make a great contribution [to the final victory]. Besides, after [the CCP] entered cities, he did some good things. For example, he led our delegation to Moscow, and he did not surrender to the pressure of the Soviet Union.[53]

Later Deng Xiaoping acknowledged his indebtedness to Mao. "Before my second fall in the CR, Chairman Mao wanted to protect me, but did not succeed. The main reason was that Lin Biao and the Gang of Four hated me very much. Their hatred toward me was not as deep as toward Liu Shaoqi, but they did not want to be soft on me. They sent me to Jiangxi to labor. In 1973, Chairman Mao transferred me to Beijing."[54] Deng acceded to the position of vice premier on 3 March 1973.

In addition, Mao personally rehabilitated many other high-level leaders. In November 1971, he exonerated those involved in the "February Adverse Current."[55] On 6 January 1971 he personally attended the funeral of Chen Yi.[56] Sensing that Mao was burying old grudges against some veteran cadres, Zhou Enlai had *Renmin Ribao* publish an editorial entitled "Punish for Future Use, and Cure the

53. Mao acknowledged that Deng had made many contributions to the revolutionary struggle as early as 1972: "I have said it before and I want to say it once again." *Zhongguo Gongchandang Lishi Jianyi* (Jilin: Jilin Chubanshe, 1982), 2:2.

54. *Qixi Niandai*, no. 10, 1980, 54.

55. The term "February Adverse Current" refers to top leaders' opposition to Mao's radical policy of allowing Red Guards to seize power. Rongzhen, *Nie Rongzhen Huiyilu* (Beijing: Jiefangjun Chubanshe, 1984), 3:859.

56. Zhou Enlai instinctively realized the significance of Mao's attendance and told Chen Yi's relatives to transmit the news to other cadres. Zhang Tianyi, *Zhonggong Dangshi* (Shenyang: Liaoning Renmin Chubanshe, 1985), 345.

Disease to Save the Patient," which boldly declared that "the old cadres steeled in long revolutionary struggles are the party's greatest treasure."[57] After that, Zhou continued to liberate some cadres and intellectuals, while improving jail conditions and banning physical torture of disgraced cadres.

While the disgraced cadres reappeared one by one, the media renewed the discussion of cadre liberation at the lower level—a theme that had been absent from public news since 1969. This time public discussion went further than before in several ways. First, discussion now focused on the cadres' rich experience of political and functional work, a characteristic of cadres that would have been denounced as counterrevolutionary. By contrast, revolutionary zeal was no longer mentioned as a necessary trait of cadres. Numerous articles describe how experienced older cadres corrected wrong decisions (presumably initiated by inexperienced young cadres), thus avoiding waste.[58] The phrase "bourgeois reactionary line" was dropped from official use, and the nature of the mistakes made during the CR—the central theme in 1969 discussions—was ignored. When the issue came up, it was only used to argue that cadres who had made mistakes once would be less likely to do so in the future.[59]

Second, primary emphasis was now given to the "bold and proper use of cadres' work ability" rather than to simple liberation. Clearly the new campaign was aimed at reinstating most of the old cadres in their jobs or in equivalent positions. One provincial newspaper declared,

> Those who have already been liberated and who are capable of normal work must quickly be given suitable work. For those who have not been properly assigned, the necessary adjustments must be made after proper investigation and study. Those who are incapacitated must be taken care of according to party policy and actual circumstances. As for those who have not been liberated, their cases must be handled without delay so that appropriate decisions can be reached.[60]

57. *Renmin Ribao*, 24 April 1972.
58. *Survey of China Mainland Press* (supplement), no. 302, 8 June 1972, 9–11.
59. *Daily Report*, 25 April 1972, B2.
60. Ibid., 3 March 1972, D3; 22 March 1972, E2.

Numerous sources reported that more than 90 percent of all old cadres had regained their positions of leadership in either party committees or revolutionary committees.[61] For the sake of properly utilizing the cadres' manpower, transferring across functional lines was officially prohibited.[62]

Third, the work of liberation was carried out by party committees, which by this time had regained their dominant position over other mass organizations including revolutionary committees. Lower-level party committees played a leading role; they set up special sections to handle cadre liberation, organized numerous work conferences to educate cadres on the "party's cadre policy," and on many occasions sent out special investigation teams to check that old cadres were appropriately employed at the basic level.[63] They arranged for work for those who were unemployed and made readjustments for those who had not been assigned to jobs suitable to their experience.[64] The official slogan at the time was, "if there is even one cadre who has not been treated in accordance with party policy, the party's cadre policy cannot be considered to have been thoroughly implemented."[65] Some party committees even organized mobile reportage teams to publicize the good results of carrying out party cadre policy. Discussions of cadre liberation seldom mentioned mass participation.

It seems that virtually all cadres at and below the county level and in basic production units had been liberated by the end of 1972. Some county committees had arranged suitable work for the "few cadres who made serious mistakes and who are not fit to carry out leadership work any more in accordance with party policy." Even the treatment of those with historical problems was changed. Special investigation teams were organized to clear up their problems as speedily as possible, and those whose cases were not yet settled were given temporary assignments.[66] Only "old and physically feeble cadres" failed to regain employment, and they were treated as retired cadres, not as purged ones. Due respect was given

61. Ibid., 30 May 1972, C1.
62. Ibid., 18 January 1973, D9.
63. Ibid., 28 April 1972, C2; 3 May 1972; 30 November 1972.
64. Ibid., 3 April 1972.
65. Ibid., 4 April 1972, C5.
66. Ibid., February 1972, D4.

to retired cadres. To make use of their experience, old cadres were allowed to take part in party committee meetings dealing with their specialties.[67]

POLITICAL STRATEGY

Having come to power by purging party leaders during the mass mobilization stage and feeling insecure about their political future, the Gang of Four used whatever formal authority they had to strengthen their power position by recruiting and promoting former rebels to leadership positions within the bureaucracy. After consolidating their own domination in one organization or area, they tried to "colonize" others, often using the news media to interfere with the operation of other organizations—in violation of the jurisdiction and command structure of each field. At the same time they vigorously defended their own exclusive jurisdiction over the propaganda machine.[68] When it was difficult to penetrate an institution, as was the case with the military, the Gang of Four tried to set up a parallel organization. Their establishment of a militia not under the control of regional PLA commanders, although obviously justified by Mao's military concept of a people's war, was basically intended to develop the Gang's own coercive forces. Having been able to control such mass organizations as labor unions, it endeavored to enhance the political influence of these organizations vis-à-vis the party committee.

In their efforts to consolidate their power positions and to obtain new positions of dominance, the Gang of Four used three different but related methods. First, they tried to promote their followers to key leadership positions of the bureacracy through renewed mass mobilization. When their method failed, they openly demanded their share of power in the government organization. In the last days they combined pressure from the top and bottom by enlisting Mao's support and mobilizing the social forces that benefited from the CR in order to get rid of Deng Xiaoping, a representative of the rehabilitated cadres.

67. Ibid., 12 January 1973, C28–29, C31, F1.
68. For instance, in September 1975, the State Council tried to publish a new journal called *Ideological Frontline*, and Mao approved the project. But because of opposition from the Gang of Four, no issues were published. *Hong Qi*, no. 8, 1978.

Renewed Mass Mobilization:
The Campaign Against Confucius
and Lin Biao

Wholesale rehabilitation renewed conflicts between former rebels
and their former victims, now rehabilitated. Since the number of
leadership positions had probably diminished because of administrative streamlining, old and new cadres now had to compete for
the limited number of positions, the former basing their claims on
their work ability and experience, the latter stressing their revolutionary zeal. Once reinstated, the old cadres reiterated their previous view that "there is no good man among the rebels." Moreover, they were inclined toward revenge. "To get even with those
who struggled against us should be considered a lenient measure.
What is wrong with venting one's spleen?"[69] To them, the CR was
"a dark night of ravaging floods and savage beasts," which had
been absolutely unnecessary. What China needed after the Lin
Biao incident was to "sweep the temple, invite the real gods, return old marshals to their posts, and send little soldiers back to
their barracks." To the radicals, the old cadres were simply waiting
for an appropriate moment to repudiate them.[70]

Related to the question of rehabilitating old cadres and the promotion of CR rebels was how Lin Biao's policy should be defined and
who should be criticized as his followers.[71] Zhou Enlai and the old
cadres regarded Lin as an ultraleftist who exploited the CR for
political gain. Zhou's characterization made the Gang of Four and
their followers vulnerable to the same charge, while justifying the
rehabilitation of the victims of ultraleftist errors.[72] The Gang of
Four viewed Lin as an advocate of ultrarightism. Thus, criticism of
Lin's mistakes could justify the campaign against the military,
which had ruthlessly suppressed the Red Guards in 1968, and

---

69. "Comrade Wang Hongwen's Report at the Central Study Class," 94–105.
70. Wang Hongwen insisted that when the old cadres "were liberated and put
back in power, they sought every opportunity to liquidate the masses." Ibid.
71. The conflict between the old cadres and the CR rebels was particularly serious in Zhejiang, where Tan Qilong, a veteran cadre who was made first party
secretary, replaced the CR radicals with rehabilitated cadres under the excuse of
"carrying out leadership readjustment." *Renmin Ribao*, 20 March 1978. For Wang
Hongwen's support of the Zhejiang rebels, see *Beijing Review*, 4 February 1977, 10.
72. "Comrade Wang Hongwen's Report at the Central Study Class," 101.

other kinds of rightist tendencies, while not raising the issue of the excesses of the mass movement or the purges it engendered.[73]

Endorsing the Gang of Four's view, Mao approved the campaign to criticize Confucius and Lin Biao, which enabled the Gang to kill two birds with one stone. By equating Lin with Confucius, who endeavored to "revive states that were extinguished, restore families whose lines of succession were broken, call back to office those who had retired into obscurity,"[74] the Gang of Four was able to challenge Zhou Enlai, who was guilty of similar offenses. At the same time they put pressure on the military leaders who had suppressed the revolutionary movement in the preceding state, but who now looked upon Zhou as a counterbalance against the radicals.

Once the campaign started, the Gang of Four pushed for mass mobilization, focusing its attack on "going through the back door," which ultimately aimed at the nepotism of veteran party and military leaders. They had particularly harsh words for local military leaders now resisting the renewed mass campaign.[75] "What is the use of building an army, if it departs from the class line, the line struggle, and the ideological revolution?"[76] Wang Hongwen was more blunt:

> Soldiers are told to obey orders unconditionally and absolutely. We must know that they are required to obey your orders conditionally, not unconditionally. They should obey whatever conforms to Marxism-Leninism and Mao Zedong's thought and rebel against whatever does not. All members of the Communist Party execute the instructions of the higher level on the basis of self-consciousness. We should judge the correctness of an order in terms of its line. We only execute correctly following the correct line. They will not be implemented if they are not correct.[77]

Apparently surprised at the radicals' reckless effort, Mao banned any discussion of "entering through the back door," but he en-

---

73. For changes in labeling Lin's mistakes from ultrarightist to ultraleftist in the official criticism, see William A. Joseph, *The Critique of Ultra-Leftism in China, 1958–1981* (Stanford: Stanford University Press, 1984).

74. *Hong Qi*, no. 2, 1978, 2.

75. "Comrade Wang Hongwen's Report at the Central Study Class," 102.

76. *Zhonggong Dangshi Jiaoxue Cankao Ziliao: Wenhua Dageming Shiqi* (Beijing: Zhonggua Renmin Zhengzhi Xueyuan, 1983), vol. 4, no. 4, 278.

77. "Comrade Wang Hongwen's Report at the Central Study Class," 99.

couraged the campaign. As the movement spread across the nation, there was no shortage of grievances. All the CR conflicts, plus the new grievances that the mass movement had raised and that had then been ruthlessly suppressed by the military, surfaced again. In addition, many decisions made by the military came under attack.

To make matters more complicated, the radicals' intention to use the campaign to "cultivate new cadres" further intensified the conflict between the rehabilitated and the newly appointed cadres.[78] After Wang Hongwen, the newly elected vice chairman of the CCP, called for training a million revolutionary successors and promoting them to posts of leadership at all levels, public discussion of cadre rehabilitation stopped. The news media began instead one-sidedly to stress the revolutionary qualities of young cadres and their contributions during the CR, while criticizing the old cadres' attitude toward the newly promoted young ones.[79] "If we fail to see this fundamental fact [that the young cadres possess revolutionary zeal] and talk of nothing but qualifications, we will not be able to select a large number of outstanding young people for leading posts."[80] Meanwhile, the radical leaders told their followers what was at stake. "Some powerholders are trying to reverse the achievements of the CR by reinstating all pre-CR leadership, irrespective of their political history or their attitude toward the CR. They made a serious error in personnel management."[81]

By this time, public discussion had made it clear that cultivating new cadres meant placing them in powerful positions, not making them decorative aides to old cadres.[82] Resistance to the promotion of young cadres ("young men are unstable, [and] men without mustaches are immature") came under increasingly severe criticism.[83] For instance, Guangming Ribao bluntly declared: "Maturity in handling things should be judged on the basis of one's class, one's consciousness of line struggle, and one's general orientation, not on the basis of one's age."[84] A thesis reminiscent

78. Daily Report, 19 July 1972, B1–4.
79. Ibid., 10 October 1973, D1; 16 November 1973, B1.
80. Ibid., 22 March 1973.
81. Guangming Ribao, 15 July 1977.
82. Daily Report, 15 October 1973, F1.
83. Ibid., 2 May 1973.
84. Ibid.

of CR rhetoric, that of the two-line struggle, was reintroduced to bolster the radicals' position. One provincial radio broadcast declared, "which line [old] cadres should follow and what stand they should take concerning the training and promotion of new cadres are questions at the heart of the struggle between the two classes, the two lines, and the two ideologies."[85] Criticisms became increasingly harsh. "Many leading cadres failed to uphold the basic line, [and] they imposed a bourgeois dictatorship on the masses."[86]

Some party committees, largely dominated by the military and old cadres, took evasive measures by simply creating new positions for the younger cadres, thus swelling their ranks in spite of the official policy of administrative simplification.[87] Others put up a strong fight.

Consequently, workers' unrest, strikes, and armed clashes between rival youth groups spread. Beijing was swamped by petitioners. The leading cadres resorted to a familiar method: some of them simply left their posts as they did at the initial stages of the CR. The economy suffered.

Determined to dislodge the veteran cadres at any cost, the Gang of Four declared that "to disrupt the production of one factory is to put a knot around the neck of the faction in authority," and that "the loss belongs to the state, the responsibility belongs to the faction in authority, and the power belongs to us."[88] Mao was not, however, in a position to sacrifice the economy for the sake of evolution.[89] Nor could he agree to the Gang of Four's view that "rebelling against the leadership is going against the tide." He reportedly declared that "the CR has been going on for eight years. It is time to settle down. The entire party and the army should unite."[90] With Mao's change of mind, the campaign came to an end.

85. Ibid., 11 June 1973, C1.
86. Ibid., 21 June 1976, T4. *Guangming Ribao*, 16 March 1977; 9 May 1977.
87. *Daily Report*, 14 March 1974, D5.
88. *Hong Qi*, no. 12, 1976, 48; *Dagong Bao* (Hong Kong), 27 January 1977, 13 December 1976.
89. "Document of the Central Committee (*Zhongfa*), No. 21, 1974."
90. *Zhonggong Dangshi Jiaoxue*, no. 4, 1983, 369.

"FORMING A CABINET":
PRESSURE FROM ABOVE

Having failed to strengthen their power base at the basic level through mass mobilization, the radicals tried to gain a large share of government positions by using the politics of confrontation at the top level. When preparation for the forthcoming National People's Congress was undertaken, Jiang Qing first pressured Zhou Enlai to hand over some government power—probably including the post of chief of staff of the PLA—to the radicals, but she failed to obtain his concession. The radicals then took their case to Mao in the city of Changsha. Wang Hongwen complained to Mao that Deng, unhappy with the CR, did not support the "newborn things" and that Zhou Enlai, although seriously ill, was always busy meeting with the other old leaders. Mao allegedly advised Wang to see Zhou Enlai often and not to form a faction with Jiang Qing. "You should be careful about her."[91]

While rejecting the radicals' bid to "form a cabinet," Mao suggested making Deng Xiaoping first vice premier, vice chairman of the party, and chief of staff of the PLA. Authorized by Mao, Zhou made the final decisions about personnel after "repeated consultation with other veteran cadres" in the hospital. He gave the ministry of culture and the ministry of physical education to the radicals, but refused the Gang of Four's demands for the ministry of education.[92] The radicals came away with very few government positions. Although Zhang Chunqiao became vice premier, second to Deng Xiaoping, only four of the twelve vice premiers could be regarded as close associates of the Jiang Qing group.

According to a Taiwanese source, the true picture was different. Mao initially supported the Gang of Four's effort to form a cabinet and obtained Zhou's agreement in selecting cabinet members. But the old cadres in the Politburo strongly opposed the idea. Zhu De allegedly said, "If Premier Zhou does not assume premiership, the position should be rotated and should come to me."[93] After work-

91. Zuigao Renmin Fayuan Yanjiusuo, ed., *Zhonghua Renmin Gongheguo Zuigao Renmin Fayuan Tebie Fating Shenpan Lin Biao, Jiang Qing Fangeming Jituan Zhufan Jishi* (Beijing: Falu Chubanshe, 1982), 92.
92. *Renmin Ribao*, 17 January 1986.
93. *Zhonggong Yanjiu* 11(23) (March 1977).

ing out their differences in secret meetings, these Politburo members collectively confronted Zhou Enlai with the threat of splitting the party center. Mao had to retreat.

Once placed in charge of the government, Deng Xiaoping proceeded to straighten out the mess created by the CR. He prepared three documents dealing respectively with industry, science and technology, and the academy of sciences. These documents not only repudiated many policies adopted after the CR but also explicitly blamed the Gang of Four for the economic dislocation. For instance, declaring that in many units power was held by "unreformed petty intellectuals, brave elements, and bad people," one version of the "Twenty Articles on Accelerating Economic Development" demanded rectification of the basic leadership. Undoubtedly the group to be rectified were the young cadres who had been promoted by the Jiang Qing group.[94] To the radicals, those whom Deng wanted to rectify were "the revolutionary intellectuals" and "those people carrying out Chairman Mao's revolutionary line."[95]

Given the explicitness of the language used in the party program, whatever hopes Mao and Zhou Enlai might have entertained of uniting the rehabilitated cadres and the Jiang Qing group were completely shattered. Now the liberated cadres and the Jiang Qing group found themselves in a situation where one group had to go. In Chinese parlance, the three documents that the liberated cadres prepared were either fragrant flowers or poisonous ones; they could not be both.

THE CAMPAIGN AGAINST "RIGHTIST REVERSAL TRENDS"

The frontal clash between the Gang of Four and the old cadres took place over the issue of educational policy. When Liu Bing, president of Qinghua University, complained that the CR educational policy lowered the quality of higher education, the Gang of Four mobilized the worker-peasant-soldier (*gong nong bing*) students, who obviously owed their place in higher educational institutions to the CR's radical admissions policy. The educational debate even-

94. *Issues and Studies*, 13(7) (July 1977):90–114.
95. *Hong Qi*, no. 10, 1977, 77.

tually developed into a public campaign against "the rightist wind to reverse the correct verdicts," which, among other things, specifically condemned Deng's three documents as the concrete manifestation of the reversal effort. By December 1975, the campaign was widely reported in the official media, and by 1976, although his name was not yet explicitly mentioned, Deng Xiaoping came under attack as the leader of the "rightist reversal wind."[96]

The death of Zhou Enlai on 8 January 1976 changed the distribution of power in the Politburo. Since Dong Biwu and Kang Sheng were dead, Zhu De and Liu Bocheng mortally ill, and Deng Xiaoping in deep political trouble, the veteran cadres' political power in the Politburo substantially diminished, whereas the beneficiaries of the CR (headed by Hua Guofeng and including Wang Dongxing, Wu De, and Chen Yonggui) emerged as the crucial bloc in the conflict between the Gang of Four and the older leaders. Mao chose Hua Guofeng over Zhang Chunqiao as acting premier, and his appointment was announced on 3 February.[97]

Understandably, the Gang of Four was unhappy with Hua's appointment, for to them he was not only behind Zhang Chunqiao in seniority, but he was also incompetent, too close to the old veteran cadres, including the late Zhou Enlai, and deeply involved in preparing one of Deng's three documents, "On the Question of Science and Technological Work."[98] The Gang of Four used the mass media they controlled to surreptitiously criticize Hua.

Although Deng's disgrace helped Hua become acting premier, Hua displayed an ambivalent attitude toward the anti-Deng campaign. He must have known about the Gang's frequent engagement in factional activities and their unpopularity in contrast to Deng's high prestige among old cadres. Mao advised him "not to be anxious and to take your time." Hua criticized Deng in such a manner so as not to upset normal bureaucratic operations: he advised provincial leaders to continue the anti-Deng campaign but cautioned that Deng's problem was "contradiction among the peo-

96. Harry Harding, "China After Mao," *Problems of Communism*, 26 (March–April 1977):1–18.

97. It is reported that Mao asked Ye Jianying to persuade Deng to submit another self-criticism and that Deng refused. Zhou Xun, ed., *Deng Xiaoping* (Hong Kong: Guangjiaojing Pub., 1979).

98. *Hong Qi*, no. 10, 1977, 72–80.

ple" and that neither Deng nor those who had supported his 1975 modernization plans should be purged.[99]

The Gang of Four, in contrast, took a strong anti-Deng line, frequently making unauthorized appearances and speeches to reinforce their position. Consequently, the campaign against Deng intensified in 1976, and posters publicly denouncing him appeared in Beijing by the end of February. In early March the Gang of Four used the name of Chi Heng to publish an article entitled "From Democrats to Capitalist Roaders," in *Hong Qi* magazine, defining the main target of the campaign as "a handful of capitalist roaders within the party who have refused to repent." The article explained, following Zhang Chunqiao's theory, how a large portion of party veterans had become "bourgeois democrats and capitalist roaders." *Renmin Ribao* also published Mao's undated statement, "You are making a socialist revolution, and yet you do not know where the bourgeoisie is. It is right in the Communist Party—those in power taking the capitalist road. The capitalist roaders are still on the capitalist road." Around this time Mao reportedly called Deng a bourgeois democrat who had never been a Marxist. "He said he would never reverse the verdicts," Mao observed. "His words cannot be trusted."[100]

The Tiananmen Square incident of April 1976 was the turning point in the Gang of Four's attack. When the spontaneous commemoration of Zhou by a large crowd gathered in the square turned into an open protest against the radicals, the Gang of Four persuaded Mao that Deng was responsible. The center made two decisions on 7 April 1976: to remove Deng from all his offices and to appoint Hua as premier and first vice chairman of the CC. Although stripped of all official power, Deng continued to enjoy the veteran cadres' support.[101]

After the Tiananmen incident, the Gang of Four expanded the scope of the original campaign with a view to replacing old cadres with young rebels. Deng Xiaoping was publicly condemned for having opposed the promotion of young cadres "because their

99. Lowell Dittmer, *China's Continuous Revolution: The Post-Liberation Epoch, 1949–1981* (Berkeley and Los Angeles: University of California Press, 1987).

100. *Xuexi Yu Pipan*, October 1976.

101. For Deng's activities during this crucial period, see *South China Morning Post* (Hong Kong), 25 February 1977, 1.

positions are high, their experience is nil, and they do not know what to do."[102] Deng's view that promotion should be made one grade at a time was criticized as a sinister attempt to "suppress the new cadres who emerged during the CR." Declaring that "a nation-wide network of the capitalist roaders had been formed," the radicals advocated the policy of dragging out "Deng's representatives in provinces" "layer by layer," and carrying out "large-scale surgery on the leadership."[103] The rehabilitated cadres were obviously their major target. Jiang Qing demanded a public apology for the rebel groups from the old cadres. Zhang Chunqiao joined her: "Every official has made mistakes and every mistake will be opposed. As a result, there is now no single county party committee member who can be trusted, no single prefectural party committee member who can be trusted; among the provincial party committee members and those of the center, no one can be trusted except Chairman Mao."[104]

During the height of the campaign against rightism, the radicals put pressure on provincial party leaders to promote former rebels to leading positions. Jiang Qing went to Tianjin and demanded that the municipal party committee adopt a quota system for young cadres. According to one source, Jie Xuemao, the first secretary, refused to carry out her wish. Yet Tianjin municipal radio reported that the municipal party committee actually made it a policy not to approve wholesale personnel appointments at lower levels unless they included the required percentage of young cadres.[105] The Inner Mongolia party committee decided that every provincial, municipal, district, and county party committee would promote two or three young people to positions of leadership by the end of 1976. Some organs without enough qualified young people dispatched teams to look for them.[106]

In some areas, many young cadres holding positions as deputies were promoted to positions as heads, while erstwhile heads became mere deputies and were forced to retire.[107] In units where

102. *Hong Qi*, no. 6, 1976, 30.
103. Ibid., no. 2, 1977, 11; *Renmin Ribao*, 19 February 1975.
104. *China News Analysis*, November 1976, 581.
105. *Renmin Ribao*, 19 February 1975.
106. *Shijian* (Inner Mongolia), January 1978, 28–37.
107. *Daily Report*, 15 October 1973, F1.

young people were not promoted, rebels holding positions of deputy chiefs openly challenged their superiors, accusing them of obstructing the movement.[108] Followers of the Gang of Four in Baoding district illegally fired three district party secretaries and appointed ninety-five young cadres above the county level.[109]

When Mao died in September 1976, three situational groups shared the power of the Politburo: the radicals with four seats, the beneficiaries of the CR with seven seats, and the survivors of the CR with five seats. Despite the obvious fact that Hua Guofeng's beneficiaries constituted almost a majority, standing between the radicals and the survivors, the Gang of Four failed to form a coalition with them. Instead, they pushed them to collaborate with the old cadres.

108. "Document of the Central Committee (*Zhongfa*), No. 37, 1977 (Part III)," *Issues and Studies*, 14(9) (September 1978): 78–100.

109. "Document of the Central Committee (*Zhongfa*), No. 37, 1977, " 142.

7

The Beneficiaries and the Victims

After arresting the Gang of Four, the coalition of CR beneficiaries and surviving veteran revolutionaries faced several urgent issues. The first was how to justify its extraordinary move against Madame Mao's radical group while at the same time establishing the authority of Hua Guofeng. Then it had to deal with how to characterize and criticize the Gang of Four's political errors and determine how best to investigate and purge it, without undermining the legitimacy of Mao and the CR. Finally, the coalition had to address the subject of the ongoing anti-Deng campaign, as well as the question of who should be rehabilitated as innocent victims of the Gang of Four. All these interrelated questions were given more concrete form in the issue of Deng Xiaoping's rehabilitation, the issue which had profound policy and power implications for Hua.[1]

From the very beginning, Hua Guofeng had few options in resolving these issues. As a beneficiary of the CR, Hua could not negate the CR or Mao. But he had to repudiate the Gang of Four and demonstrate that his ideology and policies differed from theirs. Since Hua benefited from Deng's purge, initiated by the Gang of Four, bringing him back posed a serious threat to his own political survival. In contrast, the survivors, his coalition partners, could move in either direction on all issues except Mao's legitimacy.

Given this dilemma, the possibility was slim that Hua and his followers could initiate a new ideology and policy by critically reevaluating the political decisions made during the CR. The only available strategy was to uphold Mao's legitimacy while narrowly limiting the scope of criticism, purge, and rehabilitation. In fact, Hua

---

1. For Hua's position on these issues, see "Speech on the Second National Conference on Learning from Tachai in Agriculture," *Beijing Review*, 1 January 1977, 31–43; 31 March 1978; 16 June 1978.

upheld Mao's view that a bourgeoisie existed in the Communist Party, but he condemned the Gang of Four's attack on the old cadres on the grounds that, although some veterans had indeed been in error, the radicals' struggle against them was excessive. Hua declared an end to the CR, but he defended its achievements by specifically endorsing Mao's continuous revolution, while promising to revolutionize the government's superstructure.[2]

THE ISSUE OF REHABILITATION

Hua approached the question of rehabilitation with caution. According to a Taiwanese source, a document from the central organizational department, dated October 1976, laid down guidelines for purging and rehabilitation. It specified that only "those who were rejected, attacked, removed from positions, or expelled from the party by the Gang of Four for their resistance to the [Gang of Four's] counterrevolutionary line" would be reinstated. At the same time, it refused to review cases involving "renegades, spies, Trotskyites, counterrevolutionaries, KMT elements, or degenerates," as well as all cases for which the organization had already arrived at a conclusion.[3] Anyone demanding the reversal of such cases would be punished. In brief, rehabilitation was intended for only a small number of CR victims, and even the right to reopen cases was denied to the majority of victims.[4]

The beneficiaries justified their policy in terms of defending "whatever Mao had said and decided." Otherwise, they argued, many past decisions would be challenged.

> If we always look backward, we will always be settling accounts with bygone things. We will have to negate the "Cultural Revolution," and then everything from the "Gang of Four" to the Socialist Education Movement in cities and villages, from the Lin Biao affair to the Lushan conference. If the Lushan conference is negated, we will have to negate the socialist transformation of industry and commerce, the antirightist struggle, the Great Leap Forward, and then the people's commune policy. If it were not for this tendency to look backward, there could be no such statement as, "There were mistakes

2. Ibid., 1 January 1977.
3. *Zhongyang Ribao* (Taiwan), 4 November 1976.
4. *Renmin Ribao*, 28 August 1979.

in the general line, and it is difficult to make another Great Leap Forward, the people's communes are no longer acceptable, and the 'three Red Banners are at half-staff.'" Whether this view is advanced by the masses of the people or by people in the cultural realm, I can definitely say that it is a serious mistake to make this assertion. If we settle accounts with bygone things one after another and invalidate one stage after another, how can socialism exist?[5]

The pressure to bring Deng back was, however, too strong for Hua.[6] Deng enjoyed not only the sympathy and understanding of the surviving as well as the rehabilitated cadres, but also the genuine support of the Chinese masses. Provincial leaders and Politburo members allegedly petitioned the CCP for Deng's rehabilitation. Particularly outspoken were Chen Yun and Wang Zhen, who pleaded eloquently at the February central work conference for Deng Xiaoping's rehabilitation "for the sake of the Chinese revolution and China's needs"; Chen and Wang also asked that the decision on the Tiananmen incident be revoked. Despite Hua's refusal to publish the speeches, they spread widely by word of mouth.[7] Ordinary people also expressed their wishes by placing small bottles (xiaoping) along major streets.[8] Then Deng Xiaoping wrote two letters to Hua, one promising support and the other expressing willingness to work at the front line.[9]

According to numerous sources, Deng's offer prompted a hot debate at meetings on the highest level. Most of the veteran leaders favored Deng's rehabilitation; Xu Shiyu was especially vehement. Like Hua, most beneficiaries of the CR initially objected to reinstating Deng on the grounds that Mao had approved his dismissal. Under pressure, Wang Dongxing finally agreed to bring Deng back, on the condition that Mao's decisions would not be reversed.[10] Another Chinese source reported that Hua Guofeng

5. "Zhang Pinghua's Speech to Cadres in the Cultural Field," Issues and Studies, 14(12) (December 1978), 91–119.

6. For the anti-Deng campaign after the fall of the Gang of Four, see William A. Joseph, The Critique of Ultra-Leftism in China, 1958–1981 (Stanford: Stanford University Press, 1984).

7. Dangshi Tongxun, no. 2, 20 January 1983.

8. Harry Harding, China's Second Revolution (Washington, D.C.: Brookings Institution, 1987), 59.

9. Ming Bao (Hong Kong), 9 July 1979.

10. Feijing Yuebao 1(23) (19 January 1979):65–68.

Table 27. Representation on the Eleventh Central Committee, 1977

	PLA		Cadres		Masses		Unknown		Total	
	No.	%	No.	%	No.	%	No.	%	No.	%
Full Member	54	27	112	56	25	12	10	5	201	100
Alternate Member	33	25	27	20	38	29	34	26	132	100
Total	87	26	139	42	97	29	10	3	333	100

Source. Compiled by the author from biographical information.

did not open his mouth during the debate, and when Chen Yong-gui finally voted for Deng's rehabilitation, those in favor had only one vote more than those opposed.

Deng made his first public appearance at the third plenary session held on 16 July 1977. This meeting reconfirmed Hua's appointment to the chairmanship and reinstated Deng to all of his previous positions: member of the standing committee of the Politburo, vice chairman of the CCP, vice chairman of the Military Affairs Commission, and chief of staff of the PLA. At the meeting they also decided to expel the Gang of Four from the party.

Table 27 shows how in the newly elected Eleventh Central Committee, cadre representation increased from 33 percent in the Tenth CC to 42 percent, whereas mass representation decreased from 37 percent to a mere 29 percent, and the PLA's from 30 percent to 26 percent, thereby breaking the almost perfect balance among the three groups achieved in the Tenth CC. Among the sixty-three cadres who were added to the Eleventh CC, nineteen of them were former Eighth CC members, and the rest included many rehabilitated cadres, for example, Cai Suli (Henan party committee), Yu Mingtao (central-south party bureau), Wan Li (Beijing party committee), and Kang Xien (former petroleum minister). Moreover, even such controversial cadres as Xiao Wangdong, former deputy minister of culture, and Wu Lengxi, former editor in chief of *Renmin Ribao*, who had been especially attacked during the CR, now joined the Central Committee. Altogether more than a third of the sixty-three new members were rehabilitated cadres. The majority of the remainder at the time of the CR were middle-level cadres who had survived the mass purges and obtained positions on revolutionary committees. To a striking extent, then, the Eleventh CC was composed of rehabilitated cadres.

Table 28. Survival Rate of Persons Newly Entering the Eleventh
Central Committee, as of 1982

	Twelfth CC		Advisory Commission		Failed		Total	
	No.	%	No.	%	No.	%	No.	%
Newly appointed	44	42	12	11	49	47	105	100
Leftover	64	39	26	16	73	45	163	100
Total	108	40	38	14	122	46	268	100

Source. Compiled by the author from biographical information.

Table 29. Survival Rates of Rehabilitated and Nonrehabilitated Members
of the Eleventh Central Committee, as of 1982

	Rehabilitated		Nonrehabilitated	
Status	No.	%	No.	%
Success[a]	100	97	111	46
Failure	3	3	129	54
Total	103	100	240	100

Source. Compiled by the author from biographical information.

a. Those who remained in the CC as well as those demoted or transferred to the Advisory Commission.

Table 28 examines the survival rate of those who entered the Eleventh CC for the first time and those who were left over from the Tenth CC. The difference between the two groups in terms of the percentage of those who failed to make it into the Twelfth CC is amazingly small (47 percent versus 45 percent). This may mean that Hua's preference was weakly reflected in the process of selecting cadres (except in the case of mass representatives), or else his preference did not differ very much from that of the rehabilitated. From table 28 we can also infer that Hua did not remove all of the Gang of Four's sympathizers from the committee. If so, Hua might have intentionally protected them as a potential coalition partner. Or perhaps he simply did not have enough time and organizational capability thoroughly to investigate their followers.

Table 29 shows that rehabilitation almost guaranteed survival; 97 percent (100) of the rehabilitated cadres of the Eleventh CC entered either the Twelfth CC or the Advisory Commission, whereas only 3 percent (three) of them can still be considered as purged.

Despite the large influx of CR victims, the Eleventh Party Congress as a whole still upheld Mao's thought as a guiding principle, and reconfirmed class struggle and continuous revolution as the main tasks of the socialist revolution in the revised party constitution. In his report about political work, Hua again elaborated his view of continuous revolution, condemning the "powerholders taking the capitalist road," "bourgeois legal rights," and "the sole emphasis on productive forces," while only promising to uphold "proletarian dictatorship in the various fields." It was later reported that Deng objected to a certain part of Hua's speech when he was shown a draft, and many other veteran cadres criticized Hua's wholesale praise for the achievements of the CR. Hua, however, rejected all the criticism.[11]

The Eleventh Party Congress apparently represented a moment of compromise between those who had suffered and those who had prospered during the CR. Even though many old cadres recovered their positions, Deng Xiaoping's group agreed to the rhetoric of the other side, which insisted on Mao's ideological legitimacy. But what the other side may not have foreseen was that these rehabilitated cadres, with their extensive experiences, were very skillful in political maneuvering. Moreover, increasing criticism of the Gang of Four and anyone involved with them inevitably called for a reevaluation of the soundness of Mao's thought.

PURGING THE GANG
OF FOUR FOLLOWERS

Those whom the CR had favored and those who had been victims differed on the nature of the Gang of Four's mistakes and the number of their followers. Viewing the radicals as a conspiratorial group, the beneficiaries tried to limit the scope of the purges and rehabilitation and to uphold all of Mao's decisions, whereas the victims were determined to remove their luckier or more politically adroit confreres in order to reverse any of Mao's decisions that seemed wrong to them.

11. *Dangshi Tongxun*, no. 2, 20 January 1983.

During Hua's leadership public criticism of the Jiang Qing group—which was carried out under tight control of the party organization, lest embarrassing questions for the beneficiaries were raised—underwent three different stages as Hua had originally envisioned: the first focused on the exposure of the Gang's "plot to usurp power," the second dealt with their "past criminal records," and the last condemned the "ultrarightist essence of their counterrevolutionary revisionist line."[12]

The central leadership headed by Hua prepared official criticism materials, setting the tone for each stage of the campaign. Taking cues from official materials, various units published criticism of the radicals' concrete crimes in their units. Condemning the Gang of Four as "typical representatives of the bourgeois inside the party" who had "subverted the dictatorship of the proletariat in order to restore capitalism," the first batch of official materials focused largely on their characters and class backgrounds, which they had allegedly falsified to "sneak into positions of authority." The second batch stressed the radicals' efforts to usurp political power against Mao's will since the campaign to criticize Confucius and Lin Biao, while failing to touch upon the radicals' activities in the earlier stages of the CR.[13]

The official view—that the radicals were an "ultrarightist conspiratorial" group that had betrayed Mao's instructions in an attempt to seize power—turned the thrust of the campaign to those who "endeavored to restore capitalism," while failing to correct "leftist errors" in the official line.[14] Arguing that investigating the Gang of Four would create an atmosphere favorable to capitalist trends, the beneficiaries initiated the "double-blow movement" to investigate the Gang's followers and to check the "destructive activities of the class enemy," who undermined the collective economy at the basic level.[15]

As to the question of who should be regarded as the Gang of Four's followers, the beneficiaries insisted that "only a few [had] participated in the Gang's conspiracy." In particular, the central

12. *Zhonggong Yanjiu* 12(19) (15 September 1978):99–108.
13. "Document of the Central Committee (*Zhongfa*), No. 37, 1977," *Issues and Studies*, 14(7), July 1978, 81–102.
14. *Renmin Ribao*, 7 April 1977.
15. *Beijing Review*, 1 January 1977; 10 March 1978.

organizational department specified in October 1976 who should be purged. First, only close associates of the Gang of Four were vulnerable, whereas those who "involuntarily cooperated with the Gang" were to be forgiven. Second, close associates were safe if they recanted. Third, people who had merely done or said something wrong were not be included in any punitive measures. Hua Guofeng reiterated a similar line in all his public speeches, stressing that most of the cadres who had done or said something wrong deserved education, not punishment.[16] He divided even the "backbone elements" into those who recanted by exposing the crimes of the Gang of Four and the "stubborn elements."[17] Thus, even the radicals who had genuinely sympathized with the Gang could defend themselves by insisting that their relationship was merely organizational and that "my problem was that of carrying out orders, and [the mistakes] cannot be charged to my account."[18] As for who should replace the Gang's associates, Hua reiterated Mao's five requirements for a revolutionary successor and the three-in-one formula of young, middle-aged, and old cadres.[19]

Hua Guofeng was very slow in changing the provincial leadership, either because of his limited organizational capabilities or because of his desire to protect Gang of Four sympathizers. For instance, before Deng's formal comeback in July only seven provincial first party secretaries had been replaced, while many leaders suspected of having had close connections with the Gang were allowed to stay in power.[20] Guo Yufeng, who later turned out be a Gang of Four associate, stayed on as director of the organizational department, formally heading the campaign against the radicals until the end of 1977.

Furthermore, rank-and-file cadres were not eager aggressively to pursus the Gang's followers. At that time they were confused and totally demoralized by the constant changes in official policy. Many of them had learned that making too many enemies was not

16. *Renmin Ribao*, 13 April 1977.
17. *Zhonggong Yanjiu* 12(19) (15 September 1978):99–108.
18. *Renmin Ribao*, 16 April 1978; 12 June 1978.
19. Ibid., 20 March 1978.
20. Some of the provincial leaders Hua appointed turned out to have close relationships with the Gang of Four. For instance, Liu Guangtao was made first secretary of Heilongjiang province in January 1977, only to be removed by the end of the year.

good for their careers. Moreover, the leadership of each unit was still so splintered that carrying out an objective and fair investigation was impossible.[21]

Despite the proliferating articles denouncing the Gang of Four, the campaign to "expose and criticize" did not have much impact in 1977. According to his opponents, Hua's campaign "investigated only small matters, but not big matters; investigated only the lower level, not the upper level; investigated only outside matters, not inside matters; investigated only matters tangentially related, not immediate matters."[22] As a result, only a few very well-known radicals were investigated and dismissed.[23]

As more victims of the CR were reinstated to politically influential positions, the campaign against the radicals was bound to expose Hua's tactics of "tacit discontinuity and overt defense" of the CR and Mao Zedong's thought.[24] When the public campaign expanded to touch upon the Gang's specific policies—particularly "production relations" versus productive forces and the role of profit and material incentives in economic management—it became obvious that the Gang's policy was ultraleft rather than ultraright.[25] This compelled the beneficiaries to change the official label to "ultraleft in appearance, but ultraright in essence."[26]

Nonetheless, the victims of the CR were not willing to accept the validity of this new label. For instance, Renmin Ribao questioned whether the Gang of Four carried out a "proletarian dictatorship or fascist dictatorship?"[27] Once the Gang's dictatorship was labeled fascist and its ties with Lin Biao openly discussed, it was a matter of time before the radicals were condemned as ultraleftists.[28] The change in terminology brought about an upsurge of articles de-

21. Renmin Ribao, 22 June 1978.
22. Ibid., 13 January 1978.
23. For instance, the Gang of Four's followers in Shanghai—Ma Tianxiu and Xu Jingxian—and at Beijing University—Wang Lianglong, Li Jiaokun, and Guo Conglin—were arrested and investigated.
24. Lowell Dittmer, China's Continuous Revolution: The Post-Liberation Epoch, 1949–1981 (Berkeley and Los Angeles: University of California Press, 1987).
25. For instance, see "The Gang of Four's Attack on 'Sole Productive Forces' Is an Attack on Historical Dialectics," Renmin Ribao, 11 January 1978.
26. Ibid., 6 February 1977; October 14, 1977; 7 March 1978.
27. Ibid., 11 June 1977.
28. Joseph, Critique of Ultra-Leftism, 184, 168; Renmin Ribao, 23 March 1978; 3 April 1978.

manding the correction of ultraleftism and, by implication, the Maoist line on beneficiaries. A *Renmin Ribao* article argued that if the Gang of Four's mistakes were not correctly identified as ultraleftist, there would be no way to correct them. As evidence, the article explained how Wang Ming's error in calling Li Lisan's policy ultraright justified the ultraleftist mistakes that Wang continued to make. Other articles made it plainer that without a thorough criticism of the Gang of Four's ultraleftism, the old cadres could not be rehabilitated.[29]

Public criticism eventually expanded to raise the question of those who had benefited from the CR by managing to muddle through the mass movements ("remaining faction"), by adjusting themselves to whatever was the prevailing trend ("wind faction"), and by shaking up the political structure ("earthquake faction").[30] The translations of these picturesque Chinese terms point to the questionable relationship of the beneficiaries with the Gang of Four at the early stage of the CR.

From the beginning, Deng Xiaoping advocated the removal of broader categories of radicals. In his speech to the municipal party secretaries on 27 December 1977, he established three criteria for determining who should be purged.[31] First, all those who collected materials against Zhou Enlai and Zhu De during the CR, "irrespective of intentions, positions, abilities, and political performance," should be investigated and removed from office. This applied also to the masses, who had acted without ulterior political motives. Second, all those who had developed close relationships with Lin Biao and the Gang of Four, had acted on their instructions, and had cultivated them before and during the CR were to be dismissed from positions of leadership regardless of seniority and whether or not their actions caused any bad effects. Those who did not incur the people's resentment should not be punished, but instead of staying in leadership positions, such cadres should be forced "to earn their bread through laboring." Third, all cadres who had persecuted old cadres and collected "black materials"

29. *Renmin Ribao*, 3 March 1979.
30. Ibid., 10 January 1978.
31. *Feijing Yuebao*, 21(7), January 1989, 25–30.

should be dismissed even if they had done so in the name of Mao Zedong's thought.[32]

Scrutiny of the Gang of Four's followers stepped up when Hu Yaobang assumed responsibility for the central organizational department in December 1977. He acted decisively, changing the leadership of organizational departments at lower levels and appointing newly rehabilitated cadres to leadership positions at the provincial level. Local newspapers began to criticize several provincial leaders for their close ties with the Gang of Four and for their efforts to keep the lid on the campaign against the Gang.[33] The newly reinstated cadres had many political reasons thoroughly to investigate the radicals who had attacked them. They adjusted the leading personnel on the lower levels and dispatched work teams to supervise the criticism. For instance, the new provincial party secretary of Shanxi province organized ten investigation teams with 100 cadres to check the results of the previous campaign to criticize the Gang of Four.[34] The Jilin provincial party committee first rehabilitated five old cadres who "had suffered the most from the Gang of Four's persecution" and then placed them in charge of organizing the work teams to be sent out to the various units. Even lower-level units organized and sent out work teams to subordinate units.[35] By mid-1978, the issue of how to handle cadres promoted in "the two surprise attacks" had surfaced.[36] Although official policy was to decide cases individually, it seems very likely that almost all of those who had benefited from "helicopter promotion" eventually lost their positions.

32. Ibid.
33. Xie Xuekong of Tianjin was removed from his office in June, Wu De in October, Zeng Shaosha of Liaoning and Yu Daiching of Inner Mongolia in October, Li Ruishan of Shaanxi in December, Liu Zhenxun of Henan in October, and Saifudin of Xinjiang in February. The reorganization of the State Council removed such persons as Wang Yang, Li Chitai, and Sha Feng, who were not yet criticized by name. Through the summer of 1978 a few more provincial leaders, whose connection with the Gang of Four was not very obvious, came under attack too and eventually were removed from office. Provincial party leaders who came under public attack during this period in early 1978 include Saifudin of Xinjiang, Li Ruishan of Shanxi, Lung Daichung of Inner Mongolia, and Zhang Boshan of Hunan. See *Beijing Ribao*, 7 December 1979; *Renmin Ribao*, 30 March 1978.
34. *Renmin Ribao*, 11 June 1979.
35. Ibid., 13 February 1978.
36. Ibid., 28 June 1978; 4 September 1979.

After the third plenum in December 1978, Hua Guofeng declared that the check on the Gang's followers had been completed. But rehabilitated cadres continued to stress the importance of thorough checking, and they launched what they called reexamination (*fu cha*) of the radicals.[37] More stringent criteria to verify previous campaign investigations were set up by various units. For instance, the Anshan Steel Mill Corporation organized sixteen inspection teams that used thirty criteria to see whether a unit had carried out its campaign properly.[38] *Renmin Ribao* recommended that six conditions be met before ending the campaign against the Gang of Four.[39] The rehabilitated cadres eventually put the Gang on public trial and adopted the "Resolution on Some Historical Questions," which officially acknowledged Mao's mistakes in the CR. The Gang's associates were further investigated as the "three types of people" during the party rectification campaign of 1983–85.

THE "TWO WHATEVERS" AND "PRACTICE"

The fundamental differences between the beneficiaries and victims of the CR were brought into sharp focus by the seemingly innocuous question, what constitutes the criteria for determining truth? The beneficiaries took the position that "whatever Chairman Mao said and decided" should be upheld, whereas the rehabilitated emphasized "practice" (*shijian*) as the "sole criteria for empirical truth."

The beneficiaries coined the phrase "the two whatevers" (*liang ge fanxi*) to use as "the basic weapon" for rejecting demands to reinstate Deng Xiaoping and to reverse the decision about the Tiananmen Square incident.[40] By contrast, pragmatic Deng Xiao-

---

37. For instance, see ibid., 14 April 1978 for the several investigations carried out by the Nanjing municipal party committee.

38. *Renmin Ribao*, 13 May 1978; 20 January 1979.

39. They were (1) thorough investigation of those who joined the Gang of Four to seize power, (2) criticism of the Gang's revisionist line, (3) readjusting the makeup of the leadership group by expelling Gang followers, (4) complete rehabilitation of cadres who had suffered as a result of false charges or mistaken or wrong decisions, (5) restoration of the good traditions of the party, and (6) unity and stability. *Renmin Ribao*, 5 January 1979.

40. *Dangshi Tongxun*, no. 2, 30 January 1983; *Cankao Ziliao*, 24 March 1963.

ping (who reportedly declared even before the CR that regardless of whether it is black or white, any cat that catches a mouse is a good cat) had many reasons to stress "practice." Even before his official rehabilitation, he allegedly objected to "the two whatevers" view in his letter to the party center.[41] No sooner had he been rehabilitated than he publicly argued that the essence of Mao Zedong's thought was to "seek truth from facts."

The final showdown between "the two whatevers" and "practice" views took place at a work conference organized to discuss the upcoming third plenum of the Eleventh Party Congress (held from 10 November to 15 December 1978). According to official Chinese sources, Hua Guofeng initially objected to the idea of convening the conference, and when the meeting was held, he tried to limit discussion to economic questions. Once the meeting began, however, many veteran leaders demanded that "some historical problems" be discussed. For instance, Chen Yun argued (in his speech to the northeastern group) that prior to discussing economic issues, some remaining historical cases should be resolved. "Without resolving these questions, there is no way of unifying the entire people." In particular, he raised questions about six cases: (1) the case of sixty-one counterrevolutionary people including Bo Yibo, (2) the central organizational department's seventy-seven decisions made in 1937 and the wrong decision made in 1940 about the "two political systems," (3) the problems of Tao Zhu and Wang Hoshou, (4) the Peng Dehuai problem, (5) the Tiananmen Square incident, and (6) the question of Kang Sheng. Other veteran cadres followed Chen Yun by tabling a motion to discuss the "January Power Seizure," the "February Adverse Current," the "Campaign to Criticize Deng," and even the question of the CR and Mao himself. The heated debate between the two groups lasted thirty-six days—"the longest meeting after the fall of the Gang of Four"— finally adjourning after deciding that everybody would be allowed to speak freely on these issues at the third plenum.[42]

The third plenum of the Eleventh Party Congress, which some Chinese regarded as the "Second Zunyi Conference" (Mao emerged as the supreme leader of the CCP after the first Zunyi Conference

41. *Daily Report*, 24 August 1981; *Renwu*, no. 1, 1982, 10.
42. *Dangshi Tongxun*, no. 2, 20 January 1983.

in 1935), was a watershed in many regards. It adopted economic development as the regime's ultimate goal, while promising not to use mass movements as a means to implement policy. At the meeting, the balance of power tilted toward the rehabilitated cadre group, and Deng Xiaoping emerged as the number one leader. Old cadres like Huang Kecheng, Wang Renzhong, Hu Yaobang, and Yang Shangkun regained not only their honors but also important government and party positions. Hu was elected to the Politburo and appointed third secretary of the disciplinary committee. By contrast, although many beneficiaries retained their seats on the Politburo or the Central Committee, they lost other powerful and influential positions.

In retrospect, Hua Guofeng's chance of survival was always slight. The purge of the Gang of Four, whose ideology was further left than his own, exposed him to political pressure from the right. Once their common enemy was overthrown, Hua's group did not have the leverage to keep the old cadres behind him. Although the survivors initially made efforts to bring Hua's group and the rehabilitated cadres together, they chose the rehabilitated over the beneficiaries when they were forced to make a choice, because the beneficiaries lacked deep personal ties among themselves—ties that would have reinforced political ties. Many of them had not even had work relations before being promoted to leading positions at the center, and after Mao's death they did not have any patron to bind them together. Without such informal ties, no beneficiary was willing to risk his chance to survive individually by backing another.

Neither did the beneficiaries have enough time to develop a broad power base in the party-state bureaucracy, although some had support in the provinces from which they originally came (e.g., Hunan for Hua Guofeng, Henan for Qi Denggui). Their relation to military leaders at central and local levels was very tenuous. In addition, they could not resort to mass mobilization, the method that the radicals used for inner party struggles. Moreover, they did not even have any mass constituency to mobilize (because most Chinese people were thoroughly disenchanted with the CR). The beneficiaries, therefore, pursued the strategy of defense and compromise, yielding to the pressure of their adversaries on issue after issue. In turn, the rehabilitated effectively used a guerrilla strategy of nibbling at the beneficiaries' power base and then finally destroying them as a coherent political group. The rehabilitated cadres, with more political experience, a stronger power base in the bureaucracy, and higher prestige positions, were destined to win once Deng Xiaoping was reinstated for the second time.

PART III

BUREAUCRATIC SYSTEMS
AND REFORMS

8

The Politics of Rehabilitation

One of the most amazing aspects of the CR is that despite the ten years of chaos and ruthless purging, the majority of the pre-CR elite managed to regain their political power, leading China in a direction that Mao would have regarded as revisionist and capitalist. The return of veteran cadres was possible because there was one principle that even the Maoists did not violate during the CR, namely, not executing the losers in a power struggle. The return of the old guard is also a dramatic illustration of how entrenched the bureaucrats were in China even before the CR and of their remarkable resiliency, two characteristics which will probably not change much in the coming years.

REHABILITATED, "BORN-AGAIN" REFORMERS

As a political movement the CR was a total failure; it produced many losers and very few winners. It ruined Mao's position in Chinese history. Lin Biao died as a traitor in a plane crash. The members of the Gang of Four were purged, tried, and sentenced to death only to have their sentences commuted to life imprisonment, while its followers were hounded out of office as "three types of people." Some old revolutionaries were persecuted to death, but the majority of the pre-CR political elite returned to power, leading China in the new direction that Mao had hoped to prevent China from taking when he started the CR. The ordinary Chinese people suffered greatly, coming out of the crisis with profound disillusionment, cynicism, and distrust. Active young participants in the CR became the "wounded generation"—alienated and self-centered individuals without a trace of their earlier idealism.

The enormous human suffering that the CR caused left deep scars on the Chinese people. The chaotic mass movement magnified all human follies; confusion, cruelty, viciousness, deception, and distrust ran riot. Wondering how the CR could produce such chaos in a nation proud of its long civilization, every Chinese had a share of the nightmare and is now eager to tell his or her horror story.[1] Arthur Kleinman finds a close link between the socioeconomic and political experiences that the Chinese people underwent and their high rate of mental illness.[2] For example, he traces the chronic depression of a worker in his late twenties to the deep shame and guilt that he experienced when he admitted what he had not done during the CR because he feared the public security forces. Circumstances forced many people to go against their consciences, and it seems that every Chinese harbors some secret that cannot be confessed even to his closest friends. Even Zhou Enlai, who helped many old cadres by compromising his beliefs and supporting the CR, must have had some painful reflections.

The rehabilitated cadres are the veterans who joined the party almost half a century before the CR. In their youthful and idealistic days they risked their lives by fighting against oppressors—the Nationalists and the Japanese. In their middle age, they eagerly dedicated themselves to the construction of a new China, often acting knowingly or unknowingly as "oppressors, inquisitors, and denouncers in an attempt to achieve a revolutionary transformation of the society."[3] They ruthlessly wielded the enormous powers of the party-state to suppress what they considered "class enemies." At the beginning of the CR, Deng Xiaoping regarded the students in revolt as "rightists," who, like "snakes in a hole," should be lured out of their hiding places to expose their true nature.

The old leaders were ruthless revolutionaries, willing to sacrifice their personal interests, families, and friends for the sake of the revolution and executing all who were suspected of working for the enemy. Throughout their long careers, each one's life become intertwined with the others', resulting in strong hatreds as well as

1. For example, Ann Thurston, *Enemies of the People* (Cambridge, Mass.: Harvard University Press, 1988); Nien Cheng, *Life and Death in Shanghai* (New York: State Mutual Books, 1986); Gao Yuan, *Born Red* (Stanford: Stanford University Press, 1986).
2. Arthur Kleinman, "The Interconnections Among Culture, Depressive Experiences, and the Meanings of Pain" (unpublished paper).
3. Tang Tsou, *The Cultural Revolution and Post-Mao Reforms* (Chicago: University of Chicago Press, 1986), 148.

close friendships. On many occasions they helped one another because of friendship or a shared ideology, but they also engaged in many deadly inner-party struggles.

In their late middle or old age, these veterans found themselves the victims of still another revolution in the system they had helped build. During the CR, they were subjected to violent physical abuse, forced to parade in the streets with dunce caps on their heads, and do such humiliating menial labor as cleaning toilets. They were imprisoned, interrogated, and tortured by young Red Guards who had not yet been born at the time the cases they were investigating had taken place. Bo Yibo was accused of having collaborated with Yan Xishan, a powerful warlord who had had close ties with the KMT, from 1936 through 1939 and of having surrendered to the KMT in 1934.[4] In prison he learned that his wife had committed suicide and that his children had been jailed and then sent to one of Mao's thought study classes. Liu Shaoqi, chairman of the People's Republic of China, was condemned as a renegade because he had been arrested three times in his revolutionary career. His wife spent almost ten years in prison. Hu Yaobang, who, unlike the "white" area cadres, had a flawless career record, was luckier; he spent several years at home doing reading that he could not previously afford to do.[5] Peng Zhen, the tough Beijing mayor (criticism of him had officially started the CR), was sent to a rural area in Shanxi, the province where he had done his underground work twenty years before.[6] Luo Ruiqing, former deputy chief of staff, attempted suicide, an incident that left him crippled. Other unfortunates, such as Tao Zhu, Chen Yi, Liu Shaoqi, Peng Dehuai, and He Long, died in disgrace. The fate of provincial leaders was not much better.[7]

The veterans' children suffered too. Deng Xiaoping's son was permanently crippled. He Long's children served in prison and spent a long time in a Mao's thought study class. They were under great pressure to betray their parents.[8] Old revolutionaries could not see their children for long periods of time. "When I entered the

4. *Zhengming*, October 1980.
5. Yang Zhongmei, *Biography of Hu Yaobang* (Armonk, N.Y.: M. E. Sharp, 1990).
6. *Zhengming*, no. 15, January 1979, 27–30.
7. *Dong Xiang*, May 1980.
8. *Ming Bao*, 13 November 1978.

room, a boy called me Papa and I could not recognize him. I only recognized him when he told me that he was my son, who had been eight years old when I was taken from my house."[9]

Most victims of the CR experienced similar stages of maltreatment and rehabilitation. Initally they were subjected to Red Guard interrogation and forced to attend mass struggle meetings with big signboards around their necks or dunce caps on their heads. They suffered many different kinds of physical coercion. Later in the CR they were placed in cow huts or in prisons where they underwent sustained "interrogation" by special investigation teams, managed by ad hoc committees largely composed of followers of the Gang of Four or Lin Biao. They were tortured and persecuted until they made false charges against their former comrades.[10] Some were such dedicated revolutionaries that they did not yield to torture, but many others succumbed under pressure. The brave ones who did not compromise either died or spent long periods in jail. Some were condemned as renegades and spies. Others were simply pushed aside as "powerholders taking the capitalist road." Some were sent to rural areas with their families.[11] Others were released from jail and dispersed to various localities when Lin Biao issued his infamous Order no. 1. After Lin's fall, many were allowed gradually to return to Beijing and to recuperate in hospitals.

What went through their minds? No rehabilitated senior cadre has written about his feelings and thoughts. But a few intellectuals and writers have published moving recollections of the period. Ba Jin, for example, felt regret and remorse not only for having failed to foresee the disastrous leftward drift in official policy but also for having personally contributed to the trend. The feeling of emptiness and total disillusionment stayed with him for a long time, causing him frequently to contemplate suicide. After careful objective analysis of both himself and his persecutors, he decided to spend the rest of his life trying to prevent the reoccurrence of any future political persecution in China.[12]

Old cadres must have had thoughts similar to Ba Jin's. When the

9. *Nanfang Ribao*, 5 April 1979.
10. For instance, Kang Sheng and Xie Fuzhi reportedly tried to coerce An Zuwen to produce material against Liu Shaoqi.
11. For instance, see *Nanfang Ribao*, 18 April 1979.
12. Ba Jin, "Random Thoughts," published in a series by *Huaqiao Ribao* since 17 December 1978.

initiators of thought reform and self-criticism were subjected to
these same methods, they quickly learned how arbitrary and ineffective the methods could be. They felt that they were framed by
Lin Biao and the Gang of Four for political reasons. They saw close
comrades languishing in prison because of their refusal to bring
false charges against others. And they saw how those willing to
collaborate with the Gang of Four gained political power.

Although we do not know what went through the minds of the
highest political leaders, we do know how they lived. Deng Xiaoping was confined to a small house in a Jiangxi military compound.
He was allowed to work only part time in a nearby factory: "Every
day I went to the factory and worked along with workers for half
the day, taking them as my teachers, and learning much. The experience greatly helped me to change my weltanschauung."[13] In
Shanxi Peng Zhen often mingled with ordinary peasants, learning
about their living conditions in detail. What he saw was the back-
breaking poverty of peasants—the social group who had contributed most to the success of the Communist revolution and for
whose sake the revolution had been fought. On his return to Beijing in 1972, Deng Xiaoping traveled to places where he had fought
as a guerrilla. He saw that there had been little economic improvement since liberation. The peasants complained to him: "You
made revolution and left us. We did not receive much benefit from
the revolution. What have you done for us in thirty years?"[14]

Zhang Pinghua, director of the propaganda department, who
lost his job in 1978 as a member of "the two whatevers" group,
recalled:

> When I made a stop at a commune on my way to Kaifeng in Henan
> province last year, several comrades of the commune had this to say
> to me: "How can we be interested in watching model plays after
> dinner?" [Zhang asked] "Why? If it is not good to have plays to
> watch, is it any better not to have plays to watch?" [The peasant
> replied] "When the troupe came to our front door, dinner was rum-
> bling in our belly even before the gongs and drums were beaten. We
> eat gruel twice a day and dry rice only once. After eating these
> things, we urinate but do not defecate. How can there be anybody
> who is still interested in watching plays, Director Zhang?"[15]

13. Internal documents relayed by one interviewee in Hong Kong.
14. "Zhang Pinghua's Speech to Cadres in the Cultural Field," *Issues and Studies*,
14(12) (December 1978), 97–118.
15. Ibid.

The rehabilitated cadres learned the hard lesson that propaganda makes sense only after the basic needs of the people have been met.

When these old cadres returned to positions of power in China's ruling structure after Mao's death, they became "born-again" reformers. Having shared common experiences, they formed a coherent group under Deng Xiaoping. This rehabilitated cadre group won one political victory after another over Hua Guofeng's group. There were reasons for them to be such reformers. As victims of Mao's political campaign, they were less constrained by ideological and personal ties with Mao and thus felt less responsible for past decisions.

Most important, they discovered that the sense of crisis and failure in the CCP permeated the entire society to such an extent that the party had to regain legitimacy and support from the people. In a speech given in April 1979, Chen Yun noted that since political slogans, criticism, and struggle had failed to restore the CCP's popularity, the party would not be able to maintain its political power without reforms.

> There are three methods for resolving China's increasing problems. The first method is to bring out all the problems, including those in sacred areas, asking people whether or not they want the leadership of the CCP. I think that nobody wants to do this, and it is not worth talking about it. The middle option is to carry out reform [gailiang], although not thoroughly, which would entail a large-scale readjustment of economic relations. It means to keep the present political structures and principles, while only carrying out minor surgery. Many people agree that this method can work. The third method is to maintain the present situation.[16]

The experience of having been purged and rehabilitated is the functional equivalent of elite transformation. The old revolutionaries were indeed reeducated by the CR, but not in the way intended by its originator. They saw that the system they had built could lead to disaster and that certain underlying principles, as well as actual practices, which they had strongly advocated or supported at various times, could have devastating consequences for Chinese society. The purge offered them the rare opportunity to look at the

16. *Feijing Yuebao* 10(22) (19):92.

political system from the outside—as its victims. The forced exile taught them that China needed economic development. They were compelled to ask themselves a fundamental question: why did a movement for class and human liberation develop into one of the most oppressive systems in Chinese history—what the Chinese Communists call "feudal fascism"?[17] Ding Ling pointed to the excessive concentration of political power in the hands of cadres with small-group mentalities. Hu Zhiwei, former editor in chief of *Renmin Ribao*, concluded that "unless 'democracy' inside and outside the party is fully developed, the party's system of centralism will become a 'feudal, fascist, and dictatorial system with feudal authority.'"[18]

After their return to power, the rehabilitated cadres carried out sweeping reforms, reversing the past trend toward an all-powerful party-state that imposes increasingly tighter controls over society. The reforms affected the very foundation of state power. In the economic sphere, the rural responsibility system reduces the arbitrary power of the party-state and its agents while expanding the areas open to individual decisions and economic rationality.

In the political arena, the regime has endeavored to rationalize, legalize, and institutionalize the structures of the state and party. Rules governing intraparty struggles and policy-making processes now emphasize intraparty democracy and collective leadership. Parallel efforts to separate the party from the government and the economic arena from the political arena have been made. Political control over the population has been substantially diminished, allowing ordinary Chinese citizens a certain amount of legal protection. The participation of the masses has been institutionalized, allowing popular concerns to be articulated through officially sanctioned channels.

REHABILITATION POLICY OF THE
REHABILITATED CADRES

After Deng Xiaoping's second return, the reinstated senior leaders used their positions to bring back increasing numbers of their less

17. Tang Tsou, *Cultural Revolution*, 144–88.
18. Hu Yaobang, "How to Develop Criticism and Self-Criticism in Newspapers," *Xinwen Zhanxian*, no. 6, 1979, 5.

fortunate colleagues. Hu Yaobang, who had been purged and re-habilitated twice, played a particularly crucial role in rehabilitation politics. He had personal and political reasons to push for thor-ough reexaminations of all CR-related cases and was also strategi-cally positioned for the task. After being elected to the Eleventh Central Committee, he was appointed deputy director of the cen-tral organizational department and vice president of the central party school in August 1977. Two months later, he replaced Guo Yufeng as director of the organizational department.

Sharing with other rehabilitated cadres the view that without a thorough rehabilitation "the party will not be at ease, and the people will not be at ease," Hu Yaobang moved decisively, approaching the complicated matters of investigating all the CR cases and rendering fresh judgments from several different angles. After his appointment as director of the central organizational de-partment, he first reshuffled the cadres in the department.[19] Then he mobilized more than 100,000 cadres and masses in order to make a comprehensive survey of the task and to develop several hundred model cases (dianxing). He instructed local authorities to develop their own model cases and then use them as references for actual review. At many party meetings Hu made emotional pleas on behalf of innocent victims. "Some [innocent victims'] bodies have decayed, but the criminal labels of 'spy' are still attached, and their family members are still burdened."[20]

The victims of the CR tackled the "easy case" first when the resistance of the beneficiaries to reopening the CR-related cases was still strong. Instead of demanding rehabilitation (which pre-supposed the reversal of past decisions), they advanced the slogan of "implementing the party's cadre policy," stressing the need to correct administrative ills by bringing unresolved cases to an au-thoritative conclusion.[21] Since the most obvious reason for an in-ability to draw conclusions is lack of sufficient evidence concerning whether one committed mistakes or not, it was easy to reach con-clusions based on the changed situation without reversing pre-vious decisions.

19. *Renmin Ribao*, 1 October 1977.
20. Zhonggong Zhungyang Wenxian Yanjiushi, ed., *Guanyu Jianguo Yilai de Ruogan Lishi Wenti de Jueyi* (Beijing: Renmin Chubanshe, 1986), 474.
21. *Renmin Ribao*, 19 January 1978.

The central organization department under Hu's leadership adopted several crucial decisions dealing with different groups that suffered during the CR, but all of them in a broad sense touched on the question of rehabilitation. First, it proceeded to settle five types of cases: (1) those for which no organizational conclusion had been rendered, (2) those involving incorrect conclusions, (3) old cadres who had not yet been assigned to work, (4) persons who had died before investigation was completed, and (5) cases involving problems of relatives, friends, and colleagues of purged cadres.[22]

On 3 November 1978 the organizational department issued another crucial document entitled "Several Opinions of the Central Organization Department with Regard to Intellectuals," which virtually spelled out all the concrete measures to be taken in rehabilitation.[23] Reporting that about 40 percent of all CR-related cases in science, technology, and education had been reexamined, the document insisted that "victims of put-up, false, and wrong cases should be exonerated." Even "all those who were labeled as spies [and] reactionary academic authorities" should be vindicated.[24] In addition, the document ordered that "those who died should be posthumously rehabilitated and their honors restored." All materials in the dossiers of the victims or their relatives were to be cleared; all property seized, bank deposits frozen, wages withheld, and houses forcefully occupied should be returned to the original owners.

After the third plenum, the central organization department issued another instruction, this time concerning old cadres' work. Praising the "historical contribution made by old cadres," it recommended a thorough rehabilitation. In addition to concrete measures to which every rehabilitated cadre was entitled, the documents also specified how work should be reassigned. "Old cadres who can do regular work should be quickly reassigned. Those with ability should be assigned to leadership positions. Cadres who retired during the CR should be given appropriate work, if they so desire." At the same time, it recommended a very lenient

22. "Guanyu Ganbu Zhengce Lushi," in *Zhuzhi Yu Tongxun* (Beijing: Renmin Chubanshe, 1980). The key points were published in *Hong Qi*, no. 6, 1978.
23. "Zhongyang Zhuzhibu Guanyu Zhishifenzi Zhengce de Jidian Yijian," in *Zhuzhi Yu Tongxun.*
24. Ibid. It also specified the procedures for rehabilitation.

policy toward old cadres who had made mistakes, detailing special treatment for them, which the retirement (*lixiu*) system later incorporated.[25]

Hu's energetic maneuvers behind the scene were reflected in the official media's handling of the rehabilitation issue. Or one may say that the central leadership—largely dominated by the rehabilitated cadres—intentionally fostered public pressure by widely publicizing the issue of rehabilitation. As early as October 1977, Hu Yaobang managed to have *Renmin Ribao* publish an article entitled "Rectify the Mistakes Made by the Gang of Four in Cadre Work," which reportedly drew about 10,000 letters of support from readers.[26] As the issue of rehabilitation continued to figure prominently in the official media, letters requesting reviews of cases poured in. In the two years following the third plenum, Anhui provincial authorities received 1.8 million letters concerning rehabilitation.[27] One-third of all letters received by Fuzhou municipality during the same period were concerned with rehabilitation.

Since the central organizational department did not have sufficient manpower to investigate and exonerate all wrongly handled cases, reinvestigations were carried out by the unit which had made the decisions.[28] As a Chinese maxim, "Nobody can use an axe to cut one's own body," aptly indicates, the cadres who had made the original decisions were reluctant to overturn them.[29] Lower-level leaders were also afraid of reversing decisions made by leaders higher up the ladder. In addition, many Chinese exploited the official policy of rehabilitation to demand a review of their cases. Some people wanted to change the punishment they received ten years ago and even reverse the official decision rendered on disputes among the masses. Others demanded that they be returned to urban areas and have their wages raised.[30]

Reluctance to pass new verdicts usually meant partial rehabilitation, which frequently left looser ends than the complete denial of rehabilitation. For example, a youth had been convicted as a coun-

25. "Zhongyang Zhuzhibu Guanyu Jiaqian Laoganbu Gongzuo de Jidian Yijian," in *Zhuzhi Yu Tongxun*.

26. Ibid., 1.

27. *Daily Report*, 21 October 1981, 1.

28. "Guanyu Ganbu Zhengce Lushi," in *Zhuzhi Yu Tongxun*.

29. *Nanfang Ribao*, 24 January 1979.

30. *Renmin Ribao*, 22 October 1979.

terrevolutionary in June 1977. The same court granted him conditional rehabilitation in 1978 because he had actually done no more than utter "some mistaken words." He was released. However, his original unit accepted him only as a temporary worker and continued to discriminate against him.[31] One person who had been arrested for having participated in the Tiananmen Square incident was released in December 1977, but the public security bureau that had arrested him refused to acknowledge that the arrest was a mistake. Instead, they simply changed the charge from being a counterrevolutionary to being in possession of a "yellow novel"—Tolstoy's *Anna Karenina*.[32]

Many cadres felt that it was unfair to use current standards of right and wrong to judge decisions made in the past. For instance, when some "counterrevolutionaries" demanded rehabilitation on the grounds that they had challenged the Gang of Four, cadres replied:

> The Gang of Four were members of the Politburo, and your opposition to them was a direct attack on Chairman Mao. . . . Your criticism of the Gang of Four was in reality a criticism of the CR and of the socialist system. . . . Your revolt against the Gang of Four was a little too early, and it undermined the strategic plan of Chairman Mao. . . . It should be clearly recognized that opposition to the Gang of Four was in violation of the organization principle and hence wrong.[33]

The only way to deal with such resistance was to change the leadership. After an almost two-month-long debate, the central organizational department adopted "some opinions regarding the readjustment of leadership" on September 1978.[34] Recommending the complete removal of Gang of Four sympathizers, the document urged that CR victims be promoted to high-level positions (*diao xiang*), dislodging "those cadres who lack experience and about whom the masses have many [bad] opinions"—in other words, those who had benefited from the CR. In many places, it was only after the beneficiaries were replaced by the victims that the rehabilitation work started in earnest.[35] The newly appointed leaders had

31. *Zhongguo Qingnian Bao*, 24 October 1978.
32. *Renmin Ribao*, 3 August 1978.
33. Ibid.
34. "Guanyu Ganbu Zhengce Lushi," in *Zhuzhi Yu Tongxun*.
35. *Nanfang Ribao*, 11 April 1979; *Hebei Ribao*, 4 September 1980.

no psychological inclination to protect the previous decisions made by purged leaders. The regime also specifically banned the persons who made the original decisions from becoming involved in the reviews of their original cases.

Furthermore, in order to ensure that the official policy of rehabilitation was thoroughly implemented at lower levels, the center dispatched "inspection teams" (composed of about 1,000 cadres from central ministries, the Military Affairs Commission, central organs, and the People's Congress standing committees). Local authorities also organized their own inspection teams (*fucha gongzuo ban*) with "cadres who have a very strong standpoint, who can uphold principle in all fairness, and who know history and have work ability." On the other hand, "those individuals who are seriously responsible for producing invented, false, and wrong charges and who are resented by the people" should be removed.[36] Authorized to "seek truth from facts" by correcting all mistaken cases "irrespective of when the original decisions were made, who made them, and which level of leadership approved them," the responsible teams reviewed the rehabilitation work done at the lower levels. Shanxi province organized special investigation teams involving 5,000 cadres—many of whom were the victims of previous political campaigns—and established five steps in effecting a person's rehabiliation.[37]

With a more comprehensive rehabilitation program, the official media began to question Mao's decisions. The decision on the Tiananmen Square incident, the most difficult and controversial case, was finally reversed in November 1978, when Lin Jiaohu replaced Wu De. *Renmin Ribao* published a long and authoritative article entitled, "The Rehabilitation of Trumped-Up Cases in a Historical Context," which argued that large-scale rehabilitation would prevent a total rejection of Mao such as happened to Stalin. In the absence of rehabilitation, discontented people might completely repudiate Mao.[38]

The article was followed by a flurry of other articles calling for a thorough vindication of the "framed, falsely charged, and wrongly

36. Zhonggong Zhungyang Wenxian Yanjiushi, ed., *Guanyu Jianguo Yilai de Ruogan Lishi Wenti de Jueyi*, 474.

37. *Shanxi Ribao*, 31 March 1979.

38. *Renmin Ribao*, 15 December 1978.

sentenced." Now thorough rehabilitation was officially regarded as the prerequisite for ending the campaign against the Gang of Four in each unit. The official media began to publish veiled references to Mao's arbitrary purge of many cadres. "If a certain leader made comments on the cases of certain cadres without going through an organizational approval, those comments are just his personal opinions. Those comments not corresponding to organizational principles must be rectified, if incorrect." Mao's responsibility for the radicals' actions was recognized. The Gang of Four was accused of having condemned as "renegades and spies" everyone to whom Mao had simply said, "I do not consider you a good person." Even Mao's personal approval could not prevent reversal of the particular decision. "If the party constitution and the state constitution can be amended, what excuse is there for official documents with mistakes in them to be the basis for defending wrong decisions?"[39]

By the third plenum, Hu Yaobang had exonerated all cadres under his jurisdiction. Wang Dongxing, who was in charge of the management section of the Central Committee—which in turn handled the cases of high-ranking leaders—was replaced by Yao Yilin, and the units within the management offices dealing with the rehabilitation of cadres were abolished. All cases were transferred to the central organizational department.

THE SCOPE OF REHABILITATION

Early in 1978, rehabilitation rather than "implementation of cadre policy" emerged as the predominant issue in the public media. In addition, the scope of rehabilitation expanded.[40] Several factors aided this trend. Increased criticism of the Gang of Four, which was officially labeled ultraleftist, and the notion that "practice is the sole criterion for empirical truth," implied that many leaders were merely victims of the wrong line. Growing numbers of rehabilitated cadres who assumed leadership at the provincial level aggressively investigated CR-related cases of rehabilitation.[41]

39. Ibid.
40. Ibid., 23 March 1979.
41. Ibid., 1 October 1977.

After the third plenum, rehabilitation accelerated. In 1979 the official news media carried a number of articles reporting the rehabilitation of and memorial services for those who had died during the CR.[42] Those alleged to have made mistakes during the CR and those condemned as "renegades and spies" were vindicated.[43] Finally Liu Shaoqi's case was reversed.[44] The third plenum authorized Hu Yaobang and Song Renqiong to reinvestigate, and after nine months' work, they concluded that Kang Sheng had falsified the charges against Liu. The fifth plenum (1980) approved the new findings.[45] On 19 May 1980 the center issued document 25, which revoked the previous decision against Liu Shaoqi, restoring his reputation as "a great proletarian revolutionary leader."

Reinvestigation went far beyond CR-related cases. Those purged during the Socialist Education Movement (1963–1965) (SEM) were also reinstated.[46] Even decisions made as early as 1961 were canceled. The verdict in the case of the Hu Feng counterrevolutionary group (1955) was reversed on 29 September 1980. The central organization department, probably in a review of all controversial cases since its founding, vindicated Qu Qiubai, Li Lisan, Huang Gocheng, Li Weihan, Zeng San, and Mao Mingfan.[47] By 1983, the regime had even reviewed cases decided as far back as the 1940s and 1930s.[48] Another interesting case involved former Nationalist troops, who, despite their surrender to the CCP, were nonetheless persecuted during the CR together with their children. The political consultative conference demanded that the regime vindicate this group of people.

Another group of ordinary people whose honor was restored were model workers, many of whom had been criticized as "work-

42. Those who were rehabilitated through this process include Zhang Zhichun, Xu Haidong, Wu Zhifu, Liu Changsheng, Zhang Linzhi, Wang Shiying, Liu Liumin, Liao Loyen, Xu Zufu, Hu Shihkuei, Liu Xiewu, Wang Qimei, Liu Jen, Qhien Bozan, Gao Chungmin, Tian Han, Zhang Wentian, Xu Bing, and Zhang Jingwu.

43. Revoked were previous decisions on "sixty-one persons" who had allegedly surrendered to the KMT in 1934 and on Peng Zhen, Lo Ruiching, and the "Yang antiparty group." *Shehui Kexue Yanjiu Cankao Cailiao*, no. 2, 1982.

44. *Renmin Ribao*, 19 May 1980.

45. *Feijing Yuebao*, 16 September 1979.

46. *Renmin Ribao*, 13 January 1979; *Beijing Ribao*, 15 February 1979; 24 May 1979.

47. *Renmin Ribao*, 29 September 1980.

48. *Dangshi Tongxun*, February 1985, 16.

er aristocrats with vested interests in the status quo," and "false models, and the black gang's model." Basic-level cadres initially refused to rehabilitate model workers because the masses, not official party organs, had attacked them, and there were no charges from which they needed to be exonerated.[49]

Seriously affected by the CR were former underground party workers. CR radicals had reportedly organized 339 central and 85 local investigation teams to probe into about 3,600 members of the former Shanghai underground party organization. All ninety-nine former underground party members who had reached the bureau level lost their positions, and sixty-five were arrested and investigated.[50] A similar fate befell the members of former northeast underground party organizations.[51]

The most frequently used criminal label attached to ordinary Chinese during the CR was "vicious attackers" (yadu gongji). Any disparaging remark about Mao's Selected Works and any utterance made out of "temporary discontent and anger" were used as evidence of a "vicious attack" against the party and socialism.[52] One person was condemned as a counterrevolutionary because he had said, "Jiang Qing's statement 'Defend with weapons and attack with words' promotes armed struggle." Another was jailed because he said, "Lenin said that only the dead and the unborn have not made mistakes." A cadre was condemned as a counterrevolutionary because he had left a space between the party center and Mao when he had written a poster declaring that "whoever opposes the party center and Chairman Mao is counterrevolutionary."[53]

Rehabilitation affected not only former cadres but also their relatives, colleagues, and friends. The official news media began to criticize the CR's tendency to discriminate against children of disgraced cadres as a "feudal practice." Despite Mao's directive in September 1968 that "serious historical and political problems should not affect children," punishing relatives became a widespread practice and produced such phrases as "children of the

49. Gongren Bao, 10 September 1979.
50. Renmin Ribao, 26 April 1979.
51. Ibid., 5 November 1978.
52. Beijing Ribao, 11 January 1979.
53. Wenhui Bao, 19 February 1979.

black gang" and "children of renegades." The offspring of purged cadres were discriminated against when they tried to join the Communist Youth League, enter schools, enlist in the army, or obtain jobs. Moreover, their parents' political problems were entered into their own dossiers. Each unit that rehabilitated cadres was required to notify the children's units of the decisions so that the children's dossier could be corrected.[54]

Rehabilitation was truly comprehensive. Controversial cases that had occurred before the CR were reviewed in a different and more favorable light. The united front department reinvestigated cases of its own cadres.[55] Shanxi province revoked its previous decision on "Sanshang Taofeng," a drama that the radicals condemned as an attempt to reverse the CR decision on Liu Shaoqi; the Beijing party committee revoked its decision on "The Three-family Village," which had signaled the beginning of the CR.[56] Guangdong military region rehabilitated seventy-nine officers whom the Gang of Four had persecuted.[57]

The people's courts reexamined cases—including death sentences—which they had passed judgment on before. The Shanghai court overturned previous decisions on 2,000 cases, even trying to reconcile couples whose marriages had broken up because of earlier decisions.[58] According to Jiang Hua, president of the People's Supreme Court, by May 1979, the court systems of twenty-nine provinces had corrected a total of 164,000 wrong and mistaken cases.[59]

In Yunan province, about 100,000 people were rehabilitated. The Anhui province party committee reviewed about 110,700 pre-CR cases. More than 233,000 concocted, false, and wrong decisions were rectified, and a total of 41,609 persons were reinstated in their former positions. Another 7,466 persons regained their party membership.[60] The Pijing district in Guangdong province re-

54. Through this method, Chengdu reported that about 5,200 dossiers out of 5,400 dossiers in the municipality were cleansed. *Zhongguo Qingnian Bao,* 7 October 1978.

55. *Wenhui Bao,* 19 March 1979.

56. *Renmin Ribao,* 22 September 1978; 3 August 1979.

57. *Nanfang Ribao,* 20 May 1979.

58. *Wenhui Bao,* 11 March 1979. As a result, Yangbu district court managed to help eleven cases of divorced couples to resume marital relations.

59. *Nanfang Ribao,* 28 June 1979.

60. *Daily Report,* 21 October 1981, Q1.

portedly reexamined about 3,900 cases, and three cases alone in Xinping county affected about 22,000 people.[61] Deng Xiaoping reported that 2.9 million people were rehabilitated, and if one includes relatives and friends, the rehabilitation touched almost 40 million Chinese.[62] Almost all the controversial cases that the CCP had made since 1949 were overturned. The only known exceptions, at least according to *Zhengming* magazine, were those of the Guangdong localists.[63]

PROCESS OF REHABILITATION

Rehabiliation involved many steps, each of which required decisions on how the organization should acknowledge its mistakes, compensate victims for their hardships, clear their dossiers, and assign them to new jobs. Broadly speaking, the process of rehabilitating a case involved the following steps.

First, responsibility for checking the correctness of the original decision fell on the unit that had made the decision, regardless of whether or not the disciplined person was still with the unit or requested reexamination. The party committee in each unit often organized one or several rehabilitation committees, depending on need. For instance, the history department of Beijing University, a unit that had produced a large number of rightists in 1957, organized four investigation teams, one each for former students, professors, foreign students, and research associates. A team could be further subdivided to deal with different types of problems.

The rehabilitation committee was generally headed by a deputy secretary and consisted of people who had no part in the original decision. For example, the ministry of culture organized a "rehabilitation committee with persons whose party spirit is strong, whose work style is orthodox, and who are willing to take responsibility for their actions."[64] Tianjin province mobilized 3,000 cadres to handle rehabilitation, receiving visitors and answering letters. In order to ensure impartiality, two kinds of people were barred from the investigation teams: those who had participated in armed

61. *Ming Bao,* 3 July 1978.
62. *Zhengming,* 16 January 1980, 11–23.
63. Ibid., 15 February 1979.
64. *Renmin Ribao,* 22 April 1978.

struggle during the CR and put together false cases, and the former leaders of rebel organizations.[65]

The members of the rehabilitation committee first studied official documents to familiarize themselves with official policy. Then they selected several typical cases as models. One committee chose the following three cases as models: (1) a provincial alternative secretary who had been condemned as the "root of seventeen years of the black line," (2) a director of the united front bureau who had once been arrested by the KMT as a model "historical problem," and (3) a cadre who had been persecuted to death.[66] Committees usually worked on easy cases first, leaving the most difficult cases for last.[67]

Sometimes when a person to be rehabilitated had been transferred to another unit, his rehabilitation required the work of many different units. For example, a cadre working in a provincial financial bureau was classified as a rightist and then sent down to a labor farm under the commercial bureau. In 1962 he was reassigned to a provincial department store and then retired in the same year. He had to write letters to many units because each unit passed on the responsibility to another.[68] In cases where many units had been involved in the original decision, a "combined investigation team" was set up.[69]

Each investigation team looked into the dossier of any cadre who might need rehabilitation. Investigation teams were allowed access to other dossiers in the course of their work. When the necessity arose, the committee sent out investigation teams to collect more evidence and to interview witnesses.

The party committee discussed each report and gave an organizational decision, which was placed in the dossier. New conclusions often included such statements as "no rightist remarks have been found" and "should not be considered a rightist."[70] The reasons for the changed outlook were often given. A frequently cited justification for change was that originally

65. Ibid., 24 May 1980.
66. Ibid.
67. *Nanfang Ribao*, 28 March 1979.
68. *Renmin Ribao*, 10 February 1980.
69. *Nanfang Ribao*, 12 April 1979.
70. Ibid., 13 January 1980.

several wrong statements arising from misunderstanding were accepted as evidence of antiparty and antisocialist views, [or] what one said in a free discussion was used as evidence of an antiparty clique, normal criticisms as evidence for attacking the party, what one confessed to the party as evidence of a vicious attack and a counterrevolutionary ideology, different opinions in academic research questions as evidence of anti-Marxism and rejection of Mao's thought, and suggestions to party leaders as evidence of attacking central leaders.[71]

The party secretary or another similarly responsible person explained the organizational decision, stating the concrete actions to be taken to compensate for the original wrong decision in a heart-to-heart talk. The former victim could raise questions, and leaders were encouraged to be responsive.[72] Conditions of rehabilitation entailed haggling over such issues as back payment, housing, children's problems, and medical treatment.

The victims who needed health care because of their sufferings during the CR were issued "priority cards [yudai zheng] for medical treatment." To be eligible, one had to prove that the CR was somehow accountable for one's problem; a certificate from a physician stating that the problem needed continuous medical treatment was also required.

Usually victims were entitled to partial retroactive payment of the wages they had not received during their disgrace.[73] During the CR, the purged generally received a portion of their wages, though barely enough to cover subsistence. The amount to be paid was negotiable. In some cases, units wanted to deduct the cost of feeding and lodging the victim in confinement or jail. Frequently, people who received back pay were asked to donate some of the money to their unit—sometimes this was even compulsory. Former rightists were not automatically entitled to back payment, but sometimes their salaries were raised by one or two grades to compensate for their loss. Often special arrangements were made for those in dire straits. Shanxi province reported that it had made back payments to about 2,600 original capitalists, Liaoning province to 14,000 nonparty members.[74]

71. *Renmin Ribao*, 23 January 1979.
72. *Wenhui Bao*, 19 February 1979.
73. Ibid., 11 March 1979.
74. *Renmin Ribao*, 15 April 1985.

Another matter that had to be negotiated was a person's job assignment. The basic principle was to reinstate former cadres in positions equivalent in status to their previous ones. Hunan province reported that 96 percent of those who were rehabilitated were assigned to positions equivalent to or higher than those they had occupied before.[75] "Depending on one's political situation, physical condition, and past work experience," some were promoted to higher positions, transferred to equivalent ones, or assigned to less demanding jobs. Those with health problems were allowed to retire.[76] Former rightists were not automatically entitled to their previous positions, but their new assignments were to be based on ability, physical condition, and the needs of the unit.

When both sides—the party representative and the victim—had agreed on the specific conditions of the rehabilitation package, the case was passed on to the supervisory authorities for approval. Often disagreements arose with the supervisory authorities about how to interpret evidence and what conclusions to draw from it. Since the lower level was responsible for executing the specific conditions of a person's rehabilitation, which required funding, housing, and positions, it resisted pressure from above, for instance, to declare that a particular cadre was "persecuted to death."[77] Since most workers' cases were much simpler than the cadres', often the approval of the upper echelon was waived. The appropriate unit could finalize the workers' cases, except for those that needed approval by the courts and other units. In some cases just the approval of the cadres in charge of the case was sufficient to close the matter, bypassing the party committee entirely.[78]

Quite often the implementation of the terms and conditions agreed upon produced tensions among the units involved. As an example let us suppose that a rightist who was expelled from his research unit was sent to a state farm in a different province, where he worked for almost twenty years as a guard. Who is responsible for him? His original unit wants the state farm to give the former rightist what he is entitled to—including a new job, a raise, new housing, retirement benefits, and help for his children—whereas

75. *Hong Qi*, no. 6, 1978.
76. *Renmin Ribao*, 16 September 1978.
77. Ibid., 24 May 1980.
78. *Wenhui Bao*, 3 May 1979.

the state farm insists that the research unit should take him back and do whatever it can for him. Eventually the issue has to go up to the provincial level to be resolved.

Organizational department personnel carefully went over all dossiers and removed unreliable CR-related materials. It is, however, unclear what constitutes "unreliable material." Obviously, the category includes "hearsay," evidence collected after the case was decided, and "forced confession."[79] All materials pertaining to the wrong decisions had to be removed from the dossier, and the new organizational conclusion, with its supporting evidence, was added.[80] Often material taken out of the dossier was shown to the person before being destroyed. Thus, one could see what had been removed from his dossier, but not what was left. The Chinese news media often complained that not all unreliable materials related to wrong cases were removed from personnel dossiers. The regime made it clear that past political records should not be used as a basis for future politicial discrimination by prohibiting the use of such terms as "former rightist" and insisting that former rightists, and particularly their children, should be treated like anyone else in "promotion, salary raises, wage adjustment, decisions on bonuses, and conferring job titles."[81]

All confiscated goods were returned. Sometimes monetary compensation was made for lost property. Frozen bank accounts were reactivated and houses returned.[82] The political consultative conferences cooperated with the central united front department to supervise the return of valuable goods to former owners. Many antiques that had been taken away from people—including paintings and books—were sent to libraries, antique shops, and museums.[83] From looking at the owner's names on the items, libraries and museums were able to return them. Shanghai received about $6 billion worth of gold and silver objects; about $5.9 billion worth was returned. The various units under Shanghai received about 720,000 confiscated items and 4.4 million books, which were returned to their original owners.

79. *Nanfang Ribao*, 8 June 1979.
80. *Shijian* (Inner Mongolia), April 1978.
81. *Renmin Ribao*, 17 November 1978.
82. *Ming Bao*, 30 August 1979.
83. *Renmin Ribao*, 15 April 1985.

Each rehabilitated cadre or former rightist received a rehabilitation certificate, which some people hung on their walls.[84] If the person migrated or fled to a foreign country, the certificate was sent to him.[85] Copies were also sent to units where the person's spouse or children worked. And each unit organized a mass rally to announce the rehabilitation officially so that every member of the unit would know both that the rehabilitated person had been unfairly treated in the past and that this would no longer happen.

Finally, each unit informed the units where the relatives of rehabilitated people worked. The official policy was to inform "all those who happen to be the rehabilitated cadres' relatives or children, irrespective of where they work, which units they belong to, and regardless of whether they have been affected or not." Frequently cadres working in personnel departments were dispatched to inform relatives and leaders of units where they worked. Those from far away were informed by mail. In some cases, it was necessary to inform family members scattered over more than a hundred units.[86] A factory in Beijing reported that it had convened twelve rehabilitation meetings and sent our 291 letters to relatives in the process of rehabilitating sixty-nine people.[87]

ENDING THE CLASS STRUGGLE

The idea of class struggle that Mao renewed in 1962, when he disclaimed his previous implication that violent class struggle was over in China, constituted the ideological justification for Maoist radicalism. By politicizing the concept of class, Mao justified the existence of a bourgeoisie even in China, where the ownership of the means of production had been socialized. By the time of the SEM, the term "bourgeois class" in China referred to party leaders who favored policies considered revisionist by Mao. Mao's interpretation of "class" became clearer when his thesis of class struggle underwrote the masses' attack on "powerholders taking the capitalist road" in the party, government, and military during the CR.

---

84. For a sample certificate, see *Ming Bao*, 30 August 1979.
85. *Nanfang Ribao*, 15 April 1979.
86. *Renmin Ribao*, 16 September 1978; *Nanfang Ribao*, 6 March 1979.
87. *Beijing Ribao*, 12 April 1979.

Later, Zhang Chunqiao systematically elaborated the radical meaning of class.[88]

The radicals' politicization of what they called class struggle had many undesirable consequences. It further contributed to an increase in the number of "class enemies" that every political campaign since 1949 has fostered. One 135-member brigade in Guangdong province had only one person belonging to the four-category element—landlords, rich peasants, bad elements, and counter-revolutionaries—at the time of land reform, but there were eleven by 1976.[89] A commune reported that "upon seven occasions altogether class status was reviewed and altered. More and more people became members of the 'four-category element.'" The status of those who had overseas connections was often reclassified, and the person concerned was often given a less desirable designation.[90] Sometimes original regulations were changed to make obtaining good class status more difficult. For instance, according to 1950 regulations, children under eighteen in 1949 were not to be called landlords like their parents. However, during the SEM the regulation was changed to exempt those younger than six. In some areas, children automatically inherited their deceased parents' status. Beginning with the CR, not only one's own class status but also one's family background—which was determined by the parents' and grandparents' status—was emphasized. Anyone with a bad family background was persecuted. The cadres purged during the CR formed a new category of "class enemies," and the record of their having been purged went into their children's dossiers.[91] The rehabilitated cadres had another incentive to repudiate Mao's class struggle besides all these abuses—the fact that Mao had purged them in the name of class struggle. Deng Xiaoping publicly criticized Mao's politicization of class:

> We oppose the overextension of class struggle. We do not admit that there is a bourgeois class in the party. We also do not admit that under the socialist system, after the effective elimination of the

88. Zhang Chunqiao, "On Exercising All-Around Dictatorship over the Bourgeoisie" (Beijing: Foreign Languages Press, 1975).
89. *Ming Bao*, 1 April 1979.
90. *Nanfang Ribao*, 14 March 1979.
91. *Zhongguo Qingnian Bao*, 7 October 1978.

exploiting class as well as the conditions that make exploitation possible, a bourgeois class or any other exploiting class can be produced.[92]

In addition, waging class struggle was not conducive to economic development, the regime's new goal. The third plenum of the Eleventh Party Congress thus promised to "mobilize all positive elements" for economic development while declaring that turbulent class struggle on a large scale had ended. Later Hua Guofeng declared specifically that the landlord, rich peasant, and capitalist classes had ceased to exist in China.[93] Presently class is defined exclusively on the basis of ownership of the means of production. This strictly economic definition leaves no room for the existence of an exploitative class in China. The regime, however, still refuses to declare an official end to class struggle, reasoning that there are still counterrevolutionaries and foreign agents in China.[94]

The changed official view on class and class struggle provided the theoretical justification for the abolition of discriminatory class designations. The regime decided first to remove all labels of rightists and then to reclassify most as four-category elements. This measure was intended to "mobilize all positive factors, transform negative factors into positive ones, promote stability and unity, and contribute greatly to the socialist modernizations."[95] In other words, the regime intended to count on former landlords and rich peasants, who were efficient producers, and on former capitalists, who were able managers, for economic development.

We do not know what proportion of the Chinese population had been given undesirable class designations. The official media estimated that 5 percent of the people were "class enemies," and in 1967 Mao specifically estimated their number to be about 35 million.[96] According to another source, in 1979 there were about 6 million landlords and rich peasants and half a million capitalists.[97] All of them, except for some landlords and rich peasants, received

92. Hong Qi, no. 20, 1981, 27.
93. Renmin Ribao, 26 June 1979.
94. Beijing Review, 16 November 1979, 9–13; 23 November 1979, 15–17.
95. Jiefang Bao, 29 January 1979.
96. Feijing Yuebao 22(7) (1980):42–47.
97. Zhonggong Zhungyang Wenxian Yanjiushi, ed., Guanyu Jianguo Yilai de Ruogan Lishi Wenti de Jueyi, 160–61.

new class labels.[98] Among 400,000 people who were originally labeled rightists, about 130,000 still carried the label after several readjustments made between 1957 and 1979.[99]

The decision to abolish "rightist" as a label began to take form early in 1978 when Deng Xiaoping instructed the party not to use it. The organizational, propaganda, and united front departments and the public security and civil affairs ministries jointly convened a meeting from 16 June to 22 June 1978 in Shandong province.[100] After a heated debate between the "whatever faction" and Deng's group, the meeting approved "Concrete Measures for Implementing the Decision to Remove All the Hats of the Rightists," which apparently decided to make a distinction between correcting (*gaizheng*) and granting pardons (*zhaimao*). In a "correction," the person who had been mislabeled was entitled to restoration of his party membership, his political honor, and his former salary scale.[101] For those whose cases had not involved any error, simply removing the label sufficed.[102]

It seems that the regime first planned to "correct" only the erroneous designations, but later decided to remove the stigma even from genuine rightists. Moreover, there are indications that the center put pressure on local cadres to take a broad view.[103]

Some basic-level cadres resisted the new measure on the grounds that it constituted a "rightist reversal" and a "repudiation of the achievements of the antirightist struggle." In dealing with cadre resistance, the regime emphasized that the movement was correct and generally properly directed but that some minor errors

98. Ibid.; *Zhongguo Qingnian Bao*, 8 September 1979; *Zhengming*, no. 7, March 1979, 5–8.

99. "Deng Xiaoping's Report on the Present Situation and Task," *Zhengming*, March 1980, 11–23.

100. Presiding at the meeting, Wang Dongxing set up three guidelines: (1) the overall direction of the antirightist campaign was correct, (2) the process of the movement was basically healthy, but (3) there had been some minor mistakes. *Zhengming*, 1979, 5–8.

101. Ibid.

102. Those judging whether a person had been correctly or mistakenly labeled were to rely on the "Notice of Criteria for Classifying Rightists," the document originally used in the 1957 campaign. Ibid.; *Renmin Ribao*, 23 January 1979.

103. On 3 January 1978 the central party school reported that thirty-one of ninety-seven rightists were incorrectly labeled, but only twenty days later another article reported that ninety-three of the ninety-seven had suffered from mistaken decisions. *Renmin Ribao*, 2 January 1979; 23 January 1979.

had been made in its execution. The official media defended the policy, saying it showed the success, not the repudiation, of Mao's policy of transforming rightists. As a result, by November 1978, no more rightists officially existed. The first plenary session of the newly organized disciplinary committee decided to review the implementation of the policy.

How successful was the policy implementation? The answer depends on how one defines its objectives. As far as administrative procedures are concerned, the policy was thoroughly carried out. Each person's dossier contained a note to the effect that he was either no longer considered a rightist or that the original decision calling him one had been corrected. But this left everything in the dossier, causing some people to be quite uneasy.[104] As for ridding the victims of past political campaigns of their grievances and helping them to dedicate themselves to modernization, the result is less clear. For some former rightists the new policy was not sweeping enough to make restitution for all the suffering they had endured. After all, how could the regime compensate for broken marriages, lost opportunities, and, in some extreme cases, permanent injury? For other former rightists, the removal of the discriminatory label was anticlimactic, after which they had no incentive to work hard.[105]

After dealing with rightists, the regime immediately proceeded to remove the designations of landlord, rich peasant, counterrevolutionary, and bad element.[106] Official policy toward them was not as generous as toward the rightists. The labels were not completely abolished, however, because an "extremely small number of those who are stubbornly upholding the CR standpoints and those who are not yet properly remolded" continued to merit them. Only those who met three requirements could have their class labels removed: they must have abided by state laws and regulations, sincerely labored, and not done any "bad things."[107]

After the publication of the official decision about the four categories in newspapers, the minister of public security, Zhao Zhangbi, elaborated on these conditions in an interview with journalists.

104. *Nanfang Ribao*, 11 March 1980.
105. *Tansu*, no. 5, 1979, 68–69.
106. *Nanfang Ribao*, 29 January 1979.
107. *Renmin Ribao*, 30 January 1979.

The "sincere labor" requirement would apply only to those who could perform physical labor. "Bad things" referred to such activities as "engaging in class retaliation, " "beating, smashing, and looting," and "carrying out counterrevolutionary or other criminal activities." According to Zhao, an "extremely small number of people who had done 'bad things' when Lin Biao and the Gang of Four were in power" would not be reclassified. At the same time, he emphasized that all who had been called any one of the four categories because of their opposition to ultraleftist policies and the Gang of Four would be reclassified. These included everyone "who promoted private plots and those who challenged the erroneous leadership of the radicals."[108]

The procedure for examining each case was similar to that used for rightists; it involved both leadership and the masses and required a public announcement. However, in the case of the four categories the masses' opinion carried more weight in arriving at a final decision. The public security bureaus were also involved, and final authority in each case was given to a county-level revolutionary committee. The removal procedure also involved the changing of class status, for instance, from landlord to commune member, in all written records. The class status of a person's children was also similarly changed. Grandchildren of the four categories even had their family backgrounds changed.[109]

After reclassification, former four-category elements "should enjoy all the basic rights of citizenship as specified in the constitution." No discrimination was to be practiced in such matters as entering schools, obtaining factory jobs, joining the Communist Youth League and the party, and receiving job assignments. The only proper consideration was "political performance."[110] Like former rightists, reclassified people were not to be referred to in any way by their earlier designation. Even if the reclassified person committed a crime, his former class label was not to become an issue. But no old records were removed from the dossiers.

Most of the former landlords and rich peasants had their designations removed. An example comes from the Huancheng

108. Ibid.
109. Ibid.; see also *Nanfang Ribao*, 11 March 1980.
110. *Nanfang Ribao*, 9 February 1979.

commune in Guangdong province (population 5,300 in 1979). At the time of the land reform this commune had 828 landlords and rich peasants. The number had shrunk to 608 by 1965 and to 423 by 1979, and finally only two remained.[111] In Beijing municipality, of 8,500 landlords and rich peasants, 7,800 had their designations removed. *Zhongguo Qingnian Bao* reported that only 1 to 2 percent of former four-category elements failed to obtain reclassification.[112] Another source estimates that only about 50,000 people were still considered landlords or rich peasants.[113]

By 1984, the remaining four-category elements were further reclassified. According to *Renmin Ribao*, all remaining four-category elements had their labels removed, including 28,227 landlords, 14,343 rich peasants, 16,260 counterrevolutionaries, and 20,674 bad elements. The regime declared that it had succeeded in educating and transforming about 20 million such people since the foundation of the PRC.[114]

Another group that regained full citizenship included industrialists and businessmen of the national bourgeoisie. From the beginning the CCP's policy toward them had been relatively lenient, largely because of the small size of the group. Capitalists numbered about 850,000, and of these about 150,000 were big capitalists. The rest were small capitalists, who could draw about 10 yuan per month from assets that had been taken over by the government.[115] There were about 720,000 people in the group called the "national bourgeoisie" in 1956, but the number had diminished to about half a million by 1979.[116] Even after the "peaceful transformation of industry," former industrialists and businessmen continued to enjoy their wealth; they were allowed a draw a fixed interest of 5 percent on their total verified assets, to retain private property (including houses and bank deposits), and to work as highly paid executives or technicians in the enterprises they had once owned. However, the CR not only brought an abrupt end to these economic privileges, but it also made the

111. Ibid.
112. *Zhongguo Qingnian Bao*, 8 September 1979.
113. *Beijing Review*, 21 January 1980, 14–20.
114. *Renmin Ribao*, 2 November 1984.
115. *Dangshi Yenjiu Ziliao*, 20 November 1984.
116. *Beijing Review*, 28 April 1980, 21.

national bourgeoisie vulnerable to political persecution; their private property was confiscated, and interest payments stopped. Many of them lost their jobs or suffered cuts in salary. In 1979, the regime decided to return all property, to repay them retroactively, and to reinstate them in positions where they could fully utilize their skills and knowledge.[117]

The regime's policy toward overseas Chinese and their relatives in China changed as well. When the radicals were in power, anybody with "overseas connections" was politically suspect. Such unfortunates were discriminated against in school admissions, job assignments, conscription, and recruitment into the Communist Youth League and the Communist Party. Despite the 1963 regulation that all overseas Chinese who had returned to China after the land reform should be reclassified according to their previous class status, in Guangdong province, where many people had overseas connections (there are 150,000 overseas Chinese there), radicals enacted "Six Articles on Handling Cadres with Overseas Connections."[118] These articles stipulated that no one with overseas connections could become a cadre and that incumbent cadres with overseas connections had to be investigated.[119] Many such cadres were suspected of being spies, and their houses and rooms were confiscated or occupied by force. In January 1978, the regime announced a new policy toward overseas Chinese; it promised to stop all discrimination, to return confiscated homes, to reopen special shops for overseas Chinese, and to take care of their special needs.[120] In order to supervise implementation of the new policy, the Office of Overseas Chinese of the State Council set up a reception office, which helped to resolve 13,000 cases.[121] By 1986, the regime had reportedly made restitution in 33,000 cases from the CR and 10,000 earlier cases, returned numerous houses, and promoted 17,700 overseas Chinese.[122]

The disciplinary committee reported that the number of cases involving overseas Chinese appealed and reexamined in seventeen

117. *Renmin Ribao*, 30 January 1979; 19 March 1979.
118. *Nanfang Ribao*, 12 February 1979.
119. *Ming Bao*, 20 February 1978.
120. Ibid., 3 January 1978; 27 January 1978; 29 September 1978.
121. *Renmin Ribao*, 16 July 1980.
122. Ibid., 24 February 1986.

provinces amounted to 3.26 million. The disciplinary committees of twenty provinces received about half a million letters and visits.[123] Deng and Hu Yaobang have said that rehabilitation and reclassification have affected approximately 10 billion people.[124]

The work done to remove undesirable class labels and to redress wrongs committed during the CR heralded the end both to the era of class struggle and to the practice of determining political loyalty from a family's economic status in the three years 1946–49. The amazing fact is not that the regime finally decided to end its feudalistic practice, but that it took so long to do so.

123. *Ming Bao*, 20 September 1979.
124. *Feijing Yuebao*, 22(3) 16 September 1979, 80; *Qishi Niandai*, 21 June 1980.

9

The Structure of the Cadre Corps

By the time the CCP made the historic decision to shift its main goal to economic development, China had a gigantic cadre corps shaped cumulatively by past policies. As a historical product of guerrilla warfare in the early 1940s, the socialist revolution in the 1950s, the "continuing revolutions" in the early 1960s, and the interelite conflicts during the CR, the existing cadre corps was ill-suited for the new task of the Four Modernizations (the modernizations of agriculture, industry, defense, and science and technology): it was too large in size, old in average age, low in educational level, ossified in political outlook, demoralized, and factionalized. Through their prolonged and checkered careers, the cadres learned that the best way to preserve their positions in the bureaucracy was to play it safe by refusing to take clear-cut positions on any issue, while cultivating extensive personal networks. Economic reforms and changes in official ideology that allowed a certain amount of individualism offered ample opportunity for cadres to use their formal authority for personal gain. The ordinary Chinese were bitter about the cadres' corruption. "If things continue like this, how can the party be called a Communist party and the state be called a [socialist] state?"[1]

Deng Xiaoping succinctly summarized the problems of Chinese officialdom:

> The bureaucratic phenomenon is the most serious problem for our nation and our party. The major manifestations of bureaucratism are looking down on the people, abusing political power, departing from reality, being separated from the masses, speaking empty words, espousing an antiquated ossified ideology, blindly observing absurd regulations, creating redundant organizations, having more

1. For the bureaucratic problems, see *Zhengming*, no. 52, February 1982, 11; *Renmin Ribao*, 18 September 1980; "Zhang Pinghua's Speech to Cadres in the Cultural Field," *Issues and Studies*, December 1978, pp. 97–118.

people than needed, avoiding decision-making, not caring about
efficiency, irresponsibility, betraying trust, adding red tape, behav-
ing destructively, retaliating against others, suppressing democracy,
cheating superiors and subordinates, taking bribes, and accumulating wealth.[2]

These problems stemmed from the structure of the bureaucracy in
which the cadres were operating as well as the characteristics of the
cadres themselves.[3]

THE BUREAUCRATIC SETTING

As shown in table 30, the bureaucratic machinery that the CCP had
developed after 1949 and prior to the reforms was not only gigantic
and unwieldy, but also highly stratified, with eight layers from the
central government down to an individual in the rural area. Within
each level was another set of layers. For instance, between the
municipal government and individual workers were five administrative layers including the municipal government, the commission,
the bureau, the corporation, and the factory.

Moreover, at each level there were and are several parallel
bureaucracies: party, government, military, judiciary, and political
consultative conference. Within the party and government, internal structures were further theoretically divided between executives and representative organs: secretaries, several committees,
functional bureaus, and party congresses. Government organs at
each level had similar units. In addition, about 392,500 industrial
enterprises, as well as 1 million business units, were under the
jurisdiction of the party-state organs at different levels. Some of
them were directly under the jursidiction of central government
units, while others answered to the provincial or local authorities.
Many of these units were under dual leadership of the upper echelon's bureau (*tiaotiao*) and of the local government (*kuaikuai*).

Within the bureaucracy political authority was highly centralized. The Leninist principle of democratic centralism created a
pseudo-military command structure, with authority flowing from

2. *Renmin Ribao*, 2 November 1981.
3. For structural problems of the Chinese bureaucracy, see Harry Harding,
Organizing China; The Problems of Bureaucracy, 1949–1976 (Stanford: Stanford University Press, 1981).

Table 30.   Structure of the Administrative Bureaucracy

Bureaucracy	No. of Units
Central government	
Provinces and special municipalities, including Taiwan	30
District level (*diji*)	178
Municipalities	286
District level	145
County level	141
Counties	2,080
Special districts (*qu*) directly under municipalities	552
Village (*xiang*) governments	95,000
Communes	74,000
Brigades	750,000
Production Teams	5,000,000
Industrial Enterprises	392,500
State-owned	87,100
Collective-owned	300,460
Others	387,560
Business Units	1,000,000

Sources. *Zhongguo Tongji Nianjian*, 1984, 1. For business units: *Jiaoxue Cankao*, March 1983, 20.

the Politburo down to the secretary of each party cell. Each level had a well-defined authority, responsibility, and task, but their authorities and responsibilities were not guaranteed by laws and rules. A higher authority could always encroach upon the jurisdiction of the lower level. Despite the various illegal and unofficial means (mainly passive) for resisting the higher authority, the organizational structure effectively allowed authority to flow from the center to the individual level.

All offices and cadres have well-defined rankings (see fig. 2). The uniform wage grade system of 1956 classified all cadres—from central to basic levels—into thirty grades, ranging from the top three grades for party and state chairmen and premiers, to the bottom grades for service personnel in party-state organs.[4] Although

4. Workers were classified into eight grades. Technical cadres—school teachers, public health workers, and scientists—had several different sets of wage scales ranging from 1 to 13, or 20. Cao Zhi, ed., *Zhonghua Renmin Gongheguo Renshi Zhidu Gaiyao* (Beijing: Beijing Dafue Chubanshe, 1985), 267–313.

Figure 2. Grade System of Cadres in the Party-State, 1956

Grade	National People's Congress	State Council
1	Chairman and vice chairman	Premier and vice premiers
2	Chairmen and vice chairmen of standing committees	
3		
4	General secretary, chiefs, deputy chiefs of committees	Ministers, vice ministers, chiefs, deputy chiefs of commissions, general management office
5		
6	Chiefs and deputy chiefs of offices; directors and deputy directors	
7		
8	Chiefs and deputy chiefs of committee offices	Assistant ministers
9		Chiefs and deputies of offices (*ding*); directors and deputy directors of bureaus (*su* and *ju*)
10	Division chiefs and deputy chiefs	
11		Division and section (*ke*) chiefs and deputies
12		
13		
14	Section chiefs and deputy chiefs	
15		
16		
17	Section members (*keyuan*)	Section members
18		

Grade	Provincial	County	Community (xiang) and (zhen)	Military[a]
1				
2				
3				
4				
5	Governors and vice			
6	governors			
7				
8	Chiefs and deputy chiefs of management offices; directors and deputy directors of bureaus			
9				
10				
11				Division commander
12				Division deputy commanders
19				
20				
21				
22	Administrative personnel (keyuan)			
23				
24				
25				
26	Support personnel (qinza renyuan)			
27				
28				
29				
30				

Figure 2. (Continued)

Grade	Provincial	County	Community (xiang) and (zhen)	Military[a]
13	Directors and deputy directors of divisions; chiefs and deputy chiefs of sections (ke)	Magistrates and deputy magistrates		Regiment commander
14				Deputy regiment commander
15				
16				
17		Directors and deputy directors of bureaus; section chiefs and deputy chiefs		Battalion commander
18	Section members (keyuan)	deputy chiefs		Deputy battalion commander
19				Company commander
20		Section members	Chiefs of xiang and zhen	Deputy company commander
21				Platoon commander
22				Deputy platoon commander
23	Administrative personnel (banshiyuan)	Administrative personnel		
24				
25	Support personnel (qinza renyuan)	Support personnel		
26				
27				
28				
29				
30				

Source. Cao Zhi, ed., Zhonghua Renmin Gongheguo Renshi Zhidu (Beijing: Beijing Dafue Chubanshe, 1985), 269–71.
a. Military officers are entitled to civilian-grade jobs when they are transferred to the civilian sector.

initially designed only for wage scales, the grade system codified the distribution of power and prestige within the gigantic bureaucracy. Each enterprise and business unit had, and still has, a ranking equivalent to some territorial unit. A university may be at the ministry level; in that case it would enjoy the administrative rights of ministry-level units in such areas as personnel, financing, and communication with other units. Usually research institutes corresponded to the county level, and the leaders of such an institute were considered county-level cadres, with all the appropriate privileges.

The immense size and hierarchy of the Chinese bureaucracy accentuated such well-known malaises of any large bureaucracy as leakage of authority, disputes over jurisdiction, displacement of goals, and inefficiency. There were several additional factors unique to the Chinese bureaucracy that further aggravated these problems.

The Chinese bureaucracy monopolizes political authority while not being accountable to anyone—except to top political leaders, who derive their authority from the offices they hold within the bureaucracy. The series of social revolutions—such as land reform, collectivization, the peaceful transformation of industry, and the antirightist campaign—completely eliminated any social force that could check on the bureaucracy. No forums where political issues could be discussed existed outside the party-state apparatus. Although the party-state and other mass organizations could be nominally distinguished, in reality mass organizations existed only as a "transmission belt." Despite the official position that the bureaucracy is the instrument of the proletarian dictatorship, the theoretically dominant groups do not have any direct control over the bureaucracy.

The scope of activities that the bureaucracy regulated was comprehensive and inclusive. In other words, the entire society was bureaucratized. All Chinese belong to a unit (*danwei*), each of which is organized to be as self-sufficient as possible ("big and complete, small and complete"—*da er chuan, xiao er chuan*). For example, each unit managed a wide range of support facilities for its members, such as dining halls, motor pools, repair teams, hotels, printing shops, health clinics, kindergartens, nursery schools, barber shops, bath houses, and retail shops (see table 31). Approx-

Table 31.   Distribution of Support Units by Type of Service

Source	Organizations		Persons	
	No.	%	No.	%
Dining	69	11.0	1,543	8.7
Motor pool	63	10.1	2,161	12.2
Nursery	52	8.3	2,114	11.9
Hotel	77	12.3	4,489	25.3
Public affairs	75	8.6	869	4.9
Technician	37	5.9	548	3.1
Telephone	53	8.5	630	3.5
Health clinic	62	9.9	592	3.4
Repair team	29	4.6	2,195	12.2
Printing shop	46	7.3	1,089	6.2
Conference room	28	4.5	212	1.2
Nursing home	8	1.3	264	1.5
Farm	6	1.0	377	2.1
Other	37	5.9	587	3.3

Source. *Jingji Fazhan Yu Tizhi Gaige*, no. 7, 1986, 7–12.

imately 25 percent of all personnel are employed in support services,[5] but the regime plans to reduce them to 15 percent.[6] It is said that Chinese universities have almost everything for their members' needs except a cemetery. The unit takes care of "one person's entire life from birth to death, clothing, eating, living, activities, studying culture [*wenhua*], and participating in labor; there is nothing that is unrelated to the administration."[7] Within each unit, the division of labor, specialization, and professionalization of its members are minimal, largely because of Mao's worry that functional specialization would lead to the restratification of Chinese society.

The idea of organizing each unit to be self-sufficient can also be traced back to guerrilla warfare practice. During the war period, state organs, associations, military units, and schools were dispersed in rural areas, moving around according to the changing

5. *Jingji Fazhan Yu Tizhi Gaige*, no. 7, 1986, 7–12.
6. *Zhongguo Xingzheng Guanli*, no. 4, 1986, 13.
7. *Zheng Zhi Yu Zhengzhi Kexue* (Beijing: Qunzhong Chubanshe, 1984), 95.

battle situation. Consequently, every unit had to have personnel to take care of the needs of the entire unit.[8] The practice continued after 1949, largely because of Mao's commitment to egalitarianism, his dislike of the division of labor and functions, his admiration of simplistic collectivism, and the regime's reluctance to use market mechanisms for the flow of information, materials, and service. Moreover, in Mao's view an organization and a community were indistinguishable. The organization replaced the community (*xiang*), the village became the brigade and production team, and the work unit became the basis for the residential community.

Organizing the entire society along the lines of "big and complete, small and complete" results in inefficiency and bloated personnel. For example, when all the printing shops in society are operating two or three shifts, many government printing facilities sit idle. Higher educational institutions cannot increase student enrollment because of shortages in dormitory facilities. Adding one additional car requires a new driver and support, such as housing for his family. Any cadre fired from his job loses all his support base.

In 1983, the Secretariat suggested the socialization of state support works, that is, the transfer of support works to independent enterprises, which will be managed according to economic principles by providing services to other clients. Many, however, are extremely reluctant to give their support work to independent units because "when the service industry in society is not ideal, support personnel are more important than the cadre."[9]

This kind of organizational structure does not allow much room for individuals to make decisions, but it grants a wide scope of power to the unit. Each unit makes decisions not only on matters pertaining to its tasks, but also on issues relating to the private lives of the unit members from birth to death. Theoretically, members of a unit own the unit. But in reality, it is the unit which owns the members. In turn, cadres who are officially responsible for managing the unit virtually own it.

Collectivization theoretically means collective ownership by peasants, but in reality "collective ownership" means that the collective owns

8. *Zhongguo Xingzheng Guanli*, no. 11, 1986, 16–18.
9. *Jingji Fazhan Yu Tizhi Gaige*, no. 7, 1986, 7–12.

us peasants as well as the resources we work on. The cadres who
control the collective then do whatever they please with our lives.
They behave no differently from the local bullies we heard so much
about from the recall-bitterness accounts of our fathers. However,
the strongmen of the 1930s and 1940s had no legitimate claim on the
peasants, who regarded them as excesses of the traditional society.
The cadres, on the other hand, enjoy the total authority given to
them by the socialist system. Chairman Mao once said that the scriptures were good, only that they had from time to time been recited
by priests with crooked mouths. I wonder about these scriptures; it
seems that they have distorted the mouths instead.[10]

The Chinese bureaucracy was highly politicized. Mao's idea
of "politics in command" implies that no area of human activity
should be left outside the political realm. Every decision, whether
it is political, economic, or social, is of a political nature. Thus,
political criteria—rising from the perspective of class struggle—
should be used in making decisions. No other consideration, either
of ethics or of unique laws governing the specific field, should be
taken into account when the decision is made. "Politics in command" provided the bureaucracy with ample justification for the
command style of work, which refused to be restrained by any
objective law governing separate functional fields.

The combined effect of this hierarchy, inclusive functions, and
politicization of the Chinese bureaucracy was minimal lateral contact between units. Most of the coordination and interaction of
units on the same level had to be channeled through a superior
authority, which administratively allocated most necessary resources, finances, and services to subordinate units, thereby minimizing the need for communications or interactions among units
or individuals belonging to different units. In other words, the
regime relied on political coordination while neglecting functional
coordination and coordination based on exchanges. In turn, the
absence of functional coordination further encouraged each unit to
pursue self-sufficiency in every aspect, acting like an independent
kingdom. Any kind of work that required interoffice coordination

10. Helen Siu, "Collective Economy, Authority, and Political Power in Rural
China," in Myron J. Aronoff, ed., *The Frailty of Authority* (New Brunswick, N.J.:
Transaction, 1986).

required several months because every office wanted to "research and research" and "discuss and discuss."

In addition, the party ordinarily maintains tight control over administrative as well as other functional bureaucracies, rendering meaningless organizational distinctions among the party, the state, enterprise units, and business units. The party not only has its own bureaucratic hierarchy paralleling the state structure, but it also penetrates every formal organization and institution. Party members hold key positions in government as well as in economic and social organizations. Most cadres, particularly leading ones, were party members subject to party command. Within the party bureaucracy, power gradually became concentrated in the hands of the first secretary, with party committees and congresses acting merely as rubber stamps. When the regime stressed collective decision-making, the bureaucratic system encountered a different kind of problem.

> Because of the idea of collective decision-making, numerous meetings are held. But often no decision is made, and even already decided policy is seldom implemented at the lower levels. Middle-level bureaucrats simply copy instructions from above and transmit them below. Documents are numerous, but concrete directives are very few, and the cadres do not understand the situation at the lower levels. Not all staff members attend to their work. When a general meeting of leaders is called, less than half of them attend. Even those who attend are divided in their opinions and engage in endless discussion, so that the problems remain unresolved. As for really handling matters, they just take turns signing their names on the documents and expressing their opinions, so that it takes a lot of time to circulate the documents among them. If something concerns their gains and losses, or if they are held responsible for it, it would take even more time for them to pass the documents from one to another.[11]

Although power was concentrated at the upper echelons of the bureaucracy and the bureaucracy regulated all aspects of an individual's life, the Chinese political process has never been highly institutionalized. Low-level institutionalization of the Chinese bureaucracy granted the cadres enormous discretionary power,

11. *Xuexi Lundan*, no. 2, 1983, 20.

thereby allowing them to employ their personal and idiosyncratic features in performing their official duties.

In addition, some Chinese administrative practices further increased the cadres' power. The official guidelines on any policy have always been broad and ambiguous, leaving a great deal of leeway for leading cadres at each level. Although its intended purpose was to enable the cadres to incorporate the concrete conditions of the localities in the process of policy implementation, they could easily exploit that leeway for personal gain or for local interests.

Moreover, Chinese administrative practice was to keep cadres for a long time in one position—known as the "life-tenure system"—which can be traced back to three factors. First, senior Chinese cadres are the first generation of revolutionaries who believed that "those who contributed to the revolution are justified in becoming cadres." Second, due to the unavailability of employment opportunities outside the inclusive state structure, the regime has no way of disposing of excessive personnel after a reduction in the bureaucracy or of cadres who have finished their terms. Third, the socialist state is responsible for the cadres, regardless of whether they are on active duty or not.

Although such a system provides long-term security and employment, it also produces a waste of talent, frustration, dependency, and a loss of initiative. Serving at one post for a long time may make leading cadres familiar with their own units, but it also helps develop "complicated human networks" involving superiors, colleagues, subordinates, and family members, making it easy for leading cadres to "privatize" their formal authority, while forming a "leading strata" quite separate from ordinary people throughout China.[12] As Andrew Walder succinctly demonstrates, the leading cadres frequently exploited their formal authority to reward the obedient while penalizing the disobedient, thus developing elaborate patronage networks.[13]

Even if we assume that many leading cadres have been exercising their formal authority impartially and justly according to the

12. This is why many family members work in the same unit. *Zhongguo Xing-zheng Guanli*, no. 7, 1986, 25; no. 6, 1987, 34.

13. Andrew G. Walder, *Communist Neo-Traditionalism: Work and Authority in Chinese Industry* (Berkeley and Los Angeles: University of California Press, 1987).

intention of official guidelines, the mere fact that they have jurisdiction on innumerable matters crucially relevant to the daily life of
ordinary people indicates that the Chinese masses were highly
dependent on administrative decisions. Since power in an organizational setting can be defined in terms of the "structural phenomenon of dependency," whether or not cadres made decisions
in line with the wishes and best interests of members of the unit
had no bearing on the power imbalance between cadres and the
masses.[14]

Furthermore, there was not much room for individuals to challenge the formal authority exercised by bureaucrats of the party-
state in their own units. Any challenge to an individual leader is
considered a challenge to the party-state, because, as the work
teams during the CR argued, individual leaders could claim to represent the party committee, and the lower-level party committee
could claim to represent the higher party authority. Thus, any challenge to a unit leader becomes criticism of that individual leader's
unit and is often construed as a challenge to the authority of the
party-state. No mechanism to check abuse of power by the cadres
has been formalized. Mass participation in political campaigns,
leadership participation in labor, and criticism and self-criticism became rituals without having much impact on the operation of the
overall structure.

In sum, the structural characteristics of the Chinese bureaucracy
were not conducive to the democratization of human relations
in China. On the contrary, the unique features of the Chinese
bureaucracy allowed the cadres to wield an unprecedented amount
of power as agents of the party-state. The cadres were not only the
implementors of policy decisions but also the policy formulators in
a country where there was no distinction between politician and
bureaucrat.[15] High-level cadres often exercised the formal authority of the party and the party-state and formulated official policies.
When the absence of strong leaders such as Stalin or Mao allowed
the Leninist Party to make decisions according to "democratic centralism," the preference of the lower-level cadres were bound to

14. Jeffrey Pfeffer, *Power in Organization* (Boston: Pitman, 1981).
15. For the distinction between politicians and the bureaucrats, see Joel D. Aberbach, Robert D. Putnam, and Bert A. Rockman, eds., *Bureaucrats and Politicians in
Western Democracies* (Cambridge, Mass.: Harvard University Press, 1981).

influence the policy choices of the party-state. In this process the cadres' experiences, perceptions, and values are bound to be reflected in their policy preferences. In other words, the organizational structure of the Chinese bureaucracy reinforced, rather than modified, the persistent traditional way of thinking on the part of the cadres and the ordinary masses.

It is ironic—and tragic for China—that the CCP's efforts to remove all sources of exploitation and inequality have resulted in the new system of units (*danwei*), which probably limits freedom and mobility more than traditional institutions. In traditional China, such diverse institutions as class, kinship, and community, at least, allowed each individual to identify with many different groups. But in socialist China, the practice of organizing each unit—which has its own rankings as ministry-level unit or county-level unit—to be self-sufficient in meeting most of its members' social needs, an interesting combination of the "life-tenure system" with the practice of "unit ownership" has allowed the traditional social networks and practices to enter in the operation of the unit, thus perpetuating the "feudal mentality" of the cadres. As many Chinese scholars insist, this feudal mentality is in part derived from traditional Chinese culture and in part reinforced by the "peasant mentality of the cadres," many of whom are from the poorest groups in the rural areas. But it should also be pointed out that the organizational structure in China has been as much responsible for the feudal mentality of the cadres as resilient Chinese cultural tradition. The most urgent agenda for political reform in China is the development of a new organizational structure which, instead of reinforcing the traditional political culture, will be conducive to producing a modern outlook in cadres. Without the structural changes of "department ownership," the "life-tenure system," and "big and complete, and small and complete," the feudal mentality of the cadres and the ordinary people will continue.

GROWTH AND DISTRIBUTION OF CADRES

To staff this gigantic bureaucracy, China developed about 20 million cadres by 1982 and 29 million by 1988 (see table 32). The size of the cadre corps increased steadily after 1949. In 1958, the ratio of cadres to citizens was 1:80, but it reached 1:50 in 1982. It grew by more than 370 percent from 1952 to 1982, whereas the number of people working in the administrative sector only doubled in the same period.[16] The most rapid increase occurred between 1971 and 1973, when the CR rebels were becoming cadres, whereas temporary decreases took place after the 1953 party rectification (for those employed in state and mass organs), the 1957–58 simplification of the administration, and the initial stages of the CR.

Although we do not know how the total number of cadres employed in the states were distributed by party and government organs, the table of organization the regime is setting up indicates that about 14 percent of the total authorized personnel in state organs are party cadres, 5 percent are mass organization, and 5 percent are other.[17]

The regime has managed successfully to limit the size of the State Council, although its size fluctuates largely with political movements and economic centralization and decentralization.[18] Nonetheless, the number of cadres at the provincial, district, municipal, and county levels has increased steadily, regardless of the decentralization and recentralization of economic decision-making authority (see table 33). In 1949 the regime decreed that an average-sized provincial government should have approximately 600 cadres spread over twenty offices. But the actual numbers of provincial cadres swelled rapidly. For example, Hubei province had 4,000 cadres by 1961, more than six times the originally approved ceiling; this number increased to 5,692 by the time of the CR and to 8,600 by 1982. The growth was particularly rapid immediately following the purge of the Gang of Four.[19] By 1983, the authorized manpower ceiling for Hubei increased to 6,000 persons with an eighty-office limit.[20]

The increase at district and municipal levels paralleled the

16. The administrative sector refers to the party, government, and mass organizations in the 1982 census.

17. *Zhongguo Xingzheng Guanli*, no. 4, 1986, 10–13.

18. Guowuyuan Bangongting Diaocha Yanjiushi, ed., *Zhongguo Xingzheng Guanlixue Chutan* (Beijing: Jingji Kexue Chubanshe, 1984), 45–54. The number of economic enterprises and business units directly under the State Council increased from 1,260 in 1978 to 2,680 in 1981. *Zhongguo Xingzheng Guanli*, no. 5, 1987, 27.

19. *Shijian*, no. 2, 1982, 16–17.

20. *Shehui Kexue Dongtai* (Hubei), no. 11, 10 April 1983.

Table 32. Increase in Number of Employees in Administrative Organs and Number of Cadres, 1949–88 (millions)

Year	No. of Employees in State and Mass Organizations	Cadres Administrative No.	Administrative %	Technical No.	Technical %	Cadres No.	Cadres %
1949		1.799	60	1.194	40	2.99	100
1952	258.5	3.302	61	2.043	39	5.34	100
1953	274.4						
1954	261.6						
1955	283.5	3.800	57	2.892	43	6.69	100
1956	294.3	4.200	55	3.300	45	7.50	100
1957	278.9	4.212	52	3.879	48	8.09	100
1958	246.7	4.424	48	4.773	52	9.20	100
1959	273.0	4.500	47	5.157	53	9.66	100
1960	295.4						
1961	315.1	3.832	36	5.943	64		
1962	257.2						
1963	267.7						
1964	274.9	3.352	32	7.237	68	10.59	100
1965	287.0					11.60	
1966	283.0						
1967	278.0						
1968	280.0						
1969	291.0					9.20	
1970	302.0						
1971	326.9	4.685	39	7.356	61	12.04	
1972	321.0						
1973	323.8					17.00	
1974	341.1						
1975	357.6						
1976	379.6						
1977	395.4						
1978	416.6	12.000	66	6.000	34		
1979	451.0						
1980	477.1					18.00	
1981	506.7						
1982	562.7	12.000	66	8.300	40	20.30	
1983	576.0	11.000	52	10.000	48		
1987						27.00	
1988						29.03	

Table 33. Increase in Number of Cadres by Level, 1949–85

Units	1949	1953–56	1961	1964–66	1980–85
Provincial level					
Shanghai				16,000	30,000
	(21)				(85)
Beijing	(20)				(79)
Guangxi				73,000	13,000
				(80)	(102)
Hubei			4,000	5,692	8,600
			[110,400]	[108,518]	[199,121]
Inner Mongolia				[50,000]	[137,000]
Shanxi				(66)	(112)
District (*diqu*) and municipal levels					
Average of 8 Hubei districts			370	731	1,500
Average of 11 Hubei municipalities			1,267	1,591	3,454
County level					
Taiku (Shanxi; pop.: 241,116)		195	431		827
		(25)			(56)
Infen (Shanxi)					591
	(25)	(29)			(45)
Kunshan			349		865
			(35)		(56)
Huayang (Hunan; pop.: 700,065)		629	1,470		2,023
		(27)	(46)		(90)
Average of 73 Hubei counties		236	579		1,013

Source. Collected from various Chinese official publications including *Renmin Ribao*.

Note. Figures in parentheses indicate the number of offices; figures in brackets indicate the number of cadres in all four levels: provincial, municipal, district, and county.

Sources. For all employed: *Zhongguo Tongji Nianjian*, 1984. For all cadres: U.S. Department of Commerce, *Administrative and Technical Manpower in the People's Republic of China* (International Population Reports, Series P-95, no. 72; Washington, D.C., 1973); *Guanghui De Chengjiu* (Beijing: Renmin Chubanshe, 1984), 2:23. For 1987: *Renmin Ribao*, 19 Nov. 1987. For 1988: *Huaqiao Ribao*, 16 May 1988.

Note. As of 1985, there were 4,200,000 cadres in the state organization, 1,310,000 in party and mass organizations, 12,740,000 in business units, and 10,780,000 in industrial units. They can be divided into the following generations: 3,000 joined the revolution before the Long March; 230,000 during the anti-Japanese war; 4,600,000 during land reform; 4,100,000 during collectivization; 5,400,000 during the CR; and 3,000,000 in the post-Mao period. *Shehui Kexueyan Yanjiu Cankao Ziliao*, 21 Feb. 1985.

growth at the provincial level. Before the CR, the first-class organs of the Inner Mongolian municipalities averaged between 500 and 600 people, but by 1982, there were 1,400.[21] In the early 1950s district governments started with only 100 people in six or seven sections, but by 1985 they had about 1,000 cadres in forty to fifty offices. The pattern at the county level was no different. The Taiku county government had 195 people in 25 units—with only one magistrate and four deputy magistrates—in 1956. However, by 1961, its personnel numbered 431.[22] The purge and administrative simplification carried out under the official slogan "unified leadership" during the CR reduced the number of county-level government employees to one-tenth of the pre-CR strength in some places.[23] However, after the fall of the Gang of Four, county governments first regained and then went beyond their pre-CR numbers and in many places doubled their cadre size.[24]

One of the most important factors in the proliferation of offices and the population explosion among cadres was the expanding role of the party-state, particularly in the economic arena. As China developed into a complex society and the state's functions expanded economically, the number of the organs increased.[25] For example, offices in the State Council dealing with such administrative works as foreign affairs, political-legal work, and education changed very little over time, but the number of offices in the economic arena fluctuated widely. In 1952, there were thirty-two organs dealing with finance and economics in the State Council, the number increasing to 66 by 1981.[26] Similar patterns could be seen in Beijing and Shanghai: the growth rate of administrative offices has been quite modest, but the number of offices handling economic questions increased almost 2,000 percent between 1949 and 1982. Social services offices, including education (wenjia), city planning, and environment, also increased drastically. In 1955,

21. Xuexi Lundan, no. 2, 1983, 20.

22. Zhengzhi yu Zhengzhi Kexue, 168–86.

23. For the impact of the CR on the county-level administration, see Renmin Ribao, 30 March 1968; 19 July 1968; 20 July 1968. See also Zuguo Yuekan, no. 56, 1 November 1968.

24. Zhengzhi yu Zhengzhi Kexue, 168–86; Zhongguo Xingzheng Guanli, nos. 4–5, 1986.

25. Ibid.

26. Dongyan Lunzhong (Jinan), no. 6, 1984, 27–30.

about one-fourth of county government staff dealt with the economy; the current figure is approximately two-thirds.[27]

Also China's practice of the "iron rice bowl" system, while failing to set up an effective retirement system until recently, further contributed to the increase in cadres.[28] Every political campaign increased the number of bureaucrats by promoting campaign activists to cadre positions. And those dismissed from their positions as a result of the campaigns were usually fewer than those newly recruited. Deng Xiaoping's rehabilitation policy further aggravated the bloated bureaucracy. As noted, he reinstated all of the dismissed cadres, but he did not thoroughly rid the cadres who had come in during or after CR, partly because he did not want to repeat Mao's mistake of carrying out a large-scale purge and partly because he did not have enough power.[29]

The Chinese bureaucracy was not only huge in size but also top heavy with "responsible persons." According to the 1982 census, the nationwide total of responsible cadres in party, government, and industrial enterprises and business units came to 8,130,987. This means that 1.56 percent of all employed people in China and 39 percent of the 21 million cadres had managerial duties[30] (see table 34). Another Chinese source reveals that there were 5.4 million cadres with the rank of county magistrate and deputy magistrate; among them the number of administrative cadres with ranks higher than deputy division director (fu chuzhang) of a county was about 450,000.[31] CR rehabilitation further aggravated the situation. Since most of the purged cadres' former positions had been filled

27. For the numbers of the different types of offices in Shanghai and Beijing in 1949 and 1982, see Zhongguo Xingzheng Guanli, no. 1, 1986, 3.
28. Michel Oksenberg, "Exit Patterns from Chinese Politics and Its Implications," China Quarterly, no. 67, September 1976, 501–18.
29. Zhengzhi yu Zhengzhi Kexue, 168–86.
30. Responsible persons of the state and other organs included: (1) those at the central level—the National People's Congress, the supreme court, the attorney general's office, the State Council, and all ministries, commissions, bureaus, offices, and other organs; (2) those at the provincial level—people's congresses, people's courts, people's procurators, people's governments, and various departments, bureaus, and other organs; (3) those at the district, municipality, and county levels—people's congresses, people's courts, people's prosecutor, people's governments, and bureaus and other sections. The term "responsible person" in parties and mass organs refers to leading cadres in each sector. Zhiye Fenlei Biaozhun (Beijing: Guojia Tongji Ju, March 1982).
31. Song Zhending, ed., Dangdai Ganbu Baike (Tianjin: Renmin Chubanshe, 1986), 1405.

Table 34.   Breakdown of Responsible Persons by Area and Gender, as of 1982

Level	Male		Female		Total	
	No.	%	No.	%	No.	%
State Organs						
Central	13,652	84	2,554	16	16,206	0.19[a]
Provincial	63,367	90	6,544	10	69,911	1.81[a]
						0.85
District, municipality, and county	766,949	95	41,844	5	808,793	7.80
						0.16
Total	843,968	94	50,942	6	894,910	9.94
						0.17
						11.00
Basic levels						
Cheng zhen	22,219	75	6,131	25	28,350	0.34
Urban residential committee	16,564	16	83,831	84	100,395	0.01
						1.23
Commune	257,367	96	10,563	4	267,930	0.05
						3.29
Total	296,150	75	100,525	25	396,675	0.08
						4.87
Parties and mass organs						
CCP	859,659	93	67,224	7	926,883	0.18
						11.39
CYL and labor organs	215,133	63	127,300	37	342,433	0.07
						4.20

Democratic parties	15,311	90	1,624	10	16,935	0.00 0.20
Total	1,090,103	85	196,148	14	1,286,251	0.25 15.81
Industrial enterprises and business units						
Leaders	2,442,384	93	192,645	7	2,635,029	0.51 32.40
Subleaders	2,613,959	90	304,163	10	2,918,122	0.56 35.88
Total	5,056,343	91	496,808	9	5,553,151	1.06 68.20
Total, all levels	7,286,564	90	844,423	10	8,130,987	1.56

Source. Reconstructed from census data in Guowuyuan Renkou Bucha Bangongshi, ed., Zhongguo 1982 Renkou Bucha 10% Chuxiang Ziliao (Beijing: Zhongguo Tongji Chubanshe, 1983), by combining several industries: excavation (mining and geology), construction (construction and transportation), and services (housing, health, education, science, and finance).

a. First percentage is based on the total number of employed (521 million); second percentage is based on all responsible persons.

Table 35. Distribution of Responsible Persons by Industry, as of 1982

| | Organs | | | | | | | | | Managers | | | Total | |
| | Government | | | Party | | | Mass Organs | | | | | | | |
Sector and No. Employed	No.	%a	%b	No.	%a	%b	No.	%a	%b	No.	%a	%b	No.	%a
Agriculture 384,155,030	1,788	.40	.20	50,993	11.50	4.0	3,044	.70	.80	388,567	87.4	7.0	444,392	0.1
Excavation 10,726,231	1,866	.40	2.00	90,560	20.00	7.0	975	.20	.20	356,640	79.2	7.0	450,041	4.2
Manufacture 61,668,204	438	.02	.04	379,512	17.00	30.0	1,672	.50	.40	1,882,240	83.1	34.0	2,263,862	4.0
Construction 20,990,391	4,233	.06	.04	126,551	19.00	10.0	545	.08	.10	524,474	79.0	94.0	655,803	3.0
Commerce 15,507,928	3,178	.03	.40	87,278	8.60	7.0	465	.05	.10	922,746	91.0	17.0	1,013,667	6.5
Service 8,768,002	8,415	.63	.90	107,830	8.10	8.0	1,730	.13	.40	1,213,528	91.0	22.0	1,331,503	15.0
Administrative 8,018,618	872,019	45.00	97.00	442,632	23.00	34.0	387,579	19.00	98.00	250,850	13.0	5.0	1,953,080	24.0
Others	973	13.00	.10	898	12.00	.06	455	6.10	.10	5,126	69.0	6.9	7,452	6.9
Total	894,910	11.00		286,251	16.00		396,475	5.00		5,553,151	68.3		7,130,787	

Source. Reconstructed from census data in Guowuyuan Renkou Bucha Bangongshi, ed., Zhongguo 1982 Renkou Bucha 10% Chuxiang Ziliao (Beijing: Zhongguo Tongji Chubanshe, 1983), by combining several of the industries: excavation (mining and geology), construction (construction and transportation), and services (housing, health, education, science, and finance).

a. Based on the number of responsible persons in each sector.
b. Based on the number of responsible persons in relation to the total numbers employed in the sector.

by new people, the regime simply created more deputy positions to accommodate the rehabilitated.

> In many departments or units, posts are created to suit the officials, so that there is a great number of deputies and nominal directors. Some bureaus have staffs of only a few dozen people but more than ten directors and deputy directors—in addition to numerous section chiefs, deputy chiefs and office directors. So only a few of the staff members are "secretaries" in charge of concrete work.[32]

The ministry of metallurgy had twenty-seven vice ministers by 1982.[33]

As shown in table 35, over two-thirds (68.3 percent) of this rather large group of so-called responsible persons were employed in industrial enterprises and business units; 16 percent were leaders of party organs, the size almost equivalent to the total number of government leaders at the central, provincial, and county levels. But comparing the numbers of leaders at the central and middle levels with those in the party organs may be misleading because the category of leading party cadres included leaders in the enterprises and business units. However, given the fact that a person holding both an administrative and a party position was required to report only one position in the census, the number of reported responsible persons in the party was probably on the low side. It is worth noting that the leading cadres at the middle level— district, municipal, and county—constituted 90 percent of all responsible persons in government organs.

In speaking of individual industries, if one assumes that the ratio of leaders to people in each sector is indicative of the party-state's control over the sector, the weakest area by 1982 was agriculture, where there was only one leader for every 1,000 persons (see table 35). By contrast, almost one-quarter of all those employed in the administrative sector were considered responsible. In other fields, the proportion ranges from 3 percent in construction to 15 percent in service industries. The ratio between leading cadres and workers employed in service industries is misleading as an indicator of the party-state's control, because most of the lead-

32. *Daily Report*, 2 March 1982, R4–6; *Renmin Ribao*, 19 September 1980; 19 September 1980.

33. *Asian Economics* (Japanese), no. 53, 6 March 1982, 61.

Table 36. Employment Patterns by Province, as of 1982–85

Province	Total Population	No. Employed	No. Employed by State/Party	No. of Cadres		No. of Responsible Persons	No. of Admin. Staff (banshiyuan)	No. of Scientific and Technical Personnel
Anhui	50,560,000	26,020,892	256,716	600,000	(1983)	314,012	228,046	1,004,772
Beijing	9,340,000	5,427,502	255,898	650,000	(1982)	219,116	233,540	739,509
Fujian	26,400,000	11,747,523	202,918			164,989	184,971	609,871
Hebei	54,200,000	27,498,985	549,115	800,000	(1982)	402,512	355,657	1,189,097
Heilongjiang	33,060,000	13,316,170	414,267	900,000	(1981)	431,420	414,267	1,224,903
Henan	75,910,000	39,804,811	415,326	904,000	(1983)	426,336	388,939	1,584,305
Hubei	48,350,000	25,747,496	356,064	900,000	(1983)	452,542	299,957	1,341,733
Hunan	55,090,000	28,277,496	412,975			341,576	290,614	1,157,667
Guansu	19,880,000	10,324,042	145,164	353,000	(1982)	132,224	145,164	452,864
Guangdong	60,750,000	30,673,733	560,801	1,000,000	(1983)	415,981	421,052	1,465,773
Guangxi	37,330,000	18,615,027	207,145	1,040,000	(1978)	194,128	175,481	685,936
Guizhou	29,010,000	13,987,354	204,360	447,098	(1984)	163,363	137,629	506,212
Inner Mongolia	19,550,000	9,063,281	264,943	174,558	(1982)	197,131	196,733	629,824
Jiangsu	61,350,000	34,763,115	393,249			611,999	370,513	1,815,984
Jiangxi	33,840,000	15,565,000	236,887			228,820	182,611	771,083
Jilin	22,700,000	12,130,000	213,154	570,000	(1984)	278,842	206,260	776,551
Liaoning	36,290,000	17,792,058	399,829			556,777	403,776	1,470,079
Ningxia	3,895,578	1,820,328	32,991	148,000	(1982)	30,549	30,384	109,627
Qinghai	3,930,000	1,854,349	48,367			35,961	38,095	136,680
Shaanxi	29,310,000	15,051,649	234,528	530,000	(1984)	228,683	229,195	873,529

Shandong	75,640,000	40,097,853	444,768		511,314	355,807	1,742,516
Shanghai	11,940,000	7,436,267	166,623	30,765[a]	235,715	229,145	792,770
Shanxi	25,720,000	13,075,355	267,920	480,000 (1981)	246,631	212,350	795,936
Sichuan	100,760,000	1,400,000	570,704	1,400,000 (1983)	551,736	525,216	2,047,527
Tianjin	7,890,000	4,414,054	128,252	280,000 (1980)	152,274	145,416	447,642
Tibet	1,930,000	1,016,387	36,218	33,000 (1978)	42,434	128,252	42,434
Xinjiang	13,180,000	6,138,095	154,027	422,930 (1983)	136,789	132,569	497,202
Yunnan	33,190,000	16,642,228	211,055		168,510	166,005	618,440
Zhejiang	39,630,000	20,975,899	234,282	1,140,000 (1984)	312,068	181,442	594,450

Sources. Guowuyuan Renkuo Bucha Bangongshi, ed., Zhongguo 1982 nian Renkuo Bucha Ziliao (Beijing, Guowuyuan Renkuo Bucha Bangongshi, 1982). The cadre figures are collected from Renmin Ribao, 20 Aug. 1983; Henan Ribao, 29 Aug. 1983; Nanfang Ribao, 7 Sept. 1984; Xinjiang Ribao, 24 May 1980; Hebei Xuekan, 1982, no. 4:13–20; Hunan Ribao, 26 Apr. 1982; Keyen Guanli, 1981, no. 3; Guizhou Nianjian, 1985, 291; Jiaoxue Cankao, 15 Mar. 1985; Dangde Shenghuo, 9 July 1980.

a. Shanghai figure includes only cadres employed in the municipal party and government organs.

ing cadres in that sector were managers. The ratio between all those employed and the party's leading cadres in the service sector was only 0.1 percent, the second lowest after the agriculture sector (0.013 percent). This sector had only one party leading cadre for every 10,000 persons employed, but in the administrative sector, there were 5.5 leading cadres for every 100 persons. These data again support the idea that the party maintained a tight control over the state organ.

In each province studied (table 36), the total number of cadres appears to approximate the number of people employed in the administrative sector, responsible persons, and the technical cadres.[34] I have tried to identify factors influencing the size of the cadre group in each province, using the T-test. The only significant correlations were between responsible persons as a percentage of the provincial and urban populations (P = 0.003; coefficient = 0.024), and the proportion of students in institutions of higher education (P = 0.045; coefficient = 0.08). Other variables such as gross national product, degree of industrialization, urbanization, level of education, number of hospital beds, and length of highways, railways, and waterways showed no significant correlations with the number of cadres or responsible persons.[35]

AGE

A cadre's age can be considered in two ways: his chronological age and his revolutionary age, that is, how long he has been a party member. Because most postliberation cadres joined the party after graduating from school, there is often no reason to prefer revolutionary age over chronological age because they are usually very close to each other.

The mean age of responsible persons was 44.9 years old (see table 37), which was the second highest mean age among the eigh-

---

34. There is some overlapping among these cadres; for instance, some of the responsible cadres might have been counted twice because some of them are employed in all three—the state, party, and mass organs. The same might be true with the technical cadres. Also, one has to deduct blue-collar workers employed in the state, party, and mass organs.

35. For provincial data, State Statistical Bureau, *Statistical Yearbook of China* (1983).

Table 37.   Mean Ages of Male Workers, as of 1982

By Industry		By Occupation	
Industry	Age	Occupation	Age
Agriculture	32.5	Professional	
Mining	32.4	Technical personnel	32.5
Energy	32.3	Religion	55.4
Manufacture	31.0	Responsible persons	44.9
Geological prospecting	33.4	State organs	46.6
Transportation	33.1	Party and mass organs	44.6
Commerce	34.1	Lane committees and	
Housing	34.1	communes	43.3
Health	36.9	Enterprises	44.8
Education	34.4	Administrative staff	36.3
Scientific research	38.6	Commercial personnel	33.8
Finance	35.4	Service workers	38.1
		Agricultural workers	32.3
State and party	39.1	Industrial workers	29.5
Government agencies	38.8	Unclassified	24.0
Party committees	42.9		
Mass organs	42.9		
Enterprise management	38.5		
Total	32.5	Total	32.5

Source. Tuan Chi-hsien, Yu Jingyuan, and Xiao Zhenyu, "China: Employment Status, Industrial Structure, and Occupational Composition—An Analysis Based on the 1982 Census" (unpublished paper), 127–35.

ty occupational categories used in the 1982 census (the highest was 55.4 years for those in religious occupations). Responsible persons employed in state organs had the highest mean age (46.6 years) among leading cadres. For those in party and mass organizations it was about 44.6 years. Since the category "responsible persons in party and mass organs" included the Communist Youth League and other mass organizations, the average age of a responsible person in a party organ was likely to be higher than that of his counterpart in a government agency. Leading cadres were 5.5 years older than cadres employed in the administrative sector (including some leading cadres in the sector). The age group of fifty-five and over constituted only 5 percent of all those employed, but about 13 percent of responsible cadres belonged to that group.

The mean age of responsible cadres was twelve years greater

than that of the entire work force. According to one Chinese source, about 36 percent of the 21 million cadres were under 35; cadres belonging to the group between 36 and 45 years old constituted 6.8 million; between 46 and 56, 5.4 million; and 6 percent were above 56.[36] The number of the last category is close for all cadres who began work before 1949 and who are now eligible for special retirement (*lixiu*). Men between 35 and 54, who made up 33 percent of the Chinese work force, occupied 74 percent of the responsible cadre positions. Males who were 25 to 30 comprised 16 percent of all those employed, but they accounted for only 12 percent of cadres in the administrative sector and only 4 percent of "the responsible personnel." Undoubtedly, the cadres, particularly the leading cadres, were older than the general population.

Generally speaking, the generations of cadres parallel the bureaucratic hierarchy. Most of the old cadres who joined the revolution before 1949 are believed to be above grade 18 at the moment. This was due largely to the absence of a retirement system and an emphasis on seniority in personnel management. Because of the absence of an effective retirement system, all those who had previously become officials remained in the bureaucracy. Only death or a purge removed them.[37] The seniority system helped cadres (presumably with little ability or tangible achievements) to move up further in the hierarchy.

In terms of revolutionary age, the most senior group of cadres was the Long March generation, followed by the anti-Japanese war generation and then by the civil war generation. Members of the Long March generation such as Deng Xiaoping, Chen Yun, and Li Xiannian were all well over seventy and still remained at the highest level in 1982. The anti-Japanese war generation includes Zhao Zhiyang and Hua Guofeng, who joined the party in the late 1930s. Most of the rehabilitated cadres in the central government also joined the revolutionary movement prior to the civil war. If we assume that the average age of the land reform generation was twenty in 1950, most are now in their sixties.

Before the 1982 bureaucratic reforms, the highest positions in the party were held by a gerontocracy. The average age of the six

36. Song, ed., *Dangdai Ganbu Baike*, 1405.
37. Oksenberg, "Exit Patterns."

Politburo members in 1980 was seventy, and the average age of the premier and sixteen vice premiers was sixty-nine.[38] According to a 1980 magazine article, "In some provinces the average age of secretaries and deputy secretaries is in the sixties; the percentage of district and municipal committees where the leading cadres' average exceeds sixty is over 20 percent." The age problem at the county level was as serious as at the provincial level: "The average age of leading cadres is over fifty-six in a significant percentage of counties. Because of their advanced age, many cadres cannot work eight hours every day; they are often in the hospital for treatment or recuperation."[39] Nearly two-thirds of the county-level cadres in Beijing were older than sixty.[40] Yuanping county reported that 614 (44.5 percent) of their 1,378 cadres were between fifty and sixty. Only 130 (9.4 percent) were younger than forty.[41]

EDUCATION

As for the educational background of the 21 million cadres, official Chinese sources reported that as many as 19 percent of them (4 million) were college graduates, and only 40 percent finished junior high school or less.[42] Another source reported in 1987 that 29 percent of the 21 million cadres have a college-level education (6 million), 26 percent a high-school-level education, and 45 percent an educational level lower than junior high school.[43] These figures, particularly those for college-level educations, are obviously inflated, since the current official policy of emphasizing education led the cadres to inflate their level. Nonetheless, it is amazing that about one-half of China's cadre corps had educational levels lower than junior high school.

The low level was largely due to a structural problem—the absolute shortage of educated manpower. In 1982 only eight out of 1,000 employees had a college education. When the CCP liberated the

---

38. *Feijing Yuebao*, 10(22) April 1980, 19–22.
39. *Hong Qi*, no. 11, 1980, 3.
40. *Beijing Ribao*, 27 June 1981.
41. *Zhengzhi yu Zhengzhi Kexue*, 168–86.
42. That 4 million cadres are college graduates is theoretically correct because all college graduates are allocated by the party-state and start their jobs as low-level cadres.
43. Song, *Dangdai Ganbu Baike*, 1403.

country in 1949, the total number of college graduates in the entire country was less than 210,000, including the 10,000 who had studied abroad. Between 1949 and 1984, China produced 4.11 million college graduates and 41,800 postgraduates, of whom about 34,000 had been abroad to study.[44] The CR, according to a Chinese official calculation, cost China about 100,000 postgraduate students, 1 million college graduates, and 2 million graduates of specialized middle schools.[45]

The scarce resource of educated manpower was not distributed equally by sector, level, or hierarchy. There is a close correlation between age and level of education: the older the person is, the less likely he or she will have a higher-level education (see table 38). Administrative reform intended to tap the educational potential of the younger age groups.

As noted, high-ranking cadres are older than low-ranking ones. Apparently their educational level was also lower. The educational level of cadres employed in party organizations is lower than that of cadres working in state organizations. And the educational level of the leading cadres of the party organizations is particularly low.[46] The Chinese aptly described the problem as "one high and one low"—high in age and low in education. The fragmentary information we can glean from official news media paints a vivid picture of the problems caused by cadres' lack of education: "There is not a single college graduate among the first secretaries in some provinces, districts, and counties. In some provinces and counties a large number of the top leaders have a cultural level equivalent only to primary school."[47]

According to 1982 census data, only 6 percent of all employees in the administrative sector had a college-level education, and as many as 19 percent had fewer than six years of formal education. But the 6 percent of the college graduates in administration was 12 percent of all holders of bachelor's degrees that China had pro-

44. Among them, 9,106 had studied in the Soviet Union. *Guanghuai de Chengjiu* [Glorious Achievement], (Beijing: Renmin Chubanshe, 1984), 2:407.

45. For educated personnel see *Renkuo Bucha 10% Chuyang Ziliao* (Beijing: Guowuyan Renkuo Bucha Bangongshi, 1982).

46. For instance, only 1.2 percent of the intellectuals in Qinghai and 0.9 percent of all intellectuals in China are employed in the party organizations. *Shehui Kexue Cankao* (Qinghai), 20 July 1986, 11. Eight percent of the leading cadres in state organizations have a college-level education, but only 4 percent of the leading cadres in party organizations have this level of education.

47. *Renmin Ribao*, 24 September 1980.

Table 38. Education by Age Group, as of 1984

Age	Population (millions)	Intellectuals[a]			Female Illiterate	
		No.	% of Population	% of Intellectuals	% of Population	% of Population
60+	76.6	241,460	.31	4.0	14.6	79.4
55–60	33.9	213,080	.63	3.5	15.7	67.9
50–54	40.8	386,710	.95	6.4	18.8	61.7
45–49	47.3	762,590	1.00	12.7	21.3	52.1
40–44	48.3	1,061,830	2.20	17.6	24.9	38.7
35–39	54.2	773,930	1.40	12.9	28.3	28.0
30–34	72.9	567,470	.77	9.4	28.7	26.2
25–29	92.5	755,250	.81	12.5	30.1	22.4
20–24	74.3	656,340	.88	10.9	28.7	14.3
15–19	125.3	601,870	.48	10.0	26.4	9.4
Total	666.0	6,020,530[b]	.90	100.0	25.7	

Sources. Xinhua Wenzhai, no. 8, 1984, 6–7. For illiterates: Zhonghua Renmin Gongheguo Ziliao Shouce (Beijing: Shehui Kexue Wenxian Chubanshe, 1986), 308.

a. "Intellectuals" was defined as people with a college-level education.
b. Another source reports that there were 4,417 110 college graduates as of 1982, 0.4% of the total population. Xinhua Wenzhai, no. 8, 1984, 6–7.

duced since 1949. The overall educational level of responsible persons was lower than those employed in the administrative sector: 5.7 percent of responsible persons were college graduates, and 21 percent of them were high school graduates in contrast to 31 percent of the administrative sector. Of the leading cadres, 71 percent had an educational level of junior high school or below, compared with 60 percent of those employed in the party-state.

Since the responsible persons category included some specialized cadres who had more education than the leading cadres in the administrative sector, the educational level of the leading administrative cadres might be lower than the average educational level of the responsible persons. Among the 450,000 leading administrative cadres at the county level and above, 230,000 (51 percent) had less than a junior high school education.[48] Particularly low was the educational level of political cadres, especially those at the basic level. According to one source, about 60–80 percent had educational levels lower than junior high school.[49] It seems that the quality of administrative cadres had not improved very much since 1955, because, according to one estimate, out of 3.8 million administrative cadres in 1955, 4 percent were college graduates, 34 percent had completed junior high school, and roughly 50 percent had fewer than nine years of education.[50]

Of 260,000 functional cadres (*yewu ganbu*) working in economic planning, 21 percent had a college-level education, much higher than the average of the whole cadre crops.[51] Among the leading cadres of Inner Mongolia's municipalities and counties, only 5.6 percent were college or specialized middle-school graduates. Political cadres at the municipal and county levels were less educated. Among all the standing committee members of Inner Mongolia's municipalities and districts, there were only two college graduates, twenty senior high school graduates, and ninety-six junior high school graduates.[52] In such economically advanced provinces as

48. By contrast, 45 percent of 5.4 million cadres of the same ranks, which include functional cadres, had an educational level lower than junior high school. Song, *Dangdai Ganbu Baike*, 1405.

49. *Guangming Ribao*, 22 May 1982.

50. U.S. Department of Commerce, *Administrative and Technical Manpower in the People's Republic of China*, International Population Reports, Series P-95, no. 72, Washington, D.C., 1976, 12.

51. *Jingji Jihua Yenjiu*, 25 May 1983, 30–32.

52. *Shijian*, no. 9, 1982, 19–21.

Zhejiang, the cadres were somewhat better educated: 8.4 percent of standing committee members, county magistrates, and deputy magistrates had a college-level education.[53] In contrast, Anhui province reported that of the 129 leading cadres in its twelve counties only one was a college graduate (0.7 percent); there were four graduates of specialized middle schools (3.1 percent) and seventeen high school graduates (13 percent). Some districts in the province had no college graduates.[54]

The situation in the rural areas was worse. According to one estimate, there was one college graduate for every ten communes; and there were an average of 3.7 scientific cadres for every 10,000 peasants. The educational system could not produce enough professionally competent people to replace the existing cadre corps. There were 380,000 state-owned enterprises, but only 20,000 students in all the finance and accounting colleges. Even with a full graduating class (5,000 graduates per year) it would take seventy-six years before there were enough graduates to assign one to every state enterprise.[55]

The difference in years of schooling for agricultural workers and administrative employees was 4.4 years: 4.0 years versus 8.4 years (table 39). Those employed in the administrative sector tended to have more education than responsible persons, though their 8.4 years was not much greater than that of the responsible persons (leaders) 7.9. And the difference between leading cadres and industrial workers was only 1.2 years, or 7.9 years to 6.7. Scientific researchers and teachers were better educated than responsible persons. They had 13.8 and 10.3 years, respectively.

The cadres' ignorance and poor education made them submissive to superiors, carrying out irrational orders blindly. Although incumbents claimed to have "rich practical experience and familiarity with [their] work," their lack of formal schooling made it impossible for them to raise their "practical experience to the level of scientific knowledge."

Their reliance on experience and their inability to comprehend the internal logic of matters often produced undesirable and unintended consequences. For example, Linzhou district has a large number of

53. *Zhejiang Ribao*, 25 November 1983.
54. *Xinxiang Pinglun* (Anhui), no. 7, 1980, 5–7.
55. *Renmin Ribao*, 24 September 1980.

Table 39. Educational Level of Workers by Industry and Occupation (1982 census)

By Industry		By Occupation	
Industry	Mean Years of Schooling	Occupation	Mean Years of Schooling
Agriculture	4.0	Professional and technical personnel	9.6
Industry	6.3	Scientific researchers	13.8
Energy	7.9	Managerial and auxiliary staff	9.5
Manufacture	7.0	Teachers	10.3
Geological survey	8.0	Cultural personnel	10.1
Construction	6.8	Leaders	7.9
Communications, transportation	6.8	Government leaders	8.7
Commerce	7.1	Party leaders	8.0
Housing	6.3	Leaders of urban residential committee	6.9
Health	8.9	Rural committee leaders	7.8
Education	9.8	Leaders of enterprise and institution	8.4
Scientific research	10.3	Office workers	8.5
Finance	8.7	Administrative staff	8.3
State and parties	8.4	Political staff and security affairs	8.0
State	8.6	Post and telecommunication staff	7.7
Party	9.0	Others	7.1
Mass organization	6.8	Commercial staff	7.0
Enterprises	7.8	Service trade staff	5.6
Others	6.5	Agricultural workers	3.9
		Industrial workers	6.7
		Other Nonclassified	8.5
Total	4.9	Total	4.9

Source. Tuan Chi-hsien, Xiao Zhenyu, and Yu Jingyuan, "Education in China: An Analysis Based on the 1982 Census" (unpublished paper), 42–48.

mountains and its forest is big, and that is to our advantage. But because the cadres did not understand the interdependency of forestry and agriculture, which promoted each other dialectically, and they did not understand the scientific notion of equilibrium in ecology, they carried out a policy of "taking grain as the key" for a long time. The result was the destruction of forests without any rise in grain production. Thus, an advantage was turned into a disadvantage, and weakness replaced strength. At the same time, their low educational level, their limited knowledge, and their narrow views made them slow to accept new things and move away from their ossified ideology. The same conditions made them comfortable with the old work style of issuing an administrative order and then "cutting everything with one knife" in violation of the laws of nature.[56]

With so little education to go around, it is not surprising that specialized professional knowledge is often wanting. According to Huzhu county in Qinghai province, none of its forty-two cadres in the court system had studied law. Stories of absurd episodes caused by ignorance abound.

56. Ibid.

10

Preparation for Cadre Reform

After the rehabilitated cadre group managed to make the Four Modernizations the regime's major goal, it became increasingly evident that not only the existing cadre corps (including the reha- bilitated cadres) but also Mao's five conditions for selecting cadres were not adequate for the new tasks. Nonetheless, any effort to reform the existing cadre corps was bound to offend the political interests of various cadre groups, including the veteran cadres whom Deng Xiaoping relied on for political support. Therefore, Deng approached the leadership changes cautiously, opting for a realistic alternative, in contrast to Mao's extreme policy, which aimed at bringing about wholesale change in the leadership through the mass mobilization during the CR. He first changed the criteria for personnel management from political loyalty to the abil- ity to further economic development. Departing from the Maoist practice of purging incumbents in order to create vacancies, Deng devised a special retirement system—*lixiu*—which enabled senior veteran cadres to retire with honor and privileges, and then relied on organizational methods to remove the CR radicals from cadre positions.

CHANGING CRITERIA
FOR CADRE RECRUITMENT

Hua Guofeng originally envisioned very limited personnel changes both in the purge of the Gang of Four's followers and in the rehabil- itation of the victims of past political purges. While Hua and his group were still in power, official discussion of cadre recruitment re- flected Mao's line: the news media continued to uphold his five con- ditions for revolutionary successors, while arguing that the Gang of Four had distorted Mao's cadre line for their own political gain.[1]

1. For instance, see *Renmin Ribao*, 24 August 1978.

However, after 1978, ability and productivity were frequently mentioned as important qualities for cadres. For instance, *Renmin Ribao*, on 2 March 1978, proposed five criteria for leaders: (1) support of the pragmatic policy of revolutionary cadres, (2) party spirit, (3) personal integrity, (4) ability, and (5) understanding the real-life conditions of the masses. Commitment to revolution was dropped from the requirements, and the only obvious political criterion was support for the struggle against the Gang of Four. Mao's emphasis on a cooperative spirit and adherence to the mass line was retained, but with a slightly modified sense: requiring cadres to be concerned with the masses' hardships is more specific then merely emphasizing the mass line. The former underscores the masses' real needs, whereas the latter emphasis allowed leaders to impose their own views upon the masses. In addition, new conditions specifically included work ability, party spirit— whatever that meant—and personality. Once this definition became official, it allowed a shift of emphasis from political criteria to work-related ones.

The news media soon became more explicit in saying that cadres had to have functional knowledge. For instance, the "Rules of Inner-Party Life" that the party adopted to guide its members rejected the slogan, "Outsiders can lead insiders," calling instead for every cadre to possess some practical knowledge.[2] Deng Xiaoping personally endorsed the idea in a speech in January 1980: "Regardless of position, every [cadre] has to have a certain amount of specialized knowledge and work ability in a functional field. Those without such knowledge must study. Those with some amount must continue to study. Those who cannot or are not willing to study must be changed."[3]

At the same time, the regime stepped up criticism of the Gang of Four for having exclusively emphasized "class status" while discriminating against any cadre with "bad class background," "complicated social relations," or "historical problems." The official decision to do away with the label "rightist" and abolish the term "four bad class elements" made it theoretically possible to recruit cadres

2. *Hong Qi*, no. 6, 1980, 2–11.
3. *Selected Works of Deng Xiaoping* (Beijing: Foreign Languages Press, 1984), 208–24.

from all sectors of the Chinese population.[4] While rejecting any political criteria, the new official line attached paramount importance to "ability" and "present performance," which in contrast to "past performance" refer exclusively to the expertise needed for economic development.[5]

The emphasis on ability inevitably led to questions about the relationship between ability and "seniority" (*zige*), which, although not officially sanctioned, was the most important factor in pre-CR personnel managment and in reinstating victims of the CR. The Gang of Four had challenged the emphasis on seniority by attacking veteran cadres as "revisionists." Now, seniority was again regarded as an obstacle to improving the personnel management system. For instance, an editorial in *Renmin Ribao*, entitled "Eliminate Seniority," rejected seniority as a criterion for personnel management on the grounds that although it reflected wisdom gained from experience to a certain extent, it was not the same as ability.[6]

By the end of 1979, when the public debate on the slogan "Practice is the sole criterion for testing empirical truth" had substantially undermined Hua's power base, the top leadership felt confident enough to address the problem of aged cadres. The necessity to recruit and promote middle-aged and young cadres to leading positions was first publicly raised by Ye Jianying, the eighty-four-year-old chairman of the National People's Congress, who, as a senior member of the cadres and one who had stayed in power throughout the political upheavals, was known to stand neither wholly with the victims nor wholly with the beneficiaries of the CR.[7] After Ye's speech the organizational department of the Central Committee convened a month-long conference attended by everyone of importance in the organizational field. Hu Yaobang transmitted Deng's instruction that the aim of organizational work should be changed to fit the task of modernization.[8]

Although we have no eyewitness accounts of this meeting, it

4. *Renmin Ribao*, 17 November 1978; *Jiefang Ribao*, 29 January 1979.
5. *Beijing Ribao*, 27 February 1980.
6. *Renmin Ribao*, 28 June 1980; 22 July 1980.
7. Ibid., 30 September 1979.
8. *Ming Bao* (Hong Kong), 29 October 1979.

must have mapped out a rather detailed policy for reforming the bureaucracy. Later Song Renqiong, the new director of the organizational department, explained the intended new policy of changing leadership, using age and formal education as the most important criteria.[9] Hu Yaobang further elaborated this point by declaring, "[We should] recruit cadres from the graduates of colleges, middle schools, and specialized schools or equivalent ones. [We should] generally not directly select [cadres] from among workers and peasants who have little education."[10]

Deng endorsed Hu's point in much-publicized speeches. Demanding that party leaders at the various levels select cadres primarily from the forty-to-forty-five-year-old age group, he said, "What do we mean when we talk about people around forty years old? They are the ones who entered college in the late 1950s. It has been thirty years since the founding of the nation. Those who graduated from college in the early 1960s are now forty to forty-five years old."[11]

In another long speech at a Politburo meeting on 15 August 1980, Deng advanced the slogan of making the cadre corps "better educated, professionally more competent, and younger." Although it was obvious that many of the incumbent cadres could not meet these criteria, he did not include any grandfather clauses. Neither did he claim that there was any virtue in "redness" except for the need to "preserve the four principles"—upholding Marxism-Leninism and Mao's thought, the socialist road, the party's leadership, and the proletarian dictatorship.[12] Deng's speech was sent to the lower levels with a note instructing them to forward their opinions before 15 October 1980. After his speech the news media began discussing ways to make the cadre corps fit Deng's criteria better.

With regard to promotion, the official news media recalled that in the past it had been Deng Xiaoping who had objected to "helicopter" promotions. Therefore, the media argued that promoting younger generations of cadres to leading positions was not the

9. *Renmin Ribao*, 9 July 1980.
10. Ibid., 16 December 1980.
11. "Deng Xiaoping's Report on the Present Situation and Tasks," *Zhengming*, no. 29, March 1980, 11–23.
12. *Issues and Studies*, 17(3) (March 1981), 81–103.

same as what the Gang of Four had done and that criticizing the Gang's practice did not mean rigidly to observe a step-by-step approach. "With regard to especially outstanding cadres [we] should give them a convenient elevator so they can go up fast."[13]

Rational though the Deng policy may have seemed for increasing efficiency, it obviously discriminated against most cadres with worker and peasant backgrounds. With little formal education but much experience, they could be considered "reds," but not "experts." Thus, many strong criticisms were raised in the subtle Chinese way. Some delegates to the National People's Congress complained on behalf of those cadres who "had been working hard for several decades" for the regime.[14] Others warned the reform not to "cut everything with one knife."[15] Discontented cadres characterized the policy as an attempt to "make those who conquered the world retire" and to "make all cadres from worker and peasant backgrounds step aside."[16] Some cynics summarized the changes like this: "In the past cadre selection depended on being a 'rebel.' Now cadre selection is based on writing quality [wenzhi, a derogatory term used to refer to feeble intellectuals in traditional China], and worker-peasant cadres are forced to retire."[17]

Their complaints drew a sympathetic response from Hua Guofeng, who was still premier. In his report to the third plenum of the Fifth National People's Congress, he affirmed the need to reform the existing cadre corps. But, he declared, "we should take the necessary measures to help large numbers of government functionaries and cadres to study full or part time in order acquire and increase the general and specialized knowledge they need for the Four Modernizations. These measures include special schools and training courses for cadres either at their posts or on leave."[18]

Probably having read the critical responses to his 15 August speech, Deng made many concessions to the old cadres in his speech of 15 December 1980. He added "revolutionization" as one of the goals of reform, promised the flexible application of age and

13. *Gongren Ribao*, 25 September 1980.
14. *Renmin Ribao*, 16 September 1980; 19 December 1980.
15. Ibid., 12 September 1980.
16. Ibid., 16 December 1980.
17. *Qunzhong*, March 1981, 37; *Lilun Yu Shijian* (Shenyang), no. 4, 1981, 48; *Wenhui Bao*, 14 October 1980.
18. *Renmin Ribao*, 15 September 1980.

education requirements, and indicated that implementation of reform would be carried out gradually. More important, he tried to
calm the fears of incumbent cadres: "If we depart from our present
cadre corps, we will not be able to complete any of our tasks, and it
is impossible for us to make cadres younger."[19]

An article entitled "On the Problems of Strengthening Party
Leaders" elaborated on all the points in Deng's speech. First, the
article advocated making cadres "revolutionized, better educated,
professionally more competent, and young." Second, it conceded
that age requirements should and would not be rigidly applied.
Third, it made it clear that formal education was not the only criterion for measuring cadres' ability: "If workers and peasants come
to have professional knowledge and management ability through
self-study and training, they do not naturally fall into the above
category" (of those to be dismissed from office).[20]

Fourth, the article made specific concessions to cadres of the
land reform generation. They were promised the opportunity to
receive professional training because, "Even if they stop producing
in order to study for three years, they still will be able to serve ten
more years." Fifth, the article promised the incumbent cadres a
greater voice in selecting their successors by endorsing what is
known as the "first-enter-and-then-exit" method.[21] That is, old
cadres in positions of leadership would recruit their own successors and train (or watch) them for a while; only when the successors
proved their ability (or loyalty to the old cadres) would the old
cadres retire. This procedure was designed both to minimize the
chances that the CR rebels would become leaders and to dispel the
old cadres' doubts about the younger people's ability.

Last, while making concessions to the old cadres, the article
took a tougher position toward the younger generation of cadres
who had been promoted during the radical period: "We should
resolutely remove and expel from the leading bodies those whom
the central leading comrades describe as being one of these three
types of people: (1) those who rose in rebellion with Lin Biao and
the Gang of Four, (2) those seriously influenced by the Gang of

19. *Issues and Studies*, 17(7) (July 1981), 101–19.
20. *Hong Qi*, no. 2, 1981.
21. *Beijing Ribao*, 27 June 1981; Deng Xiaoping supported a similar method.
Dangfeng Wenti (Beijing: Zhonggong Zhongyang Dangxiao Chubanshe, 1982), 68.

Four's ideology, and (3) "those who had been involved in beating, smashing, and looting."

The article symbolized an end to the Maoist practice of using exclusively political criteria for the personnel management of cadres.

THE RETIREMENT SYSTEM

China did not have a regular retirement system for cadres. In its early days, the regime had neither an immediate need nor sufficient resources to set up an elaborate retirement system. Its most senior leaders were in their early forties, and the wage system for cadres was not introduced until 1956. The only need then was to care for the wounded and sick cadres discharged from active duty. The regime adopted a series of regulations in a piecemeal fashion to deal with the different categories of sick and disabled people. Eventually, all the scattered regulations were put together into an "insurance system," which offered lump-sum severance payment to the discharged.

In 1978, the regime changed payment to a monthly pension system, which offered 40 to 60 percent of original wages. With this package of retirement benefits, the regime encouraged old cadres voluntarily to retire, glorifying retirement as the last contribution they could make to the nation. Although the official policy may have been sound, retirement was not an ideal option for the veteran cadres at that moment.

First, traditionally, incumbents of official posts are more respected than those who have retired after successful careers. To a certain extent, this is the case in every society, but in China the practice is extreme, as indicated in the proverb, "Those in power were treated as dearly as a beloved father figure, while those out of power became strangers even in the eyes of their own children." Concerned with the future careers not only of their children but also of their grandchildren, veteran cadres were reluctant to lose the personal influence that was needed to secure a better education and jobs for their offspring.[22]

Second, despite the glorification of retirement, it was not man-

22. *Zhengming*, no. 51, January 1982.

datory for everyone. Some could stay on active duty. "Our party is leading such a large nation. In the process of prolonged struggle, the party has produced some leaders who have abundant experiences and who enjoy high prestige inside and outside China. Among such old cadres, some have good health. Having such cadres remain in the leadership positions is in the interests of party leaders."[23]

Third, the uncertainty of China's political future made retirement a risky option. At that time, voluntary retirement was considered a glorious act, but if a radical faction returned, there would be no guarantee that the promised retirement benefits would continue. Fourth, the fact that retirement was not handled by a central agency—like the Social Security administration in the United States of America—but by one's original unit made retirement more risky. The retirees' future welfare depended largely on the whim of their successors. Last, the old revolutionaries were not psychologically and sociologically prepared for retirement. Accustomed to a collective life centered in their own unit and possessing neither special skills nor personal hobbies, they were afraid of being cut off from their units.[24]

Consequently, very few cadres retired in 1982, when the regime initiated the administrative reforms, except those who were physically disabled and deputies or low-ranking staff from the middle level of the bureaucracy.[25] Some old cadres changed their minds after their initial decision to retire.[26] Others wanted to continue active duty as deputies under the nominal leadership of the young cadres whom they had selected as their successors.[27]

In order to overcome the reluctance of the old cadres, the regime gradually fattened the retirement benefits by developing a special retirement for the veteran cadres known as *lixiu*, an abbreviation of *lizhi xiuyang*, which means "leaving a job to recuperate."[28] In a

23. *Lilun Yu Shijian*, 22 February 1985.
24. *Daily Report*, 15 April 82, K16.
25. During this period only cadres at district, municipal, and county levels retired. *Nanfang Ribao*, 2 October 1980; *Renmin Ribao*, 18 November 1979.
26. *Zhongguo Nongkan*, no. 12, 1981, 30–31.
27. *Beijing Ribao*, 12 March 79.
28. The practice is also known as *changqi gongyang* (long-term recuperation), *mianzhi xiuyang* (removed from active duty to rest), and *lizhi xiuyang* (leaving position to rest).

strict sense, *lixiu* is closer to a permanent leave of absence than it is to retirement.[29] Unlike retirement (*tuixiu*) that is applied to all cadres, only a limited number of veteran cadres who met specific requirements were entitled to *lixiu*. It allowed them to retire with "unchanged political treatment" and "slightly better economic treatment."

The idea of giving special consideration to old cadres who had contributed to the foundation of the Communist regime was not entirely new in China. The 1957 regulation on the "retirement of workers and staff" had a separate section for old cadres who "had started revolutionary work before the second revolutionary war." This group of old cadres was entitled to pensions up to 14 percent more than their regular wages.[30] In 1958 the regime decided to allow veteran cadres to assume honorary positions so that they could have a long-term leave of absence with full pay. Later, the regulation changed to allow them to retire with full salary.[31]

In 1963 the Secretariat of the CCP under Deng Xiaoping proposed that old and feeble cadres with the ranks of vice minister and provincial secretary be allowed to retire while still retaining all their political and economic privileges.[32] The justification for the proposal was that it would facilitate the "cultivation of a new generation of successors" by promoting young cadres to vacancies created by the policy. Two years later, the organizational department issued a tentative regulation that lowered the required bureaucratic ranks to deputy heads at the district level. When the regulation reached the State Council, it further expanded the scope of eligibility to include all veteran cadres who had joined the party before 1937, regardless of their current ranking, and all deputy secretaries who had participated in revolutionary work prior to 1945. However, the proposal was not implemented because of the CR.

In 1978 the regime for the first time set up two different retirement systems: one for cadres and one for workers. Order no. 104 of 1978, "Temporary Regulation on Settling Old and Feeble Cadres," incorporated some of the special consideration the re-

29. *Ming Bao*, May 27, 1978.
30. Chao Zhi, ed., *Zhonghua Renmin Gongheguo Renshi Zhidu Gaiyao* (Beijing: Beijing Daxue Chubanshe, 1985), 415.
31. Ibid., 423, 427.
32. Ibid., 382.

gime had previously planned to give to the veteran cadres, using two criteria to determine eligibility: work age and bureaucratic rank. The cadres who had joined the revolution before 9 September 1949 had to have the rank of deputy secretary at district level, and those who had started their work before 1945 had to have the rank of county deputy secretary. Low-ranking cadres were entitled to *lixiu* if they had joined the revolution prior to July 1939.

Large-scale rehabilitation raised the question of how to deal with victims of the CR whose health would not allow active duty, and in November 1978 the central organizational department declared that "senior cadres who joined the revolution during the second civil war" should be allowed to retire with all the privileges of their ranks retained.

> Those with financial difficulties should be given extra help. Relatives of old cadres who died should be taken care of. Government organs and party committees at the various levels should set up organs in charge of old cadres' affairs. Organs should be staffed by persons with strong party spirit. The organizational department at the county level should set up organs or assign persons to do the work of the old cadres.[33]

As the regime embarked on sweeping administrative reforms, the idea of taking care of the needs of veteran cadres developed into a vehicle to induce old cadres to retire, and the scope of eligibility further expanded. In April 1982 the party center formally adopted the "Regulation Regarding Old Cadres' *Lixiu*," which the standing committee of the National People's Congress further modified to make more cadres eligible.[34] When the regulation was finally promulgated on 7 October, eligibility for *lixiu* was further broadened to include all cadres who joined the revolution during the first revolutionary war regardless of their current bureaucratic ranking. The anti-Japanese war cadres were eligible for *lixiu* if they held the rank of deputy magistrate, or the eighteenth grade. For civil war cadres, the rank of deputy secretary at the district level, or fourteenth grade, was required.[35]

33. Ibid.
34. Ibid.
35. Minzheng bu Zhengce Yanjiushi, ed., *Mingzheng Fagui Xuanbian* (Beijing: Zhongguo Zhengfa Daxue Chubanshe, 1986), 154.

On 27 November 1982 the central organizational department decided to treat all cadres who were grade 18 or above, but who had not yet held the position of bureau director, as though they were directors. And the personnel labor department rendered an authoritative interpretation that extended eligibility retroactively to cadres of enterprises and business units. As a result, all cadres who had started work before September 1949 and who had attained grade 18 or above were entitled to *lixiu*.[36]

In May 1983, the labor ministry issued another regulation which intended to clarify the eligibility of *lixiu* but actually further widened the eligibility by removing the requirement of bureaucratic rank. Consequently, all those who joined the revolution before 30 September 1949, regardless of their official rank, became entitled to *lixiu*. Also entitled were former Red Army soldiers, all those who had worked in the liberated areas, and all those who did underground work in the enemy area.[37] People who had started as workers in factories in the liberated areas before 1949 but who later became cadres were also eligible.[38] On 7 January 1985 the central organizational department and the united front department jointly issued a "Regulation Concerning *Lixiu* Problems of the Democratic Personnel." According to this regulation, all people who joined the democratic parties before the first political consulative conferences and who supported the CCP ever since were entitled to *lixiu*. Old specialists who met specific conditions were also qualified for special treatment after retirement.[39]

The requirements now for *lixiu* are: (1) having participated in revolutionary work before the foundation of the PRC, (2) having engaged in full-time nonmanual labor work, and (3) having received payment for work in the form of wages, supplies, or a combination of the two. In brief, anyone who worked full time for the revolution before the foundation of the PRC is now entitled to *lixiu*. Even former bureaucrats of the Manchu puppet government are eligible if they surrendered to the CCP between 1 January 1943 and 2 September 1945. They are, however, treated as liberation war cadres rather than anti-Japanese war cadres.

36. Ibid.
37. Ibid., 155–57.
38. *Dangde Shenghuo* (Heilongjiang), no. 12, 1983, 15.
39. *Nanfang Ribao*, 2 October 1980; *Zhibu Shenghou* (Beijing), no. 8, 1986, 42.

As to the age requirements for *lixiu*, the 1982 regulation specified sixty-five for ministers, vice ministers, provincial secretaries, and governors, and sixty for vice ministers, provincial deputy secretaries, and vice governors.[40] Although not mandatory, the pressure to retire voluntarily was high particularly after bureaucratic reforms started in 1982. As a result of the reforms, some lost their positions while others found themselves with all their opportunities for promotion gone under the leadership of former younger subordinates.[41] In other cases, incumbents used the strategy of selecting their own successors and then requesting the approval of the upper echelon for them.[42] Those who voluntarily retired had a better chance of becoming advisers. In some cases, when a newly promoted young head suggested to his former boss—now a subordinate—that he be transferred to another place, the old cadre realized that he had to retire.[43] However, because of widespread sentiment against forcing old revolutionaries to retire, especially when new salary increases are expected, leaders of each unit are extremely reluctant to pressure old revolutionaries to retire.[44]

For the actual benefit of *lixiu*, various practices used in the past were added to make the retirement package attractive. Initially the fringe benefit was less than the perquisites the incumbent already enjoyed. For instance, according to the 1978 Order no. 104, the retirement pension, even for old revolutionaries, amounted to only 60 to 90 percent of their salary.[45] Gradually, the amount of the pension grew. Official policy now is to guarantee an income slightly higher than the regular salary for retirees, including previous fringe benefits, although the actual amount of the retirement pension for cadres varies depending on their work age.[46] All grade 14 cadres who joined the revolution before 1948 but who have not

40. *Daily Report*, 11 February 1982; Cao Zhi, ed., *Zhonghua Renmin*.

41. See, e.g., Zhao Jianming's decision to retire, in *Renmin Ribao*, 17 February 1982.

42. *Banyue Tan*, no. 5, 1983, 6–9.

43. *Renmin Ribao*, 2 July 80.

44. Interviews in China on 28 August 1986.

45. Cao Zhi, ed., *Zhonghua Renmin*.

46. The most senior ones—those who started their work before 1937—receive a fourteen-month salary per year; those who joined the work before 1942 are given a thirteen-and-a-half-month salary; those who joined the work before 1945 are given a thirteen-month salary; those who joined the work before 1949 are given the salary of twelve months. Minzheng bu Zhengce Yanjiushi, ed., *Mingzheng Fagui Xuanbian*.

reached the level of director of a bureau are treated economically and politically as director-level cadres, and all eighteenth-grade cadres—regardless of whether or not they have actually served as county magistrates—will enjoy the benefits of a county magistrate. In addition, retired old revolutionaries are given subsidies for price increases.

Retirees are entitled to housing equal or better than what they occupied as incumbents. Many units build new housing for their retirees. The units without the financial capability to do so request funding, materials, and locations from the housing authority of the upper level.[47] Housing conditions for retirees thus depend largely on the financial ability of their units.[48] Politically powerful units and units that generate profits can provide housing that meets the central guidelines specifying different sizes of housing for different ranks of cadres. Generally, it is the military units that can afford to build additional housing for their retired brass in many choice locations. On the other hand, housing conditions in academic units appear to be poor, often failing to meet the standards of national regulations.[49]

Retirees are given preferential treatment in health care. In addition to medical care covered by public expense (gongfei), they have priority for newly built and rather luxurious hospitals with the best medical facilities. Many units build new hospitals and allocate a specific number of hospital beds exclusively for retirees.[50] Some retirees receive monthly allowances for medical expenses. When sick, retirees are authorized to hire nurses at public expense. In addition, retirees have varying degrees of privilege to use automobiles from their original units, depending on their rank.[51] In some places, retirees are given monthly transportation allowances. Retirees also enjoy the same privileges as incumbents to visit their parents or children with expenses paid by the units. They are even

47. Dangde Shenghuo, no. 9, 1984.
48. Daily Report, 8 January 1982.
49. Harbin Yanjiu, no. 3, 1984, 42.
50. For various measures taken by Liaoning province, e.g., see Renmin Ribao, 24 September 1984.
51. Retirees of vice minister and above can use a car for any personal purpose, whereas former director-level cadres can request a car for such specified purposes as going to the hospital or attending official activities. When the unit cannot provide a car, retirees can hire commercial transportation and the expense will be reimbursed by the unit. Dangde Shenghuo, no. 12, 1983, 15.

entitled to subsidies for haircuts. When a retired cadre dies, his family is entitled to all subsidies due cadres of his same rank.[52]

The regime guarantees that "basic political treatment will not change" even after retirement. In other words, retirees have access to official documents, important political reports, and conferences. Many units set up new reading rooms where retirees can read official documents.[53] Retired party member cadres often form their own party branches and groups.

The 1978 order originally encouraged retired cadres to move to towns smaller than those they inhabited as cadres—from large urban centers to medium-sized cities and from medium-sized cities to rural areas. The order was also intended tightly to control any movement of retirees to such large cities as Beijing, Shanghai, and Tianjin by requiring official permission on a case-by-case basis. But the restriction has gradually been relaxed. First, the regime made exceptions by allowing cadres who had worked in remote areas—for instance Qinghai province—to return to interior (*neidi*) cities. Then retiring cadres in mountainous and desert areas were permitted to return to provincial capitals where "transportation is adequate and supplies are good." In 1984 the regime authorized cadres who had served in "front areas" to retire to medium- and small-sized cities.[54]

Dingti (hiring the child of a retiring cadre in the same unit) has not been officially recognized,[55] but an official regulation allows an old cadre to bring a son or daughter to live with him when he retires.[56] Since his unit will be responsible for finding a reasonable job for the retiree's offspring, he often manages to find a job for his offspring in his own unit. Among the 570 retired cadres in Harbin, 39 percent of them mentioned *dingti* as the reason for their retirement.[57]

Since 1978 a series of regulations gradually evolved to specify how the retirees should be managed. Basically, all retirees are managed by their original unit. An exception is made for retirees who

52. Minzheng bu Zhengce Yanjiushi, ed., *Mingzheng Fagui Xuanbian*.
53. Chao Zhi, ed., *Zhonghua Renmin*.
54. *Renmin Ribao*, 6 February 1984.
55. Interviews in China on 28 August 1986.
56. Chao Zhi, ed., *Zhonghua Renmin*.
57. *Harbin Yanjiu*, nos. 3–4, 1984.

are settled in other provinces; in these cases, management authority is transferred to the personnel or civil affairs bureaus of the local government. Low-ranking military officers are transferred to the jurisdiction of the local government, but all other officers are managed by their original military unit.[58] Each unit pays pensions from its administrative expenses.

In order to manage the retirees, the regime set up "old cadre bureaus or sections" staffed by full-time cadres within organizational departments and personnel bureaus at all levels of the administrative hierarchy.[59] Various functional bureaus and enterprise and business units have similar offices. As was the case with personnel management, high-ranking cadres of each unit are managed by the "old cadre offices" of superior units, whereas low-ranking cadres are handled by the personnel bureau of their own units.[60]

Not surprisingly, the *lixiu* system has produced many undesirable consequences. It increased the regime's administrative expenditures and set up an ironic precedent, that is, one can earn more when retired than when on active duty. Worse still, the system allowed retiring cadres to take their bureaucratic rank and status into society, thus further contributing to possible stratification of society along the lines of the bureaucratic hierarchy.

Although formally removed from official positions, retired revolutionaries continue to exert enormous political influence, some through the advisory system that the regime initiated from the top level down to the county level.[61] Although advisers are supposed to make only suggestions to the formal authorities, they are bound to exercise an inordinate amount of behind-the-scenes influence. First, in China, where the level of institutionalization is rather low, real power often lies in an individual person rather than in an office. Second, many of the newly promoted leaders often seek advice from retirees, who have had more political experience and more extensive personal connections, and to whom they owe their own promotion. More important, retired old revolutionaries are well organized into advisory commissions, disciplinary commissions,

58. *Renmin Ribao*, 18 October 1984.
59. Ibid., 24 September 1984.
60. *Wenhui Bao*, 16 June 1981; *Renmin Ribao*, 27 July 1981.
61. *Shanxi Ribao*, 21 January 1982; *Renmin Ribao*, 17 February 1982.

or party groups with their own spokesmen, constituting the most powerful political group outside the formal bureaucracy. They are officially encouraged to discuss current problems that they consider important, paying special attention to the selection of future leaders, ideological trends, and corruption, and, when the necessity arises, they convey their collective views to the appropriate authorities or write letters to newspapers.[62] Their political muscle was dramatically demonstrated in the dismissals of Hu Yaobang in 1987 and Zhao Ziyang in 1989 from the general secretaryship. Although the advisory system seems to be a temporary measure that will come to an end with the disappearance of the "founders," the old revolutionaries headed by Deng Xiaoping still exercise enormous political power.[63]

The other problem with the *lixiu* system is that it creates inequality for different generations of cadres and perpetuates the importance of seniority. Using 30 September 1949 as the cutoff date for eligibility to *lixiu*, although understandable, offers undue advantage to northerners while penalizing southerners, simply because south China was liberated in the last days of the civil war. Also due to the absence of rigorous bureaucratic formality in the chaotic period of the civil war, it is extremely difficult to determine the exact date when a cadre started work. In addition, the *lixiu* system cannot maintain equity for cadres employed in different units, since under the present system each unit is responsible for taking care of its retirees. The system also raises the question of conflict of interest as the retired cadres seek new employment in units that they previously regulated, further contributing to cadre corruption.[64]

Despite these problems, the *lixiu* system was effective in persuading old cadres to step down from their offices. The total number of old cadres who joined the revolutionary work force before 1949 is estimated to be about 2.5 million for 1982. As shown in table 40, only a fraction of them (7,260) had retired by 1982. The number

62. *Renmin Ribao*, 17 November 1984.
63. It is reported that the advisory system at the county level and below has been abolished. But it is also known that advisers at the lower levels simply changed their titles to "inspectors," while continuing to exercise their political influence both formally and informally.
64. *Renmin Ribao*, 15 April 1985.

Table 40.   Distribution of Retirees by Years

Harbin Municipality[a]			National Total[b]		
	Retirees			Retirees	
Date	No.	%	Date	No.	%
Mar. 1981	104	18.2	1982	7,260	0.3
Sept. 1982	50	8.8	Sept. 1983	470,000	21.3
Mar. 1982	25	4.3	Mar. 1984	870,000	39.5
Sept. 1982	40	7.0	1985	1,000,000	45.4
Mar. 1983	41	7.1	1986	1,200,000	54.5
Sept. 1983	152	27.0			
Mar. 1984	115	20.0	Not retired	1,000,000	
June 1984	43	7.6			
Total	570	100.0			

Sources. Harbin Yanjiu, no. 4, 1984, 27; Deborah Davis, "Unequal Chances, Unequal Outcomes, Pension Reforms and Urban Unequality," China Quarterly 114 (Jan. 1988):231.

a. Harbin figures are based on a sample of 570 retired cadres.
b. National figures are based on the approximately 2.2 million cadres who were eligible for retirement. The figures are cumulative.

of retirees increased to 21 percent of all old revolutionaries in 1983 and 40 percent by 1984. Total retired cadres in 1982 was only 0.06 percent of all retirees that included blue-collar workers. But the percentage increased to 6.6 by 1985.[65] This national trend approximated the trend in Liaoning province, which reportedly had 132,000 cadres—33 percent of the 556,777 responsible cadres— who had reached retirement age in 1984. Only 3,300 (2.2 percent) of them retired between 1978 and 1981; the number then increased to 9,130 (6.8 percent) in 1982 and to 50,000 (15 percent) in 1983. Table 40 shows the dates 570 cadres retired—a 10 percent sample of the total 5,700 retired cadres—in Harbin as of September 1984. More than 62 percent retired after 1983. The retirement of old cadres gained momentum only after 1982 when the regime initiated a special retirement package for old revolutionaries. Yunnan provinces had about 33,253 cadres entitled to lixiu; among them 14,793 have retired, and the rest are expected to retire by 1990.[66]

65. Deborah Davis, "Unequal Chances, Unequal Outcomes: Pension Reform and Urban Inequalities," China Quarterly, no. 114, June 1988, 223–42.
66. Yunnan Sheke Dongtai, May 1988, 17.

As noted, the *lixiu* system was initially designed for a small number of cadres with high seniority and ranking. However, eligibility gradually expanded to include all veteran cadres who had joined the revolutionary work before the foundation of the PRC. Old cadres who retired before the introduction of the *lixiu* system are allowed to change their status to *lixiu*. The evolution of the system clearly shows how a politically influential group forced the regime to broaden the scope of a policy beyond its original intentions. Although the retirement policy may not be a typical case because it involves the most powerful political group, veteran cadres, it may foretell how specific policies will be subjected to the influence of various interest groups in future years.

PURGING THE "THREE TYPES OF PEOPLE"

During the CR, a large number of rebels joined the party and then became cadres. Those in leadership positions had usually worked as administrative cadres for more than ten years, accumulating rich political experience and building up networks of personal connections (*guanxi*) at the basic levels. They may have lost their confidence in the Gang of Four long before its fall, but their former victims would not trust them, since former rebels could develop into a political force to challenge Deng Xiaoping and his reform programs. The Deng group therefore reinvestigated the former rebels in the party rectification. Obviously, Deng's group felt that the two previous screenings of the Gang's followers were not thorough, because they had been conducted at the time when the CR was not yet officially repudiated and Mao's mistakes were not yet exposed.

Unlike the Maoist method of mobilizing the masses, the regime relied on a carefully planned organizational method for investigating the radicals, limiting the scope of the purge to "three types of people." The first referred to CR rebels who "had seized political power 'in rebellion,' rose to high positions, and committed evils with serious consequences"; two constituent elements of this group were rapid promotion through power seizures and evil activities. The second were "factionalists in their ideas," who were defined by three constituent elements: vigorous propagation of radical ideology, factional ties with Lin Biao and the Gang of Four, and continuation of factional activities after the fall of the Gang.

The third included anyone who "had indulged in beating, smashing, and looting during the CR," broadly interpreted to include "framing, making false charges, and persecuting and torturing people to ruin their health." Not only those who had been personally involved in these activities, but also their "back-stage bosses responsible for smashing institutions, seizing files by force, and damaging both public and private properties" fell into this category. The leaders of the mass organizations who "had plotted, organized, and directed violent confrontation that resulted in serious consequences" were also included.[67]

The regime made a distinction between the "three types of people" and "serious mistakes." Those who had participated in "beating, smashing, and looting" in a "general sense," those who had joined the Gang of Four's network under the influence of leftist ideology, and those who had simply carried out the official line coming down through the Gang's communication channel were considered as having made "serious mistakes." For those who had committed serious mistakes, organizational conclusions would be drawn and "due measures" would be taken. But those who had already been investigated and punished were not reinvestigated. "Ordinary mistakes" were not investigated and did not require any organizational conclusion. The materials relating to "ordinary mistakes" did not enter into one's dossier; they were kept at the rectification office or the office of the core investigation group for the period of rectification.[68]

Old cadres who had erred during the CR were exempted from the "three types" because they had made "contributions to the people and for the revolution."[69] Their mistakes were classified as "serious mistakes," but if they had made self-criticisms for their errors, they were not expelled from the party. Also, ordinary party members "who said and did wrong things" were regarded as having made "serious mistakes" or "ordinary mistakes," for which the maximum penalty was delayed registration for party membership. The regime also excluded the public security apparatus from the investigation.[70] "If the public security field carried out the orders

67. *Beijing Review*, 17 October 1983.
68. *Zhibu Shenghuo*, no. 13, 1985.
69. *Renmin Ribao*, 26 August 1981.
70. *Zhibu Shenghuo*, no. 18, 1985.

and directives of the upper echelon according to CR policy, and even if the result was a wrong case, generally speaking the responsibility will not be pursued."[71] Rural party members and such basic-level party organs as the village (*xiang*) and the town (*zhen*) were excluded from investigation. Former middle school students were generally not investigated unless there were compelling reasons to do otherwise. Also the factional infighting of the Red Guards was not investigated unless the consequences of the fighting were serious.

In contrast, former Red Guards who had tortured people to the extent of injuring their health and those who had intentionally fabricated charges, falsifying evidence to persecute cadres and masses, were classified as one of the three types.

The basic guiding principle for the investigation was to be "firm and cautious, while not overlooking even one suspect." Mindful of the past abuse of "quotas," the regime insisted that no unit would be assigned quotas for the three types.

With these general guidelines, each unit investigated its own cases under the overall supervision of local party committees. Leaders who were suspected of having special ties with the three types were adjusted before the investigations started. The units that suffered serious damage from the CR and important cases—"cases that affect the entire unit or that involve top leadership"—were investigated first. If a case involved many people working in different units, the unit that the case affected most seriously was responsible for forming a joint investigation team with the others and for collecting materials. *Renmin Ribao* reported a case that involved forty-four units.[72]

In order to investigate events that happened more than ten years before, investigations usually divided the CR into several stages, reconstructing each event and analyzing "its start, development, and consequences." Victims' testimony was collected in order to discover those most responsible for an incident. The regime also recommended investigating only "armed struggle" (*wu dou*) rather than "struggle by words" (*wen dou*).

The last stage of an investigation involved determining whether

71. *Xuanchuan Shouce* (Beijing), January 1985.
72. *Renmin Ribao*, 31 July 1984.

or not the investigated person should be classified as one of the three types. A final decision on each case was to be made collectively by the party committee.[73] Party leaders were specifically warned not to be "too lenient" and to take great care to separate those who really deserved to be classified as one of the three types from those who had made a "serious mistake" and those who had made a "general mistake." Any final decision on the three types was submitted to the upper echelons for approval. The three types were then dismissed from their posts and expelled from the party. In addition, some of them were brought to court, even if the legal time limit for prosecution was past.

Despite the regime's stress on the careful collection of evidence and strict interpretations, many investigations were apparently conducted in an untidy and loose fashion. The multiplying factors—specific mistakes and crimes, degree of responsibility, degree of repentence, and political performance after the third plenum—that investigators had to consider, however, obfuscated rather than clarified ambiguities in defining the three-type persons.[74] Moreover, there was absolutely no guidance on the type of evidence and no rules governing its interpretation. One can, however, notice a departure from past practice on two points. First, the three types were defined by the actual damage incurred to the party and the people rather than by a person's title or membership in a particular faction during the CR. The second and more important point was that the purged did not suffer as much as in the Maoist era. "For those who are expelled but are still fit to serve as cadres, appropriate arrangements will be made; those unfit to serve as cadres should be provided with opportunities to find jobs and earn a living."[75]

However, the emphasis on consequences rather than on intentions was not much help in determining who fit the three types. It was extremely difficult to distinguish the types from beneficiaries of the CR—including those who did not actively participate in the process but were promoted simply because the large-scale purge in the CR created many vacancies that had to be filled. The ideology

73. *Gongchandangyuan*, nos. 11–12, 1985, 46–49.
74. *Zhibu Shenghuo* (Shanghai), no. 13, 1985.
75. *Dangde Shenghuo*, September 1984, 10.

of Lin Biao and Jiang Qing was an official line at that time, and not many people dared to challenge or refuse to publicize the official ideology. The phrase "beating, smashing, and looting" was as loose as the previous criteria. Most of the killing occurred in the context of factional struggles between rival mass organizations. Depending on how one defines looting, it can be applied to most of the initial Red Guards—largely composed of children of high-ranking cadres, including Deng Xiaoping, Liu Shaoqi, He Long, and Chen Yi—who had participated in the campaign against the "Four Olds"—old ideas, culture, customs, and habits. Persecution of their fellow classmates from "bad" family backgrounds can be construed as "beating."

Given the complexity of the CR and the ambiguous and contradictory official criteria, party committees at the various levels exercised enormous discretionary power in deciding who should be purged. The universities were usually lenient toward former rebels (now college students), because they kept no detailed records of their past behavior and had not enough manpower to investigate each student.[76] Investigating the three types of people in enterprises was also difficult because of the large number of personnel changes after the CR.

Basic-level cadres were not eager aggressively to pursue screening the three types. Instead, they adopted the tactics of "dragging, waiting, and avoiding." The cadres had every reason to be evasive. First, it was extremely difficult, if not impossible, to investigate—not to mention collect evidence and interview witnesses—an incident that occurred almost twenty years before. Many cadres did not want to undermine the stability of their units by reopening wounds and renewing factionalism. Also, they believed that the three types were harmless and powerless "dust in the trace of a wagon wheel."[77] The official line, however, insisted that they still

76. Interview in Beijing in 1986.
77. During the ten years of the CR, former rebels were subjected to several investigations: initially the military investigated them for their connection with "ultraleftists" and "May 16 elements"; immediately after the fall of the Gang of Four, they were again investigated for possible connection with the fallen radicals, although this phase was limited in scope; in 1982, the Deng–Hu group issued order no. 55 to investigate the "three types of people"; the bureaucratic reforms of 1982–83 removed whoever managed to survive until that moment; and finally they were subjected to a new investigation in the party rectification.

posed a dangerous threat because of their skill in mobilizing the masses. Former rebels in sensitive areas such as the organization-al, personnel, disciplinary, and legal fields had to be screened with the utmost care.

The evasive tactics devised by the former radicals compounded the difficulties of investigation. In the previous eighteen years many of them had changed their jobs and places of residence, sometimes falsifying their identities. One such case described in *Renmin Ribao* reported that the personnel dossier of one person had no trace of his activities during the CR. By changing their names, others even managed to "sneak into the third echelon, taking advantage of being young, well-educated, and professionally com-petent." Others pretended to repent by changing their attitude and behavior "one hundred and eighty degrees" to support the current official line. Some former rebels bought the protection of leading cadres through bribery and other means.[78] A word from leading cadres that "their works are not bad, and I don't see any taint of their cruelty" was good enough to save them.

Another difficulty concerned how to discern individual responsi-bility for collective actions. During the chaotic period of mass mobi-lization, the boundary between legality and illegality and between individual-initiated and organization-sanctioned actions was blurred. Most of the political violence during the CR took the form of group or mass action rather than individual behavior. Moreover, many of them were sanctioned by the official ideology and often carried out through the existing organizational channels. For in-stance, the military was ordered to intervene in the CR to restore order; in carrying out this task, it frequently resorted to violent means, sometimes inciting one faction to launch violent attacks on others. But during the investigation, the regime tried to hold indi-viduals responsible for the consequences of collective actions. Since most of the current PLA leaders—all party committee mem-bers except one in the case of the Chengdu military region—had led PLA units in the task of supporting the left during the CR, very few of them could claim to be completely innocent.

The last difficulty involved dealing with the two factions that split almost all organizations. With regard to the question of which

78. *Renmin Ribao*, 8 June 1984.

faction was correct and which was incorrect, the official line held that both factions made mistakes and that factional ties were irrelevant to the investigation of the three types of people. New party secretaries who had nothing to do with the CR were appointed to the units seriously plagued with factionalism. Nonetheless, the lingering influence of factional ties had been particularly noticeable in the personnel management of cadres. Local party cadres used factional viewpoints in investigating the three types, taking a protective attitude toward members of their own factions—by making "the big incident a small one, if their own faction was involved, and making the insignificant matter of major importance, if members of their rival faction were involved."[79]

As a result, former members of the rebel faction bore the brunt of the investigation. In contrast, the investigation did not often affect former members of the conservative Red Guards, who publicly declared that since they defended the party committee, there was nothing to investigate about them. Most of the conservative Red Guard organizations had been led by the children of former high-ranking cadres, who were now rehabilitated and returned to former power. In fact, some leaders openly pleaded that the activities of the initial Red Guards should not be investigated. "Those who made serious mistakes at the early stage of the CR, but those who made corrections of their mistakes during the middle stage of the CR, should be trusted. But those who tenaciously followed the counterrevolutionary group of Lin Biao and Jiang Qing, and those who did bad things, should never be used for important positions."[80] Many former leaders of the initial Red Guard organizations (such as the sons of Chen Yi and He Long and the daughters of Liu Shaoqi, Deng Xiaoping, and Song Renqiong) are now working in cozy positions in the state or military units or are abroad for study, whereas their adversaries are probably languishing in jail.[81]

Despite the initial estimate of 15 percent of party members slated for removal and a Hong Kong observer's speculation that as many as 4 million (4 percent of party members) would be purged, it seems that the total number of people purged as one of the three

79. *Zhengdang Yu Jiandang*, 16 April 1984, 20.
80. *Dangde Shenghou*, 1984, nos. 9, 10.
81. *Zhengdang Yu Jiandang* (Liaoning), 16 April 1984, 20.

types was very small.[82] Most of the types reported in the official newspapers were accused of having abused their cadre positions to commit such crimes as corruption and rape, in addition to their original mistakes during the CR. By bringing additional charges, the regime portrayed the three types as "bad persons" prone to irregular behavior. There is no way for outside observers to determine the official assertion. But it implies either that the former rebels were condemned when they made additional mistakes in cadre positions or that the regime falsified or exaggerated the additional mistakes to discredit the former rebels morally.[83]

Although only a small number of people were purged as the three types, a question of fairness persists. Did the investigation use well-defined objective criteria for all suspects fairly and equally? Undoubtedly, those who were condemned still feel that they were unfairly punished.

A less harsh fate for the purged cannot be much comfort for those branded as the three types because, otherwise, they would have been selected as China's future leaders. As the official news media publicly recognizes, the only difference between the three types and the candidates for China's future leadership lies in their political performances during the CR. Both the three types and candidates for the third echelon are young or middle-aged and well educated.[84] If one had a clean record during the CR, he can enter the ranks of future leaders. But those condemned as the three types lost their current positions, not to mention the chance to be promoted.

Understandably, many of the Red Guard generation are still confused. Some of them are completely disillusioned and alienated from the political process and are searching for a vehicle to express their wounded feelings and painful experiences. The more courageous ones, who are still dedicated to searching for a solution to the Chinese problem, have reached the conclusion that the basic problem with China does not lie with Mao, revisionism, old party leaders, or the innocent youth who threw themselves eagerly into the political movement, but with the political system itself. To

82. *Ming Bao*, 5 October 1983; "Zhengdang Shidian Cankao Cailiao," *Dangde Shenghuo*, 25 July 1983.
83. *Renmin Ribao*, 10 July 1984.
84. *Hong Qi*, no. 1, 1984, 1.

them China's hopes rest with democracy and a pluralism that will tolerate different views. There is no doubt that as the Communist revolution had been the definitive event of their parents' generation, so the CR was to become the event that politically defined Mao's next generation. China's first revolutionary successors came of age in that tremendous upheaval; the events of those years will color their vision. For many, it has left emotional scars that are not yet healed. But with or without healing, this generation will shoulder China's future.

11

Bureaucratic Reforms

Officially labeled a "revolution in administrative strcuture, but not against any persons," bureaucratic reform started in 1982 when the necessary groundwork was established. The reforms intended ostensibly to streamline the unruly bureaucracy and to make the leading cadres "revolutionized, better educated, professionally competent and younger in age."[1] A hidden objective was to resolve the succession problem—the question that, according to Deng Xiaoping, would determine the fate of China—by promoting a new group of leaders whose personal interests were tied to the reform policy.

This chapter examines the results of that reform, analyzes the concrete strategy followed by the regime, and discusses the political implications of the sweeping leadership change.

LEADERSHIP CHANGES, 1982–87

The regime carried out leadership reshuffling in the following sequence:

1. It changed the ministers and vice ministers of the central government in May 1982.

2. It readjusted the leadership of the functional departments of the Central Committee—such as the organizational department and the propaganda department—in the summer of 1982.

3. It appointed a large number of new members to the Twelfth Central Committee in September 1982.

4. It reshuffled provincial leadership in 1983.

5. It adjusted the leading bodies at the district and municipal levels (completed in December 1983).

1. *Daily Report*, 9 March 1982, K4.

Table 41. Reduction of Bureaucracy During the 1982–84 Reforms

Position	No. Before	No. After	% of Reduction
State council			
Offices	98	52	
Ministers and vice			
ministers	1,000	300	77
Directors and deputy			
directors	5,000	2,500	50
Persons in the state			
council	49,000	32,000	
All cadres at the			
central level	600,000	400,000	
Central party organs			
Offices			17
Directors and deputy			
directors			40
Heads and deputy heads			
of offices			14
Provincial level			
Secretaries, members of			
standing Committee,			
and governors, vice			
governors	698	463	34
Heads of bureaus[a]	16,658	10,604	
Municipal-level leaders			36
District-level leaders			29
County level leaders[a]			25

Sources. Collected from various Chinese official publications including *Dangshi Ziliao Suju Tongxun*, Mar. 1986.

a. Includes all bureau-level offices of provinces, districts, and municipalities.

6. It changed the leadership at the county level (completed in September 1984).

7. It reorganized the leadership at the enterprise levels.

8. It initiated the party rectification campaign.

9. It prepared a list of third-echelon cadres.

10. It carried out a second-round readjustment of the leadership at the central and provincial levels in 1985.

11. It promoted a large number of new generation cadres to the highest positions in the Thirteenth Party Congress.

Table 42.   Age and Education Before and After the 1982–84 Reforms

	Average Age		% College-Educated	
	Before	After	Before	After
Ministers and vice ministers	64	58	38	59
Directors and deputy directors of the state council	59	54	35	52
Directors and deputy directors of central party organs	66	62	43	53
Heads and deputy heads of bureaus of central party organs	60	54	50	56
Provincial secretaries, governors and vice governors	62	55	20	44
Directors and deputy directors of provincial bureaus	62	55	14	51
Municipal leaders	58	50	14	44
District leaders	57	50		37
County leaders	48	42	14	47
Township		39		10
Village		35		1
Industrial enterprises				
National		45		89
District[a]		52		40
County[a]		47		35
Business units				
District[a]		52		84
County[a]		47		60

Source. Collected by the author from the various official Chinese publications, including *Renmin Ribao*.

a. From Guizhou provincial figures. *Guizhou Nianjian* (Guizhou: Guizhou Renmin Chubanshe, 1985).

The results of the first-round administrative reforms (1982–84) from the center down to the basic level are tabulated in tables 41 and 42.

THE STATE COUNCIL

Administrative reforms strengthened the authority of the premier by ending the practice of placing each vice premier in charge of a specific functional area (*xitong*). The number of vice premiers decreased from twelve to two, and the new system of "State Council standing conferences" (*guowuyuan changwu huiyi*) was introduced. Many commissions (e.g., the State Agricultural Commission) were abolished, some ministries were merged (e.g., the ministries of power industries and of water conservancy), and a few new ministries were established (e.g., the ministries of aviation and of electronics). The bureaus with staff functions were combined, and some of the support functions—such as running nursery schools for the ministry personnel's children and motor pools—were transferred to newly established independent corporations, which would eventually operate on a profit-and-loss principle.[2]

The reduction of personnel was equally impressive. The total number of ministers and vice ministers—excluding heads and deputy heads of commissions, offices, and agencies—was reduced by approximately 70 percent. The average age of leaders was lowered from sixty-four years to fifty-eight, and those with college-level educations increased from 38 to 59 percent (see table 42). The reorganization also decreased the total number of directors by 40 percent and their average age from 59 to 54, while improving their educational level (those with a college-level education rose from 35 to 52 percent).[3] Most of those who had assumed leadership positions during the radical phase were removed.

CENTRAL PARTY ORGANS

Personnel changes in central party organs were less sweeping than in central government organs. According to the statistics of thirteen departments, the total number of directors and deputy directors was reduced by 40 percent, their average age was lowered from sixty-six to sixty-two, and the proportion of those with a college-level education increased from 43 to 53 percent. The heads of bureaus were reduced by 14 percent and their average age lowered from sixty to fifty-four. Those with a college-level education increased from 50 to 56 percent.[4]

2. For instance, after merging the ministries of water conservancy and of electric power, the total number of bureaus was reduced from 35 to 16 and the total number of persons from 1,500 to 720. *Zhonggong Yanjiu*, April 1982, 43.

3. Cao Zhi, ed., *Zhonghua Renmin Gongheguo Renshi Zhidu Gaiyao* (Beijing: Beijing Daxue Chubanshe, 1985), 221.

4. Ibid.

Twelfth Central Committee

Less than half of the entire Eleventh CC of members elected in 1977 (43 percent) made it into the Twelfth CC convened in 1982. The rate was lower than that of either the Ninth CC (76 percent) or the Tenth CC (62 percent), but higher than the rate of the Eighth CC. However, not all of those who failed to make it into the Twelfth CC were purged; sixty-five members were transferred to the Advisory Commission. Most of the mass representatives (seventy-nine out of ninety-seven in the Eleventh CC) failed to get into the Twelfth CC—except for those who had some credentials in addition to their activities during the CR.[5] With the Twelfth CC, the idea of having mass representatives in the Central Committee came to an end.

The PLA lost 32 percent (thirty out of ninety-two) of its Eleventh CC members. The total share of the military in the Twelfth CC decreased from 27 percent in the Eleventh CC to 19 percent, a level comparable with the 21 percent of the Eighth CC.[6] The shared characteristics of the PLA leaders who lost their seats in the CC were (1) deep involvement in the CR when the PLA was ordered to provide military training to the Red Guards, (2) support for industry and agriculture in 1967, and (3) rapid promotion to influential positions in the revolutionary committees and party organizations during the 1968–76 period.

Provincial Organs

Changes in the provincial-level leadership were sweeping. For instance, the total number of provincial party committee members, governors, and vice governors was reduced from 698 (twenty-three persons per province) to 463 (fifteen persons per province), a reduction of 34 percent (see table 41). The average number of provincial party secretaries was reduced in some provinces from fourteen to five (Sichuan and Hunan), and the standing committee mem-

5. For a detailed discussion of the Twelfth CC, see Hong Yung Lee, "Twelfth Central Committee: Rehabilitated Cadres and Technocrats," *Asian Survey* 23 (June 1983).

6. For the military's changing share in the central committee, see *Zhonggong Yanjiu*, October 1982, 114–21.

bers from somewhere in the twenties to about fifteen, depending on the size of the province. Consequently, provincial leaders with a college-level education increased from 20 to 44 percent (table 42).

The total number of bureaus at the provincial, district, and municipal levels declined from 16,658 (555 per province) to 10,604 (350 per province)—a reduction of 36 percent. The percentage of cadres in these positions with a college-level education increased from 14 percent to 51 percent, whereas their average age was lowered from sixty-two to fifty-five.[7] One-third of the new leadership was from enterprise, higher educational institutions, or research institutes, and many of them (22 percent in Qinghai province) had professional titles.[8]

District and Municipal Organs

At these levels, the total number of leaders (including secretaries, standing committee members, and bureau directors) was reduced by 36 percent; their average age was lowered from fifty-eight to fifty. Those with a college-level education increased from 14 to 44 percent and, in the case of Qinghai province, 14 percent of them had professional titles.[9]

County, Town (*Zhen*), and Village (*Xiang*) Organs

Reorganization reduced the average age of county-level leadership from forty-eight to forty-two and produced a leadership composed of forty-, thirty-, and twenty-year-old cadres.[10] The percentage of college graduates among the county magistrates increased from 18 to 43 and among the county party secretaries, from 4 to 43. More than 80 percent of the counties had either a party secretary or a magistrate who had a college-level education, and 15 percent of them had professional titles.[11]

---

7. Cao Zhi, ed., *Zhonghua Renmin*, 224.
8. Ibid., 225.
9. Ibid. *Guizhou Nianjian* (Guizhou: Guizhou Renmin Chubanshe, 1985), 292.
10. Those below forty years constitute one-third, and those above fifty were about 14 percent. Ibid.
11. Cao Zhi, ed., *Zhonghua Renmin*, 229.

Although the national aggregate figures on reforms at the *zhen* and *xiang* levels are not available, Guizhou provincial statistics may well represent the general trend. Guizhou lowered the average age of its *zhen*-level leaders to thirty-nine and *xiang*-level leaders to thirty-five. The number of those with an educational level of senior high school and above increased to 42 percent (including a college-level education of 10 percent) at the *zhen* level, and to 30 percent at the *xiang* level (including 0.96 percent of college-level education).[12] However, even after the reform the situation is not ideal because of the shortage of educated manpower.

ENTERPRISES

The regime carried out the reorganziation of key state-owned enterprises twice. The first-round adjustment replaced about 60 percent of the old cadres with new cadres—many of whom did not meet the age and educational specifications that the center set up—as a transitional measure.[13] The second-round adjustment in 1984 further improved the age and educational structure of the newly constituted leadership at that level: it was comprised of those in their forties (63 percent), those below forty (20 percent), and those above fifty (17 percent), with an average age of forty-five. Reorganization also reduced the total number of leading cadres by one-third (6.3 persons per unit) and increased those with the college-level education by 89 percent.[14] Most of the newly promoted managers "understand production, science, and technology."[15]

The quality of the new enterprise leaders managed by district organs (*diqu*) was much lower than that of the leadership in key enterprises. For instance, in Guizhou province the average age of leaders of district-level enterprises was fifty-two, and 40 percent had a college-level education. Leadership of county-level enterprises was a little bit lower: the average age was forty-seven, and 35 percent had a college-level education.[16] The average age of leaders in Guizhou business units at the district level was fifty-two, and

12. *Renmin Ribao*, 5 October 1984.
13. *Renmin Ribao*, 3 July 1983.
14. Ibid., 5 July 1986.
15. Ibid., 1 December 1985.
16. *Guizhou Nianjian* (Guizhou: Guizhou Renmin Chubanshe, 1985), 292.

those with a college-level education averaged 84 percent.[17] In county-level business units, leaders' average age was forty-seven, and 60 percent had a college-level education.

In brief, as the regime proudly declared, "after two years of structural reforms, the age, knowledge, and speciality structure of the leading bodies at various levels have improved substantially." According to another official source, about 20,000 young cadres—those "under fifty-five years old and with abundant specialized knowledge and long work experiences"—entered into leadership positions above the county level.[18]

In addition to the leadership changes examined in the preceding section, the regime prepared a list of "third echelon of cadres"—those from the younger generation already targeted for promotion to specific leadership positions. In other words, it referred not to the pool of qualified candidates from which future leaders would be selected, but to the list of cadres chosen to replace the present leaders at various levels. They were cadres "on reserve." Some of them had already been assigned to leadership positions.[19] Since even those newly promoted cadres are referred to as the "third echelon," the term is frequently used to refer to the younger, better-educated people in leadership positions.

The idea of a third echelon was apparently the rehabilitated cadres' effort to ensure political stability and continuation of their reform line after they died. "In order to ensure the stability of the state and continuity of the direction and policies of the party and state for a long period of time, it becomes necessary to start building up the third echelon."[20] In other words, the third echelon was a device to maximize political stability through planned generational change.

Reserve cadres were selected not only for politically important leading positions at each level—such as secretary, governors, and magistrate—but also for all other responsible positions in administrative, functional, and military units—including enterprise and business units.[21] The regime completed the selection of reserve cadre corps for provinces, districts, and counties by 1986. The PLA

17. Ibid. Minority cadres were 5 percent with female cadres 3.8 percent.
18. *Liaowang*, 5 October 1984.
19. *Renmin Ribao*, 29 October 1984.
20. *Deng Xiaoping Wenxuan* (Beijing: Renmin Chubanshe, 1983), 339.
21. *Gongchan Dangyuan*, no. 22, 1985, 31.

also selected its own reserve cadres.[22] Moreover, "the work of selecting, training, and managing the reserve cadre has been to a certain extent institutionalized."[23]

Although some on the list had already been promoted to leading positions in each unit, about 70 to 80 percent of the third echelon as of 1986 were assigned to deputy positions, thus prompting some Chinese to name the third echelon "deputies." Presumably, as deputies they would receive on-the-job training and would gradually assume leadership positions when they were ready. Those without much managerial experience were sent to various party schools or to basic-level units to develop "overall leadership" ability. Sichuan and Hunan provinces sent some of their third echelon to Shenzhen city "directly to witness economic reforms."[24] When the remaining third echelon will move into leadership positions depends largely on "requirements of the work."

Another component of the policy was the allocation of some college graduates to basic units so that they would be trained as future leaders "who have not only education and specialized knowledge, but who would also be familiar with the actual conditions of China and be willing to integrate themselves with the masses."[25] Probably initiated by Hu Yaobang, these young people were billed as the future leaders of China in the transition between the twentieth and the twenty-first centuries.[26] About 12,000 college graduates participated in the program, and some have already assumed leadership positions at basic levels.[27] This practice, however, came to an end in 1986.

As shown in table 43, each province and ministry prepared lists of candidates for key leadership positions at different levels. The total number at each level approximated the number of incumbents, which were probably fixed by regulations. Reserve cadres were even selected for directorships of provincial bureaus. According to an official source, a total of about 100,000 cadres were

22. *Renmin Ribao*, 10 September 1983.

23. The central organizational department set up a young cadre bureau to be responsible for preparing lists of young cadres, constantly supplementing them while dropping those proven to be unqualified. *Rencai Tiandi*, no. 10, 1985, 26–27.

24. Ibid.

25. *Renmin Ribao*, 15 October 1986.

26. *Rencai Tiandi*, no. 10, 1985, 26–27.

27. *Liaowang*, 17 November 1986, 1.

Table 43.   Number of Cadres Selected for the Third Echelon, as of 1984

Unit	Total	Provinces	Districts	Bureaus
Tianjin	1,693	18	418	2,517
Beijing	3,000			
Henan	2,919	30	797	2,108
Shandong	5,896	34	437	5,425
Shanghai	1,500			
Liaoning		25	333	
Ministry of Railways	10,877	11 (ministry level)		

Sources. *Renmin Ribao*, 5 Nov. 1984; 29 Oct. 1984; 20 Apr. 1984; 11 Sept. 1984, 24 Feb. 1984.

Note. Figures in columns do not necessarily add up to figures in the Total column because they were compiled from a variety of sources.

selected for the third echelon: approximately 1,000 for the provincial and ministerial leadership positions, 20,000 for jobs at bureau and district levels, and the rest for the county-level positions.[28]

Table 44 indicates that the average age of the third echelon selected for provincial-level cadres was about forty-five, ten years younger than the incumbents; the average age of those selected for district- and bureau-level positions was about forty; and the average age of those for the county level was about thirty-five.[29] Most cadres in the third echelon had college-level educations, including those selected for provincial- and district-level leadership positions.[30] Of the 452 cadres selected for leadership positions in one hundred and twenty-one enterprises under the ministry of coal, 86 percent were below age forty-five, 76 percent had a college-level education, and 70 percent possessed specialized knowledge, that is, had professional titles.[31] Likewise, Shanghai reported that 90 percent of its 1,500 reserve cadres had a college-level education and 70 percent had career backgrounds as professionals and specialists,

28. Ibid., 5 October 1984, 10–11; 17 January 1985, 17–18.
29. *Renmin Ribao*, 20 April 1984; 11 September 1984; 14 January 1985; 15 November 1984.
30. Ibid., 20 April 1984.
31. Ibid., 20 October 1984; 10 April 1984.

Table 44.   Characteristics of the Third Echelon

Unit	No. and Position	Average Age	College (%)	Specialized Knowledge (%)
Henan	137 for county		89	45
Shanghai	1,500 for all	42	90	70
Sichuan	173 for province	39	90	54
Gansu	district (diqu)	40	94	
	county	37	80	
Beijing	3,000 for all	96% below 45	85	
Liaoning	25 for province	45	76	70
Tianjin	18 for municipality	76% 35–45	94	
	418 for district (qu)		80	
A Ministry	452 for all	85% below 45	76	70
Ministry of Railways	1,087 for all	45	77	67
Ministry of Coal	452 for enterprise	86% below 45	76	70
Loyang municipality	1,964 for all	68% below 45	67	74
Textile bureau of	4 at bureau level	40	100	
Liaoning province	24 at division level	37	50	

Sources. Renmin Ribao, 5 Nov. 1984; 29 Oct. 1984; 20 Apr. 1984; 11 Sept. 1984; 24 Feb. 1984.

mostly in engineering fields.[32] For example, all of Shanghai's five mayors and deputy mayors were engineers.

Apparently after reviewing the results of the administrative reforms, the regime carried out a second-round readjustment at the central and provincial government levels in April 1984. Instead of an across-the-broad readjustment, the regime replaced those who had survived the first readjustment of 1982–83 with 126 younger cadres. Sixty-three percent of those newly promoted were under fifty, and 80 percent of them had a college-level education.[33] As a result, the new leadership within each office formed a "ladder-shaped" structure by including those in their sixties, fifties, and forties. The average age was lowered to fifty-three, and the educational level improved: those with college-level educations grew from 43 to 60 percent of all leading cadres at the central and provincial levels.[34]

After achieving this change in the civilian sector, Deng Xiaoping announced his plan to reduce the size of the military forces by 1 million—approximately one-half of which were officers—by cutting the number of military officers in central military organs and big military regions by 20 to 50 percent. The new military leadership has a ladder-shaped age structure: the central leaders in their sixties, leaders of strategic forces in their fifties, division commanders in their forties, and brigade commanders in their thirties.[35]

At the fourth plenary session of the Twelfth Party Congress (convened in September 1985), fifty-four full members and ten alternate members (out of 341 elected in 1982) of the Twelfth Central Committee resigned.[36] After the old cadres were removed, about sixty new cadres were added to the CC. Most of the new members were promoted to key posts in the party, government, and military and then moved into the CC when the meeting was convened. The average age of those newly added to the CC was fifty-seven, and thirty-three of them (60 percent) had career backgrounds in engineering, economic planning, or industrial manage-

32. Ibid., 19 September 1984.
33. Cao Zhi, ed., *Zhonghua Renmin*, p. 235. *Renmin Ribao*, 8 September 1985.
34. *Renmin Ribao*, 5 October 1985; 9 September 1985.
35. The average age of regional military commanders was lowered by eight years. *Liaowang*, no. 27, 8 July 1985.
36. *Renmin Ribao*, 17 September 1985.

ment. Most of the newly added made it to the Thirteenth CC with only four (out of sixty) retiring. In contrast, 91 of 152 who had been elected in 1982 retired. Only six of the alternate members who had joined the CC in 1986 retired, whereas 52 out of 98 alternate members elected in 1982 resigned.

By the time the Thirteenth Party Congress was closed in October 1987, Deng Xiaoping had achieved a generational change in China's political leadership, the goal that even Mao had failed to achieve through his CR. Most of the first generation revolutionaries retired, and a new generation of leaders rose all the way to the standing committee of the Politburo, the innermost circle of power.

Tables 45 and 46 compare characteristics of CC member in 1982 with those in the Thirteenth CC in 1987—ministers, provincial party secretaries (the first party secretary system was abolished), and governors. They are the key decision-makers in the Chinese bureaucracy. Several observations can be made in connection with these tables.

First, all ministers, provincial secretaries, and governors have seats in the Central Committee. Unlike the radicals promoted by the Gang of Four to the CC in the Ninth and Tenth CC leaders have solid power bases in the formal bureaucracies of central and provincial organs. Although their prestige among subordinates and their informal power bases are not known, the fact that they hold concurrent positions in the CC and other power organs shows that they can exert substantial political influence.

Second, the average age of the new leaders now entrenched in power organs indicates that most of them joined the revolution in the latter part of the civil war or around the time of liberation. In contrast, except for the few still remaining in government positions, usually as chiefs of central government commissions, the anti-Japanese war generation has largely been removed from active duty. By and large, the majority of the top political elite (who were around twenty-three years old in 1949) belong to the postliberation generation. Some of them may have joined the revolution in the latter stages of the civil war, but those who have college degrees would have been students at that time.

Third, the average age of the four groups is similar, thus indicating that the regime's effort to lower the age at the top level was successful. Particularly amazing is the fact that the average age of

Table 45. Average Age of Leaders, 1982 and 1987

Age	Ministers		First Secretaries		Governors		CC Members	
	1982 (30)	1987 (35)	1982 (12)	1987 (20)	1982 (12)	1987 (20)	1982[a] (139)	1987[b] (160)
Average	67	59	70	56	66	56	71	58
Median	67	59	70	56	65	55	72	61

Source. Compiled by the author from biographical information.

Note. Figures for 1982 are based on data from before the 1982 bureaucratic reforms. Figures in parentheses are numbers of cases.

a. Eleventh Central Committee.
b. Thirteenth Central Committee.

Table 46. Leaders' Work Experience, 1982 and 1987

Work experience	Year	Ministers		Secretaries		Governors		CC Members[a]	
		No.	%	No.	%	No.	%	No.	%
Engineering	1982	1	2	0	0	0	0	4	2
	1987	17	45	7	25	8	33	34	26
Economics and management	1982	2	5	0	0	1	4	6	3
	1987	9	24	2	7	4	16	10	7
Functional bureau	1982	11	26	2	7	1	4	11	6
	1987	8	21	3	11	2	8	18	13
Secretary and political fields	1982	26	60	24	83	23	84	91	48
	1987	2	5	10	36	7	30	38	29
CYL	1982	0	0	1	3	1	4	1	1
	1987	1	3	6	21	3	13	13	10
Military	1982	3	7	2	7	1	4	48	26
	1987	1	3	0	0	0	0	20	15
Mass	1982	0	0	0	0	0	0	29	14
	1987	0	0	0	0	0	0	0	0
Total	1982	43	100	29	100	27	100	190	100
	1987	38	100	28	100	24	100	133	100

Source. Compiled by the author from biographical information.

Note. Figures for 1982 are based on data from before the 1982 bureaucratic reforms.

a. Figures for 1982 refer to members of the Eleventh Central Committee; figures for 1987, to members of the Thirteenth Central Committee.

provincial secretaries is only fifty-six, lower than even government ministers. Except in the early stages, during the 1950s when the CCP was developing its institutional structures, top-level Chinese leaders have never been younger.

Fourth, their level of education appears to be quite high, although information is incomplete. It is likely that most of them have college-level educations, although only 100 CC members, sixteen secretaries and governors, and eighteen ministers have been positively identified as such. The new leaders are from the best-educated groups in China.

Fifth, 45 percent of the 1987 ministers, 25 percent of the secretaries, and 33 percent of the governors are engineers. If one adds the people with experience in economics and management, the number of those whose speciality is production increases to 70 percent of the ministers, 32 percent of the secretaries, and 50 percent of the governors. This represents the greatest change from the Maoist era. In contrast, there are only a few cadres with experience in overall political leadership—5 percent of the ministers, 36 percent of the secretaries, and 30 percent of the governors. Virtually none of the leaders has had any in-depth experience in the propaganda field. This illustrates the lessening importance of a political career as the required background for promotion to top leadership positions.

Sixth, only one person among the eighty top leaders has any career background in the military. He is Zhang Aiping, the minister of defense. In the coming years, the new leaders will probably face difficulties in dealing with the military.

Seventh, it is believed that the vice ministers, deputy secretaries, and vice governors, although not included in table 45, are younger than the other groups, as well as better educated—hence more competent functionally.

It is not only at the top level leadership positions of the party-state, but also at the basic levels and in the mass organizations that the technocrats were promoted to leadership positions. About one-half of the delegation to the Sixth National People's Congress had college-level educations, mostly in functional fields. Even the portion of intellectuals increased from 16 percent to 40 percent in the sixth political consultative conference.

According to a survey conducted by the statistical bureau of the

Ningxia autonomous government in 1985, more than one-quarter of all provincial intellectuals were promoted to leadership positions, and a majority of them were engineers and technical personnel.[37] Another source reports that by March 1983, one-third of all high-ranking intellectuals in seventy-nine central units assumed leadership positions.[38] Jiangsu province reports that 54 percent of all those who entered leadership positions in its department, municipality, and county levels were intellectuals.[39] By 1986 about a half million young and middle-aged cadres had been promoted to leadership positions at the county level or higher. This figure equals all the government cadres with similar ranks, or 10 percent of all Chinese cadres with similar ranks.[40] Most of the newly promoted leaders had studied science and technology. For instance, Shanghai reported that 70 percent of its bureau directors and 61 percent of its county-level standing committee members had majored in the natural sciences.[41]

In brief, the best term for the newly emerging elite group is "bureaucratic technocrats" because they owe their rise not to any commitment to socialism, but to possession of the knowledge, skills, and expertise that China needs for economic development. They come mostly from the postliberation generation and the best-educated section of the population. About 100 of the 160 Thirteenth CC members have college-level educations, whereas only four out of every 1,000 Chinese have received a similar level of education. Less than half of these have specialities, mostly in engineering and other production-related fields. This is largely due to the shortage of trained experts in the "soft sciences" and to the present stage of China's industrialization, where increasing production is still the major concern. As the political elite, bureaucratic technocrats have two weaknesses. Very few of them have an in-depth knowledge of economics and management—"soft knowledge" in current Chinese terms.[42] For instance, among 5,000 leaders of large state-owned enterprises, about 84 percent had career

37. *Ningxia Shehui Kexue Tongxin*, no. 2, 1986, 8–16.
38. *Shehui Kexue Yanjiu Cankao Ziliao* (Sichuan), 21 July 1985.
39. *Renmin Ribao*, 23 October 1986.
40. *Hong Qi*, no. 17, 1986, 11.
41. *Jiaoxue Cankao*, no. 3, 1988, 18–27.
42. *Shehui Kexue Dongtai* (Hubei), 1 June 1984.

backgrounds in science and engineering fields, whereas only 11 percent studied management.[43] Also, having spent most of their careers as technical staff in functionally specialized organs, they have accumulated very little experience in overall administrative leadership.

Although bureaucratic reform has replaced old revolutionaries with bureaucratic technocrats in leadership positions, it did not have much impact on the age and educational structure of the cadre corps as a whole, simply because of limited educated manpower. As far as the size of the bureaucracy is concerned, the reform is a "total failure," particularly at the provincial level and below.[44] After the reforms, the overall number of cadres increased from 20 million to 21 million and then to 29 million in 1988.[45] The increase in cadre size pushed up administrative expenditures from 4.2 percent of the total government budget in 1978 to 6.8 percent in 1982, 7 percent in 1983, and 8 percent in 1985.[46]

At another level is the fundamental problem of "offices standing like trees in a forest, organizations bloated, numerous layers, unclear responsibilities and tasks, and overstaffed bureaucracy." One Chinese scholar summarized the results of the reform in the following way:

> Units that should be abolished are not abolished. On the surface the units are merged; but internally the size has increased. The original personnel have not been reduced; instead, they were internally absorbed. People continue to create works, and as a result, the seignorial and deputy positions are numerous. At lower levels administrative units set up many "general corporations," "leading small groups," and "management offices."[47]

Some cynics argue that the reforms resulted in "three-too-manys and one-too-fews: more work, more offices, more cadres, but fewer people actually working." The effort to separate the party from the government and to develop a clear hierarchical command structure exacerbated the complexity of the bureaucracy. For in-

43. *Zhongguo Renshi Guanli*, no. 7, 1987, 1–7.
44. *Jiaoyan Cankao*, 1 February 1986; 15 April 1986.
45. *Huaqiao Ribao*, 16 January 1988. For the Anhui provincial situation, see *Zhongguo Renshi Guanli*, 3 March 1987, 1–7.
46. *Jiaoyan Cankao*, 15 April 1985; *Renmin Ribao*, 7 March 1985.
47. *Lilun Yu Shijian* (Shenyang), June 1985, 18–19.

stance, before the reforms county-level authorities had only two systems: party committees and government organizations. But now there are five different sources of authority: party committees, the government, people's congresses, political consultative conferences, and disciplinary committees. As a result, according to China's own description, the bureaucratic structure is heavy at the top, like an "upside-down pyramid. Leading cadres are too many, and those who do actual work are too few."[48]

The reform also did not change the tendency for each organization to maintain itself as a self-contained unit with a large number of support staff, virtually "owning the cadres" and workers, and practicing the "life-tenure" system.[49] Overstaffed offices continue to "stand like trees in a forest," forming numerous layers. The phenomenon of "documents and conferences forming mountains and seas" persists. Many cadres still "spend half a day drinking a cup of tea, smoking a cigarette, and reading a paper of internal circulation."[50]

REFORM STRATEGY

If one follows Samuel Huntington's distinction between *blitzkreig* and Fabian approaches to reform strategy, the Chinese case approximates the latter.[51] The regime carried out bureaucratic reorganization and leadership changes slowly but firmly, step by step, level by level, and area by area, employing a bureaucratic method to solve bureaucratic problems. Supplemented by heavy reliance on work teams sent out to lower levels, this organizational approach ensured the maximum influence of the top leaders.

The regime first readjusted the leadership at the central level and then set up a "small group to lead the leadership changes at the provincial level" with Song Renqiong as its head. This group carried out a pilot project in Sichuan province and distributed its results to other provinces as an example.[52] Accordingly, each prov-

---

48. *Zhongguo Xingzheng Guanli*, no. 3, 1987, 34.
49. *Jingji Fazhan Yu Tizhi Gaige* no. 7, 1986, 7–12.
50. *Zhongguo Xingzheng Guanli*, no. 2, 1978, 5.
51. Huntington, *Political Order in Changing Societies* (New Haven: Yale University Press, 1968), 346.
52. Ibid.

ince prepared and submitted its reorganization plan to the central group for approval. The newly organized provincial leadership in turn carried out the leadership adjustment in their subordinate units according to specific guidelines set up by the central authority. They also organized "inspection teams"—staffed by cadres in the personnel field and retired senior cadres—which interviewed potential candidates for the lower-level leadership positions and gathered the masses' opinions of them.[53]

Instead of aiming at the ambitious and risky goal of replacing all older cadres in each unit at once, the regime replaced them bit by bit, dividing each unit's potential political adversaries and dealing with them one by one. The method of "entrance first, and exit second," according to Deng Xiaoping, and "first adding and then subtracting" (xian zuo jiafa, hou zuo jianfa), in Hu Yaobang's terms, enabled the regime to reduce the total number of leadership positions in each unit, to remove some incumbents—generally those politically unreliable, physically infirm, or less capable—and then to promote the younger and better qualified. Through this method the regime could first make the newly appointed a majority in each organ and then in the next stage replace those who survived the initial readjustment with younger people.

For reorganizing the local leadership, the central authorities issued several guidelines, which set up overall goals for the reorganization of provincial-, district-, municipal-, and county-level organs. The "Notice Regarding the Opinion of Reshuffling the Provincial-Level Leading Groups" limited the number of provincial secretaries for each province to four to five, set the maximum age of the first party secretary at sixty-five, and stipulated that new leading groups should include "various specialists familiar with the works of industry, agriculture, culture, education, and science and technology."[54] Limiting the number of secretaries to three to five, the guidelines for municipal-level reforms prescribed that at least 50 percent of the municipal leadership have an educational level higher than senior high school, that none of them exceed the age of sixty, and that those under fifty constitute 50 percent. For

53. *Guizhou Nianjian*, 292.
54. *Xingzheng Guanlixue Ziliao Huibian* (Hunan: Hunansheng Bianzhi Weiyuan-hui Bangongshi, 1985), 50–78.

the district party, the standing committee member system was abolished, one-third of party secretaries and administrative heads had to have a senior high school education, and more than one-third had to be under fifty.[55] A similar guideline was issued on 1 December 1983 for the county-level leadership: the average age had to be forty-five and one-third had to have a college-level education. Even in selecting third-echelon cadres, the center apparently issued several specific guidelines with regard to requirements for age, education level, functional competency, and political reliability.

The official criteria used in selecting new leaders were commitment to reform, education level, professional competency, and age. Two of the four standards stress ability for cadre selection, whereas emphasis on the young amounts to rejecting the seniority system. Although a virtue criterion is retained, the new official criteria unquestionably marked a drastic departure from past practice by one-sidedly emphasizing political qualifications and seniority. The new standards attach more importance to ability than the Maoists did.[56]

However, we do not know how much relative weight each of the four standards carried and how they were applied for each individual cadre selected to leadership positions. But the overall results of the bureaucratic reforms allow us to examine the changing weight of virtue, seniority, and ability.

Age and educational standards are both unambiguous and objective criteria. The regime tried to make the age structure of the leadership parallel the bureaucratic hierarchy. In other words, the average age of the lower-level leadership should be less than that of the superior unit. In addition, the regime intended to keep the age structure of a particular leadership group "ladder- shaped" by including old, middle-aged, and young people—a notion similar to the three-in-one formula advocated by the Gang of Four. Thus, the age requirement depended primarily on the leadership position in question.

Table 47 demonstrates small differences in age between those who were removed and those who were newly promoted in 1982. Those who were promoted to the leadership position were younger than those whom they replaced. Many of the old CC members

55. Ibid.
56. *Renmin Ribao*, 7 August 1985.

Table 47.   Average Age of Leadership in the Four Organs After the
1982 Reforms

Organ	Survived	Newly Added	Combined
Central Committee	70	56	63
	(52 cases)	(56 cases)	(108 cases)
Ministers and vice	66	59	61
ministers	(19 cases)	(28 cases)	(47 cases)
Provincial secretaries	60	58	59
	(13 cases)	(9 cases)	(22 cases)
Directors and deputy	68[a]		
director of CC organs	(8 cases)		

Source. Compiled by the author from biographical information.

a. Because of the unreliability of information on appointment dates, this figure includes all directors and deputy directors.

were transferred to the Central Advisory Commission. But the age consideration was not applied uniformly because some cadres younger than those who stayed in official posts were nonetheless removed. The average age of the CC members who lost their seats was lower than that for those members who survived. None of the Eleventh CC members with the record of rehabilitation failed to make it into the Twelfth CC despite their old ages.

A similar pattern can be observed for those who resigned from the CC in 1985 and those who stayed. Twenty-eight of the fifty-two senior leaders who were in their seventies retired, whereas only six out of twenty-two who were in their sixties resigned. The average age of the retired members was seventy-five. Age was a factor in determining who should stay and who should retire, and seniority ceased to work to the political advantage of the older cadres. Clearly, however, a political factor was also operative. Among the thirty-five senior cadres who had entered the Central Committee at the Eighth Party Congress (all of whom were over seventy), only eighteen retired, whereas seventeen stayed in 1982. Eight of the twelve leaders who survived the CR retired, whereas only ten out of the twenty-three rehabilitated senior leaders resigned in 1982. These figures indicate that the importance of age as a factor in determining who would stay varied depending on a cadre's rank: the higher one's rank, the less important age became; for the lower-ranking cadres, however, age was a crucial factor.

Although the regime heavily publicized "ability" (nengli) as the most important standard for personnel management and although Chinese intellectuals were fascinated with the "science of talent," and set up numerous study groups to do research on the topic, in the official media "ability" is only discussed in general terms as a capacity to work "efficiently . . . to finish an assigned task . . . to be 'bold in practical spirit' . . . [and] to make an actual contribution."[57] Since "ability" can be measured only in relation to the specific task of each organ of the party-state and China has not yet achieved that level of organizational differentiation, "ability" is frequently equated with a much more easily measurable concept: educational level. This approach results in such simplistic views as the following: "the younger, the better," "the more educated the leadership, the better," and "the more persons with professional titles, the better." The regime promoted the educated and functional specialists with such zeal that it created shortages of experts in the fields in which the newly promoted had previously been working.

Professional competency is difficult to measure, particularly for outside observers. However, one can use professional titles and the possession of "practical knowledge" obtained through on-the-job training to determine the weight given to "professional competency" in the bureaucratic reforms. A large number (40 percent) of new ministers and vice ministers promoted in the 1982 readjustment had served as directors and deputy directors of functional bureaus of government ministries. If one includes those who had career experiences in functional departments at the provincial level as well as those with professional degrees—for example, engineers—in this category, the number of persons with long work experiences in a functional field rises to 71 percent. On the other hand, very few members of the State Council had a career background in the party secretaryship. Thirty-seven percent of provincial leaders in 1983 had once served as a director or deputy director of a functional department at the same level, while 29 percent were from secretary positions at lower levels.[58]

In terms of functional areas, 60 percent of the ministers and vice

57. *Rencai Tiandi*, 19 October 1985.
58. Hong Yung Lee, "Evaluation of China's Bureaucratic Reforms," *Annals of the American Academy of Political and Social Science*, no. 4, 1984, 34–47.

Table 48. Career Background of the New Leadership After the Administrative Reforms, as of 1984

Organ	Position	Ministers and Vice Ministers		Directors and Deputy Directors		Secretaries		Total	
		No.	%	No.	%	No.	%	No.	%
Government	Vice ministers	2	2	3	15	7	6	12	6
	Bureau directors	35	40	2	10	3	3	40	20
Party	Provincial secretaries	2	2	1	5	0		3	1
	Municipal, district and county secretaries	3	3	2	1	28	29	33	16
	Director of functional organs (province)	13	15	4	20	36	37	53	26
Mass	Factories	10	11	0	0	1	10	11	5
	Schools	3	3	2	10	2	2	7	3
	CYL	2	2	6	3	11	11	19	9
	Labor	0	0	0	0	1	1	0	0
	Professional	16	18	2	10	3	3	21	10
Military	Political commissars	0	0	0	0	4	4	0	0
Total		86		20		96		199	

Source. Compiled by the author from biographical information.

ministers were identified as having work experience in production fields, that is, industry, agriculture, finance, and transportation. Among the subcategories of production, the majority had experience in production rather than planning, and surprisingly few people had work experience in agricultural fields. The number of people with experience in ideological and political fields was quite low: 18 percent among government leaders. In contrast, a high percentage (42 percent) of provincial party secretaries had career backgrounds exclusively in what can be considered political fields, positions in such organizations as the Secretariat, the organizational department, secretary general offices, and party committees at the lower level. Undoubtedly, the regime promoted many specialists without any overall administrative leadership experience to high-level decision-making posts several grades higher than their original ranks.

Although the regime publicly emphasized the importance of "being revolutionized" and insisted that it could be inferred from "one's political attitude and quality, ideological work style, and ideals," the category apparently worked only as a catch-all criterion for political qualifications. More specifically, the term referred to one's willingness to support the political and ideological line of the center, which was in turn often inferred from one's activities during the CR. Those who had enjoyed rapid promotion during the Gang of Four period failed to pass the test of being "revolutionized," in spite of their appropriate age and probable sufficient professional competence. On the other hand, for the group that was promoted during the reform period, evidence that they were not actively involved in past factional politics seemed to be good enough for them to pass the political test. In other words, the political requirement for promotion during the reforms was not a positive but a negative test of loyalty. The Deng group did not seem to demand that cadres be loyal to their group, but it did demand that they not be loyal to other groups such as the radicals or Mao. The Deng group did not need to require positive loyalty, for those cadres who owed their promotion to reform policy would support the group anyway.

In a sharp departure from the Maoist era, the official news media did not suggest that an understanding of Marxism-Leninism, dedication to the mass line, or a willingness to sacrifice one's private interests should be used as indicators of political qualification. Even the "socialist principle" was infrequently mentioned. When it was, it was broadly interpreted to include any principle that "brings good fortune to the people, develops productivity, or contributes to socialist business."[59]

This does not, however, mean that political qualifications ceased to be a factor; political factors were also operative. If a cadre was comparatively young, but his political loyalty was questionable (this group consisted mainly of those who had enjoyed rapid promotion before the ascendancy of the Deng group), he was removed or transferred to the less important Advisory Commission.[60] Age did not help those with questionable political reliability—those who had enjoyed rapid promotion during the radical period. On the other hand, most rehabilitated cadres and all senior leaders who had entered the CC before the CR—including those who managed to stay in the CC up to the Eleventh CC and those who were purged and then rehabilitated to enter that CC—survived into the Twelfth CC or into the Advisory Commission. In contrast, people who first entered the Ninth CC had less chance of surviving than those who were first appointed to the Tenth or Eleventh CC.

Some conservative veteran leaders continue to regard "being revolutionized" as the most important criterion. "Those with virtue but without ability can be politically trusted. But unfortunately they cannot be given important responsibilities. It is dangerous to place those with ability but without virtue in key positions, because they can use their ability for bad purposes."[61] By contrast, reformers tended to downgrade the importance of "being revolutionized," almost equating it to the ability to carry out reforms. Decision-makers therefore could readily exploit the ambiguity of the term to select whoever shared their own political views.[62]

For a while the regime publicized the "pioneer type of personality"—the person with the courage and determination to challenge any such obstacles to reforms as "the old way of thinking, the unnecessary existing regulations, inertia, resistance, and

59. *Qunzhong*, 13 February 1985, *Dangde Shenghuo*, no. 2, 1985, 5.
60. Hong Yung Lee, "Evaluation."
61. *Renmin Ribao*, 2 October 1982.
62. *Lilun Yu Shijian*, 6 August 1986.

foot dragging."[63] The official media also defended newly promoted reform-minded younger leaders (whom the old cadres
criticised as "arrogant, impatient, and subjective") on the grounds
that "thinking independently and persisting in the correct view is
not arrogance."[64] Praise of the pioneer type—reminiscent of the
Gang of Four's "rebel spirit"—has recently disappeared from
Chinese publications.

In addition to shifting emphasis from virtue to ability, the
regime has made a great effort to broaden its search for the best
qualified candidates. It has pledged to "end the past practice of
searching secretly for candidates within each unit [by] completely
disregarding the boundary between state-owned and collectively-
owned, party members and nonparty members, regular college
graduates and the self-educated." In order to discover "hidden talent," the provincial leaders frequently sent out inspection teams,
and also divided the search among themselves.[65]

Another method employed to broaden the search was to in-
struct lower-level units to submit names of possible candidates for
positions at the upper levels. For instance, the central organizational department asked each province to recommend promising
cadres.[66] This method, if widely used, will allow the provincial
leaders some input into the selection of central leaders. In fact,
whether it is due to this process or not, many provincial leaders
recently moved to central government positions.

The selection of new leaders was supposed to be a complex process involving many different parties in order to ensure a broad
search for high quality. According to the official formula, the procedure for selecting reserve cadres involved "strict observation of
new criteria for each cadre, adherence to the mass line, screening
by the organization department, collective discussion of the matter
by the party committee, and final review by the organization office
of upper echelons."[67]

Party leaders were told not to rely exclusively on personnel dossiers, but rather personally to conduct heart-to-heart talks with

63. Renmin Ribao, 14 September 1984; Sichuan Ribao, 6 April 1983.
64. Qunzhong, 31 February 1985; Renmin Ribao, 18 November 1984.
65. Renmin Ribao, 20 November 1984.
66. Ibid., 15 February 1985.
67. Liaowang, 17 November 1986, 1.

candidates, to watch them at work, and to solicit opinions from those who knew the candidates personally.[68] In some cases, the decision on one cadre required interviews with as many as sixty persons, including "superiors, colleagues, subordinates, school classmates, chauffeurs, service personnel, and family members, as well as his political opponents during the CR period."[69] In addition, a public opinion poll was quite frequently used. For instance, the Anhui provincial party committee surveyed the opinions of more than 6,000 cadres and masses to draw candidates for provincial-level positions. Out of the several hundred candidates selected according to the poll scores, careful evaluation and screening finally produced twenty cadres for provincial top-level positions.[70]

However, despite these efforts to broaden the search for talent, retiring cadres still exerted enormous power in selecting their own successors. Furthermore, there is ample reason to believe that nepotism has been widespread in personnel management. First, the official criteria were too broad and ambiguous, and candidates meeting the official criteria regarding age and education were too numerous. Second, involving diverse groups in the selection process and listening to divergent views tended to make the incumbents' opinions more decisive in the final selection.[71] The regime's effort to formalize the evaluation of cadres by developing a multitude of criteria did not reduce the discretionary power of the incumbents. The frequently reported method of "public opinion polls" was ineffective because only decision-makers had access to the outcome of these polls, and there was no way of knowing whether the results were reflected in the actual cadre selection.

Retiring cadres frequently abused their authority despite the warning not to use their "personal feelings of like or dislike" or "whether or not a candidate complies with their personal views." "When recommending young cadres, a few old cadres do something not in line with the principle, or in obvious violation of the party principle, thereby creating controversy among colleagues and the people." Many incumbents selected their successors from

68. Ibid., 20 November 1984.
69. Ibid., 20 April 1984.
70. *Liaowang*, 17 November 1986, 1.
71. Ibid., 7 August 1985.

relatives, friends, and others whom they knew well, thus suffering from "the diseases of impression" and allowing "those who are close to the leadership to flourish."[72] According to a Chinese maxim, "a dwarf general recruits only dwarf soliders"; thus, submissive comformists among the "better educated and younger in age" had a better chance for promotion.

Understandably, ordinary Chinese were not happy with the policy of allowing retiring cadres to choose their successors as an inducement to retire, labeling the practice "the director responsibility system" (*shouzhang fuze zhi*), which was not much different from the feudal succession symbolized in Mao's statement—"with you in charge, I am at ease."[73] The practice may turn out to be a costly concession for the Leninist Party organization because it encouraged the further "privatization" of official positions by officeholders, resulting in more fragmentation of the party's authority—which economic reforms have already substantially weakened.[74]

In brief, the evidence indicates that the regime relied largely on such objective and universal criteria as age, educational level, and professional competency in making personnel changes. This use of nonpolitical and achievement-oriented criteria marked a sharp departure from the Maoist stress on virtue, which was open to subjective interpretation to such an extent that it gave rise to what Andrew Walder calls "principled particularism."[75] This time the merit-based criteria were universal, but their application gave decision-makers a chance to incorporate their personal preferences. According to another Chinese maxim, "age is treasure, education helps, but the supporter is the most important," indicating that the regime skillfully made use of the particularistic application of universal criteria in order to mollify incumbent old revolutionaries and to consolidate the reformers' power base while bringing about fundamental changes in the cadre corps.[76] As a result of the particularistic application of the universal criteria, some social groups benefited from the reform while others did not.

72. Ibid.
73. *Jing Bao*, 10 July 1985; *Renmin Ribao*, 9 June 1985.
74. *Lilun Naican*, no. 5, 1986.
75. Andrew G. Walder, *Communist Neo-Traditionalism: Work and Authority in Chinese Industry* (Berkeley and Los Angeles: University of California Press, 1987).
76. *Zhengzhi Yu Xingzheng Yanjiu*, November 1985.

The losers are the middle or low-ranking administrative cadres who are fifty to fifty-five years old, those who started their careers at the bottom of the bureaucratic hierarchy in the 1950s when they were in their early twenties.[77] As the requirements for cadre recruitment and promotion shifted to educational achievement and professional knowledge, it became obvious that this group of cadres—generally known as the "jack-of-all-trades campaign cadres"—had nothing to count on. They possess neither the necessary education level nor any special knowledge.[78] They are not liberation cadres who participated in the civil war and hence are entitled to *lixiu*; nor do they have the ability to contribute to the Four Modernizations. Worse still, they are too old according to the official age requirement. Thus, they consider themselves stuck in a "stopped elevator," "ships anchored in a harbor," or "trains stopped at the last station."

They try, however, to defend themselves by insisting that the practical knowledge that they accumulated during their prolonged careers should not be overlooked and that although their "biological age is old," ideologically they are not old. Since they have solved most of their family problems, such as raising children and getting them married, they are at the best stage in their life to concentrate their energy and attention on their work without being distracted by personal problems. Their hero is Chen Yun, who flatly declared, "Realization of the Four Modernizations should depend on the party's leadership. Some people are saying that most of our cadres are the cadres of 'medicine for all diseases.' According to my view, we cannot achieve the Four Modernizations without these cadres who are jacks-of-all-trades. We should not belittle the role of such cadres."[79] Nonetheless, the campaign cadres are losing their position and influence, although they still constitute a major portion of China's middle-level cadres. Even if they manage to remain in their positions, none of the campaign cadres has managed to reach the top level. On the whole, the top-level leadership has

77. For this type of cadre, see *Dangde Shenghou*, no. 12, 1983, 38–39; no. 13, 1983, 38–42.

78. Some science and technical cadres in the middle-age bracket feel that they have no chance of moving up; they believe in "self-survival and self-dying." *Renmin Ribao*, 17 May 1985.

79. *Dangde Shenghou*, no. 13, 1983, 42.

jumped over several generations of cadres, from the Long March generation to the postliberation generation.

The groups that have most conspicuously benefited from the new policy are the children and the former secretaries of high-ranking cadres, as well as former leaders of the Communist Youth League.[80] It is easy to understand why children of high-ranking cadres have benefited most from the system.[81] First, it was their parents who selected their own successors and who have access to information at the top level. Sometimes high-ranking cadres used their retirement as leverage to gain the appointment of their children to appropriate positions, although the *dingti* system was not officially applicable to cadre positions. Alternatively, they could use their extensive personal network by offering reciprocal favors to other decision-makers.

Most of the children of cadres could meet the official requirements of age and education. Since older cadres currently retiring are about sixty-five years old, their children fall within the forty-to-fifty-year-old age bracket. Their children were born in the Yanan period, and they finished their secondary education before 1966. Some of them went to the Soviet Union in the 1950s for further studies. In addition, these children meet the political requirements. Many of them participated in the CR at the initial stage, but they soon became targets of the mass movement as radical rebels led by children from less desirable classes rose to power. Thereafter, they were subjected to various types of political persecution during the Gang of Four era. Because of these hardships they are generally wary of excessive political struggle and disapprove of ideological orthodoxy. Furthermore, retiring cadres know that they will not be betrayed, politically or otherwise, if their children succeed them.

POLITICAL IMPLICATIONS

The bureaucratic reforms succeeded in replacing the revolutionary cadres with bureaucratic technocrats who are qualitatively differ-

80. As criticism of the special privileges of the children of high-ranking cadres spread, the regime prohibited them from assuming important leadership positions without the approval of the center. *Renmin Ribao*, 2 February 1986.

81. *Jiushi Niandai*, September 1985.

ent from their predecessors in terms of political experience, socialization, and value orientation. This rise of technical experts marks an end to the Maoist era associated with the former revolutionaries—originally recruited from the least educated and poorest segments of the population for guerrilla warfare. It also signals an end to the Maoist practice of selecting political leaders for their revolutionary potential rather than for the expertise needed to develop a modern society. Because they were chosen to help China's industrialization, bureaucratic technocrats have an incentive to continue the merit-based recruitment policy.

During Mao's era the revolutionary cadres possessed political power, whereas intellectuals with skill and knowledge functionally indispensable to the modern industrial society were not only completely excluded from political power but were also persecuted as the "stinking ninth category." To Maoist radicals, intellectual class interests were incompatible with those of poor peasants, and their knowledge enabled them to raise critical questions about the Maoist revolutionary approach. Although the CCP's bias against intellectuals originally came from Mao, it was largely supported by members who were recruited from the less educated and poorest sectors of the population. During the Maoist period, among the educated only ideologues whose major task was to manipulate Marxism-Leninism and Mao Zedong thought flourished politically.[82] Not only did this practice end with the advent of the reforms, but also for the first time in Chinese history, a social group possessing the knowledge and skills necessary for modernization came to power.[83]

Presently, bureaucratic technocrats are not completely free to exercise their political authority. Some newly promoted specialists feel that they are not given enough political authority and freedom to utilize their expertise.[84] Old cadres continue to exert political influence: a few of them still remain in the Politburo and Secretariat; others have seats in the Central Advisory Commission; and the

82. Among many absurd episodes of ideologues imposing their simplistic political criteria on educated sectors during the CR, the most revealing is that the Gang of Four rounded up about 613 professors in a surprise raid and then subjected them to a written test on politics and official ideology. Not surprisingly, only thirty-five passed. *Zhonggong Dangshi Jiaoxue*, no. 4, 1983.

83. Huntington, *Political Order*.

84. *Shehui Kexueyuan Yanjiu Cankao Ziliao*, 21 July 1985.

bureaucratic revolutionaries are still well entrenched at the middle and lower levels. The old guard's political muscle was dramatically demonstrated in the dismissal of Hu Yaobang from the general secretaryship and the recent decision to recentralize economic authority.

Nonetheless, interference by old revolutionaries is a transitional phenomenon that will decline as time passes. Unlike Eastern European countries where technical specialists were gradually coopted into state organs dealing only with economic affairs, Chinese technocrats have infiltrated the highest political offices such as the Politburo and the Secretariat of the CCP.[85] In addition, conservative leaders such as Chen Yun, Peng Zhen, and Bo Yibo were apparently not deeply involved in the selection of the new cadres. Even if they did have the power to select their own successors, to find someone who could have balanced the political and ideological requirements with the prerequisites of economic development would have been impossible. Moreover, there is ample indication that the bureaucratic technocrats are becoming more assertive vis-à-vis the old revolutionaries. The public media initially urged the old cadres to help the new generation of cadres "get on the horse and then see them sent off." But now, the slogan has changed to "help them to ride the horse and let them manage by themselves."

It is uncertain whether the bureaucratic technocrats have the leadership ability or political acumen to lead China through the multitude of contradictions inherent in these rapid social changes, while achieving unity among themselves, particularly when the senior leaders, now working as a centripetal force, disappear. Having been placed in political positions by rapid promotion that skipped several grades, many bureaucratic technocrats lack leadership experience. Some are simply unqualified for their political positions, and others are afraid of taking responsibility and so look to the revolutionary cadres to decide complex matters.[86] Furthermore, among the bureaucratic technocrats there are many different groups with different policy preferences. To make mat-

---

85. Ibid.
86. *Jingji Yanjiu Cankao Ziliao*, 8 September 1985, 32–39; *Renmin Ribao*, 12 August 1985.

ters even more complicated, bureaucratic technocrats are supposed to work collectively, but the new leaders have not yet mastered the technique of reaching consensus among specialists in different fields. Already there are signs of policy disputes among the bureaucratic technocrats, for example, on price reforms.

The important point to remember, however, is that unlike the old revolutionaries who split over the fundamental goals of the regime, the technocrats agree on basic goals but disagree on the method to achieve them. This trend of viewing policy differences among themselves as a technical matter rather than as a matter of principle will confine the disruptive consequences of inner-elite conflicts.[87] The promotion of technocrats to political positions is not based on their proven leadership ability but on the belief that their rigorous scientific training will enable them to grasp any problem in its totality and to find the solution through an analytical approach.[88] It is hoped, therefore, that as time passes, the bureaucratic technocrats will expand their horizons from those of specialists to those of generalists or will combine their in-depth speciality with a broader view, in the manner of the Chinese figurative expression of "T-shaped knowledge," thereby acquiring political wisdom and insight.[89]

Perhaps the most difficult question concerns the bureaucratic technocrats' ideology and leadership style. There is absolutely no data bearing on the direct implications of this issue, but much indirect evidence indicates that they are critical of the existing ideology. For instance, the ideological commitment of cadres since 1980 has been declining, and the younger generation is more critical of the socialist ideology than the old generation.[90]

Three factors will probably determine the political value and leadership style of the bureaucratic technocrats. Their long experiences in bureaucratic settings will have fostered an organizational mentality, but the technical work they engaged in before will also

87. For this point, see Jean Meynard, *Technocracy* (London: Faber & Faber, 1965), 134.

88. For technical training and leadership capability, see Ezra N. Suleiman, *Elites in French Society* (Princeton: Princeton University Press, 1978).

89. For the issue of unqualified bureaucratic technocrats, see *Ganxu Ribao*, 28 September 1985; *Zhongguo Xingzheng Guanli*, no. 12, 1986, 17–18.

90. *Hong Qi*, no. 17, 1988, 11–12; *Xinxiang Pinglun*, no. 7, 1982, 13–14; *Diaocha Yu Yanjiu*, no. 12, 1986, 11–13.

have preserved an outlook derived from their professional training. Moreover, their own understanding of the role of political leaders will affect their actual behavior. Although it is obvious that bureaucratic technocrats as political leaders will experience cross-pressures between the demands of their professional backgrounds and their political role, there is no way of knowing the relative weight of these factors. However, if one uses Frederic Fleron's distinction between "cooptation" and "recruitment" as a measure of determining their outlook, the bureaucratic technocrats were co-opted rather than recruited. According to Fleron, those co-opted into the political elite after serving a long time in a specialized professional position tend to bring their professional attitude to the new political roles.[91]

One point is very clear. The bureaucratic technocrats have a better understanding and better qualifications to deal with such prerequisites of industrialized society as functional specialization, coordination of various parts, rational decision making, and problem solving. Moreover, as Thomas Baily argues, all "technical intelligentsias" are pragmatic in the sense that they resent the bureaucratic rules that have constrained their work in the past, attach priority to "getting the job done," and view ideology not as a dogma but as something to be interpreted flexibly for the economic goal.[92] Similarly, it seems that bureaucratic technocrats in China share a relative indifference to politics and ideology, accompanied by the urge to get on with the accomplishment of professional tasks.[93] Thus, they will probably prefer structured and orderly environments, opting for technical and piecemeal rather than comprehensive political solutions to China's problems.

Compared with old revolutionaries, the new leaders are more self-confident, less dependent on the party for guidance, urban-oriented, forward- and outward-looking, and with minimal emotional ties to or understanding of the rural peasants.[94] At the same time, the new leaders also lack personal moral integrity and com-

91. Frederic Fleron, "Representation of Career Types in the Soviet Political Leadership," in R. Barry Fareell, ed., Political Leadership in Eastern Europe and the Soviet Union (Chicago: Aldine, 1970), 123–38.

92. Thomas Baily, The Technical Intelligentsia and the East German Elite (Berkeley and Los Angeles: University of California Press, 1974), 85.

93. Ibid., 262.

94. Xueshu Jiaoliu (Heilongjiang), no. 2, 1982, 38.

mitment to the Communist ideology that the old revolutionary cadres possessed. In the eyes of old revolutionaries, this quality has caused the widespread corruption and abuse of political authority for private gain by the new generation of leaders.[95]

Being pragmatic does not mean being politically liberal. As "intelligentsia" rather than "critical intellectuals," using Alvin Gouldner's terminology, the new Chinese leaders are authoritarian in their political outlook and will utilize their expertise to improve and maintain rather than innovate and change the existing system.[96]

Yet, a caveat: the new leaders are co-opted precisely because they promised to create new institutions and to promote economic development at a time when the old Maoist system was being thoroughly discredited. In this sense, they are quite different from the Brezhnev generation in the Soviet Union and the technical intelligentsia of the Eastern European countries who were recruited by the old leaders to run the existing system more effectively.[97] The bureaucratic technocrats' lack of ideological commitment will help them to push for structural reforms.[98] Moreover, in contemporary China, age and level of education are closely correlated with support of reforms: the younger and better educated are more likely actively to participate in reform efforts.[99] The reason is simple: the better educated are more innovative, less persistent in old habits, and more cost-efficient, thereby benefiting more from reforms. In addition, the bureaucratic technocrats know that their political future is inextricably tied to the success of the Four Modernizations. Since the political ideology has been discredited and the party's charisma is fading, the bureaucratic technocrats must build legitimacy by delivering the promised economic benefits to all the Chinese people.

95. *Ningxia Shehui Kexue Tongxin*, no. 2, 1986, 8–16.
96. Alvin Gouldner, *The Future of Intellectuals and the Rise of the New Class* (New York: Seabury Press, 1979).
97. Jerry Hough, *Russia and the West: Gorbachev and the Politics of Reform* (New York: Simon & Schuster, 1988).
98. For the relationship between level of education and willingness to take risks, see *Zuohao Zai Zhishifengzi Zhong Fazhan Dangyuan Gongzuo* (Beijing: Xinhua Chubanshe, 1985).
99. For the relationship between education and attitude toward reforms, see *Xueshi Yu Shijian*, May 1985, 5.

12

Rebuilding the Party

Since Mao's death, the CCP has taken a series of measures designed to restore its credibility and legitimacy. As noted, it has rehabilitated the victims of past purges, reversed some past decisions, and upgraded the quality of the cadre corps. More important, it has critically appraised its past record in "The Resolution on Historical Questions."[1] The party's willingness publicly to "correct its own mistakes," however, proved to be insufficient to regain the people's confidence. By the time the regime started the party rectification in 1984, the CCP was still so demoralized, factionalized, and confused that "the crisis in faith" had to be publicly discussed.[2] Because of disenchantment and alienation, the ordinary Chinese person was apathetic and cynical, while the courageous openly declared their intention to "cut ties" (*juejiao*) with the party.[3] The intensive ideological education, careful screening, and reregistration of each party member in the three-year rectification campaign from 1984 to 1986 did not improve the party's organizational capability. When Deng Xiaoping wanted to suppress the student movement in 1989, he realized that the military, not the party, was the only reliable instrument for such purposes.

This chapter analyzes, first, the existing structure of the party membership; second, the new recruitment policy; third, the party's effort to revitalize itself through the rectification campaign; and, last, the basic dilemma facing the Leninist Party as it tries to lead China to economic development while maintaining its Leninist tradition.

---

1. For the document, see *Beijing Ribao*, 6 June 1980, 10–39.
2. *Wenhui Bao*, 13 June 1980; *Beijing Ribao*, 31 January 1980.
3. *Dangde Shenghuo*, no. 1, 1984, 18; *Zhengdang yu Jiandang*, 16 April 1986, 26.

Table 49.   Distribution of CCP Members by Occupation, 1981

Occupation	A (millions)	B (%)	C (millions)	D (%)
Peasants	17.77	45.5	377	0.4
Workers	7.34	18.8	83	8.8
Military	1.90	4.8	4.2	45.0
Service	0.93	2.4		
Specialists	3.09	7.8	26.0	7.8
Administrative cadres[a]	8.20	20.6	12.0	6.6

Source. Diaocha Yu Yanjiu, no. 144, 2 November 1982.

Note.
  A: Number of party members in the category (total: 39 million).
  B: Percentage of party members in relation to total party members.
  C: Number of persons employed in the category.
  D: Percentage of party members in relation to the workers employed in the
    category.
  a. Estimated.

CHARACTERISTICS OF PARTY MEMBERS

As of 1985, the Chinese Communist Party had about 42 million members in 2.57 million branches.[4] Organized by geography and function, party branches exist in every locality and functional unit, except in places (such as government ministries) where the party core group (dangzu) exercises leadership. Most of them are male, and the percentage of females ranged from 13.5 percent in Sichuan province to 12 percent nationwide.[5]

DISTRIBUTION

As table 49 demonstrates, most party members are peasants: 17.77 million (45.5 percent). Despite the impressive statistics they are still underrepresented: only 0.4 percent of the total peasant population are party members. In contrast, 8.8 percent of all Chinese workers are party members. The membership rate in the military is quite high; if one assumes that the total PLA strength is 4.2 million, almost of half of all those in uniform are party members. If one

4. Nongmin Ribao, 4 December 1985.
5. Renmin Ribao, 1 December 1983 ; Sichuan Ribao, 30 June 1984.

takes into account the difference between enlisted men and officers, it is very likely that almost all officers are party members.

About 9.9 million party members (25.5 percent) are unaccounted for. In all probability, the remaining group consists of party members among cadres. If so, the membership rate among administrative cadres (12 million) is 83 percent. This estimate approximates Zhao Ziyang's report that 69 percent of all cadres in the state organs are party members and that the rate of membership is much higher among the leading cadres of the state organs.[6] Inner Mongolia reports that all provincial-level leading cadres, all mayors and deputy mayors (except for two) in twelve municipalities, and all magistrates and deputy magistrates (except for two) in 100 counties are party members. Among directors and deputy directors of the approximately 100 bureaus that are directly under provincial supervision, only fourteen are nonparty members, and nine of these are newly retired.[7]

The percentage of party members among specialists is reportedly 3.09 million (7.8 percent), which constitutes only 13 percent of all specialists (26 million in the 1982 census). Another source reports that about 23 percent of 10.18 million functional cadres were members in 1983.[8] At 23 percent, the party membership rate is higher than in other occupational groups, but much lower than among administrative cadres.

Distribution of party members among the functional areas varies from sector to sector.[9] The membership rate is higher in the industrial sector, for instance, than in educational institutions. Membership among high school and middle school teachers is only 8 percent, whereas it ranges from 25 to 40 percent in industrial enterprises.

In individual enterprises, the membership rate varies greatly from factory to factory. On the whole, the rate is higher in heavy industry than in light industry. For instance, only 4.1 percent of workers in the Shanghai Seventeenth Textile Factory are party

6. *Renmin Ribao*, 17 March 1989.
7. *Shijian*, no. 6, 1982, 8–10.
8. In 1981, the total number of those who were specialized technical people (*zhuanye jishu ganbu*) was 8.35 million, 1.85 million (22.2 percent) of whom were party members. Zhongong Zhongyang Zuzhibu, ed., *Zuohao Zai Zhishifenzi Zhong Fazhan Dangyuan Gongzuo* (Beijing: Xinhua Chubanshe, 1985), 65.
9. *Gongchandangyuan*, nos. 11–12, 1985, 22.

Table 50. Party Membership of Workers and Cadres in Eleven Enterprises, 1983

Unit	Total No. of Workers	Worker Party Members		Total No. of Cadres	Cadre Party Members	
		No.	%		No.	%
Third Construction Corporation of Beijing	6,975	569	8.1	1,520	616	40.5
Zhengzhou railway branch	41,058	6,349	15.4	4,889	3,212	65.6
Dalian shipyard	13,051	1,737	13.3	3,771	2,047	54.2
Shanghai First Department store	2,273	165	7.2	163	100	61.3
Angang's thirteen units	11,017	2,120	19.2	1,671	1,113	66.6
Yungding Minging	7,018	872	12.4	1,125	460	40.8
Daqing Oilfield's thirteen units	11,985	2,423	20.2	3,015	2,045	67.8
Naning Wireless Factory	3,688	372	10.0	1,817	524	28.8
Shanghai 17th Textile Factory	8,439	346	4.1	795	382	48.0
Zhangchun First Automobile	35,625	4,622	12.9	10,992	5,150	46.8
Guangzhou Sea Transportation Company	8,776	5,822	66?	3,858	1,692	43.8
Total	149,995	25,393	16.9	33,616	17,341	51.5

Source. Zhonggong Zhongyang Shujichu Yanjiushi Lilunzu, ed., *Dangqian Wuguo Gongren Jieji Diaocha Ziliao Huibian* (Beijing: Zhongyang Dangxiao Chubanshe, 1982), vols. 1–2.

members, whereas almost 66 percent of workers in the Sea Transportation Company are reportedly members (see table 50). The low level of party membership in the textile factory can be attributed to the fact that the majority of workers in this sector are female—a group with a low rate of membership. The second lowest rate was found in the Shanghai Department Store—also composed of female workers. Within each factory, the membership rate of management is almost three times higher than that of workers, and the difference appears to be growing. In the Anshan Steel Mill (*dangang*) and in the Daqing Oilfield, two of every three management cadres are party members.

Table 51 reflects the changing emphasis in the regime's recruitment policy. The rate of membership among production workers reached its highest point (26 percent) in 1978, probably reflecting the Gang of Four's leftist recruitment policy, whereas the rate in 1981 dropped substantially to 17.9 percent. The current party membership rate among production workers is likely to be lower than the indicated figure. The percentage of technical personnel has been rising steadily, thus indicating that the Gang of Four's anti-intellectual policy did not affect a technocrat's chance to join the party. What is most striking is the fluctuation of party membership among management personnel. Undoubtedly due to the leftist policy of the CR, the percentage among them reached the lowest point (43.5 percent) in 1978, but it increased to 67.2 percent by 1981. At the moment, it is likely that the percentage has increased among management cadres, as well as among technical cadres. It is worth noting that the ratio of party membership to management personnel has been consistently higher than that of any other category.

Among intellectuals, the membership rate varies depending on the age group. For instance, 48 percent of older intellectuals (those who graduated from college before 1949) are party members, whereas only 20 percent of those who graduated from college between 1950 and 1966 are members in Shanghai.[10] Twenty-five percent of those who graduated from college after 1978 are members. Two factors account for this variation. First, age is closely related to professional ranking. In the past few years, the regime has endea-

10. Zhongong Zhongyang Zuzhibu, ed., *Zuohao Zai*, 183.

Table 51. Party Members Among Employees in Eleven Enterprises,
by Type of Work for Three Different Periods

Type of Work	1965		1978		1981	
	No.	%	No.	%	No.	%
Production field						
Workers	75,634		151,979		181,216	
Party members	13,210	17.5	39,607	26.0	32,470	17.9
Support field						
Workers	7,955		26,908		21,534	
Party members	1,037	13.0	2,669	9.9	2,788	12.9
Technical field						
Personnel	8,068		11,570		11,553	
Party members	721	8.9	3,062	26.4	4,040	40.2
Management field						
Personnel	15,659		33,478		34,328	
Party members	8,788	56.1	14,570	43.5	23,070	67.2
Total						
Staff and workers	107,316		223,933		24,863	
Party members	23,756	22.1	59,908	26.8	62,977	25.3

Source. Zhonggong Zhongyang Shujichu Yanjiushi Lilunzu, ed., *Danggian Wuguo Gongren Jieji Diaocha Ziliao Huibien* (Beijing: Zhongyang Dangxiao Chubanshe, 1982), vols. 1–2.

vored to recruit famous intellectuals—many of whom are old—for obvious propaganda purposes. The second factor is the recruitment policy at any given moment. The relaxed policy toward intellectuals up to 1957 explains the high proportion of older intellectuals.

The distribution of party members among college students varies from college to college and from year to year (see table 52). Before the CR, the membership rate was rising steadily through 1958 (9.7 percent) but then it gradually dropped. In 1980, the percentage of party members among the 1.28 million college students was 3.8; after graduation of classes that had entered college in 1977 and 1978, the percentage dropped to 1.9 percent in 1982.[11] The membership increase to 2.5 percent in 1983 was largely due to students in special training classes, which included many party-

11. Ibid., 67.

Table 52.   Party Membership Among College Students

Years	University Students	Party Members	
		No.	%
Shanghai universities			
1956	39,859	3,302	8.3
1957	38,663	3,263	8.4
1958	45,840	4,457	9.7
1959	55,913	3,450	6.2
1960	63,435	3,632	5.7
1961	63,648	3,872	6.1
1962	58,575	2,811	4.8
National universities			
1980	1.28 millions		3.8
1982	1.13 millions	210,000	1.9
1983	1.20 millions	300,000	2.5

Sources. Shanghai data: Li Yungjin, "Zhongshi zai Daxueshengzhong fazhan dang-yuan," *Ma'anshan Gangtie xueyuan Gaojiao Yanjiu,* no. 2, Apr. 1985, 89; cited in Stanley Rosen, "Survey Research in the People's Republic of China: Uses and Limitations." National data: Zhonggong Zhongyang Zhuzhibu, ed., *Zuohao Zai Zhishifenzi Zhong Fazhan Dangyuan Gongzuo* (Beijing: Xinhua Chubanshe, 1985), 67, 89.

member cadres.[12] In 1983, the membership rate among students of Shanghai's three universities and Tianjin's seven colleges was less than 1 percent, ironically less than the rate during the KMT era.[13]

The most striking feature in the distribution of party members by province is that the membership rate does not vary much (see table 53). Available figures for the 1980s vary from 2.2 percent in Guizhou to 7.9 percent in Beijing. The average rate is about 3.5 percent to 3.9 percent. The high membership rate in Beijing is understandable because it is the capital where all high-ranking cadres live. High membership rates in Shanghai (6.3 percent), Tianjin (5.7 percent), and Liaoning (5.5 percent) indicate that they bear a significant correlation with the degree of industrialization. The rather high rate in Yunnan (7.7 percent) and Qinghai (4.4 percent) is probably due to the presence of a large number of military personnel. The rather even distribution of party membership

12. *Jiefang Ribao,* 29 September 1984.
13. Zhonggong Zongyang Zuzhibu, ed., *Zuohao Zai.*

Table 53.   Distribution of Party Membership by Province

Province	Population	Party Members	% of Population
Anhui	50,560,000		
1983		1,440,000	2.85
Beijing	9,340,000		
1985		740,000	
1985		675,000	
1982		650,000	
Fujian	26,400,000		
1979		630,000	2.39
1959		245,000	
Hebei	54,200,000		
1985		2,000,000	3.90
Heilongjiang	33,060,000		
1983		1,299,016	3.90
1979		1,082,629	
1971		726,245	
1960		544,200	
1959		450,000	
1956		378,806	
Henan	75,910,000		
1956	47,195,000	509,540	1.08
Hubei	48,350,000		
Hunan	55,090,000		
1982		1,980,000	3.60
1977		1,700,000	
1957		285,790	
1956	35,222,000	282,000	0.80
1955		210,000	
Guansu	19,880,000		
1981		700,000	3.52
1959		352,713	
7/1956		216,000	
1956	12,852,000	200,000	
Guangdong	60,750,000		
1978		1,800,000	2.96
1979		1,700,000	
12/1961		907,000	
9/1959		740,000	
12/1957		500,000	
7/1956		350,000	
6/1955		240,000	
12/1954		200,000	
1949		40,000	
Guangxi	37,330,000		
1977		1,050,000	2.81
1956	19,447,000	108,598	
Guizhou	29,010,000		
1985		640,000	2.20

(*Continued on next page*)

Table 53. Continued

Province	Population	Party Members	% of Population
1956	16,273,000	139,000	0.88
6/1956		110,000	
In. Mongolia	19,550,000		
1985		680,000	
1960		255,000	
6/1959		232,639	
8/1956		167,000	
1956	8,164,000	151,756	
Jiangsu	61,350,000		
1985		2,300,000	3.75
12/1977		1,700,000	
11/1976		1,600,000	
1956	43,904,000	600,000	1.36
Jiangxi	33,840,000		
1984		1,130,000	3.34
1956	17,997,000	250,000	1.30
Jilin	22,700,000		
1956	12,130,000	195,720	1.60
Liaoning	36,290,000		
1985		2,000,000	5.50
1984		1,900,000	
1980		1,640,000	
1956	23,891,000	400,000	1.60
Ningxia	3,895,578		
1982		147,500	3.70
Qinghai	3,930,000		
1983		157,923	4.40
1976		128,291	
12/1966		77,665	
1956		41,609	
1951		2,267	
Shaanxi	29,310,000		
1982		1,240,000	4.23
1977		1,100,000	
1956	17,381,000	200,000	1.15
Shandong	75,640,000		
1982		3,000,000	3.97
2/1981		2,900,000	
10/1976		2,400,000	
1956	51,042,000	1,120,000	2.19
Shanghai	11,940,000		
1985		7,537,000	6.30
1956	6,669,000	150,000	2.25
Shanxi	25,720,000		
12/1956		300,000	
Sichuan	100,760,000		
1983		3,300,000	3.27
2/1979		2,800,000	2.78

Table 53.   Continued

Province	Population	Party Members	% of Population
Tianjin	7,890,000		
1984		450,000	5.70
Tibet	1,930,000		
10/1977		54,000	2.79
Xinjiang	13,180,000		
1956	5,384,000	68,000	1.30
12/1954		1,169	
Yunnan	33,190,000		
1981		256,000	7.70
1956	18,553,000	182,000	1.00
Zhejiang	39,630,000		
1981		1,090,000	2.70
4/1980		1,030,000	
5/1978		950,000	
1957		300,000	
1956	24,462,000	190,000	0.70
1952		24,000	

Sources. All 1956 figures are from Franz Schurmann, *Ideology and Organization in Communist China* (Berkeley and Los Angeles: University of California Press, 1968), 156. Other figures are from *Heilongjiang Provincial Information* (Investigation Research Office of Heilongjiang Provincial Government); *Xinjiang Ribao*, 24 May 1980; *Keyen Guanli*, no. 3, 1981; *Hebei Xuekan*, no. 4, 1982, 13–20; *Hunan Ribao*, 26 Apr. 1982; *Renmin Ribao*, 20 Aug. 1983; *Henan Ribao*, 29 Aug. 1983; *Tianjinshi 1984 nian Shehui Kexue Keti Diaocha Chengguo Xuanbian* 2:45; *Nanfang Ribao*, 7 Sept. 1984; *Shijian*, no. 11, 1985, 4–9.

among the provinces implies that a centralized control mechanism coordinates recruitment in different areas.

AGE

The age of party members is not available, but it is fair to assume that as a whole they are much older than the population. According to an official source, 26 percent were below the age of twenty-five in 1950, but the same age group constituted only 2.25 percent in 1983, and in some areas (e.g., Zhunhua county in Hebei province) the percentage is as low as 1.3. But by 1984 the proportion increased to 3.2 percent because of the stepped-up effort to recruit young people.[14]

As of 1981, ony 6.8 percent of 39 million party members had

14. Ibid., 89.

joined the party before 1949—2.65 million including 10,000 senior members (ones who had joined during the great revolutionary period and 300,000 who had joined during the anti-Japanese war). Fifteen million (38.6 percent) joined the party between 1949 and 1966. The CR generation comprises 16 million (40.6 percent), and those who joined after the Gang of Four total 5.64 million.[15] Since it is fair to assume that most members joined when they were young (in their mid-twenties), the distribution by generation indicates that the average age was very old, even in 1981. For instance, the average age of those who joined before 1949 was over sixty-five. Those who joined between 1949 and 1966 were sixty-five to forty-five. Those who joined during the CR were forty-five to thirty-five.

Table 54 demonstrates young people's apathy toward joining the party. Among workers who were employed after the Gang of Four, only 3.6 percent are activists, whereas the rate goes up to 12.2 percent for those who began work before the CR. Among technical cadres, the percentage of activists rose from 8.1 percent during the CR to 15.1 percent in the post-Mao era. This may be because young technical cadres see membership as a way to enhance their career potential, whereas young workers have less incentive to join the party. Young peasants are less interested in joining the party than their urban counterparts, despite the official effort to recruit them.[16] Among 2,926 party members in the three counties of Jiangsu, only sixty-three are under twenty-five (0.15 percent of the age group). Another village (*xiang*) has a total of 2,877 people in the age group eighteen to twenty-three. Among them only twenty-five have applied for membership (0.83 percent).[17] Only 0.8 percent of the rural population are nonmember activists; the official goal is to raise the figure to 3 percent.[18]

EDUCATIONAL LEVEL

The overall educational level of party members is rather low. Only 4 percent have a college-level education (see table 55). The majority

15. *Renmin Ribao*, 30 June 1986. For young workers' political attitude, see *Sixiang Zhengzhi Gongzuo yanjiu*, no. 3, 1984, 20.
16. Zhonggong Zhongyang Zuzhibu, ed., *Zuohao Zai*, 35.
17. *Nongcun Gongzuo Tongxun*, July 1985, 7–8.
18. *Gongchandangyuan*, no. 12, 1985, 10–14.

Table 54. Party Members and Activists Among Workers and Technical Cadres, by Starting Work Period

Type	Total		Before 1949		1949–56		1957–65		1966–76		After Gang of Four	
	No.	%	No.	%	No.	%	No.	%	No.	%	No.	%
Workers												
Party members	25,393	16.9	1,083	33.6	5,483	37.4	5,665	20.4	1,399	2.3	1,763	4.4
Nonmembers	123,602		2,139		15,045		22,070		57,440		37,854	
Activists	10,950	7.3	113	5.2	1,850	12.2	2,707	12.2	4,891	8.5	1,389	3.6
Total	159,945		3,335	2.1	22,378	13.7	30,442	18.5	63,730	39.2	41,006	26.5
Technical cadres												
Party members	17,341	51.5	2,044	69.1	5,519	62.8	4,382	49.9	4,507	23.0	889	3.5
Nonmembers	16,275		912		3,269		4,394		15,049		1,651	
Activists	3,698	22.0	89	9.7	1,014	31.0	1,111	25.2	1,234	8.1	250	15.1
Total	37,314		3,045	8.8	9,802	26.1	9,887	26.1	20,790	31.3	2,790	7.6

Source. Zhonggong Zhongyang Shujichu Yanjiushi Lilunzu, ed., Danggian Wuguo Gongren Jieji Diaocha Ziliao Huibien (Beijing: Zhongyang Dangxiao Chubanshe, 1982), vols. 1–2.

Table 55.   Educational Level of CCP Members, as of 1985

Educational Level	A (millions)	B (%)	C (millions)	D (%)	E (millions)
Graduated from college	1.60	4.0	4.5	35.5	1.2
Specialized middle school and senior high school	5.52	13.8	54.8[a]	10.0	7.3
Junior high[b]	12.00	30.0	135.5	8.8	37.6
Primary school	16.88	42.2	179.1	9.4	135.7
Illiterate	4.00	10.0	147.3	2.7	
Total	40.00	100.0			

Source. *Zuo Hao Zai Zhishifenzizhong Fazhan Dangyuan Gongzuo* (Beijing: Beijing Xinhua Chubanshe, 1985), 58.
Note.
   A: Number of party members.
   B: Percentage of party members with the educational level.
   C: Number employed with the educational Level.
   D: Percentage of party members among people with the educational level.
   E: Number of students enrolled in 1983.
a. Figure includes only senior high school graduates. If estimated graduates of specialized middle schools were added, the percentage of the total (D) would decrease to about 8.6 percent.
b. All figures are estimated.

of members have only a primary school education (42.2 percent), and about 10.1 percent are illiterate. Three or four out of every ten college graduates are party members. One surprise in table 55 is that more primary school graduates (9.4 percent) are represented than junior high school graduates (8.8 percent). Based on this information, the table identifies the regime's past recruitment policy of emphasizing class background and political contribution. The national average appears to approximate the provincial situation quite closely. For instance, party members with a college-level education are 5 percent in Liaoning and 3.2 percent in Guangdong.[19] In Heilongjiang, party members who have a primary school education or who are illiterate comprise 41 percent of the total membership.[20] The overall educational level of the CCP members in 1985 is similar to that of the Soviet Communist Party in

19. Zhonggong Zhongyang Zuzhibu, ed., *Zuohao Zai*.
20. *Dangde Shenghuo*, no. 5, September 1985, 12–13.

1937, when 24 percent of its members had less than four years of education, 45 percent had four to seven years, 12 percent had twelve years, and about 7 percent had sixteen years.[21]

The educational level of rural party members appears to be worse than the national average.[22] Among 230,000 rural party leaders in Hubei, those who are illiterate or have a primary school education constitute 63 percent. About 20 percent of the rural branches do not have any members with a junior high school education. Particularly low is the educational level of the first and second secretaries in rural areas.[23] Among party members in three villages, there are about twenty-four with a college-level education (0.81 percent), about forty-nine (1.6 percent) who attended a specialized middle school, and about 343 (12 percent) who attended senior and junior high school.[24] Of fifty-three party committee members in Xiangying village, all are illiterate, except for seven with a primary school education.

In addition to a low educational level, the age structure of rural party leaders is dismal. In Hubei province 40 percent of its rural members are over forty-six, and 30 percent of secretaries in branches are sixty or older.[25] Of eleven secretaries in branches, only two are under thirty, three have a middle school education, and four are illiterate.[26]

Having joined the party during the land reform era, collectivization, and the Great Leap Forward, most rural members are accustomed only to class struggle and "blind commands, cutting everything with one knife, and issuing administrative orders." They lack the education to understand the new official policy.[27] As a result, "rural leaders are not capable of leading the rural economy with commodity production. A new group of leaders is needed."[28]

21. Jerry Hough, *Soviet Leadership in Transition* (Washington, D.C.: Brookings Institution, 1980), 28.

22. *Zhengdang Yu Jiandang*, 1 January 1986.

23. Among the basic-level party leaders in Hebei, about 63 percent have a primary school education or are illiterate, and about 20 percent had a junior high school education. *Hebei Xuekan*, no. 2, 1986, 8.

24. *Nongcun Gongzuo Tongxun*, July 1985, 7–8.

25. *Renmin Ribao*, 11 December 1984.

26. *Zhibu Shenghuo* (Beijing), December 1984, 50–51.

27. Ibid.; *Hebei Xuekan*, January 1985, 108–10.

28. *Hubei Xuekan*, January 1985, 100–110.

NEW RECRUITMENT POLICY

It is a widely accepted axiom in the social sciences that the membership characteristics of an organization largely determine its goals, and at the same time any drastic change in organizational goals requires personnel turnover.[29] Even a Leninist party is no exception to this rule: it has to maintain a certain congruence between its ideological outlook and the interests of its members. In the past, the Maoists' emphasis on class background in cadre and party member recruitment reinforced the CCP's revolutionary goals. Drawn largely from the lowest rung of society, the party members supported Mao's notion of permanent revolution.

With the CCP assuming economic reconstruction as its main task, it became obvious even to such conservative leaders as Chen Yun, not to mention more reform-minded ones such as the late Hu Yaobang, that the party was ill-equipped for the new tasks and needed to readjust "all recruitment work to that direction."[30] The majority of party members are too old, too wrapped in Maoist ideology, and too low in educational level. Nonetheless, it is not feasible for the party to expel those members with little education and to recruit new members in large numbers as the Gang of Four did.[31] Therefore, the party has decided on "selective recruitment" to improve the quality of membership over a long period. Its overall plan is to recruit approximately 2 million specialists by 1990 by admitting about 300,000 to 400,000 every year. In this way a higher percentage of party members will have received a college or specialized middle school education.[32]

It was not an easy task for the CCP to change the criteria for membership recruitment in operation for such a long time. As noted, the practice of emphasizing class background and political loyalty started from the very foundation of the CCP and continued—except for a brief period during the second united front —even after 1949, giving weight to increasingly narrowly defined political criteria. Most current CCP members owe their membership to political qualifications. In order to switch from political loyalty to ability, the regime had first to replace the old cadres in

29. Philip Selznick, *Leadership in Administration* (New York: Harper & Row, 1957).
30. Zhonggong Zhongyang Zuzhibu, ed., *Zuohao Zai*, 47–57.
31. Ibid., 34.
32. Ibid., 76.

the organizational departments at the various levels with reform-minded young ones, because only party members have the authority to recommend new members. Every year the central organizational department has held national conferences on organizational work, issuing instructions concerning the recruitment of a specific group. It issued a "Report on Strengthening the Recruitment of Intellectuals" in 1982 and an "Opinion Regarding the Strengthening of the Work of Recruiting College Students" in 1983.[33] In 1984, the center instructed local party committees to resolve the difficulties intellectuals faced in joining the party. After central conferences, each province convenes its own meeting to transmit and explain the specific organizational task of the year.[34]

Recruitment planning appears to work in the same way as economic planning. Every year the central organizational department develops a recruitment plan on the basis of activist lists prepared by the lower levels. The plan is broken down and sent to the next level, which in turn assigns a specific quota to individual units. Although "the plan developed in this way can be reliable," it has its share of problems.[35] Once a quota is assigned to each party organization, the unit feels compelled to meet the assigned quota regardless of whether or not there are qualified candidates. On the other hand, once the quota is filled, even deserving candidates cannot be admitted. Therefore, some party leaders want to abolish this method, but it seems unlikely that the regime will give up its control over broad quantitative targets.[36]

The party has also gradually changed its recruitment criteria, shifting its emphasis from political to functional abilities. Although not officially admitted, in order to join the party it is now required for cadres and workers to have a senior high school education and for soldiers and peasants to have a junior high school education. Exceptions are allowed for minority candidates and those who live in mountainous areas, but as a rule the illiterate are not recruited, and secretaries of rural party branches must have a junior high school education.[37]

At the same time, the regime has been relaxing its political

33. Ibid., pp. 63–178; *Neimong Ri Bao*, 10 March 1983.
34. *Neimong Ribao*, 10 March 1983.
35. Ibid.
36. *Dangde Shenghuo*, no. 6, 1984, 39.
37. *Gongchandang* (Liaoning), no. 12, 1985, 12–14.

requirements. The previous practice of looking at family background, social relations, and historical records to ascertain a person's political attitude is now discouraged or eliminated. Instead, commitment to the Four Modernizations and support of the official policy are stressed. "Anything that brings luck to the people and that contributes to the development of productive forces" is accepted as socialism. The CCP has removed some of the old regulations that specifically barred such types of people from joining the party as former members of the People's Livelihood Party (Minshengdang) and the KMT Youth Corps.[38] However, "those with strong religious feelings" are still disqualified. Even those who made mistakes during the CR can join the party if "they have made sincere self-criticisms and their performance since the third plenum is good."

Beneficiaries of the new policy are the young and educated groups, which largely overlap. The party has also stepped up recruitment of the most underrepresented groups, namely, "females, minorities, workers in the first line of production, and staff in industry, finance, and trade." Another group with educated manpower are returnees among overseas Chinese. Although there are about 2 million returnees with about 20 million family members, only a small fraction of them are party members because of previous discrimination.[39]

The regime's effort to recruit intellectuals and young people frequently encounters subtle opposition from party leaders, particularly at the middle and basic levels, where old members who were poor peasants are still entrenched. "Not yet freed from the ossified thinking of the leftists" or from their old habit "of looking at seniority, natural age, date of filing an application, date of participating in work, and ranking of technical titles to determine a candidate's qualifications," they regard young people as "only expert but not red," "arrogant," "detached from the masses," "seeking the bourgeois life-style," and "immature and unstable." They continue to believe that intellectuals, being "outsiders [and] the target of reform, can be used but not trusted," and that "if they are recruited, the party will change its characteristics." Others feel that

38. Zhonggong Zhongyang Zuzhibu, ed., *Zuohao Zai*, 235.
39. Ibid., 109–12.

admitting them is similar to "adding wings to tigers," who will threaten the old party members' vested interests and their "iron chairs." Some are more straightforward: "You [intellectuals] have culture, and I have a party ticket; you have knowledge, and I have seniority; you know your affairs, but as far as your joining the party is concerned, I will lead you." Frequently cited reasons for rejecting the intellectuals' applications are that they are "arrogant" or "their social relations are complicated."[40]

Resistance to the new policy is rather subtle. When old party members are pressured to admit the young and educated, they take the "three nos" posture: not taking notice of the application, not cultivating activists, and not helping the applicants. Others embarrass the party by publicly declaring that "from now on, anyone without a junior high school education cannot be recruited." This raises the question of what to do with peasants and workers who are politically qualified but lack the educational requirements.[41] The muted official answer states that the party has room for both peasants and intellectuals. This explanation does not assuage the resentment of peasant and worker party members. "The 'stinking ninth category' now smells fragrant, and the 'all-purpose cadres' stink; those with literary training now smell fragrant as do those below forty while the worker-peasant cadres encounter disaster."

The party responded to resistance from lower levels by strengthening its supervision of the work of recruiting intellectuals. Party committees at various levels are instructed to prepare a list of intellectuals applying for membership. Control over the list follows the ranking of the applicants: the provincial authorities supervise the recruitment of high-ranking intellectuals—those above associate professor, associate researcher, and deputy medical doctor; the district authorities are responsbile for the middle-ranking ones— lecturers, assistant researchers, engineers, and head physicians (zhuzhi yishi); and first-class party organs at the county level manage the applications of low-level intellectuals. In addition, party committees frequently dispatch inspection teams to check the work

40. Renmin Ribao, 27 June 1984; 17 April 1985. Some cultural units in Gansu recruited intellectuals for the first time in thirty years. Renmin Ribao, 17 August 1980.
41. Dangde Shenghuo, no. 16, 1985, 41.

of recruiting intellectuals at subordinate units. In February 1984, the Sichuan provincial authority organized about 8,000 cadres into 2,000 inspection teams and sent the teams to the basic levels to check the implementation of recruitment policies. In order to encourage intellectuals to apply for membership, one county party organ in Sichuan even wrote individual letters, urging intellectuals to join. Xinfeng district of Raoping county dispatched twelve teams to search for the right candidates for membership.[42]

The regime's endeavors appear to have produced some positive results. In the five years between 1978 and 1983, slightly more than half a million specialists were recruited. The percentage of intellectuals among new recruits has steadily risen: 8 percent in 1979, 19 percent in 1980, 21 percent in 1981, 24 percent in 1982, 37 percent in 1983, and about 40 percent in 1984. In 1984 alone 1.4 million "advanced elements," one-third of whom were "labor models, advanced staff, outstanding teachers, pacesetters in the New Long March, and three-good students," were admitted. Those with a college-level education numbered 230,000 (17 percent), a figure almost equivalent to all college graduates in that particular year (only about 10 percent of all college graduates lack membership). Forty-five percent of the new members have specialized middle school or high school educations.[43] About 50 percent of the 1 million recruited in 1985 are considered intellectuals.

The recruitment rate of intellectuals in provinces parallels the national trend. Henan reports that about 21 percent of its intellectuals are members, and Guizhou brags that it has recruited more intellectuals in the five years between 1978 and 1983 than in the past thirty years since 1949.[44] According to various reports, more than half the recruits in various units are young or middle-aged.[45] Most of the young people were recruited through the CYL, which reportedly sent 590,000 of its members to the party in 1984.[46]

Recruitment of intellectuals has taken place mostly in business units that failed to admit them in the past, often rejecting their

42. *Shantou Ribao*, 22 May 1985.
43. *Renmin Ribao*, 25 September 1985.
44. *Sichuan Ribao*, 27 June 1984; *Hangzhou Shifan Xuebao*, 15 January 1985.
45. For instance, Beijing reported that one-third of these 1984 recruits were under twenty-eight, and about 50 percent of them were younger than thirty-five. *Xuanchuan Shouce* (Beijing), no. 13, 1985, 3–4.
46. *Dangde Shenghuo*, no. 13, 1985, 38.

applications repeatedly. One professor, who had reportedly submitted his application forty-one times, and a dancer, who had gone through the process forty-three times, have now been admitted.[47] Apparently, many old and middle-aged intellectuals have taken advantage of the new policy. Among intellectuals, those in the natural sciences are more eagerly sought after than those in the social sciences and humanities. In 1984 Beijing accepted the largest number of scientists, engineers, and technicians ever recruited in one year, a figure equivalent to "one-third of all new recruits in the central organs in the past several years."[48]

In many places the newly admitted are readily promoted to cadre positions. One province reports that 39 percent of the newly admitted intellectuals (10,942) have been assigned to leadership positions at the district, municipality, county, and village levels. Liaoning province has appointed "scientists, veteran teachers, engineers, technicians, and medical health workers" to positions as division and section chiefs of the provincial government.[49] By March 1983, among 12,862 high-ranking intellectuals, 4,088 (31 percent) assumed leadership positions in seventy-nine units at the central level.

In rural areas, the party has eagerly courted young and educated groups, which it had formerly neglected for being "ideologically immature and politically unreliable."[50] Since the young and educated constitute the largest portion of specialized households, it is not surprising that many of them are being admitted into the party. Jilin county reports that 59 percent of its new members come from specialized households,[51] which probably expect to protect their political liabilities by joining the party.[52]

Initially, the regime justified active recruitment of specialized households and "10,000 yuan households" (yiwan hu) on the

47. A county immunizaton station reportedly recruited only one person since its establishment. In some university departments not one single person was recruited into the party in the past twenty-four years, and only one person was accepted between 1960 to 1983. Renmin Ribao, 1 December 1984; Hangzhou Shifan Xuebao, 15 January 1985, 15–20.

48. Xuanchuan Shouce, no. 13, 1985, 3–4.

49. Daily Report, 16 January 1979, 13.

50. Hebei Xuekan, no. 1, 1985, 108–10.

51. Nongcun Gongzuo Tongxun, 5 July 1985.

52. Lilun Yuekan, no. 8, 1985, 56–58.

grounds that they were "the most advanced elements." "Advanced youth and specialized households are the outstanding elements among the peasants, and they are a new type of peasants with a pioneering spirit. They have culture and knowledge, are ideologically sensitive and less conservative, and have the creativity necessary for forming a socialist rural area with Chinese characteristics." By recruiting them into the party and promoting them to rural leadership positions, one county increased the number of specialized households from 8,000 to 32,000.

The regime appears, however, to have had second thoughts about specialized households.[53] "Admitting the advanced elements of specialized households is acceptable. But one should take a careful attitude toward this action, seeking truth from facts. Their admission should not be avoided, and [we] also should not be passive about admitting them." The current policy is to accept only those specialized households meeting political qualifications, which include: (1) a willingness to struggle to realize the great ideals of communism and the general line of the party at the moment, (2) the ability to lead the masses to get rich together, and (3) the potential to contribute to the state and collectives.[54]

This cautious approach reflects the reluctance on the part of old party members, who believe that "admitting that kind of person encourages individuals to get rich."[55] Many old party members still insist that "enlightened party members will not get rich, and rich party members are not enlightened."[56] At the same time the regime apparently has been putting increasing pressure on party members to help others to become rich or to move jointly toward wealth. Now rural party members are portrayed as a "basic skeleton" (zhuxin gu) or "a bridge" for the masses to become rich. Party members who became rich in the rural areas are urged to "sign contracts" to help one or two poor households.[57]

Meanwhile, the regime's effort to promote the young and educated to rural leadership positions continues. Now village secre-

53. Dangde Shenghuo, no. 11, 1984, 19.
54. Gongchandangyuan, no. 17, 1985, 31; Lilun Yuekan, no. 12, 1985, 40–41.
55. Dangde Shenghuo, no. 7, 1983, 22; Zhibu Shenghuo (Beijing), no. 7, 1985, 52–53.
56. Nongcun Gongzuo Tongxun, 16 November 1985.
57. Dangde Shenghuo, no. 13, 1983, 27.

taries are required to have at least a primary school education, and the majority of branch members should be young. Town party committees are required to have at least one person with a college education, and those with a senior high school education should constitute a majority in party branches. The rural branches are instructed to select "reserve cadres" from among party members who are below thirty-five years of age and who have a junior high school education.

Since there are not many qualified persons among old party members in terms of age and level of education, newly admitted young members are quickly promoted to leadership positions.[58] Through this method, one county was able to lower the average age of its branch members from forty-five to thirty-seven, increasing the numbers of those with a college or senior and junior high school education to 63 percent and the proportion of specialized households to 30 percent of the entire leadership. Today, the expectation for anyone who joins the party to become a cadre is so great that members without cadre positions are ridiculed as the members with low status (baiding dangyuan).[59]

Although the regime's effort to upgrade the quality of rural party members is necessary, it also creates new problems. The recruitment and promotion of economically successful peasants polarizes rural members along generational lines. Many old members remain in poor households.[60] "They have deep feelings about the party, their sense of discipline is strong, and their desire to play a positive role is great." But because of their advanced age, low educational level, and lack of specific skills, they have difficulty in understanding the commodity economy and in leading the people to become rich. Some party members endeavor to enrich themselves by "abusing their offices, occupying property belonging to collectives, and misusing public funds," while neglecting their responsibilities or wishing to withdraw from the party. "Such situations exist in every place." In turn, the masses say that "we do not respect such party members and cadres, even though they got rich."[61]

58. Daily Report, 16 January 1979, 13.
59. Dangde Shenghuo, no. 6, 1984, 24.
60. Ibid., no. 15, 1985, 11.
61. Zhengdang Yu Jiandang, 16 January 1986.

Although they have "enthusiasm and are courageous in pioneering," the newly recruited and promoted have their share of problems as well. Lacking "the party spirit and the party's work style" and practical experience in rural work, they neglect ideological work and command instead of educate and persuade. Few of them are simply incompetent. The regime promises to resolve these problems by training "reserve cadres."[62]

RECTIFICATION

While trying to improve the overall quality of its members by admitting only educated people, the CCP carried out party rectification from 1984 to 1986 in order to achieve "ideological unity," to strengthen party discipline, and to purify its organization.[63] During the rectification the qualifications of each party member were reviewed on the basis of one's attitude in studying party documents and in making self-criticism, with those failing the test being expelled.

The method used in the rectification was an organizational approach, an extremely realistic and pragmatic method largely designed to ensure tight control over the process by the top leaders. Hu Yaobang publicized the plan for a party rectification at the Twelfth Party Congress (held in September 1982), but rectification actually started one year later when reorganization of the ruling structure as well as personnel changes almost up to the county levels were completed. The CCP prepared a careful plan for the campaign by carrying out the rectification in a selected unit to create models (*dianxing*) and by collecting information on basic problems of party life and appropriate methods to be used nationally. For instance, the Heilongjiang provincial party committee prepared a very detailed report entitled "Reference Materials on the Experimental Party Rectification Work."[64] On the basis of information and recommendations forwarded by provincial authorities, the second plenum of the Twelfth Central Commit-

62. *Hubei Ribao*, 4 November 1985.
63. For this decision, see *Renmin Ribao*, 13 October 1983.
64. "Zhengdang Shidian Cankao Cailiao," *Dangde Shenghuo* (Heilongjiang), no. 14, 25 July 1983.

tee (held on 11 October 1983) adopted "The Decision of the Central Committee of the CCP on Party Consolidation."[65]

The center produced a set of documents with specified goals, targets, processes, and criteria in unprecedented detail. In addition, party rectification leading groups were set up at all different levels with the Central Commission Guiding Party Consolidation at the top.[66] Authorized to issue special instructions, the commission issued numerous notices on specific problems as they occurred in the process, which drew the attention of party members to the particular experiences it deemed worthy.[67]

The concrete sequences stipulated by the decision were also based on an organizational approach. "It will proceed from the central level to grass-root organizations, from the top downward, stage by stage in groups. Rectification of the party organization of each unit will start with the leadership body at the top level."[68] After rectifying themselves, the leadership bodies supervised the process at the next level, thus ensuring that the entire process of rectification was conducted in an orderly fashion. Moreover, the rectification was first carried out in central government organs, the leading bodies of the provinces, and large units of the PLA (which included 380,000 members in 159 units). Only after completing the rectification in the first batch at the end of 1984 did the regime move to the second batch (which included district- and county-level party organs as well as business and enterprise organs of that level, with a total party membership of about 13.5 million).[69] The last group to undergo rectification consisted of rural party members at the level below the county. The entire process was officially completed in the spring of 1987.[70]

In addition, the CCP also relied heavily on work teams in order to ensure organizational supervision. Since dispatching the teams had generated intense controversies during the CR, the regime tried to define their authority in such a way that they would not

65. *Renmin Ribao*, 13 October 1983.
66. For its members, see ibid.
67. *Gongchandangyuan*, no. 24, 1985, 4–66; no. 7, 1985, 4–5; no. 10, 1985, 4–5.
68. *Renmin Ribao*, 13 October 1983.
69. Ibid., 23 December 1984.
70. *Gongchandangyuan*, no. 12, 1985, 10–14.

push aside the existing leadership but would act as an effective watchdog for the center. Although described as liaison offices, which would report directly to the Central Commission on the local situation and transmit instructions from the upper echelon to the lower units, the work teams were at the same time held responsible for "meticulously implementing official policies" and not compromising with the existing leadership on "matters of principle."[71] Moreover, the head and deputy head of the work teams, or ordinary members designated by them, were authorized to attend the meetings of the existing leadership.[72] Work team members were carefully selected from "old cadres with long experience in party affairs" or "those who understood the rectification." Selection of the head and deputy head of the work teams had to be approved by higher authorities, and all members of the teams were given intensive training, sometimes lasting eight days.[73] In addition, the party organization at a higher level was specifically instructed to supervise the rectification work of its subordinate units. To perform this supervisory function properly, the higher-level leadership had to inform subordinate organizations of the progress of the rectification in its own unit. No rectification work could be completed without the careful checking and explicit approval of the higher authority.[74]

All party units uniformly followed the concrete steps laid down by the central authority. First, party members spent ten to twenty days reading the relevant materials—including *The Selected Works of Deng Xiaoping*, some of Mao's writings, a collection of important documents published since the third plenum, and *A Must for Party Members*.[75] For this study—intended to raise members' understanding of "their responsibility, the party's new tasks, and the new policy line"—members were divided into several groups according to their level of education. For instance, in the ministry of chemical engineering the group with a college education read a million characters, averaging 7,000 characters per hour, whereas

71. *Renmin Ribao*, 12 December 1983; "Zhengdang Shidian Cankao Cailiao," 20, 23; *Renmin Ribao*, 23 December 1983.
72. *Renmin Ribao*, 12 December 1983.
73. "Zhengdang Shidian Cankao Cailiao," 19–20; *Renmin Ribao*, 23 December 1983.
74. *Renmin Ribao*, 13 October 1983.
75. Ibid., 10 October 1983; 14 October 1983; 24 October 1983.

the group with a lower education studied materials containing 200,000 characters. Party committees also organized and trained people to read and explain the materials to illiterate party members. Despite the massive energy and time spent studying these materials, many units apparently conducted the study "perfunctorily."

The second stage was "comparing and checking," in which each party member examined his own ideology, past record, and present performance against the standards specified in the official documents.[76] All participants made self-criticisms and submitted their writings to the party committee for collective discussion and approval. First party secretaries at all levels were to set an example by participating in the meeting of the party core as an individual member, by making thorough self-criticisms, and by assuming responsibility for their units' work. Self-criticisms were not limited to one's ideology, degree of compliance with official policies, or adherence to party regulations. They also touched upon corruption, bad work habits, bureaucratism, or any other irregularity resented by the masses.[77] When a leading cadre's self-criticism—which was often prepared with the help of work teams—was approved, it was reported at the membership meeting at that level, as well as to the leadership group at the next level.[78] This measure was to ensure that superior and subordinate units would supervise each other to prevent perfunctory performances.

Although the rectification was basically an internal matter, party leaders had to solicit the opinions of nonparty members, using such methods as the exchange of opinions, opinion polls, and heart-to-heart discussions.[79] However, the regime repeatedly stressed that the mass mobilization methods of the CR—allowing the masses to expose cadres' mistakes, to write accusatory letters, to exchange experiences across unit boundaries—should be avoided. In order to underscore the fact that the rectification was not a political campaign like the CR where the leaders and upper-level organizations made many arbitrary decisions affecting indi-

76. "Zhengdang Shidian Cankao Cailiao," 31; *Sichuan Ribao*, 11 August 1984.
77. For self-criticisms of the government ministers, see *Renmin Ribao*, 16 March 1984.
78. *Sichuan Ribao*, 12 March 1984.
79. *Renmin Ribao*, 2 November 1983.

viduals, the regime promised not to use the "four methods," while observing the "four principles." The party would not (1) grab pigtails, (2) put hats on the accused, (3) beat with a stick, or (4) put materials in personnel dossiers. The principles allowed the accused to (1) defend himself, (2) explain the specific circumstances of the incident investigated, (3) reserve his own opinion, and (4) change his own view.[80]

The last stage of the rectification was registration.[81] The party could make one of four decisions regarding each individual member: (1) to register, (2) to postpone registration, (3) to persuade individual members to voluntarily withdraw from the party, or (4) to expel. Each party member had to evaluate his own qualifications for membership, specifying his strengths and weaknesses after having a heart-to-heart talk with a party representative. Those who passed the test pledged "unconditionally to carry out a party member's obligations" and were sworn in at the designated registration place.

The regime insists that no fixed quota for those to be purged was sent down to the lower level.[82] Only two categories of people were to be expelled: the "three types of people" and those members with serious economic, ideological, organizational, and work style problems. For those unwilling to reapply for membership, party committees were instructed to use neither force nor persuasion. When a negative decision was made about a member, the person was allowed to defend himself and to appeal his case to higher authorities, who promised to handle such cases with special care.[83] The names of party members whose registrations were postponed or refused were submitted to party organs at the next higher level for approval.

Despite the tight supervision by a higher authority, the overall result of the rectification appears to be disappointing. The party summarized the net results by saying that there was "some interference, some mistakes, some achievement, and some progress." However, the Chinese people used a cryptic but more cynical phrase to sum up the results: "The results of three and a half

80. *Hong Qi*, no. 13, 1984.
81. *Renmin Ribao*, 13 October 1983; 20 November 1984.
82. Peng Xueshi, Wang Hongfu, and Lu Xianfu, eds., *Xin Shiqi Zhengdang Jianghua* (Beijing: Xinhua Chubanshe, 1984), 94.
83. Ibid., 92.

years of rectification is neither salty, nor bland. After the rain, the ground is wet, but the wind blows away the fog. Mr. Hu trembled at the strength of the leftist wind, and confusion changed the reform plans. Wine and sex are added to wealth. When will a real improvement come?"[84]

In retrospect, it seems that from the beginning the party's effort to rebuild itself through ideological education of its members was unrealistic. In order to achieve "ideological unity," the CCP had to have a coherent ideology that clearly defined its role in leading China to economic development, while justifying economic reforms in terms of Marxism-Leninism-Mao Zedong thought. However, it was impossible for the party to formulate a well-defined and coherent ideology that would justify the various reform measures that it initiated out of practical necessity, while preserving whatever it regarded as the core value of socialism.

Moreover, the party had could not insulate itself from the impact of rapid change in the society that reform engendered. The prerequisites of economic development compel the regime to relinquish some of its authority over economic and administrative matters and to manage cadres according to task-oriented criteria rather than political ones. As the regime encourages individual Chinese to become rich ahead of others, career opportunities outside the bureaucratic structures of the party-state open up. Consequently, party membership becomes less attractive than before, even for career advantages within the party-state apparatus. Nonetheless, the ruling Leninist Party deems it necessary to rebuild itself in such a way that it can insulate itself from the undesirable influences of society, while making it effective in leading China to achieve the Four Modernizations.

Top party leaders disagreed among themselves over the extent to which ideological orthodoxy should be sacrificed for the sake of reform. This dilemma was crystallized over the concrete question of which should be the main objective of the rectification: ideological purity of the Leninist Party or facilitating reforms. The conservatives viewed the rectification as a means to maintain the Leninist Party's ideological orthodoxy, whereas the reformers saw it as a means to facilitate the reforms.

84. *Jing Bao*, July 1987, 76–78.

THE PARTY'S DILEMMA: IDEOLOGY

Ideology has played a more crucial role in China than in any other political community. In traditional China, Confucianism, the official ideology, provided the basis for consensus among the political elites with regard to basic standards of right and wrong and acceptable and unacceptable behavior. In so doing, throughout most of Chinese history, Confucian official ideology performed an integrative function by keeping the diverse groups and localities together within a unified political community. This success in Confucianism's integrative function led the Chinese ruling elites to believe that the most effective way to rule China was to develop an official ideology. Apparently, it also created a psychological need in the Chinese people for a comprehensive ideology.

The functional importance of an official ideology and some specific ideas of Confucianism (such as emphasizing man's rationality, looking at human actions in totality, and regarding education as a means of raising human potential) persisted in the CCP's mode of thinking. The fact that China lacked an "industrial proletariat" made it more necessary for the CCP to stress a correct ideology to proletarianize the peasants. Thus, from the beginning, the CCP accepted Marxism-Leninism as the official ideology which defined and offered a concrete strategy for its political goals, but not a deterministic "law of social development." Mao's emphasis on the creative application of the "universal truth of Marxism-Leninism" contained the seed for the ideas of his "politics in command."

Mao pushed the traditional tendency of stressing human will to an extreme during his last years, further radicalizing the revolutionary theory of Marxism-Leninism. Mao's thought as the official ideology was extremely radical in the following ways. First, the content—exemplified by the notion of permanent revolution—was more radical than the original doctrine of Marxism-Leninism because it rejected its materialistism and deterministism by stressing human will over the material foundation of society. Second, Mao's thought became the highest authority, often totally disregarding the functional necessities of party organization and society. Third, because Mao was the sole guardian and interpreter of the radicalized official ideology, he and his followers could exploit the official ideology for their own partisan political interests. Fourth, the official ideology was frequently translated directly into official programs and policies, leaving little room for any concrete policy to depart from the official ideology or to accommodate the practical needs of society; in other words, there was a smaller gap between theory and practice. Fifth, the domain of the official ideology was comprehensive, leaving no human action outside its control. Last, the radicalized official ideology was uniformly imposed on everyone, often backed by the ruthless coercive power of the state and the masses.

When the victims of Mao's purge returned, they initially tried to liberate people's thinking from "the ossified leftist view" by advancing the slogan of "practice is the sole criterion of the truth." It was quite effective in dislodging Mao's thought from the position of official ideology and discrediting the Maoists including "the two whatevers" faction. But it could not offer a basis for developing a new official ideology acceptable to the Communist leaders, who had not given up their claim to Marxism-Leninism. As popular demands challenged the party, Deng Xiaoping laid down the four principles (Marxism-Leninism-Mao Zedong thought, the socialist road, the people's democratic dictatorship, and the leadership of the party) as the core values of the party-state. The specific contents of the principles, however, are so ambiguous that they have given party leaders the freedom to crack down on anything they deem unsocialistic. The principle was effective as a control mechanism for the top leaders, but not as the basis for forming a new ideological consensus.

Meanwhile, the regime has been carrying out reforms not out of any ideological motivation but from the practical necessity of economic development. Although such development undoubtedly reflects the aspirations of the Chinese people, as a Communist party, the party must justify the goal of economic development in Marxist terms. But the party has so far been unable to do so except for the simplistic view of "scientific socialism" or "the primary stage of socialism."

Consequently, the main objective and focus of the rectification changed during the campaign. At its initial stage, the regime underscored the need to correct "all erroneous 'left' and 'right' tendencies."[85] While advocating what amounted to a "struggle on

85. Ibid.

two fronts," the regime viewed the party rectification and reforms as two separate matters because the rectification was essentially an internal affair, whereas reform was the concern of the state.[86] However, when the campaign against spiritual pollution, which had been designed to criticize the notion that the early Marxist theories of humanism and alienation could be applied to socialist China, came to an abrupt end in 1984, references to the danger of "right tendencies" disappeared from the official news media, and the emphasis of rectification shifted from the abstract notion of ideological unity to the resolution of such concrete problems as corruption and other issues that most concerned the masses.[87] The new official formula urged party members to carry out the "rectification on one hand and reform on the other."[88] At the same time, official criticism of the "left" tendency and the CR were stepped up. All party members were urged to spend a fixed period of time repudiating the CR.

By the time that Premier Zhao Ziyang made a long report on structural reform at the Sixth Plenum of the Twelfth Party Congress, the distinction between rectification and reform had completely disappeared, and the original objective of achieving ideological unity was subordinated to the goals of reform. The reformers invented the phrase "ideologies to guide the functional work" (*yewu zhidao sixiang*) in order to stress a functionally oriented perspective and to encourage local leaders to carry out reforms without being constrained by the official ideology. The difference between "ideology" as used in the previous official documents and "ideologies to guide the functional work," although very subtle, was profound. "Ideology" refers to political ideology, comprehensive in applicability, and socialist in content. In contrast, the meaning of "ideologies to guide the functional work" is closer to the notion of "laws and rules" inherent in each functional area, for example, economic laws and rules. In this sense, the term refers to the functional expertise of each functional field rather than a general com-

---

86. "Zhengdang Shidian Cankao Cailiao"; *Renmin Ribao*, 6 December 1983; 12 December 1983.

87. For the antispiritual pollution campaign, see Thomas B. Gold, "Just in Time! China Battles Spiritual Pollution on the Eve of 1984," *Asian Survey* 24(9) (September 1984); *Renmin Ribao*, 21 December 1983; 1 April 1984.

88. *Renmin Ribao*, 1 March 1984.

mitment to socialist ideology. Any inherent ambiguity in the term was later further clarified. It was officially declared that the "correctness of ideologies to guide the functional work" would be evaluated in terms of their contribution to the general task and goal of the party, that is, economic development. By the time some ministries were ready to make a final report on party rectification, the implementation of reforms rather than the unity of ideology became the main criterion for judging achievements of the rectification. For instance, the ministry of coal was evaluated in terms of whether its decisions corresponded with the new tasks of economic development and reforming economic structure.[89]

Furthermore, the reformers publicly argued that the main objective of the rectification was to facilitate the reforms. Hu Qili declared:

> Party rectification is intended to ensure and promote reforms. There can be no doubt whatsoever about this major goal. Apart from reforms, which are the main task of the party-state, the rectification has no other realistic goals or meaning. . . . Without party rectification, which will remove obstacles in ideology, work style, discipline, and organizations, reform proposals, regardless of how good they are, cannot be carried out smoothly and can even produce confusion as a result of distortions and changes.[90]

If the reformers were prepared to sacrifice ideological orthodoxy, the conservatives were not ready to give up the idea of unifying party members on the basis of a well-defined official ideology. They saw official ideology and reform as completely different matters, more often in conflict with each other than in harmony. In Bo Yibo's view, the rectification of the first batch achieved substantial positive results in correcting the "ideologies to guide the functional work," but no tangible improvement "in the area of unifying the *ideology*." Later he publicly repudiated the reformers' view:

> Correcting ideologies to guide functional workers is an important aspect of unifying the [official] ideology, and this point is proven correct by practice. . . . [However] when we summarized the results of the first batch of the rectification, [we discovered] that the formula raises some problems. Some units promoted only "the correction of

89. Ibid., 25 June 1984.
90. Ibid., 15 July 1985.

the ideologies guiding the functional work," while neglecting other objectives of the rectification.[91]

Reformers and conservatives agreed that cadre corruption—which was widespread—was a serious problem, deserving attention in the rectification campaign. But they disagreed over what should be considered corruption, how to explain its sudden rise, and how to deal with it. Such conservatives as Bo Yibo and Chen Yun tended broadly to define "unhealthy trends" to include all the undesirable consequences of reforms (including inflation). They also traced "unhealthy practices" to the policy of reform and opening up China to the outside world. In their view, reforms gave rise to the "capitalist philosophy that 'if one does not promote self-interest the sky and earth will collapse,'" and it allowed the Chinese people to "think of money in everything they do in the guise of 'invigorating' and 'reforming.'" By contrast, the reformers tended to define corruption narrowly. To the conservatives the only remedy was to reassert the socialist ideology. Bo Yibo explained: "In some localities and units, . . . leading bodies and party-member cadres have forgotten the Communist Party's lofty ideal of waging a lifelong struggle for the socialist and Communist cause, and for the party's fundamental goal of wholeheartedly serving the people." He prescribed the strengthening of political and ideological work by upholding the four principles and criticizing the "lefitst" as well as the "rightist" views.[92]

Probably, the issues of reform and rectification were heatedly debated in top-level party meetings. Later, Bo Yibo quoted Hu Yaobang as having said that "only talking about functional work, but not talking about political ideology, will not work."[93] Meanwhile, as cadre corruption became more pervasive, the original ambitious goal of achieving ideological unity was diluted to combating the "new, unhealthy trends" that structural reforms produced.

Although the conservatives are wrong in believing that cadre corruption can be rectified through ideological education, they are right in tracing corruption to the structural conditions of society. In

91. *Hong Qi*, no. 20, 1985, 3–7.

92. *Renmin Ribao*, 15 July 1985. For Chen Yun's view, see *Hong Qi*, no. 19, 1985, 35–37, 40–44.

93. *Hong Qi*, no. 20, 1985, 3–7.

the present Chinese economic system, which is neither a free market nor a state-controlled economy, with dual price structures, some party members are in the position of enjoying access to decision-makers, as well as to the resources, capital, and information necessary to get ahead in the market. Official policy encourages party members to lead the masses in becoming rich. Party members, however, are more interested in enriching themselves.[94] The classic phrase, "being the first to assume responsibility but the last to enjoy the benefits," is often evoked to remind party members of their duties. However, its effectiveness is doubtful in present-day China where "seeking money in everything" is the prevalent mood.[95]

Nonetheless, the regime continues to urge party members to promote "the revolutionary spirit of serving the people wholeheartedly" and not to "seek personal gain by taking advantage of one's power and position." The incentives the party promises to its members continue to be based on old revolutionary values that have no practical relevance to the social values that the party is trying to establish. The statement, "Our party has no particular interest of its own other than the interests of the working class and the masses of the people," does not resolve the dilemma. As an ideological statement, it completely disregards the fact that the Communist Party as a corporate entity is supposed to have its revolutionary interests defined by Marxism-Leninism and Mao Zedong's thought. Moreover, as a collective composed of concrete individuals, the party has a tendency to develop its own organizational interests.

Consequently, the party is losing its attractiveness to the people, particularly to the young.[96] As its control diminishes over economic resources, the areas subject to political decisions, and revolutionary idealism in the official ideology, the party is left without much that can attract new members. In fact, some members even want to withdraw from the party in order to concentrate on their careers in society. This disillusionment makes it difficult for the party to maintain strict discipline among its own members.

94. *Hong Qi*, no. 2, 1987, 36–39.
95. *Xuexi Yuekan*, July 1985, 12–13.
96. For low-level membership in factories, see *Sixiang Zhengzhi Gongzuo Yanjiu*, no. 7, 1985, 5–6.

The problems are particularly serious in rural areas where the rural responsibility system has changed the basic rules of the game. Many rural members now engage in more profitable sideline businesses, for examples, hauling cargo, manufacturing, and specialized farming. Hubei reports that one-third of its 1.5 million party members are pursuing new forms of economic activity, which require them to travel outside their residential areas.[97] As a result, when branches convene meetings, usually less that half the members attend. Those members who skillfully exploit the new opportunities are usually young and capable and with the "most progressive ideology." They form what the party regards as "the backbone of rural party organizations."[98] They are, however, reluctant to serve as party cadres because they can earn more money in society. For instance, five members of a village party committee resigned from their posts to engage in a sideline business that pays four or five times more than cadre positions. In a survey one-third of Hebei rural cadres thought that being a cadre entailed a loss of income.

While failing to offer a comprehensive official ideology, the regime encourages low-level cadres to continue their ideological work. Yet because of its close association with the Gang of Four and the declining relevance of ideology to daily life, the propaganda apparatus within the party is so demoralized that no one wants to do ideological work. They complain that they cannot work "with an empty mouth" when all their other powers are taken away.[99] Moreover, there is one supreme irony at the moment: the propaganda workers find themselves preaching the very ideas they had condemned in the past as capitalist ideology.

> In the past we talked about "politics in command" and propagated that "first, big and second, public" [yi da er gong] was socialism; presently distribution according to labor and dispersed management is said to be socialism; in the past the three freedoms and the one guarantee [san zi yi bao] was criticized as capitalism. Now assigning a contract to each family is said to be socialism. Each view has its own logic, but each is confusing to the people.[100]

97. *Zhengdang Yu Jiandang*, 10 January 1986.
98. *Dangde Shenghuo*, no. 2, 1983, 29–30.
99. *Renmin Ribao*, 6 October 1984.
100. "First, big and second, public" refers to the belief that the bigger the size of

The regime insists that the focus of ideological work is to edu- cate the people about the necessity of reform. Ordinary Chinese people do not need an ideological education on reform because they know what they want, and if they are left alone, they will follow the reforms' direction. The group of people that really needs an ideological education are the party cadres, who dedicated their entire life to building the Maoist version of socialism and whose vested interests are tied to the existing system.

To summarize, unable to develop a coherent ideology, the party leadership tended to emphasize an organizational principle in order to deal with the increasing uncertainty that economic re- forms created. This principle justifies a given official policy not in terms of the official ideology, but in terms of the structural legi- timacy of the decision-making body and its due processes. Thus, according to the organizational principle, the official ideology is whatever the party decides it to be through the established decision-making procedures. In order to ensure their reform poli- cy, the reformers are recruiting into key leadership positions a group of people whose ability and interests coincide with economic development.

As far as the official ideology is concerned, the following trends are discernable. First, the vocabulary used in the official media has been changing from Marxist categories of "class struggle, revolu- tion, and socialism" to such traditional Chinese phrases as "lofty idealism" and "purpose" (*zhongzhi*), which appeal to nationalism, patriotism, and self-imposed noblesse oblige.[101] Second, as the sources of official ideology diversify, different political groups vie with one another to present their views as the official ideology. Official recognition that each area of society has to be regulated autonomously according to its specific laws and rules has already laid down a foundation for ideological diversity. Third, the existing official ideology is losing its immediate relevancy to the regime's specific programs and policies; the gap between theory and prac- tice is widening. Last, the party's ability to rely on ideological sym-

---

a commune and the more it owns, the more socialist it is. "The three freedoms and the one guarantee" refers to the policy of permitting the expansion of private plots, free markets, and sideline enterprises, and fixing quotas by individual households. *Dangde Shenghuo*, no. 16, 1985, 41.

101. *Renmin Ribao*, 1 January 1985.

bols to recruit the members needed for new tasks and to keep the party as a whole disciplined and committed to Marxism-Leninism is diminishing. Eventually, the party has to come out with more tangible incentives—in terms of power and prestige—to make itself attractive to the better-educated section of the Chinese population.

PART IV

THE PERSONNEL MANAGEMENT SYSTEM

13

The Personnel Dossier System

Personnel management (*renshi guanli*) deals with a wide range of specific tasks such as recruitment, training, appointment, assessment, promotion, transfer, demotion, dismissal, and retirement, in addition to wage and fringe benefit questions. Decisions have to be made and implemented on these issues for each individual cadre; then they are entered into a personnel dossier, a file of written materials on an individual that the regime keeps on every cadre, every party member, and every Communist Youth League member.[1]

PRIOR TO THE CR

Keeping written records is, as Max Weber argued, one of the basic traits of any bureaucracy; all governments normally maintain files on employees. However, the most striking aspect of the Chinese personnel dossier system is the comprehensive scope and political nature of information stored in each file. Cadres have only one personnel dossier, which includes all information on them, although sometimes the regime maintains two versions of a dossier; one is the original (*zhengben*), which contains all relevant

---

1. "Dossier" in a broad sense refers to a file containing systematically collected materials on any subject. The types of dossiers often referred to by the Chinese news media are personnel, historical, scientific, and enemy dossiers. Different units maintain and control each type of dossier. Access to and secrecy surrounding them varies from one dossier to another. However, when used in cross-checking, dossiers provide the regime with a very powerful control mechanism. It maintains some kind of personnel dossier on everyone except peasants. For English sources on the dossier system, see A. Doak Barnett, *Cadres, Bureaucracy, and Political Power in Communist China* (New York: Columbia University Press, 1967), 49–50; Melanie Manion, "The Cadre Management System, Post-Mao: The Appointment, Promotion, Transfer, and Removal of Party and State Leaders," *China Quarterly*, vol. 102, June 1985, 203–33.

material, and the other is a partial duplicate (*fuben*), which has only a summary of the materials.[2]

Obsessed with the cadres' political loyalty, the party-state during Mao's era insisted that

> [We] have to examine whether or not one has unlimited loyalty to the party and people and one's political and historical records, ideology, personality, and attitude toward study. [We] have to examine them regularly. Only when we have made a detailed examination of each cadre's political history, political conditions, political quality, ideology, work style, work performance, and ability in a systematic way, can we systematically understand cadres, correctly recruit, and use them.[3]

During Mao's era the personnel dossier system performed two important functions for the regime. First, it formed the foundation for managing cadres. Through the documentary materials in the dossiers the leadership were able to make rational decisions on recruitment, promotion, assignment, transfer, and so on for each cadre. In this sense, the personnel dossier system constitutes an indispensable part of the broader personnel management system in China. For this purpose, each cadre dossier contains information on: (1) organizational relations—records of party or CYL life, (2) administrative relations—materials on career background, present positions, and educational background, and (3) supply relations—salary grade and other fringe benefits.

Second, the personnel dossier system enabled the regime to maintain tight political control over the cadres.[4] For this purpose, any information even only tangentially pertinent for checking cadres' loyalty to the regime, to the party, or to any particular faction in power at a given moment was collected. Each of the many campaigns that the regime has carried out since 1949 has generated huge amounts of information for dossiers: the 1941 party rectification yielded a large amount of material that eventually formed the

---

2. The level directly above a cadre keeps the original, the cadre's unit, the simplified version. In the past, material in a dossier was not limited to reports about job performance. Wang Faxiong, *Renshi Dangan Guanli Gailun* (Hubei: Hubei Renmin Chubanshe, 1984), 31.

3. *Guangming Ribao*, 14 November 1957.

4. Ibid.

basis of personnel dossiers; the land reform, about landlords; the Three Antis and Five Antis, facts about people working in commerce and finance; and the antirightist campaign, data on intellectuals. The regime carried out in 1956 the first nationwide investigation of each cadre's file, cross-checking contents against the information provided by the masses and from files seized from the Nationalist Party.

The importance of the personnel dossier system for each cadre cannot be overemphasized. Whether one was recruited, promoted, or demoted, whether one entered college or went abroad for study, whether one survived a political campaign, who would be chosen as a target in a particular political movement—the outcome of all these largely rested on the contents of one's dossier.

Because personnel dossiers are so all-inclusive, they can work to the advantage or disadvantage of each cadre, depending on the information they contain and the users' intentions. The dossier may offer the regime a solid basis for selecting cadres according to the criteria emphasized at a given moment, or it may offer an excuse to persecute anyone the regime may choose to. In 1957, during liberalization, many intellectuals charged that "the party has two record books; one record is a good one, the other is a bad one; when you are needed, the good record is used; when you are a problem to the party, the bad record is used."[5] The regime did not deny that the dossiers can be two-edged.

Although the cadres have always been concerned about the personnel dossier system, they did not dare to criticize it publicly. Only when political control was relaxed did the system become a focal point of criticism. During the Hundred Flowers campaign, many intellectuals condemned the dossier as "a registrar for life and death," "secret document bags," "benefactor roster" (*enming an*), and "ammunition cartridge" (secret reports prepared through dubious channels).[6] Intellectuals believed that "nobody can be completely liberated [*fanshen*] unless the dossier system is abolished."[7]

The party may have inherited the dossier system from the Soviet

5. *Renmin Ribao*, 27 July 1957; *Wenhui Bao*, 27 October 1957.
6. *Changjiang Ribao*, 22 August 1957.
7. *Wenhui Bao*, 27 October 1957.

Union, for it has as long a history as the party itself.[8] However, specific norms for the personnel dossier in terms of format and handling gradually evolved. The first national conference held in 1956 apparently systematized the varying practices and laid down standard procedures for collecting, arranging, and putting materials into the dossiers and maintaining and utilizing them. In the ten years up to the CR, the system was expanded further with the enactment of more specific rules on cadres' dossiers.[9]

Personnel dossiers are state secrets.[10] Any mention of them in the media has been general and ambiguous, often only indicating their existence. When someone dies, the regime keeps the dossier for another five years at least, then transfers it to the government dossier bureau.[11] No individual is supposed to have access to his own or a relative's dossier, and those who work with dossiers are forbidden to reveal their contents. When critics of the regime demanded public access to personnel dossiers, the regime gave three reasons for their being kept secret. First, an individual's privacy must be protected from other individuals (but not from the state). Second, dossiers include facts that have been verified as well as suspicions, rumors, and other pieces of potentially damaging, but unconfirmed, information that should certainly not be made public. Third, a dossier's confidentiality prevents unnecessary disharmony among the people.[12]

CONTENTS

Each personnel dossier includes official forms, documents, and materials. Most are ones that each individual has provided, and the rest is either evidence collected or opinions rendered by the organization.[13] The most frequently included forms are one's Summary Career History (*jianli piao*), Promotion to Cadre (for newly appointed ones), Cadre Registration (when assigned to a new

8. A director of the dossier bureau of the State Council started his career as a code operator in 1927. *Renmin Ribao*, 7 January 1980.

9. Wang, *Renshi Dangan*, 75.

10. *Zhengming*, no. 3, 1980, 74.

11. Zhonggong Zhongyang Zhuzhibu Yanjiushi, ed., *Dangde Zhuzi Gongzuo Wenda* (Beijing: Beijing Renmin Chubanshe, 1984).

12. *Guangxi Ribao*, 10 August 1975.

13. Ibid.

unit), and Application for Party Membership. Supporting materials also appear. The formats of these documents vary, although they all have columns for certain specific kinds of information.[14]

The contents of most of these forms overlap. As is the case with those distributed by most bureaucracies, spaces are provided for such data as name, age, sex, birthplace, family origin, dates of employment, cultural level, and party membership. Party members must describe when, where, and by whose recommendation they first joined the party, also explaining whether or not the spouse is a party member and what position he or she holds.[15] A closely detailed explanation can be provided, if necessary. In addition, each cadre must give an account of the economic conditions of their families, in detail, before and after liberation. They also have to specify their family background (*jiating chusheng*), for until recently this was regarded as the most crucial factor in personnel management. All classifications are based on what a cadre's father did between 1946 and 1949 (or, for veteran cadres, on when they participated in the revolution). Those who were adopted are required to write the occupations of their legal parents rather than that of the natural parents, although the natural parents' background is also taken into consideration. The justification for this rule is that family upbringing directly influences one's political attitudes.

For family background, the regime provides detailed categories based on economic as well as political criteria for all Chinese except ethnic minorities.[16] Though the detailed official categories may be thorough, they are not sufficient to cover China's complex reality. Moreover, there has always been a strong incentive to make one's family background look as good as possible. Even Zhang Chunqiao's description of his father changed from "small staff" to "middle peasant," "handicraft worker," and "medical doctor" in different forms.[17] Detailed explanations of one's family background may be included on the form or they may assume the freer style of autobiography. In addition to writing about their families, each

14. "Central Document, No. 10, 1977," *Zhonggong Yanjiu* 14(7–8) (July–August 1980):80, 165, 172, 163.

15. Ibid., 80, 165, 172, 163.

16. For further details on the categories, see Richard Klaus, *Class Conflict in Chinese Communism* (New York: Columbia University Press, 1981).

17. "Central Document, No. 10, 1977," 167–69.

cadre must also write about their own status, based on what they have done since becoming economically independent.

After the section about family background and personal status, most forms require people to list their "key family members." There are detailed regulations on who constitutes a key family member. Both parents and children are regarded as key family members, whether or not one is living with his parents. But if a woman is married, her parents are relegated to mere "key social relations," and her parents-in-law are considered the key family members.

People must also write about their key social relations. Close friends, classmates, colleagues, and relatives who are not key family members are in this category, whose definition is hazy compared with that of key family members. A cadre has great latitude about whom he lists; but if he leaves someone out—particularly someone who has once been politically active—the organization may question him if suspicion arises.

Most official forms also include specific questions about whether a person or a family member has ever been arrested, jailed, or executed by the CCP. If so, the person filling out the form is unlikely to go far in the party. More information is required about the one who was arrested, jailed, or executed. Did he ever "join a reactionary organization or reactionary military and surreptitious religious organization? What position did he hold? Present relations? Any references?"[18] Last, the form asks for a brief statement about the compiler's career background, including academic training. Each school attended and each place of employment must be given with references and addresses.

After filling out all the official forms, one must write a detailed autobiography (*zizhuan*), which covers the writer's life from the age of seven on, in particular, focusing on such politically relevant activities as demonstrations, publications, and any association memberships. The autobiography is expected to reveal how its author's thought has developed, but it must also include all political relationships. Discussion of friends is not needed except in a political context.[19]

18. Ibid., 164.
19. For an example of autobiography, see *Guancha Zhe*, January 1980, and *Zhongguo Chingnien Bao*, 9 February 1980.

The finished autobiography is scrutinized by the small group to which the person belongs as well as by the party committee. If satisfied with the content, the committee will include the auto-biography in the dossier. However, everyone is required constant-ly to supplement his autobiography. For example, if something of political significance happens to a key family member or if a sister emigrates, then this change should be reflected in the personnel dossier. A supplement to the existing dossier may be ordered by the organization when a minor mistake is discovered or when an individual volunteers information out of a guilty conscience.[20] All these materials are arranged in the order specified by the guide-lines of the central organizational department.[21] Only the depart-ment has the authority to put materials into the dossier; indi-viduals cannot collect materials or demand that the department put any particular piece of information into their dossier.[22]

MAINTENANCE

Although in the past, ultimate authority over personnel matters lay with the party committee, the actual management of the files was handled by the organizational department of the party and the per-sonnel bureau of the government. Staff members working in both organs were usually party members, and quite often they held positions in both organs concurrently.[23] A party secretary or stand-ing committee member normally supervised personnel work. When the party committee was small, one deputy secretary was in charge of personnel management. Thus, unlike a personnel unit in an American organization, which is considered a staff department, both the party's organizational department and the government's personnel bureau have substantial influence over personnel mat-ters. Consequently, the personnel bureau draws sharp criticism whenever there is any political relaxation.

Following the principle of managing the cadres in a "unified, level-by-level, and field-by-field" fashion (see chapter 14), the par-ty committees at the various levels keep the dossiers on the cadres

20. *Wenhui Bao*, 27 October 1957.
21. Wang, *Renshi Dangan*, 133–38.
22. For instance, testimony by other people certifying one's starting date of rev-olutionary work is not allowed in the dossier. Ibid., 10.
23. Barnett, *Cadres*, 46–65.

over whom they have personnel authority. Generally speaking, the party unit at one level has authority over the dossiers of the high-ranking cadres belonging to the next lower unit. Thus, the dossiers of the highest provincial and municipal leaders are kept in the organizational department of the Central Committee. The provincial organizational departments manage the dossiers of the cadres over whom the provincial authority has jurisdiction. The county party committee is the lowest unit that is allowed to maintain personnel dossiers.[24] This elaborate division of jurisdiction within the hierarchy is designed to prevent any cadre from keeping his dossier under his own jurisdiction, while making it easy for those who make personnel decisions to have access to the information.

Although it is unclear how authority is divided between the party's organizational departments and the government's personnel bureau, it seems that the division of power between the two depends on the cadre's rank. The organizational department of the Guangdong provincial party committee maintains dossiers for leading cadres (above grade 12) of all organs directly under the provincial government. The personnel bureau of the provincial government keeps dossiers for middle-echelon cadres—those between grades 12 and 18 (between division chief and section chief)—of all the organs directly under the province. According to one informant, the personnel bureau of Guangdong provincial government maintained about 5,000 dossiers at the time of the CR. The cadres below grade 19 have their dossiers kept in the personnel section or the organizational department of the bureau level. The same principle may apply to the units below the provincial level.

At each unit, except probably in small enterprises, dossiers are kept in a specially designated dossier room. One person is accountable for approximately every 1,000 dossiers. To be allowed to work with dossiers, a person receives close scrutiny of his political reliability and party spirit.[25]

On the dossier's outer envelope are written the person's name, dossier number, sex, unit, birthplace, date of birth, family background, individual status, date of first engaging in revolutionary

24. Zhonggong Zhongyang Zhuzhibu Yanjiushi, ed., *Dangde Zhuzi*, 279.
25. Wang, *Renshi Dangan*, 57–62, 110–32.

work, status, position, and address. Each dossier is given a serial number, the first two digits specifying the field to which one belongs, and the other digits assigned by seniority. Files are organized according to serial number. In order to facilitate retrieval, each personnel department maintains a directory arranged according to the number of strokes in the last name. In addition to normal updating of dossiers, custodians are required to check the serial numbers once every six months and to index them annually.[26]

Before the CR, there was a well-established set of rules to access dossiers, and these rules have recently been reinstated.[27] Two people must carry out any investigation of a political problem in the personnel dossier. In order to have access to the dossier for cadres above section chief, both of the investigators have to be party members, and at least one must be of a higher rank. If the cadre being investigated is below section chief, one investigator can be a nonparty member, although this is very rare. When a party committee wishes to check a dossier held by another unit, it has to write a letter of introduction for its investigators. The letter specifies the investigators' ranks and positions and whose file they are authorized to see. After registering with the persons in charge of the dossier, the investigators leave the letter, which is later added to the dossier. Questions raised about the contents of a dossier are also put into it.

Investigators are allowed to see dossiers of those specified by the letter only in the designated dossier room. No mechanical duplication of a dossier is allowed except for a simplified version of the dossier. When part of a dossier is copied, it is verbatim; no summarizing or paraphrasing is allowed. The person in charge of the dossier must authenticate every page copied and the entire package.

Control over copied materials is strict because they can enter the dossiers of others as supporting evidence. To ensure proper control, the regime authorized each unit maintaining dossiers to set up more detailed regulations.[28] As for lending dossiers, "as a rule, a dossier cannot be checked out. But under special circumstances, it can be lent with approval [of the party committee]. However, lend-

26. Ibid.
27. Ibid., 32–34.
28. Ibid., 33, 43.

ing should follow strict registration, and those borrowed should be returned within the due date."[29]

A personnel dossier always follows a person when he is transferred. In the early 1950s the transferred cadre could carry his own dossier in a sealed envelope. This practice allowed many people to change the contents in order to secure a better job. Thereafter, all dossiers were required to be sent out only through "confidential transportation," and now only cadres in organizational departments above the county level may carry them.

INVESTIGATION AND ASSESSMENT

The two most important functions of the party committee were the investigation of the contents of a dossier (*shencha*) and the assessment (*jianding*) of a cadre's performance in both work and politics. Three occasions precipitate an investigation. First, anything questionable in the autobiography requires further investigation. Second, the reexamination of a cadre's dossiers occurs when the organization receives accusation letters (*jiancha xin*). Before the CR, this kind of letter would not automatically have initiated a full-scale investigation unless the charge was serious and the letter was signed by the sender. However, during the CR, any suggestion of wrongdoing, either in an anonymous letter or in an oral accusation, frequently brought about an investigation. The present leadership is ambivalent toward an anonymous letter; on one hand, it admits that fear of reprisals leads people not to sign letters, but, on the other, it warns that malicious people often use the method to lay "false charges."[30]

The third occasion for investigation is a political campaign. Then, the personnel bureau or organizational department examines dossiers carefully, selecting ones with problems and reporting them to the party committee,[31] which decides whether a cadre's problem is serious enough to make him a target. The same method was used in the last party rectification campaign of 1984–86, which intended to punish former radicals for what they did almost twenty years before.

29. Zhonggong Zhongyang Zhuzhibu Yanjiushi, ed., *Dangde Zhuzi*, 281.
30. *Dangde Shenghuo*, no. 8, 1983, 37; no. 8, 1984, 10.
31. *Qingdao Ribao*, 14 September 1957.

To find falsification, investigators look for inconsistencies, particularly in the many versions of a cadre's autobiography. Any inconsistency is cause for investigators to suspect that a cadre has deliberately falsified his dossier. Discrepancies are entered in the dossier and dealt with during the next political campaign.

If a case requires further evidence, the party committee may decide to send out its own investigation team. In this case, the regulations stipulate that at least two people (sometimes three if they need to travel a long distance) must be dispatched together. Otherwise, any evidence collected is inadmissible. The investigators, who are usually selected from personnel agencies, ensure the reliability of information collected from witnesses.[32]

After returning to their respective units, the investigators write their reports, including corroborating testimony from witnesses, and submit them to the party committee. If the discrepancy between the new findings and what is reported in the personnel dossier is not serious, the committee will not make a case immediately, but the entry noting the discrepancy remains. In the next campaign, the party committee will try to verify the materials again.

During the CR, the Red Guards nominally followed the same procedure, quite often using the pretext of investigation for sightseeing trips. Due to an emphasis on "class struggle," suspicion on such trivial matters as class background resulted in sending out numerous investigation teams. As one observer argued, China must have wasted enormous amounts of money and energy on these trips. Moreover, most of the investigators merely collected evidence to support already-formulated conclusions.[33]

Apart from investigations, the party committee regularly assesses a cadre's work competence and political performance. The assessment can be made: (1) at the end of each year, (2) when the cadre is transferred to a new unit, or (3) at the end of each political movement. During Mao's era, the assessment focused on and emphasized political qualifications rather than functional work competency.[34]

Standard procedure for making an assessment requires, first,

32. For a documentary example of this kind of evidence, see "Central Document, No. 10, 1977."
33. Zhengming, no. 9, 1983, 55–56.
34. Wenhui Bao, 10 August 1957.

that each individual write his own assessment, detailing salient points and focusing on his own political performance and attitudes, strengths and weaknesses, achievements and mistakes. Second, the self-evaluation is read and discussed in a small group, which consists of colleagues who know one another very well.[35] Third, on the basis of the self-evaluation and the small group's report, the party committee writes an evaluation that is added to the dossier. Sometimes the evaluation has to be approved by an upper-level party committee. Assessment materials make up a large portion of the dossier.

Those being evaluated have a pretty good idea of the contents of the assessment. They know what they have written and what suggestions were made in the small group discussion. Cadres sometimes have access to the summaries of assessments made by the organizations. They were required to sign their names on the organizational assessment, and they have the right to reserve opinion on that portion with which they disagree. The assessment becomes effective only when the units and those evaluated sign together.[36] Despite this rule, many cadres complain that "party organizational assessment about cadres is surrounded by mystery."[37] During the CR many units stopped making assessments, and in places where they continued, coercion replaced objectivity. Recent regulations have revived the old practice of requiring the signature of the person being assessed.

Administrative control over the personnel dossier was well institutionalized in pre-CR China. The dossiers were strictly regulated, and there were at least well-established administrative practices, if not uniform rules, regarding the types and processing of information that went into the dossiers. These guidelines also applied to the maintenance and investigation of dossiers, as well as to rendering organizational judgments on the contents and on each individual cadre's performance. Thus, the dossier provided the party with accurate information on each cadre, enabling it to carry out recruitment and promotion in an orderly and justifiable way.

35. For a detailed description of the small group operation, see Martin Whyte, *Small Groups and Political Rituals in China* (Berkeley and Los Angeles: University of California Press, 1974).
36. *Renmin Ribao*, 10 August 1957.
37. *Wenhui Bao*, 27 October 1957.

The pre-CR personnel management practice, however, had several serious weaknesses, which subsequent politics magnified. First, there was no external mechanism to stop the party from abusing its authority in the area of personnel management. Whatever restraints there were, they were internal ones, whose effectiveness depended on goodwill. For instance, each cadre was granted the right to appeal to the upper echelon of the bureaucracy. But this right was generally ineffective in guaranteeing a fair review opportunity for the cadre because, as many Red Guard newspapers asserted, the upper echelon of the bureaucracy frequently showed more sympathy to the lower level than to an individual cadre.

Second, the heavy reliance on personal testimony—in contrast to the Western judicial practice of attaching importance to material evidence—and the lack of strict rules with regard to the admissibility of evidence and its interpretation offered even more room for abuse. The Chinese practice of interviewing those who knew the investigated person and using their testimony in written form as evidence reflected in part the cultural tradition and in part technical backwardness in dealing with material evidence. The effectiveness of this practice as an investigation method largely depended on an assumed mutual trust and a consensus on what was right and wrong among the people involved in the process. When the CR shattered the consensus on fundamental values, the practice degenerated to producing a large number of false charges and framed-up cases.

Third, the Chinese emphasis on "confession," which was epitomized in the official slogan, "lenience to those confessing, but harsh punishment to those refusing," contained a seed of abuse and excess. The notion that people would honestly confess their mistakes also indicated the utter lack of philosophical distinction between public and private domains, a distinction that led in the United States to the Fifth Amendment, granting the individual the right to refuse self-incrimination. As was the case with witness testimony, confession can work as an effective mechanism for justice only when all the participants share common criteria for right and wrong. When the official criteria changed during the CR, coercion, torture, and other types of physical punishment were widely used to force the purged to "confess" their crimes or to write accusations against others. A family member, relative, or other acquaintance was subject to the same abuse.[38]

Fourth, the principle of double jeopardy has never been firmly established in China. Even a case over which the party committee had rendered a final conclusion could be reopened when new evidence—reliable or not—became available. Many people were persecuted several times for the same reason.[39] As a result, there has been enormous pressure for reversals of past decisions and for the rehabilitation of victims, particularly when policies have changed with new leadership. By discrediting the organizational legitimacy of the party, the CR gave rise to demands to reverse previous decisions. One group of political leaders at the top level could then utilize such demands for their own political gain. As a result, the Chinese people are justifiably worried that if any drastic policy change occurs, what is regarded as virtue today—in Chinese a "red-color dossier"—will turn out to be a liability—a "black-color dossier."

IMPACT OF THE CR

From the beginning of the CR, the personnel dossier was the focus of attention, although no one publicly challenged the system per se. When Mao pressured the party into launching the CR, it sent out work teams to school campuses. Largely composed of cadres from outside the campus, the work teams examined the dossiers of each cadre and student and then classified them into rightist, middle roader, or leftist. When the work teams themselves came under public attack for having diverted the main targets from the party leaders to the masses, Mao ordered the materials collected by the work teams (generally known as "black materials") to be burned. However, some work teams hid materials among the personnel dossiers and other confidential party materials for future use. This offered the Red Guards an excuse to seize personnel dossiers under the pretext of searching for "black materials."

As the dossier rooms became less inviolable to the Red Guards,

38. *Shehui Kexueyuan Yanjiu Cankao Ziliao* (Sichuan), no. 10, 1983, 20–23; *Ming Bao*, 21 August 1981; *Guangming Ribao*, 8 January 1979.
39. For instance, see *Zhonggong Gongchandang Lishi Jiangyi*, 3d ed. (Jilin: Jilin Renmin Chubanshe, 1982), 2:182.

party leaders improvised various methods to protect the dossiers. In Guangdong, Zhao Ziyang, then the first provincial party secretary, moved all the dossiers under his jurisdiction to the Guangdong military command. The military kept the Red Guards at bay all through the CR by insisting that personnel dossiers were military secrets. At Zhongshan University, the party committee moved its dossiers to the school library, which was closed to students. However, Red Guards raided the library, seizing and destroying some of the dossiers.[40] Personnel dossiers for high-level cadres (those above section chief) survived intact, but the dossiers for lower-level cadres sustained some damage.[41]

In February 1967, the center ordered that mass organizations should not raid or seize personnel dossiers, that seizure of power in dossier rooms should be carried out exclusively by the rooms' original personnel, and that people unsuitable for the work should be transferred according to regular procedures (which required upper-level approval). Realizing the danger of seizing dossiers but suspicious that other factions might obtain access to them, warring factions in many units negotiated to seal the dossier rooms. Denied access to official personnel dossiers, the Red Guards began to build up their own by collecting materials and carrying out investigations.

The mass organization's inability to look at official dossiers, however, put them at a great disadvantage vis-à-vis PLA representatives. The latter often used their privilege of having access to dossiers in order to promote partisan political interests by supporting cadres of their choice, while rejecting cadres supported by the mass organizations. By contrast, the mass organizations had to rely on their own less reliable materials or on the opinions of the PLA representatives for the selection of "revolutionary cadres." In some cases PLA representatives allowed the mass representatives to look into cadres' dossiers in order to promote consensus, although that was a clear violation of pre-CR practice. Once the revolutionary committee was formally established, it assumed jurisdiction over dossiers.

40. Hai Feng, *An Account of the Cultural Revolution in the Canton Area* (Hong Kong: Union Research Institute, 1971).
41. *Dangde Shenghuo* (Tianjin), no. 18, 1980.

When the CR began "purifying class ranks" in 1968, the main thrust of the mass movement was turned against "hidden class enemies"—those who were suspected of having falsified their class backgrounds and of covering up their past ties with the KMT. The witch-hunt atmosphere was so intense that every Chinese, including the top leaders, became obsessed with the dossiers. Even Zhou Enlai was accused of once having surrendered to the Nationalists, and his case was not closed until Mao personally intervened.[42]

Radical leaders had their share of blemishes; Jiang Qing worried about the materials concerning her starlet life in the 1930s; Zhang Chunqiao had to protect his wife, who had once been captured by the Japanese, in addition to accounting for his past ties with the Nationalist secret organization *Fuxing She*; Yao Wenyuan had to cover up the fact that his father was labeled a rightist in 1957.[43]

According to its critics, the Gang of Four used every conceivable means to destroy any materials detrimental to themselves, while collecting, distorting, and manufacturing evidence to incriminate their political opponents. They are accused of having used deception, coercion, and torture for their purposes. Subjected to their abuse were not only the persons suspected, but their relatives, colleagues, subordinates, casual acquaintances, and even innocent bystanders who had any knowledge either of the Gang of Four's past or that of their political enemies. For instance, a librarian at Shanghai University discovered by accident some materials on Jiang Qing's 1930 career in the stacks; because of this, he languished in jail.[44] Even the Red Guards, who accidentally discovered more background on the Gang of Four, were persecuted for having "collected black materials against the central leaders." The story of how Yao Wenyuan handled the "black materials" reveals the radicals' obsession with them. When Yao received materials on Zhang Chunqiao in a sealed envelope, he wrote: "Contents are not opened and are not known. Ask for instructions from Comrade Zhang Chunqiao and Wang Hongwen. Handle according to party regulations." But Yao kept the materials in his house for almost

42. *Dangshi Yanjiu*, no. 1, 1980, 14.
43. *Renmin Ribao*, 6 July 1977.
44. "Central Document, No. 10, 1977."

seven years until his arrest. It appears that at that time the only rule governing politics was that one needed materials to purge others. But there were absolutely no rules about how to determine the materials' reliability or how one obtained them. As a result, "materials" could have an explosive effect, regardless of their reliability.

In brief, the series of continuous political campaigns after 1966 largely destroyed the normal administrative procedures of personnel management. Regular authority and procedures for decision making on personnel matters were abandoned. The rule that only party members could have access to dossiers was completely discarded, as many nonparty member rebels were promoted to positions that allowed for handling the dossiers. As a result of the simplification of the administrative structure, the sections in charge of the personnel dossiers were abolished. When the establishment of proper criteria for recruitment, promotion, appointment, and purging became the major focus of contention among the various political factions, materials in the dossier proved to be irrelevant. The scale of personnel changes during the same period was also gigantic. About 18 million new party members were recruited during the CR, whereas about 2.9 million people were purged. About 2 million workers, soldiers, and peasants were promoted to cadre positions while retaining their previous occupation status, the practice known as using peasants as cadres (*yinong daigan*) and using workers as cadres (*yigong daigan*).[45] For instance, workers who were promoted to revolutionary committees continued to keep their former grade. As a result, the positions they actually occupied and their grades (which determine salary) did not match.

Were all of these changes recorded in the personnel dossiers? Where were the materials of self-criticism and the records of being accused and investigated kept? What happened to the huge amount of materials collected by the mass organizations? There is not enough information to answer these questions systematically. Fragmented information allows for a few general observations.

Although no specific regulation was issued by the center, the materials collected by the mass organizations were kept separately from personnel dossiers in order to be checked for reliability later.

45. *Renshi Guanli* (Beijing: Beijingshi Renshiju, 1985).

However, it is also very likely that many unauthorized materials entered the dossier.[46]

> In the ten years of calamity, when right and wrong were reversed, the cadres' personnel dossiers, which were not perfect, were further destroyed. Merit became a liability, mistakes became merits, and facts were reversed. Many false materials entered the cadres' dossiers. . . . So much unnecessary and false information entered the cadres' dossiers.[47]

Moreover, any decision rendered by the organization through the organizational process was entered in the dossier, even if it was reversed later. The verdict made by the Ninth Central Committee on Liu Shaoqi probably was in his dossier. Also, numerous self-criticisms made by the highest leaders—for instance, Deng Xiaoping—were probably included in their dossiers.

A more serious problem was the accumulation of unsettled cases. Even after the reconstruction of the party organization, the party committees at the various levels were unwilling or unable to render organizational conclusions on many cases, largely due to the unreliability of the collected materials, the absurdity of charges made, and the lack of guidance from the center during the chaotic ten years of the CR. The personnel dossier system was in disarray when the Gang of Four was ousted.

REFORM

Immediately after the Gang of Four's fall, the regime tried to restore the pre-CR practice. First, party committees at various levels regained their exclusive authority over personnel matters. Then, the regime issued several regulations about dossiers, for example, "Regulations on Cadre Dossier Work," "Methods of Handling Cadre Dossiers," and "Regulations for Personnel Working on the Dossier System." Even though the contents of the rules are not known, the section dealing with dossiers in "Questions and Answers on the Party's Organizational Work" reveals that these new regulations are quite similar to what had existed before the CR.[48] They intended to tighten organizational control over dossiers

46. *Daily Report*, 21 October 1981, 1.
47. *Zhibu Shenghuo* (Shanghai), no. 18, 1985, 24.
48. Zhonggong Zhongyang Zhuzhibu Yanjiushi, ed., *Dangde Zhuzi*, 276–80.

rather than protect the individual's rights by specifying rules with regard to collecting materials, investigating their reliability, placing them in the dossier, and arranging them in a certain order. For instance, now only materials "approved by the organization" can enter the personnel dossier. Any materials needed for evaluating cadres can enter the dossier if they are approved by the organization. Such materials as records of speeches or results of opinion polls and reports, that the organization has not yet examined, can be kept separately in the personnel departments. Moreover, the regime has organized nationwide conferences on personnel dossiers and endeavored to give specialized training to all people dealing with dossiers.[49]

In addition, reforms initiated since Mao's death have had direct consequences for personnel management. As noted, the emphasis in recruitment and promotion has shifted from political reliability to ability, particularly technical and professional competency, and largely measured in terms of formal education. The removal of class designations such as counterrevolutionary, rightist, and landlord has made class origin and past political activities less relevant to personnel management. On the whole, documentation of actual performance rather than past performance is now more heavily weighed in personnel decisions. Some measures have been taken to protect individual rights in the state constitution, the party constitution, and the party rules and regulations. The new rules grant individuals the right to "put forward their statements, appeals, accusations, and defense at party meetings or to party organizations at a higher level, right up to the party committee." Also, party members have access to any decision made by the party organization on "appraisals, verdicts, and punishments."[50] The new criminal code considers it a punishable crime to make false charges or accusations.

The second national conference on cadres' dossiers held in 1982 decided to check every dossier, updating the contents to make them accurately reflect the personnel changes after the CR, and, most important, to "cleanse" personnel dossiers by destroying all materials collected since the CR. The Shanghai organizational de-

49. Wang, *Renshi Dangan*, 43.
50. "Guiding Principle for Inner Party Life," *Beijing Review*, 7 September 1980.

partment assigned ten cadres to straighten out the personnel dossiers.[51] Despite these efforts, some cadres are still complaining about the inaccuracy of the information stored in their dossiers.

> Even after four years since 1980, still some of the cadre dossiers are not yet cleansed. . . . Still some problems exist with the dossier work. For example, some dossier materials reflect only good news not the bad news, or they reflect the bad news, while failing to report the good news. Most information in the dossier reflects the situation at a given moment, their contents are old, failing to reflect the entire history of a cadre, his work achievements and real conditions.[52]

To rehabilitate victims of the CR and former rightists completely, the regime issued an official certificate of rehabilitation or removed rightist labels. In order to prove the regime's sincerity, on some occasions the party committee has shown the concerned individual the materials to be removed from the personnel dossier and then destroyed them. However, wondering whether or not all incriminating materials have been removed, some individuals have demanded to see the entire contents of their dossiers. The party committee, of course, will not allow that. The cadres' apprehensions appear to be justified because the policy of cleansing the dossier is not categorical. On the contrary, official policy specifies types of materials to remain in the dossier. They are "materials accurately reflecting historical reality and useful for understanding cadres," "materials related to the investigation, reinvestigation, and rehabilitation of a person's historical problems," and "the organization's conclusion and its supporting material." Understandably, this makes some Chinese nervous about what is left in the dossier.

Moreover, the removal of rightist, counterrevolutionary, capitalist, or other class enemy labels does not mean erasing past records. Most official forms used for cadres still include columns for family background and individual status, and in filling the class origin column, each individual is required to report his former class labels—no one is allowed to change his family background or individual status without approval of the organizations—and to add

51. *Zhibu Shenghuo* (Shanghai), no. 18, 1985, 1–18.
52. *Daily Report*, 28 September 1981, P1.

his present occupation.[53] This is the case with the children of the former exploiting class. In other words, the regime has not yet stopped soliciting information on class background but simply promises that it will not be used as a criterion for personnel management. Thus, this practice, plus keeping the traits of past political decisions, makes concerned individuals uneasy about the possibility that when the political wind changes, their records can be used against them.

In fact, it seems that the regime continues to rely on information stored in dossiers whenever the necessity to check a cadre's political reliability arises. For instance, whether or not one is "revolutionized" is largely determined on the basis of materials in the dossier. The investigation of the "three types of people" relied heavily on materials stored in dossiers. In addition, new materials are constantly being generated for dossiers.[54] For instance, every decision made in the party rectification of 1983–86 entered the dossiers—including delayed and denied registration. The sentence that one has made "comparatively serious mistakes during the CR" can enter one's dossier.

As the scope of reform in other fields expands, the existing dossier system poses some serious problems. For instance, the system comes in conflict with the current policy of utilizing China's limited resources of technical cadres efficiently by making it easier to transfer them across administrative boundaries and by allowing individuals to seek employment and transfer on their own initiative. At present, no organization will accept anyone without first going through his or her dossier. However, unless one is officially transferred, it is extremely difficult to persuade a unit to send a dossier to the new unit.[55] Anyone who controls the personnel dossier of a particular cadre actually controls the cadre. When several units compete for a particular person, the unit that has access to his dossier can have the person because the other competitors cannot make a decision on him or her without looking at the dossier.

To sum up, the regime has not yet fundamentally changed the

---

53. Zhonggong Zhongyang Zhuzhibu Yanjiushi, ed., *Dangde Zhuzi*, 287. But other sources indicate that after June 1979 one can write his present occupation in the column (*geren chengfen*). *Dangde Shenghou* (Tianjin), no. 20, 1980, 9.

54. *Zhibu Shenghuo* (Shanghai), no. 13, 1985, 26.

55. *Zhengming*, no. 9, 1983, 55.

practice of collecting detailed information on each cadre and storing it in a personnel dossier, although a serious effort is made to check the potential abuse of materials. When some Chinese demanded the abolition of the dossier system on the ground that "since the basic goal of the regime has changed, there is no need for the dossier system," the official view insisted that "on the contrary, when the party's main task changed, the personnel dossier became more important, and its utility increased."[56] Nonetheless, it seems that decentralization of personnel decision-making power and transferring it to the government personnel bureau are changing the administrative practice of managing dossiers. When the civil service system is thoroughly implemented, the personnel bureau of the government will manage all personnel dossiers for functional civil servants, leaving only the dossiers of political civil servants with the party's organizational departments. Instead of abolishing the personnel dossier system, the regime seems to intend to strengthen administrative control over files and to use them more rationally (e.g., entering examination scores). Consequently, a cynical Hong Kong observer asks: "China is economically and politically the most backward; but it has the most advanced personnel dossier system in the world. Is it a blessing or a curse for the Chinese?"[57]

There is absolutely no sign to indicate that the regime is concerned about possible infringements of individual rights through the dossier system. The utter lack of concern with individual privacy was again revealed when Qien Xuesen, a renowned Chinese scientist, suggested a few years ago that the Chinese computerize their personnel dossier system. The ostensive objective was to make the personnel management system rational, enabling the government to select easily the best qualified persons for the most suitable jobs.

> By using combinations of centralized but grade-by-grade management, we can simultaneously evaluate a thousand, ten thousand persons, and we can select the best-qualified people from several tens of millions of personnel dossiers. The old method of checking personnel dossiers one by one cannot do that. Already there is a

56. Wang, *Renshi Dangan*, 44.
57. *Zhengming*, no. 9, 1983, 55–56.

system of examining dossiers by computer and even dossier investigation can be automated. A computer can work several thousand times faster than man. Once the criteria for selection are set up, a computer can automatically select the most suitable persons. Since the dossiers are recorded on magnetic tape, they can be supplemented: work condition, masses' and leaders' opinions of a person, and his health record can enter the dossiers through the regular process.[58]

Given the present level of science and technology in China, it would be extremely difficult to develop a comprehensive system of classifying and coding all the necessary information on personnel management of cadres in the foreseeable future. However, in some units computerization of dossiers has started. It is chilling even to think of a computer that contains all conceivable physiological, biological, medical, and psychological information on every one of the millions of Chinese people.

58. "Engineering in the Socialist Manpower Field," *Hong Qi*, no. 2, 1982. Also for computerizing personnel dossiers, see Wang, *Renshi Dangan*, 184–85.

14

The Party's Changing Role in Personnel Management

All Leninist parties maintain their authority over cadres in order to control not only the vast bureaucracy but also access to elite status. The CCP regards its monopoly of personnel management as "the basic source of authority that our party needs to fulfill its political mission at each historical stage, [and that] renders the organizational guarantee for the successful completion of a new democratic revolution, a socialist revolution, and a socialist construction."[1]

The party-state vigorously defends its monopoly over personnel, reacting violently whenever social forces challenge this prerogative. During the Hundred Flowers campaign the intellectuals' demand to share authority over cadres prompted the top leaders to initiate the antirightist campaign. Similarly, it was only when Polish workers called for abolition of the *nomenklatura* system that the military stepped in to repress the Solidarity movement.[2]

The phrase "the party manages the cadres" justifies the CCP's monopoly. "State cadres are the party's cadres, and all cadres should be managed according to the party's direction and policies and the principle of unified management." More specifically, the principle implies that the party has the exclusive right to set up the "line, direction, and policies" relating to personnel management, no one can challenge the party's prerogative, and no regional variation can be tolerated. All cadres, whether party members or nonmembers, administrative or technical, are to carry out the party's line and program under the CCP's leadership. Furthermore, the principle also states that only party organs at the various levels

1. Cao Zhi, ed., *Zhonghua Renmin Gongheguo Renshi Zhidu Gaiyao* (Beijing: Beijing Dafue Chubanshe, 1985), 7.
2. Takayuki Ito, "Controversy over *Nomenklatura* in Poland" (unpublished paper).

can select, assign, and utilize cadres. However, the principle does not tell how the party should exercise its authority.

PAST PRACTICE

From its foundation to 1949, the CCP directly managed all cadres under a principle of "unified management" without sharing its prerogative with any other government agency.[3] At each level, party committees made all major decisions on personnel matters while the party's organizational departments handled all administrative aspects of cadre management. Moreover, the system was highly centralized, with upper-level party committees making most decisions on cadres employed at the lower levels. This centralized system was suitable to the revolutionary war period when the size of the cadre corps was small and the CCP was engaged in a desperate struggle with the KMT.

When China started its first five-year plan in 1953, the regime modified its management of cadres to fit the tasks of economic development and socialist construction. As the cadre corps grew and the types of work they were required to perform multiplied, it became more difficult for the organizational departments to manage all the cadres, much less develop a long-term plan for cultivating specialized cadres.[4] Therefore, the CCP decided in 1953 to manage cadres "department by department and level by level" (*fenbu* and *fenji*) under the unified management of party committees and organizational departments. All cadres were grouped into ten functional categories (*xitong*): (1) culture and education, (2) agriculture, forestry, and water conservation, (3) united front, (4) party and government organs, (5) industry, planning, labor, and statistics, (6) finance, economics, commerce, banking, and grain and supply cooperatives, (7) transportation, telecommunications, and postal service, (8) public security, civil affairs, judiciary, court, and procuratorate, (9) foreign relations, foreign trade, and overseas Chinese, and (10) mass organizations such as labor unions, the CYL, and women's associations.[5] The various functional depart-

3. Cao Zhi, ed., *Zhonghua Renmin*, 7.
4. Ibid., 7–8.
5. Wang Jianxin, Yang Shugui, Jin Guoliang, and Yan Zhuanyu, eds., *Ganbu Guanli Gailun* (Liaoning: Liaoning Dafue Chubanshe, 1984), 44; Cao Zhi, ed., *Zhonghua Renmin*, 417–18.

ments, established under the Party committees, managed the cadres working in their fields.

Level-by-level (*fenji*) management meant that each level managed the cadres of its subordinate units down to two or three levels below. The center was responsible for ministers, vice ministers, directors, and deputy directors of the central government and party organs, as well as for leading cadres of provinces and districts. Provincial party committees were in charge of their own middle-level cadres and leading cadres of districts (*diqu*), the municipality, and the county. District party committees handled leading cadres of the county and village (*xiang*), in addition to their own middle-level cadres (heads of division and sections). County committees looked after their own middle-level (section and team) cadres and the leadership group of village, town (*zhen*), and hamlet (*cun*).[6]

Paralleling the party's organizational departments were personnel bureaus, set up in the government, enterprises, and business units to "assist" (*xiezhu*) the organizational departments.[7] Generally speaking, the personnel bureaus managed low-ranking cadres and workers or took care of the administrative work of personnel management, whereas the organizational departments worked as the administrative arm of party committees. Compared with previous practice, the new system was reportedly more suitable for "investigating, observing, and understanding more deeply the political quality and functional competency of the cadres . . . thus helping to fulfill the first five-year plan successfully."[8]

In order to implement the state constitution, all cadres appointed by the central government or the State Council were screened by the organizational departments before any formal announcement. The cadres to be elected by the state or party organs had to report to the proper authorities before the election.[9]

By 1955, the center completed the lists of cadres (*nomenklatura*) whom it directly managed. The lists included "all cadres assuming nationally important positions."[10] The appointment or transfer of any cadre on the list had to be approved (*pizhun*) by the center,

6. Cao Zhi, ed., *Zhonghua Renmin*, 8.
7. Ibid.
8. Wang et al., eds., *Ganbu Guanli Gailun*, 44.
9. Cao Zhi, ed., *Zhonghua Renmin*, 156–63.
10. Ibid., 143.

which also instructed the local committees and their functional departments to prepare lists of cadres under their jurisdiction, using the principle of "managing fewer and managing better" and considering the importance of the post rather than the incumbent.[11] The lists included a brief description of the major responsibilities of each post. Thereafter, every year the organizational department must update the list.

For conflicting jurisdictional claims over units under the dual leadership of the central functional department and the local party committee, the center urged the involved parties to negotiate through the management offices—for example, the organizational departments—rather than through responsible persons.

Whenever a new question arose with regard to jurisdiction, the regime ruled on a case-by-case basis. For instance, in March 1953 the center placed the leaders of the Sino-Soviet Friendship Association and the Chinese Writers' Association under the propaganda department. The higher learning institutes were placed under the various central party departments according to the functional areas of the schools; thus, agricultural and forestry colleges fell under the jurisdiction of the central agricultural work department, and cadres of nationality institutes were given to the united front department.[12]

Thus, the pre-CR personnel management system took into consideration to only a small degree the type of unit the cadres belonged to (*fengong*) or the level in the bureaucratic hierarchy they occupied (*fenceng*). The system lacked any notion of classifying the cadres according to the type of work they performed (*fenlei*). Although such terms as "party, state, and mass organization cadres," "business cadres," and "enterprise cadres" (classified according to the type of organ where the cadres were employed), or "political cadres," "administrative cadres," and "specialist cadres" (classified according to the type of work the cadre performed) were used, these categories had no practical ramifications for managing the cadres. The party committees managed all cadres, using uniform criteria for different types of cadres.

How to classify the cadres according to the type of work they

11. Ibid., 144.
12. Ibid., 419–21.

did, how to manage different categories of cadres using different criteria, and how to distribute personnel authority among the different state organs—for example, the party, government, and enterprise—were questions that were never raised until the 1982–87 reforms.

Nonetheless, a modus operandi for making decisions on personnel matters evolved from 1953 to the CR, nominally involving four parallel hierarchies—that is, decision-making and executive organs of the party and state—although the party had the final say.[13] The system was not designed as a master plan; rather specific regulations dealing with concrete problems were accumulated, thus producing the general structure of the system.

The chaotic CR, however, destroyed whatever regulations and rules that existed at the time and abolished the personnel bureaus in the government units. As may be inferred from table 38, about 6.4 million joined the cadre ranks without going through formal procedures.

INITIAL ADJUSTMENTS

After the fall of the Gang of Four, the regime restored the pre-CR system whereby each party committee managed the cadres two levels below it. It reissued cadre lists to be managed by the center.[14] In addition, the regime clarified the issue of jurisdiction over enterprise and business cadres: the central organizational department would manage leading cadres of the enterprises directly under the center in coordination with the party core group (*dangzu*) of the relevant government ministries.[15] Management of middle-echelon cadres in the enterprises was generally assigned to the enterprise and business unit party committees. For enterprises

13. Wang et al., eds., *Ganbu Guanli Gailun*, 54–56.
14. Cao Zhi, ed., *Zhonghua Renmin*, 147.
15. The party core group was set up right after 1949 in all government agencies when many administrative heads were nonparty members. Existing separately from the party committee at the same level, it was appointed directly by the higher party committee to which it was accountable. *Xinhua Wenzhai*, no. 11, 1978, 1–6; *Zhongguo Shehui Kexue*, no. 6, 1987, 3–22. Consisting of three to five persons and a group secretary, the party core group maintains the list of people over which they have authority. John Burn, "China's *Nomenklatura* System," *Problems of Communism*, September–October 1987, 36–51.

subject to dual jurisdictions—the central party department and the local party committee—"the higher-level party committee will be in charge, and the lower-level party committee will help with observation, examination, training, education, and investigation." With regard to appointment, promotion, transfer, reward and punishment, the lower-level committees could make only suggestions.[16]

With regard to the division of work between the party's functional departments and its organizational departments, the regime instructed each provincial authority to decide in a way that would uphold the principle of "unified management," while making the system flexible by allowing each functional department to manage cadres in its own field.[17]

Soon the two-level management by the superior party committee proved to be too highly centralized to work effectively. The regime gradually decentralized the personnel authority by transferring some cadres from central to local jurisdictions. In 3 February 1979 the organizational department authorized nine central organs to manage their own deputy heads. On 24 December 1980 a notice issued by the central organizational department transferred to provincial authorities the jurisdiction over district party secretaries, directors of provincial bureaus, and responsible persons of some enterprise and business units. Provincial party committees were required simply to notify the center of their decisions.[18] The same notice divided the cadres on the center's lists into two categories. Category A included only the leading cadres of the center and provinces.[19] All those not listed in category A belonged to category B. When appointing or dismissing members of category A, the party functional departments or the party core groups in the government ministries and the other relevant organs first had to seek the opinion of "the central leaders or vice prime ministers in charge of the units" and include their opinions in the report submitted to the central organizational department. For cadres under

16. Cao Zhi, ed., *Zhonghua Renmin*, 148.
17. Ibid.
18. Ibid.
19. According to John Burn, this category included about 5,000 of the most senior people throughout the country. For a sample of the list, see Burn, "China's *Nomenklatura* System."

dual leadership, the dominant unit would first seek the opinion of the other side and then report both opinions to the center.

For the posts included in category A but whose incumbents were selected through election, the list of candidates had to be reported with the information specified in the "Form for Reporting Cadre Appointment and Dismissal" to the center for examination before an election. The results of the election also had to be reported to the center for approval. Cadres on the B list were transferred to provincial authorities, who reported their decisions to the center for record keeping.[20] Thus, cadres on the B list were in fact transferred to provincial jurisdictions.

Any appointment or dismissal of cadres, which required the State Council's approval, had first to be forwarded to the party center. After reviewing the request, the organizational department notified the ministry of labor and personnel of its decision. Only then would the case be submitted to the State Council to formalize the changes according to the regulation. For provincial leaders, whose appointment and dismissal required approval of the local People's Congress, the relevant authority—that is, the provincial organizational departments—first had to consult with the standing committee of the local People's Congress and then report to the central organizational department or to the State Council. These complicated rules were designed to keep personnel authority in the party organs while following constitutional and other legal formalities.

For cadres belonging to category B, each provincial and municipal party committee as well as the various central party organs, the various ministries, and the various people's organizations had to make nominations in written form, explaining in detail the reason for the appointment or dismissal to the center.

The "Regulation Regarding Reform of the Cadre Management System," adopted on 5 October 1983, finally formalized the scope of cadre management by party committees at the various levels. According to this regulation the center managed only "the first-class leadership" of the provincial organs. It also managed ministers, vice ministers, members of the party faction in government ministries, and directors and deputy directors of bureau-level

20. Chao Zhi, ed., *Zhonghua Renmin*, 149.

organs. Control over the rest of the cadres was given to provincial authorities.[21] On 14 July 1984 the organizational department issued more instructions in order to clarify the previous decisions and to solve the problems arising in the process of implementing the decisions. Thereafter, provincial and prefectural party committees prepared the list of cadres they controlled while others were sent down one level below.

The new system is called "managing according to ranks and having each echelon responsible" (*fenji quanli, cengceng fuze*). This system decentralized the personnel management authority to a certain extent. Each level manages the one directly below it, instead of two levels below. The organizational department issued a "Notice Regarding the Revised Cadre Post List Under the Center's Authority," which retained only one-third of the cadres on the previous list. The rest were transferred to a lower level. Each state organ reprepared the list for which it was responsible. The new lists, according to an official claim, enable each central ministry and local party committee more effectively to "supervise, check, and discover the talents" for the positions for which they are responsible. The party committees survey personnel changes in the positions listed under their jurisdiction twice a year and report them to the organizational department.

However, overlapping claims on cadres continue, particularly among government ministries, which exercise functional leadership (*yewu lingdao*) over their subordinate enterprise and business units scattered nationwide, and local party committees, which have "leadership relations" with the same units. The functional leadership is often called "line" (*tiaotiao*), and the leadership that the local party committee exercises over the enterprise and business units is known as "area" (*kuaikuai*). The division of work in the area of personnel management between *tiaotiao* and *kuaikuai* is particularly unclear and gives rise to situations where both pass the buck and both check each other.

Generally, there are three types of arrangements for the claims of the *tiaotiao* and *kuaikuai*. The first type is dominated by the central ministries: their party core groups are responsible for appointments, transfers, examinations, investigations, assess-

21. *Huaqiao Ribao*, 14 July 1987, 1.

ments, promotions, and dismissals. Local party committees assist the work of the various central departments, assuming major responsibility only for the political, ideological, and functional education of the cadres.[22] The local party committees also supervise the administrative side of personnel management as well as such party functions as convening party conferences, electing party committees, and examining (*shencha*) candidates for committee membership.

The second type is dominated by local party committees: they are mainly responsible for personnel management, whereas the upper organs provide functional leadership and make suggestions only on personnel matters. The third type involves the conflicting claims between local party committees and enterprise and business units under the local authority. For this case the involved parties are supposed to divide their work through negotiation and bargaining.

In addition to the limited decentralization of personnel authority along the party hierarchy, the regime also tried to rationalize the methods of managing personnel matters.

RECRUITMENT

All cadres in China are "appointed" (*renming*) by superior organs (*shangji*), and this method has not changed in any meaningful way, despite the frequent misuse of authority by leading cadres.[23] Instead, the regime has endeavored to improve its operation by emphasizing careful screening by the organizational departments and collective decision making by party committees. Officially, any important decision about cadres should involve "democratic nomination, consultation with a wide range of opinions, selection of candidates with care, investigation by organizational departments, collective discussion by party committees, reports to upper echelons, rechecking by organizational departments, and final approval by party committees one level higher."[24] In addition, the

22. Wang et al., eds., *Ganbu Guanli Gailun*, pp. 48–49; Cao Zhi, ed., *Zhonghua Renmin*, 422–23.
23. *Shehui Kexue Pinglun*, 5 September 1985.
24. *Renmin Ribao*, 2 February 1986.

regime has experimented with several other methods to improve the effectiveness of the appointment system.

One remedy is to make appointments only after soliciting recommendations from the masses and after careful organizational investigation (*kaocha*).[25] The regime now encourages the masses, low-ranking cadres, and retired cadres to recommend qualified persons for specific cadre positions. Even if fully utilized, this method will not change the appointment system; it only broadens the pool of candidates from which party committees will make final selections. So far it seems that only retired cadres effectively use their "right to recommend" to influence the final selection for their benefit.[26]

Another remedy is a kind of election, primarily used to select administrative heads for small enterprises and business units. For instance, Guangdong province reportedly used an "election" to select the managers of the Jianmen Beverage Factory and the Friendship Store of Shenzhen, as well as the department heads of the Central-South Institute.[27] Viewed as a means of "finding competent persons" rather than of electing representatives, the "election" resembles an opinion poll because the outcome must be approved by a proper party committee. Despite its experimental nature, some old cadres are openly critical of elections on the grounds that they aggravate factionalism, and "talent [*rencai*] will not necessarily get the most votes."[28] It is, therefore, very unlikely that "elections" will become an important mode of selecting cadres.

For recruiting specialist cadres, some units use an "invitation system," in which each hiring unit and individual applicant bargain, negotiate, and make a contract that contains specific terms on tenure, remuneration, and type of work to be done.[29] The regime tolerates a limited labor market for specialist cadres because of the need to utilize scarce manpower effectively and to allow peripheral regions and rural areas to attract much-needed specialists. To criti-

25. Ibid., 12 October 1982.
26. Ibid., 7 August 1985.
27. *Guangzhou Yanjiu*, no. 3, 1985, 41–42.
28. *Renmin Ribao*, 21 March 1985.
29. Guangdongsheng Renshiju, ed., *Shenzhen Ganbu Renshi Zhidu Gaige* (Beijing: Laoding Renshi Chubanshe, 1984).

cism that the system undermines state planning and brings back the "capitalist labor market," proponents respond by stressing that specialists, once hired, become "co-owners" of the means of production and that the system induces specialists to improve their knowledge and to raise their productivity. By offering attractive terms, Guansu province managed to draw about 8,800 specialists from outside the province, and a poor county in Henan province invited about 700 outside technical personnel.[30]

In July 1984, the center designated three provinces, two municipalities, and three scientific organizations to experiment with the invitation system (*pingren*).[31] Shaanxi province reportedly used this method to select the leading cadres of six provincial organs.[32] The invitation method is widely used for choosing village and township-level cadres.[33] Hubei province reportedly recruited 15,000 people for leadership positions at that level.[34]

In some places, an examination is used to recruit people for low-level functionary positions in such sectors as banking, taxes, industry, commerce, prison work, and legal fields.[35] Initially, tests were administered to only a fixed number of candidates designated by the recruiters, but the regime promises to change the method to "open invitation, self-application, firmly upholding test results, evaluation of virtue, intelligence and physical conditions, and selection of the best." The city of Shenyang has used the "open invitation and test" method to appoint leading cadres of its science and technology commission, measurement bureau, and tourist corporation.[36] By 1987, Zhejiang province reportedly recruited 13,900 people through the examination system.[37] Seventy-five percent of the newly recruited or promoted were from units other than where they assumed leadership positions.[38]

30. *Jiaoyanjiu Cankao Ziliao*, 1 February 1986; Guowuyuan Bangongding Diaocha Yanjiushi, ed., *Zongguo Xingzheng Guanlixue Chutan* (Beijing: Jingji Kexue Chuban-she, 1984), 55–81.

31. *Renmin Ribao*, 29 March 1985.

32. *Shaanxi Ribao*, 6 February 1985.

33. Altogether about 60,000 were invited. *Renmin Ribao*, 15 October 1984.

34. Ibid., 1 June 1985; *Chiangjiang Ribao*, 1 June 1985; 23 June 1985.

35. *Renmin Ribao*, 8 November 1980.

36. *Jianzhou Shiyuan Xuebao*, 10 April 1985; *Liaowang*, no. 39, 1984, 5.

37. *Beijing Review*, 31 August 1987, 8.

38. For instance, a local school teacher of economics became the head of Ningpo city's price bureau. Ibid.

EVALUATION

The merit-based personnel management system requires impartial and rigorous appraisal of performance, the system which many Chinese scholars believe to be the key to solving the problems of the "iron rice bowl [and] eating from a big pot." The regular assessment that the CR had ended has been restored by the regime and is now conducted once every two years.[39]

However, the criteria and procedures for assessing performance have not yet been systematized or standardized. Currently, cadres are assessed in four areas: virtue, ability, diligence, and achievement. The meaning of these four terms is ambiguous, and the effort to clarify them produces only more numerous subcategories and indicators. For instance, one Chinese writer divides virtue into four subsets: personality, moral and ethical standards, professional ethics, and political attitude. Each of these subcategories is further divided into three indicators. As a result, the evaluation of virtue requires the examination of twelve indicators.[40] Similarly, ability, diligence, and achievement are divided into several dozen indicators. When more than fifty indicators are graded in terms of four categories—excellent, fine, fair, and poor—the evaluation becomes too complicated and confusing.[41] Shanghai reportedly developed forty standards with which to evaluate each cadre, and the scores on each criterion obtained by surveying superiors, subordinates, and colleagues were coded and stored in a computer.[42]

These multiple categories allow an inordinate amount of discretionary power to evaluators.[43] Therefore, leading cadres frequently rely on simple criteria such as age, education, and their impression of the candidate. Despite an official emphasis on "pioneering spirit," cadres with such spirit often offend the powerful and "cannot stay on the job for a long time," but "those with ordinary ability can manage very well." The best way for the Chinese bureaucracy to manage is to take a cautious middle position on every issue: "Swimming at the upper end of the stream receives punishment,

39. Cao Zhi, ed., *Zhonghua Renmin*, 174.
40. Wang et al., eds., *Ganbu Guanli Gailun*, 189.
41. The "Provisional Regulations of the Civil Servant" prescribes the same procedure for evaluation. *Liaowang*, 17 June 1985, 26–27.
42. *Renmin Ribao*, 19 September 1984.
43. Wang et al., eds., *Ganbu Guanli Gailun*, 187–94.

swimming at the lower end of the stream maintains the present position, and swimming in the middle is blessed."

As part of a planned civil service system, the regime experimented with a new evaluation system in three different units. One was a year-end assessment of political cadres in Zhejiang in 1987, and it plans to test the same method in eighteen provinces and municipalities in 1988. A guideline issued on 8 July 1987 for assessing county-level cadres followed the existing personnel management procedure. The authority to assess the county secretary and magistrate is in the hands of a special committee organized by the district-level party secretary or administrative heads.[44] For a year-end assessment of administrative cadres, the regime plans to test a new method in Huangbu district and the commerce bureau of Shanghai. Also, some central government ministries are slated to experiment with the new evaluation method.[45] The "Provisional Regulations of the Civil Servant" specifies that any evaluation of cadres of division (*chu*) level or above should include the opinion of the masses as collected through an "opinion poll."

Responsibility System

Since Deng Xiaoping's speech in March 1983, which stressed the need to specify tasks, people, quantity, quality, and time needed to complete every project, the center has issued a series of directives and organized numerous conferences to exchange experiences to establish a system for defining responsibilities.[46] By 1984, about 20 percent of the provincial organs and about 50 percent of the district- and municipal-level organs in twenty-three provinces had allegedly established some kind of responsibility system.[47] By 1987 about 93 percent of districts and municipalities and 94 percent of county governments had established some kind of responsibility system.[48]

Understandably, defining the authority, responsibility, and task for each of 27 million cadres is a mammoth undertaking in China

44. *Zhuzhi Renshixue Yanjiu*, no. 2, 1988, 36–38.
45. *Renmin Ribao*, 11 December 1987.
46. *Lilun Zhanxian* (Anhui), 15 January 1984, 13; *Sichuan Ribao*, 14 March 1984.
47. *Lilun Zhanxian*, 5 January 1984, 4–5.
48. *Zhongguo Renshi Guanli*, no. 9, 1987, 20.

where even systematic and effective tables of organization are non-existent. Instead of issuing general guidelines on how to set up the responsibility system, the center encourages each unit to develop its own system on the basis of its concrete conditions. Most systems reported in the newspapers include one or another attempt to delineate authority, responsibility, and the main task for each office and post, thus tying performance to some kind of reward-and-punishment scheme. Liaoyuan municipality divided its entire workload into "routine work and important work," assigning twenty points for the first and eighty points for the latter. One county categorized its entire workload into three types: specific tasks assigned by the county party committees, the task of developing spiritual civilization, and the objective of improving work style. Fulfillment of the first task deserves sixty points, and the completion of either of the other two is worth forty points.[49]

Broadly speaking, there are four types of responsibility systems. For leading cadres whose job involves many different kinds of work, "position, responsibility, and tasks" are taken into account during assessment.[50] Jiangyan district of Wuhan municipality, with 2,800 cadres in sixty-three units, has reportedly defined the responsibility, authority, and task for each unit and each individual. Now, each cadre keeps his "work record" which is used as a basis for assessment.[51]

The method of contracting out specific tasks with a fixed number of people, a deadline, and points to earn is used for the leading cadres of rural areas. "Managers and other cadres of enterprises sign contracts on such specific economic indicators as production value, profit, quality, and sales, etc., and when all these targets are met, they are rewarded."[52] This responsibility system based on contracting out for technology is used for technical persons in functional fields and basic research units.

It remains to be seen whether a written job description for each position will improve the efficiency of the Chinese bureaucracy. Although this practice marks a sharp break from the Maoist practice of stressing internal remedies based on ideological incentives,

49. *Xin Changzheng*, no. 9, 1984, 30–32.
50. *Shehui Kexue Yuan* (Liaoning), no. 33, 1984, 5.
51. *Renmin Ribao*, 11 November 1984.
52. *Gongren Ribao*, 6 June 1981.

it seems very unlikely that the regime's present one-sided emphasis on external remedies, based on quantifiable achievement records, will work. Moreover, the responsibility system can produce the desired results only when it is combined with a rational incentive system that links performance to promotion and salary increments.

To summarize, the regime initially tried to rationalize the personnel management system by first strengthening the authority of higher levels and then decentralizing, while restoring the party committee's authority over personnel matters. But all these attempts were made in a piecemeal fashion with the knowledge that the party would directly manage all cadres. Consequently, the personnel management authority still remains too centralized and very rigid—"recruiting persons are separated from managing persons and managing persons from managing affairs." It continues to be a "closed-door system": each *tiaotiao* and *kuaikuai* sets up its own system, and any horizontal coordination between the two is extremely difficult. The system, however, cannot be rationalized without resolving the broader question of how to separate the party from the government and other functional units.

SEPARATING THE PARTY
FROM THE GOVERNMENT

In post-Mao China, virtually all Chinese leaders have agreed that the past practice wherein party committees directly managed administrative and economic work should be changed. In fact, the regime has already corrected for the excess of Mao's era. The Maoist practice of having one person concurrently holding leading positions in the party and the government has come to an end.[53] Many functional departments of the party and its core groups in government organs were abolished. The offices of such government heads as minister, governor, and magistrate have been substantially strengthened: they are less dependent on party committees at the same level, and their capacity to develop rational policy has been substantially enhanced with the increase of specialists among their staff and the establishment of numerous research

53. *Renmin Ribao*, 26 November 1987.

offices. Within the state the People's Congress system has been restored, and the court system apparently enjoys more independence now than at any other time in its history.

With regard to the party committee's functions at the lower level, numerous articles published in the official media suggest the following tasks: (1) supervising the implementation of the party line and policy, (2) leading ideological and political work, (3) managing the party's internal affairs, (4) making decisions on "important matters," and (5) managing the personnel matters of cadres.[54]

First, no one disagrees with the idea that ideological work belongs under the party committee's jurisdiction, but whether the committee should limit its work to ideological work or not is open to debate. This is especially true when the significance and relevance of this work to other functional tasks is diminishing as the regime subordinates politics to economic development, while failing either to define the meaning of "socialism" or to develop a coherent official ideology.

Limiting the party's main task to its own internal work, such as managing and educating its members, is not problematic. But a persistent question is whether the CCP, a Leninist ruling party committed to a one-party dictatorship, can afford to restrict its activities to such a narrowly defined range.

The problem with the term "important work" (generally defined as "affecting the fate of the entire people") is that it does not specify how and who will determine which matters are important in a specific case.[55] The highly centralized bureaucratic structure in China does not leave many "important matters" for the county party committees to decide. Thus, it is not surprising that after extensive debate on what constitutes "important matters," a county party secretary and magistrate decided to consider all issues jointly.

Authorizing party committees to supervise government and enterprise units in the implementation of official decisions is not controversial. But it does not resolve the technical questions of what supervision means in concrete terms, how to supervise the operation of government agencies and enterprise units without taking over their tasks, and how much and what kind of power party

54. *Shaanxi Ribao*, 26 October 1983.
55. *Hebei Ribao*, 21 October 1982.

committees need for supervision. Lower-level party secretaries insist that "without substantial authority, there is no way to supervise and guarantee that work will be done correctly."[56] Managers are also unhappy with the supervision: "If they trust secretaries and do not trust managers, it is better to make the secretaries managers." When a manager is higher than his secretary in education, there is no reason to supervise.[57] In addition, the formula raises other complicated questions. For instance, should a party secretary be held responsible for the profit and loss of an enterprise? If the answer is no, does that mean that they are not entitled to a bonus when the enterprise makes a profit?[58] On the issue of supervising authority, conservatives and reformers split. Reformers reject the idea of giving supervisory authority to party committees because it could constrain the manager responsibility system.[59]

The official guideline on how to separate the party from the government at the lower level is not only ambiguous but contradictory. While criticizing party committees' involvement in functional work, top party leaders still insist on the principle of "the party leading everything." On one hand, party committees are instructed not to manage economic issues directly. On the other, superior party committees urge lower-level party committees to "spend 70 percent of their time on economic matters."

The issue of separating the party from the government and enterprises requires the redistribution of political power, thus directly touching on the political interests of party secretaries at the middle and lower levels, most of whom were recruited after 1949 from peasant and worker activists and demobilized soldiers. Therefore, party cadres exploit the ambiguity in the official policy in order to resist the official effort to separate.[60] They often resort to defensive tactics such as foot-dragging and rearguarding. Some old party cadres are more straightforward: "If the first party secretary does not concurrently hold the first position of the government, that

56. *Lilun Yu Shijian* (Shenyang), no. 13, 1985, 34–35; *Tianjinshi 1984 nian Shehui Kexue Keti Diaoyan Chengguo Xuanbian* (Tianjin Renmin Chubanshe, 1985), 11:411–27.

57. *Xuexi Yu Yanjiu*, no. 11, 1985, 15–17.

58. *Hubei Caizhengxueyuan Bao*, no. 4, 1985, 41–42.

59. *Lilun Tantao*, no. 2, 1987, 76.

60. *Zhengzhi Yu Xingzheng Yanjiu*, November 1985, 18–32.

means that the party will not have power, and the idea of the party leading everything becomes an empty slogan." Others play on the fear of "dispersionism and independence [of the government] from the party."[61]

Results in County Governments

Numerous investigation reports prepared by Chinese scholars after their fieldwork at the county level indicate that party committees still dominate administrative organs. Usually, the county party committees and their government counterparts jointly issue orders and convene meetings. County party committees still discuss a wide range of issues from economics to party affairs, spending most of their time on economic issues. Although they are supposed to meet only once a month, they usually meet more frequently. On the other hand, "the management committee" of the magistrates—which is supposed to meet weekly—rarely convenes because "there is not much left for the government to decide, and the management office of the government is redundant."[62]

In addition, magistrates, who are usually deputy secretaries subordinate to the first party secretary in the party hierarchy, now act more like representatives of the party committee rather than heads of the government unit. The party core group (*dangzu*) rather than the directors continue to exercise the real power in county government bureaus. Consequently, "the party secretary presently does the work of the magistrate, and the magistrate does the work of the director of county bureaus."

Party committees continue to dominate not only the executive organs but also the People's Congress and its standing committees, which theoretically are representative organs of the entire people. Leaders of the standing committees (*changwei*) of the People's Congress are organized into party cells, which are subordinate to party committees. Most standing committee members are semiretired party cadres. As a result, many Chinese satirize the county standing committee of the People's Congress (which they call "the nurs-

61. *Jiefang Ribao*, 30 October 1983.
62. *Jingji Yanjiu Cankao Ziliao*, 25 April 1986, 32–39.

ing home") by saying it is "big in three items and empty in one item": its constitutional right is big, the sign board of its office is big, the age of its members is big, but its power is empty.[63] Party committees, not the People's Congress, prepare economic plans. And if the standing committee rejects the plan, the party committees can overrule it.[64] Until recently, the party's disciplinary committees investigated government corruption. According to a Chinese expression, "the county party committee writes the scenario, the government performs, the People's Congress watches, the political consultative conference comments, and the disciplinary committee judges."[65]

The turf fight is particularly fierce over economic issues, which make up 60 percent of government tasks. At the moment, whether or not a county party secretary makes a decision on economic matters largely depends on the personality of the secretaries and managers. Whenever a secretary is capable and enjoys high prestige, even magistrates look to him to make all major decisions. Thus, it seems that appointing able persons to secretaryships, ironically, tends to hinder the separation of the party from the government.

Since there is no separation, the question of how to share personnel management authority is premature. County party committees have not relinquished their prerogative over personnel management. According to an investigation by Chinese scholars, county party committees manage all the important leading cadres of first-class organs (ministries [bu], commissions [wei], bureaus [ju], and villages [xiang]) and second-class organs (sections [tuan] and certain enterprises), or they handle all the leading cadres of the first-class organs while allowing the personnel bureau under the magistrates to manage the cadres of the second-class organs. Believing that managing cadres is their most important responsibility, county party committees spend most of their time on personnel matters.[66] Although its authority over certain government cadres is constitutionally guaranteed, the People's Congress remains a rubber stamp.

63. *Zhengzhi Yu Xingzheng Yanjiu*, November 1985, 18–32.
64. *Jingji Yanjiu Cankao Ziliao*, 25 April 1986, 32–39.
65. *Makesi Zhuyi Yanjiu*, no. 4, 1986, 7.
66. *Jingji Yanjiu Cankao Ziliao*, 25 April 1986, 32–34.

RESULTS IN ENTERPRISES

The situation in enterprise units is much better than on the county administrative level. Despite the strong opposition of party cadres, the manager responsibility system has been gradually implemented in most state-owned factories in the past few years, thereby substantially weakening the party secretaries' power.

However, the manager responsibility system has not yet completely resolved the controversy over personnel management authority, despite bitter complaints from managers that the existing system constitutes the most serious obstacle to the efficient management of enterprises, more serious than the shortage of raw materials.[67]

Reformers advocate *fenggong guanli*, that is, authorizing managers to manage administrative cadres, while limiting the party committee's authority regarding party cadres in order to make the managers' authority and responsibility coincide and to enable them to exercise "uniform leadership with regard to production, management, and administrative management."[68] Viewing the proposal as a serious threat to the party's prerogative over personnel matters, the conservatives raised objections at every stage of the development of the manager responsibility system.

The battle over the issue is fought on three specific questions. The first is to what extent party committees will share personnel authority with managers. The second is the managers' right to "form cabinets." The third concerns jurisdiction over middle-level administrative cadres.

The conservatives do not oppose the idea of giving some personnel authority to managers because they are well aware of the shortcomings of the past, but they still insist on the principle of "the party managing cadres" and have tried to keep as much authority as possible in the party committees. The central organizational department usually sides with the secretaries by reiterating that the party committee is responsible for the "recruitment, alloca-

67. Zhongguo Jingji Tizhi Gaige Yanjiusuo Conghe Diaochazu, ed., *Gaige: Women Mianlin de Diaozhan Yu Xuanzhe* (Beijing: Zhongguo Jingji Chubanshe, 1986), 137.

68. *Zhengzhixue Yanjiu Tongxung*, no. 4, 1983, 7–13.

tion, evaluation, and supervision of cadres."[69] Pervasive cadre corruption strengthens the conservatives' position that party committees—as collective decision-making bodies under the tighter supervision of the upper echelons—rather than the one-person manager are more suitable for safeguarding the state's interests and for screening the political quality of cadres, preventing those "lacking loyalty to the revolutionary business" from being promoted.[70] By contrast, reformers insist that "the party managing cadres" does not mean that party committees manage everything directly; rather it means that under the principle of the party's "unified management," some concrete work can be delegated to government and enterprise units.

Once the regime decided to give managers personnel authority, the next question is to what extent the party committee should be allowed to influence a manager in exercising his authority over personnel matters. The reformers want to prevent the party committee from interfering with the managers' authority, but they cannot state their position in such a blunt way, lest it be construed as an open challenge to the CCP's authority. Instead, they argue that managers should use their authority wisely, paying attention to the opinions of the masses and the party committees. By contrast, conservatives try to guarantee the party committees' influence in personnel matters. One compromise requires managers to consult the "management committee" on personnel matters. Since the committee usually includes members of the party committee, as well as the disciplinary committee and labor unions, both of which are under the party committee, this option allows the secretaries to continue to exert influence over personnel matters. In fact, whenever the party committee objects to the choices made by managers, there is no way for the manager to prevail. The party secretaries still retain veto power.

Pushed by reformers, the regime publicized the idea of allowing managers to "form their own cabinets" for a while. Several differ-

69. Guojia Jingwei Jiceng Zhengzhi Gongzu Bangongshi, ed., *Shixing Changzhang Fuze Zhi Hou Qiye Dangwei Ruhe Gongzhu* (Beijing: Jiefang Zhengzhixueyuan Chubanshe, 1985), 37–49. See also *Gaige Qiye Lingdao Zhidu Shixing Changzhang Fuzezhi* (Beijing: Nengyuan Chubanshe, 1986), 34–42.

70. Guojia Jingwei Jiceng Zhengzhi Gongzu Bangongshi, ed., *Shiping Changzhang*, 21–36.

ent methods of "forming cabinets" were practiced between 1984 and 1985. The manager either nominated or appointed deputy managers as well as all heads of administrative positions, who in turn nominated their own deputies and ordinary cadres. Or managers appointed deputy managers, who in turn appointed administrative heads, who selected their own deputies and ordinary staff. Another method required the approval of the organizational department of the upper echelon and the workers' congress of the enterprise to finalize the appointment.[71]

The procedure for forming a cabinet included the following steps. First, the manager, the party secretary, and the chairman of the relevant labor union discussed the matter in advance and set up the method of forming the cabinet. Second, they formulated the criteria to be used for cadre selection. Third, the manager solicited comments from various sectors, including ordinary workers. Although the party secretary and labor unions were involved in the process, it was the manager who made the final decision. In this sense, the system marked a departure from past practice.

To the conservatives, allowing the manager to form his own cabinet clearly violated the principle of the "party managing cadres" and precipitated factionalism.[72] Moreover, the practice threatened the personnel authority exercised by the party committee one level higher as specified in the *nomenklatura* system. Despite the reformers' vigorous defense, which sometimes twisted logic, they apparently lost the battle on this particular issue. The regime finally decided not to use the term "forming a cabinet."[73] Apparently, the central organizational department believed that the practice of managers choosing their own deputies posed too serious a threat to the entire personnel management system.

Over the third question—the manager's authority over middle-level administrative cadres—the reformers apparently obtained what they wanted.[74] Whether or not it was due to Zhao's insistence, the regime announced revised regulations, which, among other things, specified the manager's authority over middle-

71. *Jingji Gongzuo Zhe Xuexi Ziliao*, 1985, 24, 8–31.
72. Ibid.
73. *Xuanchuan Shouce* (Beijing), July 1985.
74. *Zhengdang Yu Jiandang* (Liaoning), 1 June 1986, 30.

echelon cadres, although it allowed the party secretary to make suggestions.[75]

To summarize, it seems that a compromise has been reached: although they failed to obtain the right to form their own cabinets, managers have the authority to manage middle-level administrative cadres. However, the controversy over personnel authority is likely to continue because party committees are not clearly excluded from managing even middle-level cadres. It is officially recognized that party committees are responsible "for observing cadres, examining the political qualifications of candidates, organizing discussion meetings, and carrying out public opinion polls in order to provide accurate information to managers."[76] Managers are granted authority over certain cadres, but their authority has to be used in consultation with the party committees: "On the matter of using persons, managers should rely on the party committee, should rely on the masses. . . . Managers should listen to the opinion of the masses, and then decide."[77] Consequently, many party committees and their organizational departments refuse to transfer personnel authority to managers, who bitterly complain. Despite resistance, the general trend is to weaken party leaders' authority in enterprises. One indication of this trend is the fact that jurisdiction over party committees in enterprises is being transferred from committees of government bureaus (tiaotiao) to territorial committees, a transfer that helps limit the work of the enterprise party committee to managing party members.[78]

PLANNED CIVIL SERVICE SYSTEM
AND ITS IMPLICATIONS

The Chinese personnel management system was originally copied from the Soviet Union. However, although the USSR has modified its system, China's has remained relatively unchanged.[79] Because any debate on the system is bound to question the party's lead-

75. Zhongguo Renmin Gongheguo Gongbu, no. 1, 30 January 1987, 9–12.
76. Guojia Jingwei Jiceng Zhengzhi Gongzu Bangongshi, ed., Shixing Chang-zhang, 47.
77. Zhengdang Yu Jiandang (Liaoning), 1 June 1986, 30.
78. Zhengzhi Tizhi Gaige (Shanghai: Shanghai Renmin Chubanshe, 1988), 43.
79. Zhengdang Yu Jiandang (Liaoning), no. 3, 1984; 30 June 1984, 1–4.

ership, the public did not demand reform until 1986, when the regime itself publicly recognized the need for structural reforms. To many Chinese, changing the personnel management system was the main goal of political reform: "Whether or not the structural reforms can be carried out and their results consolidated is largely dependent on cadre reforms."[80] The need to utilize scarce scientific and technical cadres efficiently further justified demands for a change in the Maoist system.

At the Thirteenth Party Congress newly elected General Secretary Zhao Ziyang announced the regime's plan gradually to introduce a civil service system. According to this plan, a mere 4.2 million out of the existing 29 million cadres—only those who were employed in government agencies—will be classified as civil servants.[81] In other words, cadres employed in both the judicial and the legislative branches of state organs as well as those working in the party, enterprises, and business units will be excluded from the civil service system.

All leading cadres who legally constitute "governments," ranging from the center to county levels, and whose appointments require the approval of a People's Congress will be classified as "political" (zhengwu) civil servants. Thus, this category will include the premier, state councilors, and ministers of the central government, governors and vice governors, mayors and deputy mayors, magistrates and deputy magistrates, and some bureau directors.[82] Regarded as "policymakers," political civil servants will be elected for fixed terms as specified in the existing constitution and in the organizational laws of local governments; therefore, they lose "life tenure," although there are no laws limiting the numbers of terms they can serve.

The rest are functional (ye wu) civil servants, "the implementors of policy," who are further classified as either "administrative" or "specialized technical." Their selection will be made through "open, equal, and competitive" examinations. Candidates for examinations are limited to graduates of "higher educational institutions" who are twenty to thirty years old and who "support the

80. *Zhengzhixue Yanjiu Tongxun*, no. 4, 30 December 1983, 4–7.
81. *Renmin Ribao*, 31 October 1988.
82. Tan Jian, ed., *Guojia Gongwuyan Shouce* (Beijing: Shehui Kexue Wenxian Chubanshe, 1988), 7.

leadership of the CCP [and] love the socialist motherland." Possessing "certain political conditions" is a prerequisite, but many writers insist that party membership is not required. Specialists will be selected from among those possessing certificates demonstrating specialized technical training. All those who pass the examination are required to go through one year of training at the basic level. Only after a successful training period can they become regular civil servants.[83]

Moreover, these civil servants are to be promoted grade by grade. To assume leading positions, one has to meet additional requirements: section chiefs have to have an educational level higher than senior high school and at least four years of work experience; division chiefs (*chuzhang*) need a college or specialized middle school education and seven years of work experience; bureau directors require a college education and ten years' work experience; and ministers need a college education and at least fifteen years of work experience.[84] In addition, before assuming these positions, civil servants must receive further training at administration institutes that the government is setting up at various levels.

A provisional regulation guarantees job security by ensuring stable working conditions, reasonable pay, and protection from arbitrary dismissal. Besides the standard rights and duties listed in similar laws of other countries, the regulation also stresses the career civil servants' right to "criticize and make suggestions to their leaders" and the duty to "carry out the party's and the state's line, directives, and policies."[85]

The regime plans first to experiment with such a system in several central government ministries, provinces, and municipalities and then to implement it in all the state organs.[86] The first step in establishing the system is to classify positions, which will determine the task, responsibility, and pay scale of each cadre. At the moment, the regime estimates that it will take five years for these five units to set up "the frame" of the civil service system and an additional ten years to implement the system nationwide.[87]

83. "Temporary Regulation of State Civil Service System."
84. Ibid.
85. Ibid.
86. *China Daily*, 20 July 1988.
87. *Renmin Ribao*, 31 October 1988.

This provisional regulation fails to resolve the most crucial obstacle to creating an efficient personnel management system— the party domination over the government. On this question the provisional regulation itself contains many ambiguous and contradictory points. For instance, it does not grant political neutrality, even to career civil servants. On the contrary, they are specifically required to demonstrate a certain level of "socialist consciousness" and to follow the political leadership of the Communist Party.[88] However, many Chinese scholars argue that although Chinese civil servants are required to be loyal to the party, the regulation protects them from future policy fluctuations resulting from leadership changes or power struggles among the top leaders. Insofar as the career civil servant faithfully carries out any policy directed by the party, he will not be held responsible for its correctness or incorrectness. This will be an improvement over the situation during the CR when many low-level cadres were purged because they had implemented "revisionist policies" handed down to them through legitimate channels of hierarchy.

Another ambiguity in the regulation and official writings concerns the party committee's authority over personnel matters; on the one hand, it will give up its prerogative over cadres, but, on the other hand, it will continue to exert a substantial amount of authority over political civil servants and "important cadres."[89] According to Zhao Ziyang, "the party center and the local party committee will nominate political civil servants to the People's Congress at various levels and will supervise and manage political civil servants with party membership."[90]

A particularly troublesome aspect of the regulation is the role of the party's organizational departments. Although core groups in government agencies were abolished, the central organizational department still keeps a party core group in the personnel ministry. Furthermore, it is likely that as long as the party maintains organizational departments along the administrative hierarchy, the turf fighting between the party and the government over even the functional civil servants will continue. If the provisional regulation

88. Tan Jian, ed., *Guojia Gongwuyan Shouce*, 10.

89. Nie Gaowu, Li Yichou, and Wang Zhangtian, eds., *Dangzheng Fenkai Lilun Tanlu* (Beijing: Chunqiu Chubanshe, 1988), 17.

90. Su Yudong, ed., *Guojia Gongwuyuan Zhidu Jianghua* (Beijing: Laodong Renshi Chubanshe, 1988), 13.

is thoroughly implemented, the party organizational departments will have nothing to do except manage their own cadres and the "political civil servants," which altogether would number less than a thousand. The party may claim jurisdiction over party member officials, as indicated by Zhao Ziyang. If so, an interesting question would be whether or not the party's claim would be limited to the "organizational life" of party member officials, while the government manages their "work relations." The party may argue that unless it has authority over employment conditions of party member cadres, it will not be able properly to supervise their "organizational life." To make matters more complicated, each cadre's personnel dossier includes materials on his party membership, as well as his work relations. Unless the dossier is broken down into two parts, each of which is managed by either the party or the government, however, the organizational departments would have an excuse to avoid relinquishing their authority over personnel matters.

Having agreed to share its power over personnel with other appropriate authorities—be they government leaders, managers, or administrative heads of business units—the party is extremely reluctant to give up its influence over cadre management completely. Now, instead of directly managing cadres, the party is helping other appropriate authorities make the right decisions by recommending qualified persons and supervising their handling of personnel matters. This change has taken place at a time when the party is relinquishing direct control over economic resources. Any weakening of the party's control over the economy makes it more difficult to resolve the persistent question of how to change the structure of personnel decision making in such a way that the new system can maintain a balance between two conflicting goals: ensuring the party's control while managing the cadres efficiently, thus making the system flexible but not creating chaos, and preserving a national planning perspective while allowing lower units to be autonomous even in personnel management.

As noted, the result of the official effort to separate the party from the government has so far been rather limited. In structural terms, the regime completely separated the party from the government and other functional units. But the official formula, in which the party "ensures and supervises" the work of administrative heads, has failed to clarify ambiguities in terms of power distribution. The most important reason is that the party has not yet re-solved important theoretical as well as practical questions. The theoretical questions are what role basic-level party committees will assume and how they will justify their continuing existence when the Leninist Party has declared an end to class struggle and has adopted efficiency as the ultimate criterion for evaluating orga-nizational performance. The practical question is how to maintain the Leninist Party's prerogatives while allowing autonomy in gov-ernment agencies and economic enterprises in order to promote economic development.

A possible option followed by many Eastern European countries is to abolish the party committee system in functional areas. As many liberal reformers argue, these are "unnecessary political organizations detrimental to efficient economic management."[91] But the Leninist Party in China is not yet ready to do so. The other option is for factory managers to hold concurrently party secretary positions. This seems to be taking place in many enterprises. In some enterprises selected for experimental purposes, managers take charge of even ideological and political works, thereby depriv-ing party secretaries of using their authority over these works to interfere with managers' decisions. This experiment is obviously designed to weaken the party secretaries' power and eventually to abolish the party committee system in economic enterprises.[92] However, at present in most enterprise and business units, the dual structure of the administrative and functional hierarchy on the one hand and the party hierarchy on the other still exists.

The continuing existence of this dual structure raises another puzzling question: what qualifications and career backgrounds are necessary to be appointed to the party and other administrative positions? Different career experiences and personal backgrounds among party secretaries and managers can aggravate conflicts.[93] But, at the same time, using the same criteria for selecting party secretaries and administrative heads and managers makes the dual system only redundant without any tangible benefits.

Available data on this question indicate that career differentia-

91. Guojia Jingwei Jiceng Zhengzhi Gongzu Bangongshi, ed., *Shixing Chang-zhang*, 35–36.

92. *Fazhi Ribao*, 26 September 1988.

93. *Lilun Tansu*, no. 2, 1987, 31–36.

Table 56.   Educational Level of Enterprise Cadres, as of 1986

Cadres	Level[a]
Managers	3.36
Deputy managers	3.32
Deputy secretaries	3.04
Secretaries	2.83
Advisers	2.68

Source. Zhongguo Jingji Tizhi Gaige Yanjiusuo Zonghe Diaochazu, *Gaige: Women Mianlin de Diaozhan Yu Xuanzhe* (Beijing: Zhongguo Jingji Chubanshe, 1986), 273–74.

Note. Educational levels were assigned as follows: 1 for primary school graduates, 2 for junior high school graduates, 3 for senior high school graduates, 4 for college graduates.

tion between the two positions is narrowing. According to a survey of 900 enterprises conducted by the Institute for the Reform of the Chinese Economic Structure in 1985, when the initial readjustment of the enterprise cadres was completed, managers were found to be slightly younger than their counterparts in party committees. The average age of managers is forty-five, whereas that of secretaries is forty-seven.[94] As shown in table 56, managers are better educated; indeed, they are the best educated; the second best educated are deputy managers; third deputy secretaries; and least are the secretaries and advisers. These differences are quite small. Since the educational level of cadres is closely correlated with age—the younger are generally better educated—the differences in education between the two groups may reflect age rather than job differences.

Most managers and deputy managers are promoted from technical, functional, or lower-level managerial positions: 85 percent of them have experience in technical, 72 percent in functional, and 71 percent in basic-level managerial work. By contrast, secretaries and deputy secretaries are largely selected from administrative ranks (54 percent) and from among demobilized soliders (71 percent).[95]

94. Zhongguo Jingji Tizhi Gaige Yanjiusuo Conghe Diaochazu, ed., *Gaige: Women*, 270–305.
95. Ibid.

Despite career differences, there is a powerful trend that may mitigate the conflict between managers and secretaries in the long term; that is, the career backgrounds of party secretaries are changing. Not only has a new type of enterprise cadre emerged, but the desire to obtain professional knowledge is pervasive even among party secretaries. When enterprise leaders were asked about the type of qualifications that enterprise cadres should have, many cited functional over political knowledge. Enterprise leaders were also keenly aware of their own shortcomings, that is, they lacked technical expertise.[96]

Another mitigating factor for possible conflict between party and administrative cadres is that the actual leadership type is also changing from what the Chinese call the "personality and virtue type" (*pingde xing*) to the "ability type" (*nengli xing*). As noted in chapter 11, bureaucratic technocrats are replacing revolutionary cadres even in the highest political positions. The official ideology is in disarray as a result of economic reforms. New types of party members are being recruited. The regime has been co-opting experts in decision-making bodies, thus providing tangible incentives for the transformation of party secretaries. Many informants report that able party cadres are eager to move into government positions. The younger generation tends to embrace the values and outlook of the technocrats, not the revolutionary cadres. Thus, it seems that revolutionary cadres cannot find successors like themselves.

Despite many uncertainties, after thirty years of revolutionary turmoil, which entailed the recruitment of cadres on the basis of political qualifications, China has finally come to emphasize ability by recruiting government officials through open and competitive examinations. The fact that the regime is planning to introduce a civil service system indicates its willingness to end the Maoist practice of selecting officials through mass campaigns and on the basis of class backgrounds, and instead to develop rational, efficient, and competent administrative bureaucrats. The term "civil servants" itself implies that government officials are "public servants" who will manage public affairs as the guardian of public interests, whereas the term "cadres" refers to those with certain leadership

96. Ibid.

abilities necessary to lead the masses in revolutionary struggles for social change. The term "civil servants" also connotes a merit-based recruitment, whereas the cadre's role requires political skills and ideological consciousness. The introduction of a planned civil service system also represents the regime's intention to separate government employees from party cadres, thus ending the previous practice of managing the party and the government cadres together (*dangzheng ganbu*) in some manner and allowing the government to manage its employees. In fact, the provisional regulation stipulates that the "personnel ministry and bureau" will manage the civil servants [performing functional works] "according to laws."[97] The recruitment of government officials through the examination system also rules out the possibility of any input from the populace along the mass line model emphasized during Mao's era.

Apparently, the regime is preparing a separate set of regulations regarding party cadres, enterprise unit cadres, and business unit cadres. Although the contents of these regulations are not known, the planned regulations for party cadres will probably stress election or some other method that allows rank-and-file party members to select their leaders. For the selection of enterprise and business unit cadres, the planned regulations will probably try to blend different methods, such as "appointment, examination, invitation, and election." However, it is extremely unlikely that the regulations will explicitly deny the party any voice in personnel management. As long as the concept of public ownership continues, the party will consider itself justified in retaining some authority over personnel management.

The impact of introducing a civil service system is not limited to the party-state's bureaucracy. As many studies of Western European bureaucracies have demonstrated, a merit-based recruitment of administrative elites tends to offer undue advantage to the middle class.[98] As the competition for government employment shifts in emphasis to ability, educational institutions will become the springboard for entering official positions. China's new education-

97. "Temporary Regulation of State Civil Service System."
98. Ezra N. Suleiman, *Politics, Power, and Bureaucracy in France* (Princeton: Princeton University Press, 1974), 72–99.

al policy of attaching priority to academic achievement and spending large amounts of the state budget for key schools will accelerate the stratification of educational institutions. Middle-class students have the advantage of entering better high schools and then highly competitive colleges, from which they can land cadre positions.[99] Actually, middle-class values are more congruent with the role of technocrats than that of revolutionary cadres.

In this way, the state bureaucracy will lose any claim to representing a broad range of social classes, but it can still be responsive to society.[100] This nondemocratic characteristic will, however, be compensated when the regime steps up its effort to professionalize state employment. The rigorous training of civil servants, the development of an esprit de corps, and a trend toward professionalization will make the administrative elite act more as guardians of the public interest than as representatives of their original middle-class backgrounds.

As the evolution of Western European civil service systems demonstrates, creating an efficient state bureaucracy is the first step toward reducing the patrimonial power of a monarchy. In Prussia, the absolute monarchy created a civil bureaucracy largely staffed by the landed aristocracy. As the bureaucracy gained power and status, joining the civil bureaucracy offered upward mobility for the newly emerging bourgeoisie. Meanwhile, by claiming to represent the public interest, the civil bureaucracy gradually became independent of the monarchy. As the monarchy collapsed, it was replaced by elected politicians, who, on behalf of the people, supervised the administrative bureaucrats, while the administrative structure began resembling Weber's ideal type of bureaucracy, one staffed by specialists and neutral to the political process.[101]

In China, the party-state created a large corps of cadres as a tool for revolutionary change. During Mao's era, the party maintained tight control over this group, preventing them from developing into an administrative instrument. Now, the regime is trying to transform the cadre corps into administrative bureaucrats by granting them more autonomy. In this sense, the introduction of a civil

99. Ibid., 79–92.

100. Ibid., 386.

101. Hans Rosenberg, *Bureaucracy, Aristocracy, and Autocracy* (Boston: Beacon Press, 1958).

service system—even though at the moment the civil servants' political neutrality is not yet recognized—may be the first step toward separating the party from the administrative hierarchy.

However, such questions as what controls the party will maintain over the administrative bureaucrats and to whom the latter will be held accountable still persist. Since in most non-Communist countries, democratically elected politicians supervise the administrative bureaucrats, one may predict that the party leaders at various levels will act likewise. In other words, the party leaders will become "political managers" and "powerbrokers."

PART V

CONCLUSION

15

From Revolutionary Cadres
to Bureaucratic Technocrats

This study is based on the simple premise that the less institutionalized a political system, the more likely political elites will
bring the ideology, experiences, and outlook of the social classes
from which they came into the political process.[1] This assumption
is particularly true of the new socialist China that emerged after the
disintegration of the traditional order and prolonged warlordism.
As Tang Tsou noted, political elites played a most critical role in the
reintegration of China as a political community, leaving their mark
on political, economic, and social organizations.[2] Even after the
establishment of the People's Republic of China, revolutionary
momentum and incessant inner elite conflicts over ideology,
policy, and power hindered institutionalization and routinization,
allowing the political elites' idiosyncrasies to affect the political
process.

Although originally recruited largely from poor peasants with
a low level of education for the specific task of fighting guerrilla
wars, the former revolutionaries became the ruling elite in 1949
and thereafter dominated the Chinese political process for almost
three decades. Only since 1982 have the revolutionary cadres
been gradually replaced by bureaucratic technocrats. Selected from
among the best-educated segment of the population, the new
Chinese leaders have their academic training mainly in engineering and production-related fields and their career backgrounds in

1. The correlations between elite type and policy outcome in more stable Western democratic political systems are weak. For instance, see Moshe M. Czudnowski, ed., *Does Who Governs Matter: Elite Circulation in Contemporary Societies* (DeKalb:
Northern Illinois University Press, 1982); Moshe M. Czudnowski, ed., *Political Elites
and Social Changes: Studies of Elite Roles and Attitudes* (DeKalb: Northern Illinois University Press, 1983).
2. Tang Tsou, *Cultural Revolution and Post-Mao Reforms* (Chicago: University of
Chicago Press, 1986), 5.

specialist positions at functional organizations. Now in the 1990s, they face the challenging task of reforming the totally discredited old system. Just as the Maoist system reflected the old revolutionaries' experiences, goals, and understanding of China's needs, the newly emerging system will reflect the bureaucratic technocrats' training, work experience, and ideological outlook.

THE MAOIST SYSTEM

Chinese politics during the Mao era largely reflected the former revolutionaries' rural orientation. As the founders of a new regime, the former revolutionaries continued to recruit officials from lower social classes, using political loyalty rather than ability as the main criterion. Since the structure of the party-state that gradually evolved granted maximum discretionary power to leading cadres, the political elites continued to bring their views to Chinese politics, thereby enabling the CCP to sustain the revolutionary momentum for a long time after its successful political revolution. In turn, the regime's primary task—socialist revolution—reinforced its cadre policy of emphasizing class background, its leadership method of mass mobilization, and its commitment to revolutionary change. In other words, the Maoist version of socialism reflected the system of cadre recruitment and promotion adopted during and after the revolution, and the cadres so recruited further bolstered the Maoist version of socialism. In retrospect, it seems an extreme historical irony that Mao's very success in mobilizing poor peasants to capture political power turned out to be a major obstacle in shifting the CCP's focus from revolution to nation building and economic development after 1949.

REVOLUTIONARY CADRES

The upper echelons of China's leaders during the Mao era started their careers as guerrilla fighters during the anti-Japanese war and the Chinese civil war. Recruited largely from poor peasants and hired laborers, they were high in revolutionary potential but their level of education was too low for them to understand the functional requirements of industrialized society. With nothing to protect in the existing society and much to gain from a revolution, they created a new political structure and continued to pursue radical social revolution even after 1949.

The former revolutionaries continued the practice of recruiting cadres from among political activists on the basis of their political reliability. Each political movement, such as land reform, collectivization, the antirightist campaign, the Great Leap Forward, the Socialist Education Movement, and the CR, produced activists who eventually joined the party and became cadres. Despite their low level of education, they gradually moved up the bureaucratic hierarchy, becoming the leading cadres at all levels of the bureaucracy.

The personnel-management system during the Mao era reinforced the image of officials as heroic revolutionary cadres. After 1949 political loyalty (virtue) gained increasing importance, whereas the relative weight of achievement and expertise (ability) declined to such an extent that Susan Shirk called the system a virtuocracy.[3] Political loyalty, frequently inferred from class background, was first defined in terms of party membership; but as the party ranks swelled with new recruits from the most disadvantaged social groups, the criterion changed to support for Mao's thought. Although applicable to every Chinese—except those with undesirable family backgrounds—such a criterion tended to be subjective, allowing the evaluators wide discretionary power and encouraging "faked" activism.

The party-state not only jealously guarded its prerogative over the personnel management of cadres but also exercised that authority in a highly centralized fashion without developing any meaningful classification scheme for the gigantic cadre corps. Authority over personnel was exercised by superior organs two levels above a cadre. Party committees and organizational departments managed all the cadre corps, using political criteria. The personnel dossier system allowed the superior organizations to control cadres under their jurisdiction, further reducing the cadres' job mobility and the effective use of scarce human resources, as well as contributing to a unit's ownership of cadres. The politicization of the cadre-management criteria made cadres fear the contents of

3. Susan Shirk, *Competitive Comrades: Career Incentives and Student Strategy in China* (Berkeley and Los Angeles: University of California Press, 1982).

their dossiers, while those with access to the dossiers gained enormous leverage over the other cadres.

The Maoist personnel-management system could not, however, prevent senior political leaders from abusing their authority for private gains. Instead, the highly politicized and centralized personnel-management system, together with the life tenure system, provided individual political leaders with ample room to develop personal power bases.[4] The only effective control that this system could achieve was to prevent intellectuals from going into politically influential positions.

Although founded by the best-educated group, the CCP developed a bias against the educated sector of the Chinese population for several reasons. First, in the 1950s most intellectuals came from the exploiting classes and tended to develop their own views, independent of the official orthodoxy. Second, having been symbol manipulators themselves, high-ranking cadres tended to view intellectuals as ideologues and propagandists rather than technocratic specialists. Third, CCP leaders, including Mao, felt that they knew best about China's conditions and its course for the future. The party's success in capturing political power reinforced its leaders' self-confidence and led them to overlook the intellectuals' potential contributions to the new society. Fourth, even when the regime recognized that intellectuals possessed expertise necessary to the regime's goal, it wanted to use their knowledge without having to tolerate their political views. The party, therefore, compared intellectuals to peacocks—which frequently change color—suggesting that the party should control them firmly but not too tightly, lest they suffocate, and not too loosely, lest they fly away.[5] Consequently, only intellectuals willing to espouse the official orthodoxy were allowed to flourish, whereas intellectuals critical of the regime were suppressed without mercy. Most specialists stayed in functional positions without any political influence in the bureaucracy and worked under the leadership of revolutionary cadres who were without any professional knowledge, as exempli-

---

4. In traditional China, the imperial court controlled personnel matters, but allowed local officials (which it had appointed) a substantial discretionary power in policy areas. As the Qing court lost its vitality, powerful officials frequently used their authority to develop personal power bases by placing their own followers in strategically important positions within the official bureaucracy. This process eventually led to the warlordism.

5. From an interview in Beijing in 1988.

fied by Mao's slogan that "outsiders [nonspecialists] lead insiders [specialists]."

Although Mao was personally responsible for this anti-intellectual attitude, it also reflected the opinion of most revolutionary cadres, who were resisting the pragmatic leaders' attempts to focus on economic development. During the land reforms of 1947, poor peasant cadres in some party organizations spontaneously took over leadership from intellectual cadres. During the Hundred Flowers campaign, some intellectuals questioned the party's cadre line, which favored certain class backgrounds and political loyalty; the top political leaders mobilized newly recruited peasant party members and cadres to suppress the challengers, purging almost 10 percent of all the intellectuals.

To make matters worse, the regime neglected to provide on-the-job training to the revolutionary cadres. The cadre educational program that had begun immediately after the revolution came to an end with the Great Leap Forward. As a result, many old cadres could boast of their long seniority and their wide range of work experience, but they tended to remain generalists rather than develop a speciality.

In contrast, Eastern European Communist leaders selectively co-opted a new generation of specialists and then gradually relinquished political power to them while trying to maintain a balance between the Leninist tradition and the goal of economic development. Even Stalin cultivated members of "the proletarian technical intelligentsia" in the 1930s and promoted them to political positions vacated by his purges.[6] By failing to co-opt its intellectuals, China refuted the general assumption that all revolutionary Leninist regimes go through the same stages of transformation, consolidation, and adaptation or inclusion.[7] Instead, the CCP attempted to consolidate its own political structure, first through social transformation and then through adaptation. Consequently,

6. Sheila Fitzpatrick, *The Commissariat of Enlightenment* (Cambridge, Mass.: Harvard University Press, 1970); Sheila Fitzpatrick, "Cultural Revolution in Russia, 1928–1932," *Journal of Contemporary History*, January 1974, 33–52; Sheila Fitzpatrick, "Stalin and the Making of a New Elite, 1928–1939," *Slavic Review* 38(3) (September 1979): 376–402.

7. Samuel Huntington, "Social and Institutional Dynamics of One-Party Systems," in Samuel Huntington and Clement H. Moore, eds., *Authoritarian Politics in Modern Society* (New York: Basic Books, 1970), 3–42; Kenneth Jowitt, "Inclusion and Mobilization in European Leninist Regimes," *World Politics* 27(1) (October 1975): 69–78.

the Chinese political process during the Mao era displayed cycles of radicalization and deradicalization, while moving in a more radical direction.[8]

STRUCTURE OF THE PARTY-STATE AND
REVOLUTIONARY CADRES

The party-state structure that gradually evolved in the 1950s and 1960s reflected the founders' experiences, including "their own pre-1949 experience in conducting revolutionary struggle and administering 'liberated areas.'"[9] Other factors such as "the theoretical Leninist model of 'democratic centralism,' the post-Leninist model of Soviet society," and "China's centuries-old tradition of authoritarianism, elitism, ideological orthodoxy, and bureaucratic administration" also helped shape the organizational structure of the PRC.[10] These factors were, however, filtered through the founders' rural orientation, which stressed subsistence and self-sufficiency, moralized politics, distrusted exchange through a market mechanism, and knew little about the functional prerequisites of modern society.

The scope of the activities directly regulated by the Maoist party-state was all-inclusive.[11] In the name of the socialist revolution and transformation, the party-state gradually expanded its control over not only coercive instruments but also all economic and human resources, including the goods and services that the Chinese people needed in their daily lives.[12] As the party-state took over the

8. For the policy cycles, see G. William Skinner and Edwin Winckler, "Compliance Succession in China: A Cyclical Theory," in A. Etzioni, ed., *A Sociological Reader on Complex Organization* (New York: Holt, Rinehart and Winston, 1961); Edward Winckler, "Policy Oscillations in the People's Republic of China: A Reply," *China Quarterly*, no.68, December 1976, 734–50.

9. A. Doak Barnett, *Cadres, Bureaucracy, and Political Power in Communist China* (New York: Columbia University Press, 1967), 427. For an attempt to explain the post-1949 policy in terms of the preceding revolutionary experiences, see Theda Skocpol, *State and Social Revolution* (Cambridge: Cambridge University Press, 1979).

10. Barnett, *Cadres, Bureaucracy, and Political Power*, 427.

11. For a characterization of the Maoist system and its transformation by 1982, see Michel Oksenberg and Richard Bush, "China's Political Evolution: 1972–82," *Problems of Communism*, September-October 1982, 1–19.

12. For the evolution of the powerful party-state in China, see Tang Tsou, "Reflections on the Formation and Foundation of the Communist Party-State in China," in his *Cultural Revolution*, 259–334.

functions traditionally performed by social organizations and individuals, personal autonomy shrank and dependency on the state increased. The socialist transformation resulted in a state command economy, in which the party-state controlled all aspects of economic activities "from planning and financing to the circulation of a product and the allocation of labor" (*jihua shang dabao dalan, caizhengshang tongshou tongzhi, liutongshang tongguo tongxiao, laodongshang tongbao tongpei*).[13] The elimination of the labor market and the introduction of the centralized allocation system enabled the party-state to control all social mobility. Since the party-state rejected exchange relations as a mode of social interaction on the grounds that they were capitalistic, power and authority relations—as controlled by the party-state—permeated every aspect of interaction.[14]

Despite the party-state's comprehensive jurisdiction, structural differentiation was minimal during the Mao era, largely because of Mao's concern that functional specialization would foster a new social stratification. The rural population was organized into communes—multifunctional organizations that performed political, administrative, social, and economic tasks—thereby strengthening the traditional cellular boundaries of each village community.[15] Even economic enterprises and universities were encouraged to be self-sufficient in meeting the needs of their members. Instead of encouraging specialization and professionalization, the regime urged individuals to perform multiple tasks just as the old revolutionaries had during the guerrilla war era.

The party's "monistic leadership" reduced structural differentiation further. Although initially introduced in 1942 as "a means of resolving the lack of coordination between the various organizations of the party, government, and military that were scattered all over the guerrilla base areas," party committees came to dominate every organization, whether political, economic, or

---

13. *Shehui Kexue Yanjiu*, no. 2, 1983, 35–42.

14. Whether the state used its capability for the people's benefit is irrelevant because power is a "structural phenomenon" of dependency. For this view of power, see Jeffrey Pfeffer, *Power and Organization* (Boston: Pitman, 1981).

15. Vivian Shue, *The Reach of the State* (Stanford: Stanford University Press, 1988); and Helen Siu, *Agents and Victims in South China* (New Haven: Yale University Press, 1989).

otherwise.[16] The party core group (*dangzu*) system—originally introduced in government ministries as a temporary measure in 1949 when a large number of government leaders were nonparty members—continued to dominate government decision-making bodies until recently. Moreover, after 1957 the party moved to manage the business of the functional organs directly with the slogan "the party leads everything in the seven areas of work: agriculture, industry, commerce, education, military matters, politics, and party affairs." In response to the increasing power of party committees and secretaries, the boundary blurred between the party on the one hand and state organs and social organizations on the other, and the party-state's accountability to society declined.[17]

In addition, the official ideology, although not fully internalized by cadres, operated as a structure in the Althusserian sense by limiting the policy choices of the political elite.[18] Mao's "politics in command" exemplified the uniform imposition of the official ideology on all sectors of the party-state and society. The Maoist version of socialism—which attached paramount importance to distribution rather than production and stressed egalitarianism over efficiency in order to provide minimum material needs for all Chinese—took precedence in decision making in all functional fields.

The renewed emphasis on class struggle revitalized discrimination against such former exploiting classes as landlords, rich peasants, and capitalists—despite the fact that their political influence was so meager that Mao called them "fleas in Buddha's palm." The antirightist campaign produced still another category to be excluded from the political process, the "rightists." The CR added "powerholders taking the capitalist road" and the "stinking ninth category" of intellectuals to the list of enemies.[19] Nevertheless, despite an official emphasis on the class nature of the party-state, the regime's policies did not further the interests of the working class. Although the cadres were largely drawn from this class,

16. *Xinhua Wenzhi*, no. 11, 1987, 1–5; *Zhongguo Shehui Kexue*, June 1987, 3–22.
17. Ibid.
18. Louis Althusser and Etienne Balibar, *Reading Capital* (London: New Left Books, 1970).
19. The nine categories include landlords, rich peasants, counterrevolutionaries, bad elements, rightists, renegades, enemy agents, and capitalist roaders.

they obviously failed to act as its representatives. Their class "situation" was probably stronger than their ties to the class in which they originated.[20]

The increase in the magnitude of political activities, without accompanying structural differentiation and functional specialization, resulted in enormous discretionary powers for the leading cadres of each unit. The absence of a market exchange and the low level of functional interdependence meant that horizontal coordination and communication between two units had to be conducted through the top leaders of each unit or through a higher echelon with jurisdiction over the two units. Since each unit was organized to be self-sufficient, providing most if not all the services needed for its members, the leading cadres had authority over a wide range of matters directly affecting even the daily lives of its members.

Despite the emphasis given to the mass line, no institutional mechanism existed to check cadres' abuses of authority. Complaints about leading cadres tended to end up on their target's desks because there was no investigation system independent of the party committees. The masses' lack of a normal channel by which to criticize cadres accounted for many of the violent attacks on political leaders during the Socialist Education Movement and the CR.

Although revolutionary cadres had enormous discretionary power, they were not allowed to represent any particular social group or class. As revolutionaries and as administrators, politicians, and bureaucrats,[21] they were expected to play conflicting roles. The cadres were hierarchically organized with grades, official positions, and salaries, all specified by rules and regulations. They were subject to the personnel decisions of their superiors. The Leninist priniciple of democratic centralism created a pseudo-military command structure with authority flowing from the Politburo down to the secretary of each party cell. As agents of the state, the cadres were expected to carry out every policy faithfully

20. Nicos Poulantzas, "The Problem of the Capitalist Class," in Robin Blackburn, ed., *Ideology in Social Science* (London: Collin and Sons, 1972).

21. For the distinction between the politician and the bureaucrat, see Joel D. Aberbach, Robert D. Putnam, and Bert A. Rockman, *Bureaucrats and Politicians in Western Democracies* (Cambridge, Mass.: Harvard University Press, 1981).

regardless of its popularity with the masses or its conformity to the perceived interests of the masses. As revolutionaries, they were expectecd to represent working class interests through the mass line, but the top leaders largely predetermined what those interests were, ignoring input from the lower levels.

As politicians, the cadres were required to energize the policy-making process by mobilizing and inspiring the masses through propaganda, education, and personal example. But unlike politicians in Western democracies, they were not allowed to represent sectarian interests or work as arbitrators of conflicting sectarian interests. Cadres were instructed to investigate the concrete conditions of China's reality, but the findings of these investigations were not allowed to affect the general policy direction that the top leaders had adopted using ideological criteria. To perform the conflicting roles of revolutionaries and bureaucrats the cadres needed the support of the masses, but they were not allowed to represent the interests of the units they led.[22] Consequently, the Chinese bureaucratic system was a strange mixture, very different from Max Weber's ideal type. It was organized hierarchically with full-time cadres, but it lacked the characteristics of impersonality, technical expertise, and political neutrality.

The effective operation of the Maoist system depended mainly on the cadres' ideological commitment. Therefore, Mao subjected the cadres to constant ideological campaigns, refusing to grant any legitimacy to their personal interests. His approach did not work, however, because his expectations were too high. As the campaigns were repeated, the process became ritualized. According to the Maoists' ideal vision, cadres were supposed to forfeit their personal interests to the higher cause of the revolution, but in reality they frequently resorted to what Andrew Walder calls "principled particularism" in order to protect their personal interests and neutralize conflicting pressures.[23]

Although failing to forsake their personal interests, the revolutionary cadres generally acted as the state's agents. In many cases,

22. For different views on whether the basic-level cadres could protect the local interests from the state, see Shue, *The Reach of the State*, and Siu, *Agents and Victims in South China*.

23. Andrew Walder, *Communist Neo-Traditionalism* (Berkeley and Los Angeles: University of California Press, 1986).

as the first in their family to obtain an official position with prestige and a regular salary, the cadres owed the party-state not only their job but also their power, income, and status. As the beneficiaries of the new order, they were eager to defend it, doing whatever the party told them as long as the commands were transmitted through the organizational channel. In addition, some of them genuinely believed in the party.[24] Whatever their motivation, they found an accord with Mao's version of and his approach to building socialism because of their own successful experience in mobilizing the masses for such specific tasks as fighting guerrilla wars and promoting land reform or collectivization. They could appreciate the Maoist method of evaluating cadres in terms of political rather than achievement-oriented criteria. To the revolutionary cadres, dedication to cause, obedience, diligence, conscientiousness, and intention were more important than ability, efficiency, innovation, and actual results.[25]

The revolutionary cadres' blind subscription to the Leninist principle of democratic centralism produced the unintended consequence of blending policy debates with the struggle for power. Since the principle assumes that there is only one correct policy for the party, dissenting views cannot remain as alternative policy options. Moreover, because losing a policy debate was equated with being ideologically incorrect, policy debates frequently ended with political purges. Conversely, once an official policy was adopted, it became extremely difficult to adjust or change the policy without victimizing the cadres who had benefited from, supported, and earnestly carried it out. It is an extreme irony that the Leninist principle, which was originally devised to achieve a unity of leadership, produced the unintended consequence of encouraging factionalism.

The structure of the cadre corps and the Maoist system reinforced some of the more rigid and maladaptive features of China's two-thousand-year-old tradition of feudal bureaucratism. Despite the Maoist radicals' antibureaucratic rhetoric, the concentration of decision-making authority in the party-state and the absence of social forces counterbalancing the bureaucracy intensified the tradi-

24. *Dangde Shenghuo*, no. 12, 1983, 32–39.
25. *Weidingkao*, July 1986, 25–28.

tional pattern of a centralized ruling elite monopolizing power. And the rigid hierarchical structure of the party-state and the cadre grade system produced a stratification within the cadre corps, thus reinforcing the elitist tradition. The party-state's total domination of civil society left a career in the bureaucracy as the only channel for social mobility, further intensifying competition for the limited number of cadre positions that commanded not only political power but also economic resources and social prestige.

Traditional views persisted among leaders who were supposed to act as guardians of collective interests and to set an example by forfeiting private interests. The idea that political leaders could improve themselves by self-cultivation continued in the practice of criticism and self-criticism. The traditional view that the moral force of doctrinal orthodoxy legitimized power justified the use of coercion to impose the official ideology. The life tenure system allowed cadres to privatize their offices, blurring the boundary between the authority derived from an office and the power of the cadre as a person, thus fostering further the paternal exercise of power.[26]

THE IMPETUS FOR CHANGE

The Maoist system had problems because of its rigidity and over-concentration of power. The expansion of the party-state's control over human activities and the elimination of resistance from civil society did not end social conflicts and tensions. Instead, it turned them into an inner-party struggle.[27] The ideal was the replacement of an impersonal and erratic market mechanism with political authority that would make rational decisions, but in reality the command economy, which had only a "strong thumb [and] no fingers," enhanced the power of the well-entrenched cadre corps.[28] Mao's attempt to moralize cadres' power through ideological education politicized morality and ethics rather than humanizing

26. For this point, see Lloyd Rudolph and Susanne Rudolph, "Authority and Power in Bureaucratic and Patrimonial Administration," *World Politics*, 1979, 195–227.

27. For this point, see James Townsend, "Intra-Party Conflict in China: Disintegration of an Established Party System," in Huntington and Moore, eds., *Authoritarian Politics in Modern Society*, 284–310.

28. Charles Lindblom, *Politics and Markets* (New York: Basic Books, 1977).

power relations, adding further ideological legitimacy to the cadres' domination. Paradoxically, his effort to resolve these intrinsic dilemmas by mobilizing the masses in the CR strengthened the party-state's domination.

The CR symbolized the profound crisis within the first generation of revolutionaries over the issue of revolution versus economic development and the concomitant issue of cadre recruitment.[29] Bureaucratic modernizers such as Liu Shaoqi and Zhou Enlai wanted to improve the overall quality of the cadre corps by co-opting intellectuals from undesirable classes into the power structure. They also tried to develop functionally specialized organs and to secularize the official ideology. Mao viewed the co-optation of intellectuals as a betrayal of the Chinese revolution at the expense of disadvantaged social groups. Worried over the possibility that the cadre corps might emerge as a new ruling class, he insisted that officials continue to act as selfless heroic revolutionaries, willing to submit themselves to the masses. Political considerations also entered the complex political maneuvering and countermaneuvering at the top level. After the failure of the Great Leap Forward, some of Mao's former colleagues questioned the validity of his approach to economic development, and his popularity within the bureaucracy declined.

When Mao removed the party's control over society and allowed the masses to mobilize freely, all the social conflict that the powerful party-state had managed to suppress erupted and threw China into chaos. Although the official targets of the CR were the "powerholders taking capitalist roads," the factionalized mass organizations targeted all "powerholders." With the purge of a large number of leading cadres who, in effect, symbolized formal authority, the entire authority structure of the party-state collapsed.

When the mass mobilization phase of the CR ended in 1968, the basic cleavages within the elite ran between the situational groups produced by the preceding two years of mass mobilization: the initiators, the beneficiaries, the survivors, and the victims of the

29. For the issues over which the old revolutionaries split, see Tsou, "The Cultural Revolution and the Chinese Political System," in Tang Tsou, *Cultural Revolution*, 67–94.

CR. These four groups, each with its own distinctive support base, held disparate views on the CR and its policy agenda. As a military man, Lin Biao's power base was limited to a few select military officers. The Gang of Four resorted to the revolutionary method of mobilizing discontented social groups against the establishment. It recruited and promoted young CR rebels into the bureaucracy in order to strengthen its own power base while resisting the rehabilitation of the purged cadres. In contrast, the beneficiaries approved of some rehabilitation but resisted the return of Deng Xiaoping. The survivors advocated large-scale rehabilitation. The maneuvers and countermaneuvers, coalitions, and conflicts of these four groups ended with the victory of the rehabilitated cadre corps after Mao's death.

The impetus of reform can thus be traced back to the senior leaders' personal experience of humiliation, imprisonment, and purges. As victims of the very system they had, until 1966, helped to create, they now saw its flaws. And when forced to live with peasants and labor with workers, they witnessed the prevalent poverty—an experience that changed their perception of China's reality and the masses' desires. Moreover, by the time the rehabilitated cadres regained political power, they realized that the system's legitimacy was so weak in the eyes of the Chinese people that drastic measures had to be taken to restore popular confidence in the CCP. Consequently, the former-victim-now-rehabilitated cadres became born-again reformers.

Once reinstated in leading positions, the veteran cadres shifted the party's major task from revolution to economic development—a goal that required sweeping reforms of the system. However, the existing cadres were ill equipped for the new task; they were "too old, too poorly educated, and too ossified in their thinking." The only way to improve the quality of the corps was to promote the educated to leadership positions, which required two preparations: improving the political status of educated people and creating vacancies for them to move into.

By the time the CR officially ended, with the purge of the Gang of Four, the powerless Chinese intellectuals had been thoroughly persecuted and abused. At one point, the Gang of Four—called petty intellectuals by their adversaries—rounded up the professors of Beijing's universities and subjected them to a test on Mao's thought and other ideological questions. Many of the professors failed that test, and the radicals used their poor performance as evidence of their "parasite nature."[30] Many scientific research institutions were disbanded and their staffs were sent to the countryside to reform themselves. Subsequently, "those specializing in rocketry were assigned to be custodians, remote control specialists were turned into butchers, those trained in computer science were employed in distilleries, entomologists were engaged in industrial design, mathematicians and foreign language specialists became fuel sellers or bakers."[31]

After 1978 the regime attempted to improve the political standing of the intellectuals. Publicly conceding that modernization was impossible without knowledge, the regime for the first time cited the possession of technical knowledge rather than the ability to manipulate symbols as the intellectual's most salient characteristic.[32] For instance, Deng Xiaoping, the architect of the 1958 antirightist campaign, publicly declared that since engineers and technicians participated directly in the creation of surplus value, they were "a part of the working class."[33]

The regime conducted a comprehensive nationwide survey of scientific and technical personnel so that it could effectively utilize these scarce human resources.[34] It also took steps to improve the intellectuals' working and living conditions. First, it assigned scientific and technical persons to appropriate positions when their jobs did not match their speciality.[35] Second, it resolved the problems of about 720,000 couples living separately.[36] Third, Hu Yaobang, the director of the organization department, initiated measures to rehabilitate intellectuals victimized in the CR.[37] Fourth, the regime took several actions to raise the income of some intellectual groups, giving special attention to intellectuals' hous-

30. *Zhonggong Dangshi Jiaoxue Cankao Ziliao: Wenhua Dageming Shiqi* (Beijing: Zhongguo Renmin Zhengzhi Xueyuan, 1983), vol. 4, no. 4, 284.

31. *Ming Bao*, 15 May 1978.

32. *Jiaodang Cankao* (Anhui), 15 May 1983.

33. *Wuhan Daxue Xuebao*, no. 2, 1985, 63–66.

34. *Daily Report*, 26 June 1978, E11; *Hebei Xuekan*, no. 1, 1985, 1.

35. *Shehui Kexue Yanjiu Cankao Ziliao* (Sichuan), 21 July 1985.

36. *Renmin Ribao*, 3 November 1980.

37. In some cultural units, intellectuals, specialists, and experts constituted 60 percent of all purged in the CR. *Jiaoxue Cankao* (Hebei Construction Institute), no. 203.

ing difficulties. Fifth, in order to boost morale and raise professional prestige, the regime created professional titles for specialists.
Sixth, for the sake of utilizing scarce resources effectively, the regime gradually relaxed its "unified recruitment and unified allocation" while legalizing a limited labor market for specialists.[38]

In order to clear the way for a new cadre corps, the regime developed a special retirement system (*lixiu*), which allowed old
cadres to retire with all their perquisites intact. Consequently, the
majority of the senior political leaders—those who had joined the
revolution as guerrilla fighters, founded the new regime, created
the huge bureaucratic machine and occupied its leading positions,
sustained the revolutionary momentum, experienced the purges as
"powerholders taking the capitalist road," and regained power as
rehabilitated cadres—finally retired. The regime proceeded to
promote a new breed of cadres, who were "better educated, younger, professionally competent, and revolutionized," while purging
the former CR rebels–turned-cadres as representative of the "three
types of people." Thanks to the pragmatic and incremental
strategy of changing the cadre corps step by step, level by level,
and group by group, a new generation of bureaucratic technocrats
finally replaced the revolutionary cadres as China's political elite.

BUREAUCRATIC TECHNOCRATS
AS NEW LEADERS

China's new leaders belong by and large to the postliberation generation, which came of age in the new socialist China—a group
known as the third generation (after the first generation, which
joined the revolution before the Long March, and the second generation, which participated in the anti-Japanese war).

Selected from the best-educated segment of the Chinese population, most of China's new leaders studied natural sciences in
college and worked as specialists in production-related fields in
bureaucratized organizations. Thus, the new leaders are not "critical intellectuals" who, by virtue of their knowledge of tradition,
values, norms, or ideology, tend to act as critics of the existing
system. With their career backgrounds as engineers and specialists

38. *Liaowang*, 21 January 1985.

trained in hard science—possessing narrowly defined technical knowledge related mainly to a formal rationality that helps to choose the best means once the basic goals of the society are agreed on—the new leaders will likely see their mission as improving and perfecting the existing system.[39] The technocrats' political proclivity may have helped them rise to the top political positions. Or the selection of bureaucratic technocrats as China's new leaders may simply reflect China's shortage of trained experts in the soft sciences and its concern with production outputs.

Although we cannot assume that the bureaucratic technocrats form a homogeneous group with a shared ideology and policy preferences, they are on the whole quite different from the revolutionary cadres in many aspects.

First of all, the criteria used in selecting the bureaucratic technocrats are different. At the lower level some were selected by election, contract for a limited term, examination, and other methods. The revolutionary cadres owed their position to their ideological reliability, whereas the bureaucratic technocrats are promoted on the basis of their "ability," usually inferred from such objective and universal criteria as age, educational level, and professional competence. The rise of bureaucratic technocrats, therefore, marks a sharp departure from the Maoist practice of stressing "virtue."

Even though political qualification was used in selecting the new leaders, its contents have changed. During the Mao era, it included such ideological criteria as an understanding of Marxism-Leninism, a dedication to the mass line, and a willingness to sacrifice one's private interests. Now political qualification refers to one's dedication to the "socialist principle," which is broadly interpreted in turn to include any principle that "brings good fortune to the people, develops productivity, or contributes to socialist business."[40]

The universal, achievement-oriented criteria, however, are not uniformly applied to every qualified candidate; personal connections also operate, thereby resulting in "unprincipled universalism," in contrast to what Andrew Walder calls the "principled

39. Alvin Gouldner, *The Future of Intellectuals and the Rise of the New Class* (New York: Seabury Press, 1979).

40. *Qunzong*, 13 February 1985.

particularism" of the Mao era. Because of the particularistic ap-plication of universal criteria, some social groups benefited from the reform while others lost.

Second, available data (although scarce) indicate that, like their counterparts in Western Europe, the bureaucratic technocrats are less committed to any political ideology—whether a broadly de-fined socialism or Mao Zedong's discredited thought—than the disappearing revolutionary cadres. Some veteran revolutionaries, therefore, openly fear that the new leaders' understanding of "the basic principles of Marxism" and "the good party tradition and work style" is so limited that they will not "use the Marxist per-spective to solve present problems." Moreover, free from "the par-ty's fine tradition of the Yanan period," they are more susceptible to new ideas and foreign trends. If the bureaucratic technocrats have any common ideology, it is the simple pragmatism necessary to get the job done.[41] To them, socialist ideology is not a dogma but something to be interpreted flexibly for an economic goal.

Third, the revolutionary cadres and the bureaucratic technocrats differ over the range of policy alternatives considered feasible. Although an ideologically inspired policy option was a real alter-native for the revolutionary cadres, it may not be so for the bureaucratic technocrats, whose primary concern is China's im-mediate problems. The technocrats prefer a structured and orderly environment and technical, piecemeal solutions rather than com-prehensive political solutions dictated by ideological goals. Criteria for judging policy options are also different. The revolutionary cadres tended to view policy options as morally right and wrong, ideologically correct and incorrect, whereas the bureaucratic tech-nocrats, less concerned with abstract ideals, look at technical and administrative feasibility in making a final choice. They evaluate even political decisions in terms of actual outcome rather than ideological value. In developing a range of policy options, each of which carries only different costs, benefits, and feasibilities, this way of thinking inclines the bureaucratic technocrats toward com-promise and bargaining.

Fourth, on the whole the bureaucratic technocrats are more supportive of reform than the retiring revolutionary cadres were.

---

41. Ezra Suleiman, *Politics, Power, and Bureaucracy* (Princeton: Princeton Univer-sity Press, 1974), 380.

Many of them served in technical positions without influence, watching uneducated political leaders make arbitrary decisions and use bureaucratic rules to constrain their own professional work. Some were condemned as "bourgeois experts." Even those from the lowest class of preliberation China have diminished gratitude to the party because of their experiences with past political turmoil.

Fifth, having been promoted rapidly from low-level technical positions scattered all over China, the new political leaders, with the probable exception of those who studied in the Soviet Union, do not enjoy the close and extensive informal ties that the revolutionary cadres developed during their prolonged careers. The lack of such informal ties—which helped the senior political leaders to run the bureaucracy smoothly despite its departmentalism and lack of horizontal channels of communication—may compel the new leaders to rely more on formal procedural rules when making decisions and thereby facilitate the institutionalization of the Chinese political process. Then again, weak personal ties might turn out to be a decisive liability that prevents these leaders from reaching any compromise and leads instead to division and stalemate. A particularly obvious weakness is their lack of close ties with the military as an institution.

Last, having spent most of their careers as part of the technical staff in functionally specialized organizations, even bureaucratic technocrats who have reached the top political positions have accumulated very little experience in the overall political apparatus, which includes administration, propaganda, and mass works. Thus, a question crucial to China's future politics is whether bureaucratic technocrats at the top will see themselves as bureaucratic administrators or politicians.[42]

---

42. The separation is bound to take place, although the differences between the two are beginning to fade elsewhere, even in places like Western Europe that have traditionally kept the roles distinct. The bureaucrat generally acts as an equilibrator by taking ideologically centrist positions, mediating interests, and minimizing conflicts, whereas the politician acts as an energizer by mobilizing the support of social forces. Articulating the broad, diffuse interests of unorganized individuals, politicians tend to be passionate, partisan, idealistic, and innovative, whereas "the bureaucrat approaches a policy question with a predisposition toward harmony; he is prepared to compromise in order to promote unity and cohesion within the organization and to broaden its external appeal." John P. Roche and Stephen Sachs, "The Bureaucrat and the Enthusiasts," *Western Political Quarterly*, 1955, quoted in Aberbach et al., *Bureaucrats and Politicians*, 257.

There is not enough empirical evidence to render a definitive judgment on how the new leaders' specialized technical knowledge will help them acquire political wisdom and insight. The existing literature points in two different directions. One school suggests that the technocrats will bring their professional perspective to the role of politician by "treating the ideological argument with condescending indifference, [while] upholding the conviction that social problems are susceptible to technical solutions."[43] The other believes that the complex roles required of politicians will change the technocrats' behavior in political positions, forcing them to take partisan and politically motivated postures. Data available in China, although scarce, indicate that those who have reached the highest positions of the Chinese bureaucracy—for instance, Jiang Zemin and Li Peng—will act more like coordinators, conciliators, and managers than like politicians representing the interests of the various social groups, developing long-term visions, and manipulating symbols to rally popular support.

Although on the whole quite different from the revolutionary cadres, the bureaucratic technocrats do not form a homogeneous group with a shared ideology and policy preferences. Since the process of selecting future leaders has involved nepotism and corruption, it is fair to assume that different groups within the new leadership owe their rise to senior leaders with different policy preferences. They have also worked in different fields, and they are divided by a generation gap too wide to make shared attitudes the basis for unity. The older technocrats, many of whom have studied in the Soviet Union, tend to be more conservative than the younger ones.

How will the bureaucratic technocrats resolve their internal differences? Will they be able to use compromise, bargaining, and negotiation—which presuppose a more tolerant attitude toward dissent—to iron out differences without resorting to the methods used by the revolutionary cadres? Direct evidence is unavailable. But one can infer from their overall traits—including a minimal commitment to a well-defined ideology, a lack of personal net-

43. Stephen Cohen, *Modern Capitalist Planning: The French Model* (Cambridge, Mass.: Harvard University Press, 1969), 46, cited in Ezra Suleiman, *Politics, Power, and Bureaucracy* (Princeton: Princeton University Press, 1974), 380.

works, and a perception of themselves primarily as adminis-trators—that China's new leaders will be more prone to bargain and compromise. There are additional reasons for this cautious optimism. Given their political style and the rapidity of their rise in the past few years, it is very unlikely that any bureaucratic technocrat—including Jiang Zemin, whom Deng Xiaoping desig-nated as his successor—will come to exert as much "real power and influence" (*shiquan*) as Mao or Deng did. With no paramount leader, the policy-making process may result in division, stale-mate, and immobility. But it is more likely that the bureaucratic technocrats will feel compelled to develop a collective style of lead-ership and formal procedural rules in making decisions—the very steps needed for political institutionalization. Any decision made this way will likely be less innovative and less revolutionary than one made by a dictator. But such a decision-making process will less frequently result in power struggles, purges, and counter-purges.

Even though the bureaucratic technocrats' preferences on speci-fic policy issues are not yet known, the replacement of revolution-ary cadres by bureaucratic technocrats signifies an end to the revolutionary era in modern China, an era characterized by the classes from which members of the political elite were recruited, their personal experiences, and their career backgrounds. The rev-olutionary cadres differed from the traditional political elite, whose dual interests made it a buffer between the state and society. Re-cruited mainly from the landlords and wealthy families, members of the traditional elite felt the need to defend their social and eco-nomic interests from state encroachment. As scholar-officials who received appointments from the imperial court after passing the civil service examination, they also represented the state's author-ity. As the term "gentry-scholar-officials" implies, wealth, knowl-edge, and power converged in their hands, ensuring perhaps the longevity of the traditional system. In contrast, in socialist China knowledge was separated from power; the Maoist political elite possessed only political power (with which they controlled wealth) but not knowledge.

China is now returning to the time-honored practice of selecting its political leaders from the best educated in the population, a practice that had ended with the abolition of the civil service examinations in 1905. Future historians may well view the revolutionary era as a temporary aberration in the long Chinese tradition of choosing members of the political elite from the best-educated group. Now bureaucratic technocrats—who have a better understanding of and better qualifications to deal with such prerequisites of industrialized society as functional specialization, the coordination of parts, rational decision making, and problem solving—have replaced the revolutionary cadres. However, it is an altogether different question whether the new leaders have the ability and the political acumen to lead China through the multitude of contradictions created by the reforms of the post–Deng Xiaoping era.

DIFFICULTIES OF REFORM AND THE TIANANMEN INCIDENT

What makes reforming any socialist system difficult is that its various parts—including its political, economic, and social systems—are so tightly integrated that changing any one requires simultaneous changes in the others. For instance, the state command economy presupposes the existence of a Leninist Party which, as the agent of the working class, will supervise the operation of the state machinery. The Chinese leaders tried to circumvent this difficulty by adopting a gradual, step-by-step reform strategy. They started with reforms of the economic rather than the political system—whereas the Soviet Union and Eastern Europe started with political reforms—the rural rather than the urban economy, and, within the economic arena, industrial management rather than the price system. Such a strategy, which did not require a master plan at the beginning, proved effective in preventing potential opposition forces from coalescing. But the strategy's ultimate success depends largely on the success of each stage of reform.

By 1988 the incremental approach in China encountered serious challenges because of the mixed results of the steps taken so far. Over the previous ten years, reforms had raised the living standards of most Chinese steadily, but the population's expectations were outstripping the system's capabilities. The overheated economy produced superinflation, undermining stable prices and employment opportunities, the only advantages that the Maoist system offered equally to all social groups. The dual price structure introduced as a transition to price reform aggravated official corruption, thereby weakening the regime's legitimacy further. And by not separating political from economic authority, the decentralization of the decision-making authority resulted in a fragmented bureaucracy, allowing lower-level units to use political authority for their own economic gain and to act as "independent kingdoms." At the same time, the reforms had opened the political process sufficiently to allow newly rising social groups to air their demands.

These immediate challenges forced the Chinese leaders to confront the more fundamental but unresolved questions that they had hoped to avoid by adopting the incremental reform strategy: How far should the economy be free of political control? How should state planning be combined with market control, and what is the optimal combination? How can the Leninist Party deal with the social forces liberated by the reforms and maintain its political hegemony while leading China toward economic development? In the final analysis all these questions can be reduced to the question of how to separate politics from economics.[44]

On this essential question, one can identify four major schools of thought, located along the ideological spectrum represented by the influential political leaders. The first school regards political reform as a prerequisite for further economic reform. In accord with what Andrew Nathan calls the "functional benefit of democracy," it insists that only political democratization can resolve China's pressing problems by regulating political conflicts, strengthening the regime's legitimacy, and improving the quality of the bureaucracy.[45] This view draws support from critical intellectuals and college students.[46] Among the top leadership, Hu Yaobang has stressed the importance of a democratic atmosphere in inner party life as well as in politics in general, while indicating that Marxism-Leninism has become outdated or irrelevant to China's present-day problems.

The second school, represented by Zhao Ziyang, gives priority

44. *Ziliao Yuekan*, no. 4, 1988, 3–11.

45. Andrew Nathan, *Chinese Democracy* (Berkeley and Los Angeles: University of California Press, 1985).

46. Su Shaozhi, "The Problems of the Political Reform in China," *China Information* 3(3) (1988): 32–37.

to continuing economic reforms, including price reform, an elimination of the dual price system, and further marketization. Although Zhao Ziyang has never explicitly advocated privatizing the ownership system, he was apparently willing to accept eventual and inevitable privatization.[47] In the political arena this school subscribes to the idea of "new authoritarianism"—the ideas developed by Zhao's young brain trusters on the basis of the Four Asian Dragons' experiences. The "new authoritarianism" differs from the notion of "the people's democratic dictatorship." The former envisions the necessary political leadership as coming from the intellectuals and experts, whereas the latter stresses the political leadership of the working class. The first is devoid of any commitment to socialist ideology, whereas the second presupposes its acceptance.[48] Zhao Ziyang reportedly not only prohibited the official ideology from interfering with economic reforms but also "went so far as to say that he himself did not really know what the socialist road was."[49] To Zhao, official corruption has nothing to do with spiritual pollution and therefore should be considered the price that China has to pay in the transitional period.

The third school is represented by Deng Xiaoping, who is pragmatic in economic policies but authoritarian on political issues. As implied by his remark "whether it is a white or a black cat does not matter; any cat that catches mice is a good cat," Deng Xiaoping is willing to try either state planning or marketization—whichever works. He supported Zhao's economic reforms by expanding the meaning of the "socialist road" to include any method that brought prosperity to the Chinese people. He is, however, not committed to marketization to the extent of accepting the risks of inflation, unemployment, and budget and trade deficits. Nor is Deng committed to the separation of politics and economics to the extent of excluding the central government's administrative control over the economy.[50]

In the political arena Deng Xiaoping regards party leadership as a precondition for a stable and strong central authority and is un-

47. *Daily Report*, 6 July 1989, 21.

48. As a result, the new authoritarianism is condemned as elitist. See *Chengming*, March 1989, 55–56; *Chengming*, April 1989, 42–46.

49. *Daily Report*, 25 August 1989, 7.

50. For his instructions on these three points, see ibid., 21 April 1989, 33–35.

willing to allow social forces to interfere with what he considers the party's internal affairs.[51] More committed to Leninist principles than to Marxist ideals, Deng tends to see the official ideology as the means of achieving leadership unity. In fact, as his approach to cadre reform demonstrates, he has operated as an organization man, relying on hierarchical authority rather than ideological legitimacy to control the lower levels. Although he has been flexible in defining the four principles when necessary, Deng has also tolerated conservative ideologues such as Hu Qiaomu and Deng Liqun, self-appointed guardians of correct socialist ideology and spokesmen for the workers, peasants, and the former revolutionary cadres.

The fourth group is led by Chen Yun, who rejects the Maoist method of mobilizing the masses for economic development while continuing to believe that China should preserve at least the basic structure of state planning in order to maintain an equilibrium between—for instance—government revenues and expenditure, agriculture and industry, exports and imports, and the supply of and demand for major commodities.[52] He acknowledges the utility of the market mechanism, but only as a supplement to a planned economy. Thus, to Chen economic reform should seek to improve the mechanism of state planning—his analogy is expanding the cage to give the bird more space instead of allowing it to fly at will. According to this school, the excessive marketization under Zhao Ziyang led to a structural imbalance, which in turn resulted in a high rate of inflation. Chen Yun has not elaborated on his view of political authority, but the very idea of the state-planned economy with a large portion of the means of production collectively owned implies that political authority should possess a certain revolutionary quality. Moreover, as a senior revolutionary cadre, he tends to emphasize the moral integrity of the political leaders; for this reason he has been very popular among older cadres as an incorruptible elder politician.

Although the bureaucratic technocrats are more supportive of reform than the retiring revolutionary cadres were, they are not

51. A probable exception was his support for the 1978 democratic movement in order to weaken his political adversary Hua Guofeng.
52. Harry Harding, *Chinese Second Revolution: Reform After Mao* (Washington, D.C.: Brookings Institution, 1987).

democrats politically. Because of their training, they are averse to uncertainty and the slow process of decision making, the inevitable consequences of political democratization.[53] Because they are primarily concerned with "doing," not "dreaming," and because "by definition, the status quo is 'do-able,'" the bureaucratic technocrats tend to show more tolerance for the shortcomings of the existing system than critical intellectuals do.[54] In addition, as the products of the new China the bureaucratic technocrats have benefited from the existing political system.

The bureaucratic technocrats' preference for economic policy seems to vary according to previous career experience and current official position. Those with career backgrounds in the state-planning apparatus may share Chen Yun's concern over the possible loss of state control over the economy. Those in managerial positions at the factory level may prefer Zhao Ziyang's approach. Among party secretaries of local governments Deng Xiaoping's economical pragmatism and political Leninism may be popular. Among the three highest-level bureaucratic technocrats, it is believed that Jiang Zemin and Li Ruihuan, who actively pursued economic reforms as the top leaders of major municipalities but took a hard-line approach to the student demonstrations, are less doctrinaire than Li Peng.

Nonetheless, all the bureaucratic technocrats share one common interest: their personal and career interests are tied to a program of economic development. The raison d'être for their promotion was economic development. They cannot base their legitimacy on the claim of representing the working class, as the revolutionary cadres did, and they will not be able to maintain their elite status unless they deliver the promised economic benefits to the Chinese people. Without continuing the reforms, they cannot lead China to economic development. It thus seems very likely that the departure of the senior revolutionary leaders will free the bureaucratic technocrats to seek increased levels of production rather than equal distribution and efficiency rather than social justice.

By 1988 China's worsening economic condition added another

---

53. Gouldner, *The Future of Intellectuals*.
54. Richard Rose, "Political Status of Higher Civil Servants," quoted in Aberbach et al., *Bureaucrats and Politicians*, 257.

element to the already-existing policy dispute. After heated debate in a series of meetings, the regime decided to deal with the rampant inflation by strengthening central authority over economic matters and using administrative authority to tighten financial control. This policy shift signaled defeat for the reformers headed by Zhao Ziyang. At that time it was widely feared among Chinese and outside observers that further reforms were stalled and Zhao Ziyang would be eventually eased out.

It was at this moment of political uncertainty in the spring of 1989 that Chinese students initiated a protest movement—an almost unavoidable turn of events, given the social, economic, and political problems that China had experienced in the ten years of reform. In turn, the student demonstrations further deepened the already-existing cleavage among the top leaders. Li Peng, supported by the old cadres, insisted on harsh measures from the beginning, whereas Zhao Ziyang pursued a more flexible and conciliatory policy. Li Peng did not want to make concessions to the students because they would have amounted to conceding the correctness of Zhao's policy position. After an unsuccessful plea to the hard-liners to moderate their course, Zhao took his position to the public, hinting that he had no free hand in dealing with the crisis.[55] This revelation made Zhao Ziyang, who had been considered largely responsible for the inflation and corruption, an overnight hero in the eyes of student demonstrators. To the hard-liners, Zhao's activities constituted a betrayal, an open challenge to the basic principle of the Leninist Party. Understandably, the basic-level cadres were confused and furious: "Zhao Ziyang plays the good guy at the top while we play the bad guys at the grass roots."[56]

Why did Zhao Ziyang insist on moderation in dealing with the student demonstrators even at the risk of invoking the old leaders' resentment? Zhao might have concluded that increasing pressure from old comrades would force Deng Xiaoping to make him a

---

55. Li Peng sarcastically said to him: "The students are all against you. They want to arrest those 'official speculators' to arrest your sons." *Daily Report*, 12 May 1989, 22–23.

56. He did so first in his May Fourth speech to the representatives of the Asian Development Bank and later in his 19 May speech to the students in Tiananmen Square. He told Mikhail Gorbachev on 17 May that "an important decision of the first session of the 13th CPC CC" was to refer "all important matters" to Deng Xiaoping. *Daily Report*, 6 July 1989, 26.

scapegoat for the policy failures, for which Deng himself was as much responsible as Zhao, and that his—Zhao's—fall would seal the fate of the entire reform movement.[57] Or Zhao might have thought that by capitalizing on the students' demands, he could strike back at the adversaries conspiring to remove him and turn back the clock on reform.[58] Zhao might have calculated that he would be better off, at least in the future, if he took the issue to the public, even at the risk of breaking the Leninist principle.

The leadership split prevented the regime from taking coherent and consistent measures with regard to the student protest. As the stalemate between the regime and the students continued, the protest expanded to draw the support of other Beijing social groups, allowing many different grievances to converge.[59] Not only some government employees but also many party members openly showed sympathy for the student movement, "quite a number of them" acting as leaders of the protest and others publicly stating their withdrawal from the party.[60]

Among the social groups, the private entrepreneurs and individual business households that had benefited most from the reforms supported Zhao and the students most enthusiastically.[61] Unfortunately, this group has yet to develop the strength to be an independent political force, and it lacks sufficient common interests with the workers and peasants to form a broad coalition. Probably the workers and peasants have resented the high income of private entrepreneurs and individual business households, believing that the gain was obtained at their expense.[62]

Some individual workers showed sympathy for the students, particularly after Li Peng's unpopular decision to declare martial law. But it seems that they never participated in the demonstra-

57. Although Deng Xiaoping was initially inclined to protect Zhao, the pressure from the old cadres was too heavy particularly after the Tiananmen incident.

58. *Daily Report*, 8 May 1989, 19.

59. A survey of 865 residents conducted by students in six districts of Beijing in early May indicated that 51 percent of them expressed "strong support" for the student movement, 44.5 percent expressed sympathy, and only 1.1 percent said they were opposed.

60. *Daily Report*, 28 July 1989, 19.

61. Ibid., 18 August 1989.

62. For the workers' role in the demonstration, see Anita Chan and Jonathan Unger, "Voices from the Protest Movement, Chongqing, Sichuan," *Australian Journal of Chinese Affairs*, no. 24, July 1990, 1–21.

tions in any organized fashion.[63] Although the workers resented the official corruption and inflation, they apparently had few interests in common with the students and intellectuals, who acted as a self-proclaimed social elite. Neither the "new authoritarianism" nor the manager-responsibility system offered many benefits to workers. This lack of sympathy might be the reason that Li Ruihuan in Tianjin and Jiang Zemin in Shanghai could mobilize workers to control the student demonstrations.

The educated sectors of the population were more supportive of the student movement, even at great risk to personal safety. Although no conclusive evidence is available, it is very likely that among the educated, younger persons were more sympathetic while older persons were more cautious because they remembered the CCP's past practice of retaliating against dissidents. Another factor determining the degree of support was the type of work unit. People employed in the media and in research institutes with more direct contact with the students were more supportive of the student protest. As for the students themselves, those trained in humanities and social sciences tended to become more involved than those majoring in natural sciences.[64] When the regime retaliated against the student movement by curtailing the number of freshmen at Beijing University, departments such as International Politics, Sociology, History, and Philosophy were not allowed to admit any freshmen in the 1989–90 academic year.

During the 1989 student movement, some of the bureaucratic technocrats might have felt sympathy with the demands for democracy, particularly at the initial stage of the movement; but all the available evidence indicates that they did not actively participate in the mass demonstrations or support Zhao Ziyang. For instance, after the June incident, Jiang Zemin praised "the scientists and technicians [for having] given a good account of themselves."[65] Song Jian, state councillor and minister of the State Science and Technology Commission, declared that "the great majority of scientists and technicians have lived up to the expecta-

63. *Daily Report,* 22 May 1989, 81 .
64. For instance, even among the twenty-one leaders of the movement, fourteen majored in humanities and social sciences and seven were identified as majoring in natural sciences. Ibid., 13 July 1989, 20.
65. Ibid., 29 August 1989, 33.

tions of the party" and proved themselves "a completely reliable force of the party and people."[66]

However, the brutal killing of innocent students by the PLA made it impossible for even bureaucratic technocrats who preferred strong government action to end the chaos to defend the specific measures taken and the ensuing political repression. At the same time, the scope and intensity of discontent among the Chinese population must have surprised many bureaucratic technocrats; if so, the experience will discourage them from initiating any bold economic measures whose long-term political consequences they cannot estimate. At the moment, the bureaucratic technocrats seem to be keeping a low profile, waiting for the hardline old revolutionaries to finally pass away.

Despite the 4 June tragedy, the bureaucratic technocrats have continued to replace the revolutionary cadres, thereby assuming most of the leading positions in the Chinese bureaucracy from the central to the lowest level. Among the members of the standing committee of the Politburo, for instance, Li Peng, Jiang Zemin, and Li Ruihuan are bureaucratic technocrats. Although the old revolutionary leaders could still exert an undue amount of political power in late 1986 when Hu Yaobang was removed and in 1989 during the student demonstrations, they will fade away within a few years. Soon the core of the highest leadership will not be a senior leader from the preceding generation—like Hu Yaobang or Zhao Ziyang—but Jiang Zemin, who belongs to the same generation.[67]

By using naked force the regime managed to suppress the protest movement and restore a semblance of order, but now the bureaucratic technocrats face almost impossible tasks: to consolidate their power base while regaining the people's confidence and to reimpose socialist ideology while continuing economic reforms and the open door policy, at a time when many Chinese feel that the regime has lost its mandate to rule China. The only way for the regime to regain some of its legitimacy is to produce tangible economic development.

However, the official policy following the Tiananmen Square incident—which the remaining old revolutionaries continue to

66. Ibid., 12 July 1989, 29.
67. *Renmin Ribao*, 13 November 1989.

dictate to the bureaucratic technocrats—is not promising. The regime has recentralized economic authority, adopted a tight monetary policy, and initiated a campaign to "improve economic order and rectify the economic environment." Instead of price reform, which even liberal economists believe could not be carried out because of superinflation, the regime intends to perfect contract systems. In general, state planning has regained control of the economy and the idea of privatizing the ownership system is officially condemned.[68] Although these actions have been publicized as temporary measures designed to "deepen the reform," many liberal economists worry publicly that "reform is marking time [and] no reform means no future."[69]

Politically, the regime has reverted to repressive measures. It is attempting to strengthen the CCP by restoring the party core group in the government ministries and bolstering the party secretary's authority in businesses. The effort to separate the party from the government has been reversed; the current official position is that the party and the government organizations will not have separate organizational structures but merely separate functions.[70]

Attributing the student demonstrations to Zhao's neglect of ideology, the regime has tightened its control. Ideological orthodoxy is now emphasized; the regime vows to develop "socialism with Chinese character," frequently mentioning class struggle and warning against the dangers of the "peaceful evolution of socialism." Li Peng even plans to assign one political cadre with a professional job title to every hundred workers and staff members.[71] College students are required to study "ideals, discipline, and ethics, as well as Marxist-Leninist theories," and to be "steeled" in rural areas or factories before assuming cadre positions.[72] In personnel management, the practice of emphasizing skill and ability is criticized. For instance, Li Peng promises to pay more attention to political ideology, practical experience, and leadership skills.[73]

The current policy of slowing economic reform and reimposing

68. *Daily Report*, 13 September 1989, 37.
69. Ibid., 7 September 1989, 29.
70. Ibid., 28 August 1989, 16.
71. Ibid., 21 July 1989, 8.
72. Ibid., 14 September 1989, 15.
73. Ibid., 7 September 1989, 29.

repressive political control may deal with the immediate problems of inflation and social unrest, but it will not resolve China's basic problems. Particularly unworkable are present efforts to control the party and ordinary Chinese by ideological education. Ideological education proved ineffective during the thirty years of Mao's rule. The regime tried the same approach during the three years of the party rectification campaign, but failed again. The social changes that China has experienced in the past ten years are too great for such an archaic method to work: the Chinese people's expectations are too high, cynicism is too deep, the society too complex and diversified, the regime's legitimacy too low, and the official ideology too incoherent and too irrelevant for China's mounting problems. Most important, as *Renmin Ribao* publicly concedes, a reassertion of ideological orthodoxy clashes with the regime's avowed policy of reform and international cooperation.[74] Zhao Ziyang's tolerance of ideological liberalization was not due to his personal preference but rather to the requirements of economic development. "Ideological confusion" in China has not arisen from a neglect of ideology; rather, it reflects the very social values that the regime has tried to promote for the sake of economic development.[75] Moreover, the present coalition of bureaucratic technocrats and such old ideologues as Deng Liqun and Ho Jingzhi, who are greatly resented by the critical intellectuals, is unstable and will not last long.

In the past ten years, the CCP has undergone subtle but irreversible changes. In order to lead China to economic development, the party found it necessary to raise the educational level of its members by co-opting the intellectuals.[76] The party changed its recruitment policy: to join, a senior high school education was required for workers and junior high school for peasants. Although the party members' task was redefined to help others get rich, they preferred to enrich themselves first. As official corruption spread, the gap between official ideology and actual policy widened, and

74. Ibid., 22 September 1989, 12.
75. Ibid., 22 August 1989, 11.
76. There are two different methods of co-optation. The first brings specialists into the framework of the party. The second shares power by granting them the status of consultants. Both attempts are being used in China. For the two methods, see Philip Selznick, "Cooperation: A Mechanism and Organizational Stability," in Robert K. Merton, ed., *Reader in Bureaucracy* (New York: Free Press, 1967), 135–39.

the Chinese were swept away by a fever of getting rich. The Leninist Party's claim to a legitimacy based on socialist values lost moral ground in the eyes of many Chinese. Critics see the party as a privileged group that uses socialism simply to defend its privileged position. An indication of the party's demoralization and disarray is the massive support that the student democratic movement enjoyed in Beijing, where eight out of every hundred citizens are party members.[77] Even the effort to investigate members' behavior during the protest demonstration has encountered difficulties, as the basic-level party leaders protect those who showed sympathy to the movement by "turning big problems into small problems and small problems into no problems at all." It will be impossible for the bureaucratic technocrats to rebuild the party—with its 47 million members—as a coherent revolutionary force dedicated to socialism.

There are some reasons to believe that the present hard-line policy is a defensive and temporary measure taken in response to what the top leaders perceived as a serious threat to the survival of the regime rather than an indication of a total reversal of the reform policy. For instance, the regime's current defense of socialism stresses China's unique socioeconomic and political conditions rather than its inherent and universal virtue. The planned civil service system continues to be experimented with in selected areas, even though it is obviously in conflict with the renewed emphasis on political qualifications.

UNCERTAIN FUTURE

If the policies adopted after the massacre have been temporary measures intended to prevent the collapse of the regime, what kind of political system will the bureaucratic technocrats create when they are completely free from the interference of the old revolutionary cadres? Is a pluralistic democratization or a return to the Maoist system likely? Any speculation on these questions should take into account such mutually reinforcing factors as China's economic performance in the coming years, the distribution of the costs and benefits of reform among social groups, Deng Xiaoping's longev-

77. See table 53.

ity, and the sweeping and dramatic changes taking place in other socialist countries.

Impossible as it may be to foresee China's immediate future, one can create several scenarios by drawing on insights from the past; the inevitable historical trend toward ideological secularization, functional specialization, and reviving societal strength; and the prerequisites of economic development.

It is unlikely that China will return to the Maoist system, as that system was the product of several accidental factors that no longer exist.[78] The social forces unleashed by ten years of reform are too strong to accept a return to Maoist practice; the social structure, functional differentiation, and regional differences are too great. Moreover, the bureaucratic technocrats, particularly the younger generation who have gone through the CR, are too sophisticated to subscribe to Mao's values of a simple life, hard work, self-sufficiency, and economic development by human labor. Even if these values continue to dictate policy choice, the bureaucratic technocrats will be less willing than the peasant cadres were to blindly carry out policies made by the top leaders. The technocrats will be more inclined to use their own expertise and judgment rather than the structural legitimacy of the party organization to evaluate a policy's validity. Even Deng Xiaoping warned against returning to this old way: "China cannot possibly return again to the previous closed era."[79]

Nor is there much chance that China will evolve gradually into a group of autonomous regional governments like the ones that existed during the warlord period of the 1920s, even though the present situation appears explosive because of the widespread discontent, defiance of the intellectuals, and intensifying economic conflicts between the central government and the localities and among the regions. If the military splits, regional rivalry will be compounded and China may face a real danger of disintegration. The possibility of such a scenario is minimal, however, because the provincial authorities have shown little ability to collaborate with one another. Moreover, the long tradition of a unitary government,

78. Lowell Dittmer, *China's Continuous Revolution* (Berkeley and Los Angeles: University of California Press, 1987).

79. *Daily Report*, 17 July 1989, 16.

bitter memories of warlordism, and the military's inability to run the economy without support from the technocrats and the population at large further reduces the chance of such an outcome.

Another possible scenario is a total democratic revolution and total economic reform by peaceful means. As noted, even before the Tiananmen incident, college students and some critical intellectuals argued that democratization of the regime would enable China to carry out economic reforms including price reform and, eventually, privatization of ownership. Paradoxically, the tragic events of Tiananmen Square and the events in Eastern Europe have probably reduced the possibility of such a change in the short run. But how the memory of the government's brutality will work out in the long term is uncertain. The Tiananmen incident may herald a democratic revolution just as the Russian Bloody Sunday in 1905 heralded the 1917 Bolshevik revolution.

At the moment, a democratic revolution led by social forces outside the system—such as the Democratic Front of China organized by exiled critical intellectuals and students overseas—is also implausible, although not impossible. No revolution will succeed in China without the support of the workers and peasants; but with the democratic forces in exile already prone to fight among themselves to control the movement and the best course of action, the chances of their coalescing with the workers and peasants appear very slim. On the whole, the social forces pushing for democratization are too weak and still too dependent on the party-state economically. Before political democratization is possible, China may have to develop economically, so that more differentiated social groups and classes can possess not only functional autonomy but also their own economic resources independent of the state. At the moment, the main obstacle to such a development is the work unit (*danwei*) system. Although the regime recognizes that the unit ownership system has "refeudalized" China, efforts to change the organizing principle of society have not yet made much progress. The only way to change the work unit system is to introduce a market principle.

In addition, some economic reforms appear to be mutually exclusive with political democratization. For instance, one may argue that price reforms preclude political democracy. In socialist countries, where shortages of goods are normal phenomena, free price setting inevitably leads to inflation. If price reform is combined with a privatization of ownership, it will lead to the bankruptcy of many inefficient enterprises and an increase in the unemployment rate. Ownership reform may be incompatible with political democracy in the socialist countries where the working class is accustomed to egalitarian distribution and a guarantee of minimum subsistence.

Many scholars argue that three steps are necessary for the political democratization of an authoritarian regime. The first step involves a fragmentation of the political elite, because "political democracy is produced by stalemate and dissensus rather than prior unity and consensus [among the political elite]." The second requires one group to go outside the ruling circle and mobilize the masses for its political cause. During the third, the political elite agrees on an institutional arrangement by which policy will be determined.[80] Agreement on procedural rules for decision making increases the uncertainty about which policies will be adopted. At present China seems to have reached the stage where leaders at the top level can articulate the interests of their constituencies but cannot mobilize their constituent groups in order to bring pressure on colleagues in the policy-making process. Zhao Ziyang attempted such a mobilization during the demonstrations, and he failed.

Moreover, the propensity of bureaucratic technocrats is not toward democratization; memories are vivid of Mao's mobilization of the masses against his adversaries during the CR. More impressed by the cases of Japan before World War II and of contemporary Taiwan and South Korea, where authoritarian regimes led their nations to successful economic growth—which in turn produced social groups and a middle class capable of leading the process of political democratization—the bureaucratic technocrats will probably argue that at present China lacks the conditions for political democratization.[81]

Yet another possible scenario is that the bureaucratic techno-

80. Adam Przeworski, "Some Problems in the Study of the Transition to Democracy," in Guillermo O'Donnell, Philippe C. Schmitter, and Laurence Whitehead, eds., *Transitions from Authoritarian Rule* (Baltimore: Johns Hopkins University Press, 1986), 3:47–63.

81. Tun-jen Cheng, "Democratizing the Quasi-Leninist Regime in Taiwan," *World Politics* 41(4) (July 1989): 471–99.

crats will carry out economic reforms culminating in a market economy, while limiting political changes to a bare minimum, thereby
producing "political authoritarianism" and "social pluralism" in
Scalapino's phrases.[82] This is, in fact, what Zhao Ziyang originally
advocated. According to this view, China needs a strong and
powerful political authority in order to create the preconditions for
a market economy and to overcome the resistance of the Chinese
people, who "are neither prepared to give up the advantages of
socialism, nor willing to take the risk entailing the market mechanism, while wanting to preserve the benefits gained under the old
system."[83]

There are several reasons that China may move in this direction.
First, the elitism of the bureaucratic technocrats supports the belief
that only an authoritarian regime staffed with efficient bureaucratic
administrators will be able to push economic reform step by step
toward marketization while dealing effectively with all the problems arising in the process. Second, when the next major leadership change occurs—probably after the power struggles that will
follow Deng Xiaoping's death—the winners will be more liberal
bureaucratic technocrats than the leaders they replace, and they
will have a better understanding of the democratic aspirations of
the Chinese population and the importance of a market economy.
Third, whether or not Zhao Ziyang returns to power, it is likely
that some of the victims of last year's purge will be rehabilitated.

Finally, as the bureaucratic technocrats learn how to use macroeconomic leverage and improve their ability to control the economy in times of crisis, they will be more willing to introduce
market mechanisms and reduce the scope of the economic activities that the party-state regulates. Li Ruihuan's defense of the present policy of recentralization, subtly different from Chen Yun's
analogy of the bird cage, hints at the possibility of moving in this
direction. "What we are trying to do is fly a kite, not set it free.
When we are flying a kite, it is still controlled by our hand. We can
have many ways to control it. Our controlling ability is expressed
by how far and how flexibly we can fly it."[84]

82. Robert Scalapino, "Asia and the United States: The Challenges Ahead,"
Foreign Affairs, 1989/90, 89–115.
83. *Daily Report*, 7 September 1989, 21.
84. Ibid., 20 September 1989, 7.

The only crucial obstacle against China's moving in this direction is socialist ideology, but the regime has several options. The first—and it is very unlikely—is to replace Marxism-Leninism and Mao Zedong's thought with another ideology. The second is to "refunctionalize" the official ideology by incorporating "numerous elements, concepts, and categories" from modern social theories.[85] The third is to separate "the goal culture" from "the transfer culture" (or "pure ideology" from "practical ideology," in Franz Schurmann's terms) by remaining committed to socialism as defined by Marxism-Leninism and Mao Zedong's thought but modifying the means to achieve socialist goals in light of the specific Chinese needs and conditions.[86] The fourth is to deideologize the entire political process. This option is very unlikely, given the crucial integrative role that official ideology has traditionally played in governing the massive Chinese population. The most likely option is the third, which would diminish the ideology's coherence. Eventually it would approximate what Juan Linz calls a "mentality," a "way of thinking, attitude, or psychic disposition" that is vague and formless enough to enable diverse elite groups to work together while retaining the loyalty of the masses.[87]

China will not be able to separate the party from the government unless it changes its economic system. Under the present arrangement, the state is unaccountable to the people even though it directly manages the means of production, which are theoretically owned by all the people. Because the power of the state is potentially so great, the party must maintain a tight control over it. For instance, because the present work unit system gives too much power to individual factory managers, it provides a reason for the party to interfere with the managers' authority while claiming to represent the workers.

Only when the state frees itself from the practical difficulties it faces as the owner of the means of production will it be able to limit its main functions to balancing the conflicting interests of social

85. Peter Ludz, *Changing Party Elites in East Germany* (Boston: MIT Press, 1972).
86. Franz Schurmann, *Ideology and Organization in Communist China* (Berkeley and Los Angeles: University of California Press, 1968).
87. Juan Linz, "Totalitarianism and Authoritarian Regimes," in Fred Greenstein and Nelson Polsby, eds., *Handbook of Political Science* (Reading, Mass.: Addison-Wesley, 1975) 3:175–357.

groups, guaranteeing the minimum economic well-being of all social groups, and developing a long-term economic plan and an
effective macroeconomic leverage. The state should be changed, in
Janos Kornai's words, from a "maximum state" to a "medium" one
by retaining responsibility for only (1) active macropolicies for stab-
ilization, full employment, and balanced economic relations with
the outside world; (2) activities to combat adverse externalities and
ensure an appropriate supply of public goods; and (3) a redistribution of income to provide social justice and support the poor and
weak.[88] Once the state's role in the economy is reduced, the CCP
can serve as the intermediary between civil society and the state,
thereby resolving its dilemma of how to separate itself from the
state and still maintain its political hegemony. Some Chinese scholars have already argued that the party's role should be to aggregate civil society's diverse demands and forward them to the state
as "guidance inputs" (zhidaoxhing) for the state to use in making
authoritative decisions for the civil society.[89]

If the party wishes to maintain its politically dominant position,
it will eventually have to drop its claim to be a class-based party in
order to accommodate diverse interests and rising social forces.
Gramsci's theory is pertinent here.[90] Gramsci distinguishes between "transformism hegemony" and "expansive hegemony." In
the former, the party neutralizes hostile social groups and prevents
the development of specific demands by articulating their interests, thereby producing a "passive consensus."[91] The latter involves "the creation of an active and direct consensus as a result of
the party's willingness to adopt the interests of the popular classes
as if they are the party's own, thereby producing a genuine
'national will.'"[92] According to Gramsci, the second type of hegemony leads to the creation of a "collective will," which fuses and
synthesizes all partisan interests. At present, the CCP, by actively
promoting a united-front policy, demonstrates its interest in creat-

88. Janos Kornai, "Individual Freedom and Reform of the Socialist Economy,"
European Economic Review, 32, 1988, 233–67.
89. Nie Gaomin, Li Yizhou, and Wang Zhongtian, eds., *Dangzheng Fenkai Lilun
Tantao* (Beijing: Chunqiu Chubanshe, 1988).
90. Chantal Mouffe, "Hegemony and Ideology in Gramsci," in Chantal Mouffe,
ed., *Gramsci and Marxism* (London: Routledge and Kegan Paul, 1979), 168–204.
91. Ibid., 182.
92. Ibid., 183.

ing an expansive hegemony as a means of ensuring its own political survival and its own dominant role in modernizing China.

Marketization and economic development will entail a further structural differentiation of political, social, and economic institutions. The viability and efficiency of a complex society with a multitude of functionally specialized organizations depends on the society's capacity for integration.[93] In the case of China the mixed nature of the Chinese economic system—neither totally controlled by state planners nor operating in a perfectly free market—intensifies the need for coordination. The bureaucratic technocrats in party positions can fulfill this need by coordinating specialized organizations staffed by "experts" and resolving the conflicting interests of diverse social groups, becoming what Jowitt calls "political managers."[94] Many Chinese leaders have already suggested that party cadres will even play the role of coordinators "among the various parts of the power organs of the state, and economic organizations, and the cultural organizations," as well as among the managers, the labor unions, the Communist Youth League, and the workers' congresses.[95] This type of broadly defined coordination will require the political managers to be more receptive to the wishes of various groups and to rely on their own ability to manipulate needs and symbols. It seems that the new generation of cadres, with its technical background, is better prepared than the former revolutionary cadres for this type of mixed political and technical coordination.[96]

The concept of the political manager also presupposes a more democratized party, which would allow its leaders to air differing views on policy agendas and options. Despite the temporary setback following the massacre on 4 June, the political elite will become more pluralistic as its members are drawn from diverse social groups on the basis of their career backgrounds and skills. In fact, it has already become increasingly acceptable for political leaders to

93. Lindblom, *Politics and Markets*.

94. Jowitt, "Inclusion and Mobilization in European Leninist Regimes."

95. Zhao Ziyang, for instance, stresses the party's coordinating roles. *Renmin Ribao*, 26 November 1987; *Sixiang Zhengzhi Gongzuo Yanjiu*, no. 10, 1985, 12–14; Zhonggong Hunanshengwi Dangxiao Dangjian Yanjiushi, ed., *Zhizhengdangde Lingdao Wenti Gailun* (Beijing: Zhonggong Zhongyang Dangxiao Chubanshe, 1986), 59–60.

96. Suleiman, *Politics, Power, and Bureaucracy*, 380.

bring the partisan interests of social groups into the policy-making process and draw support from different segments of the bureaucracy. If this trend continues, it will combine with the bureaucratic technocrats' pragmatic orientation and inclination toward compromise to gradually change the basic rules of the Leninist Party. The party may become like the Japanese Liberal Democratic Party, with various factions that hold slightly disparate policy preferences but work together within a broad ideological consensus. The CCP will reach this stage when the opinion groups now existing within it are allowed to develop. It is more likely that China will move in this direction than that it will develop a genuine multiparty system. And even if the party does not go quite this far, there is no doubt that having learned the limits of political power in transforming society, it is now more permeable to social influences than in any previous period.

A broad historical review of the Chinese revolution reveals a paradox. An elitist revolutionary party staffed and supported by poor peasants carried out the Communist revolution in China, where the Marxian preconditions for a socialist revolution did not exist. After capturing political power, party leaders set up a powerful party-state, which ruthlessly attempted to carry out a socialist revolution. After socializing the means of production, the party-state used its political authority to manage the economy and rejected exchange relations as a means of organizing even economic activities. The justification for this approach lay in Marx's view that economics and politics are inextricably interrelated and that exchange relations, which use the medium of money, distort genuine human relations.[97]

Marxism as originally formulated contains humanistic elements. Karl Marx, who lived at the early stage of capitalism, resented the commercialization of human relations and dominance of money and capital over humanity. He therefore urged that human relations not be mediated by capital and money, which tend to exploit human labor. But both the Soviet Union's and China's efforts to construct a society without exchange relations through money and capital failed completely. Their attempts to regulate social relations

97. For Marx's criticism of capital, see T. B. Bottomore, ed., *Karl Marx: Early Writings* (New York: McGraw-Hill, 1963).

resulted in societies dominated by political power, and exploitation by political power turned out to be more ruthless than exploitation by capital. Moreover, their state-planned economies proved ineffective for economic development.

China now recognizes the dysfunctional consequences of applying a political approach to all human problems. It is therefore extremely unlikely that the country will return to the Maoist approach of regulating almost all human activities through power and authoritative relations. Instead, it is now trying to make up for lost time by reducing political authority in the economic arena and expanding the range of human activities regulated by exchange relations. But finding the right mix of authority and exchange relations will not be easy, for in China the Maoist version of socialism has reinforced a long-standing bureaucratic tradition.

Index